Competency-Based Assessments
in Mental Health Practice

Competency-Based Assessments in Mental Health Practice

Cases and Practical Applications

Susan W. Gray

John Wiley & Sons, Inc.

Library of Congress Cataloging-in-Publication Data

Gray, Susan W. (Susan Walker)
    Competency-based assessments in mental health practice: cases and practical applications / Susan Gray.
       p.; cm.
    Includes bibliographical references and index.
    ISBN 978-0-470-50528-1 (pbk. : alk. paper)
       1. Psychology, Pathological—Case studies. 2. Diagnostic and statistical manual of mental disorders. I. Title.
    [DNLM: 1. Diagnostic and statistical manual of mental disorders. 2. Mental Disorders—diagnosis—Case Reports. 3. Clinical Competence—Case Reports. 4. Disability Evaluation—Case Reports. 5. Mental Disorders—classification—Case Reports. WM 141]
    RC465.G73 2011
    616.89'075—dc22

                                                                                          2010039795

Printed in the United States of America

10 9 8 7 6 5 4 3 2 1

To my beloved husband,
Kenneth E. Gray, JD
. . . again, again, and now once again.

Contents

Preface

INTRODUCTION

An estimated 26.2% of Americans ages 18 and older or about one in four adults will experience a diagnosable mental disorder in a given year making it the most common problem you can expect to encounter in practice (Kessler, Chiu, Demler, & Walters, 2005). For quite some time now, practitioners such as social workers, mental health counselors, marriage and family therapists, and psychologists have been recognized as being primarily responsible for assisting with the provision of mental health services in the United States, including assessment, and this trend is expected to continue (Gray, 2008; Miller, 2002; Newhill & Korr, 2004; Pace, 2008; Thyer & Wodarski, 2007). Beginning with the advent of managed care during the early 1980s and up to the recent health-care legislative initiatives, the different disciplines within the health- and mental health-care fields have been rapidly changing to keep up with the demands of providing effective services to those with major mental illnesses. Efficiency and cost containment dominate the contemporary service delivery landscape and exert a strong influence on the way that care is provided. The effects of this direction are viewed with mixed emotions. For instance, practitioners are now facing the challenges of budget cuts and increased costs while continuing efforts to provide quality care to clients (Cohen, 2003). The exigencies of providing mental health care also influence core professional activities, including how mental health problems are articulated. As the mental health field of practice moves toward more efficient and cost-effective delivery of services, quality care dictates that formal mental health diagnoses be provided (Thyer & Wodarski, 2007). The *Diagnostic and Statistical Manual of Mental Disorders* or *DSM* is the primary tool used to make this diagnosis. It contains a language that is universally understood across the professions. This book is about helping the diverse yet similar mental health practitioners become more proficient in formulating a differential diagnosis using the classification system delineated in the *DSM* while maintaining the century-old practice of acknowledging client strengths and resilience.

Assessment in the field of mental health practice is an ongoing process intended to collect data aimed at fostering the understanding of the individual who requires help in the context of his or her environment (Jordan & Franklin, 2003). Seen as a competency-based assessment, this book offers a constructional approach to the systematic exploration of the multiple factors that play a role in a client's life. Each person's unique experience with mental illness is considered and the assessment process focuses on a parallel evaluation of assets and pathology in order to set the stage for realistic optimism about the possibilities for change.

The *Diagnostic and Statistical Manual* and the Competency-Based Assessment

The *Diagnostic and Statistical Manual of Mental Disorders* is a publication of the American Psychiatric Association (2000) and commonly referred to as the *DSM*. Until the next major revision is published, a text revision of the manual, known as the *DSM-IV-TR®*, was issued in 2000 (American Psychiatric Association, 2000). The *DSM* lists all mental disorders and includes a detailed description of each diagnostic category along with specific criteria in order to help the practitioner make reliable assessments of mental disorders.

Despite its popularity and consistent use as a resource within the mental health field, there have been a number of long-standing criticisms of the *DSM* that essentially call for more of an emphasis on the client's social, situational, and environmental factors (see, for example, Bentall, 2006; Honos-Webb & Lietner, 2001; Widger & Sankes, 2000). A common misconception associated with the *DSM* is that its classification system tends to classify people and less attention is given to the individual's unique experience with a particular disorder (APA, 2000).

Although the *DSM* does pose some problems for professionals, nevertheless it remains as the major format by which the mental disorders are organized. The *DSM* comes from the medical model; that is, individuals are labeled with an illness. Based on this perspective alone, you might lose sight of the fact that clients have strengths and successes despite a serious mental illness. Although a diagnosis is useful, it can have the effect of diminishing the client as a whole person. Each person's experience with mental illness is different. Certainly those individuals that we work with have a right to expect and receive services consistent with prevailing practices in the mental health field and related ethical standards (Reamer, 2006). This level of professional accountability includes the need to know how to make an accurate assessment. To remain consistent with this time-honored orientation to practice, this book puts the competency-based assessment together with the *DSM* to provide a framework for an individualized assessment of human behavior within an ecosystems perspective; one that includes the biological, psychological, and social and environmental including cultural variables in the client's life (Gray, 2006; 2008). By including the competency-based assessment, the client focus includes a simultaneous understanding of both problems *and* resources. Obstacles are often in the "eye of the beholder." What may initially be perceived as an obstacle may actually be a positive feature if reframed. The competency-based assessment shifts the assessment away from a dysfunctional conceptualization of problems to include the more helpful instrumental aspects of the person's life.

Mental health practitioners have a unique role in the assessment and diagnostic process (Pace, 2008). Each profession maintains a distinctive philosophical orientation to practice, but they come together around how to use the diagnostic assessment system found in the DSM (Dziegielewski, 1998; 2002). By offering a common language, communication among practitioners in the mental health field is facilitated by using the diagnostic classification system outlined in the DSM. The DSM is considered as the gold standard for assessments and offers the most comprehensive explanation of diagnostic categories. It is also the language of insurance companies and other funding sources. In order to be effective in today's current practice environment, you need to know and be able to appropriately utilize this assessment tool.

The competency-based assessment offers a number of advantages to the assessment process. As many of us already know, most clients typically pursue a variety of other options before seeking professional help. They may try to solve problems on their own or look to family and friends for help. Without a doubt the decision about receiving assistance is not always an easy one. In fact, some individuals are mandated to accept our services; for example, state legislation that requires intervention when someone is severely depressed and thinking about suicide. We do not always have the opportunity to see people at their best. In these instances, the person's expectations about what will happen to them and how they will be evaluated will influence the assessment process. In addition, the extent to which the goals, expectations, and values of the practitioner match those of his or her client will also play a role in the assessment process. The competency-based assessment provides the foundation for a clear description of presenting concerns and related factors along with the identification of personal assets that will more than likely make the assessment process of value to clients (and their families) and ultimately enhance participation and involvement.

A unique feature of the DSM is its multiaxial system for evaluation. This fits well with the competency-based assessment where the multiple factors in the client's life are examined. By merging the competency-based assessment with the DSM, the diagnostic assessment becomes a process that focuses on client strengths, coping capacities, and those environmental stressors that can exert an influence over the debilitated patterns of relating and behaving. This broad-based approach to assessment is not intended to replace the DSM but to help balance the tensions inherent in formulating a diagnosis. The competency-based assessment complements the DSM's classification system and offers a structure that incorporates a strengths-based perspective. Alex Gitterman, a noted social work educator, observes that the competency-based perspective "views mental illness through theoretical lenses that attempt to move away from treating a 'disease' to capturing people's unique experiences with mental illness . . . a person is much more than her or his diagnosis" (Gray, 2006, pp. vii–viii).

THE BOOK'S ORGANIZATION

This book presents a brief overview of the major mental disorders that you will likely encounter in your work with clients followed by a series of case studies and practical applications. This is intended to set the stage for connecting the competency-based assessment with the diagnostic classification system outlined in the *DSM* and provide opportunities to practice your assessment skills. To help you to ascertain the accuracy of your skills, the specific competency-based assessment and the *DSM* multiaxial classification for each case study are included at the end of each chapter.

You may not always agree with my assessments and the proposed diagnoses should not be seen as infallible. Instead, I hope that the cases will familiarize you with the terminology found in the *DSM* and stimulate your critical thinking around the assessment process. The cases are drawn from my clinical practice experience and from working with supervisors, students, and fellow colleagues in the field. These experiences bring to life the reality that diverse populations can be affected by mental illness and this shows up in the book's discussion. The identities of the clients presented have been disguised to protect confidentiality. Details such as the client's name, occupation, locale, and/or age have also been altered. You will find the case studies, along with the practical applications, to be educational and also fun to read.

The first chapter introduces the competency-based assessment and the major features of the multiaxial classification system found in the *DSM*. The competency-based perspective provides a strengths-based lens for assessment in the field of mental health and is not driven by any one particular theoretical orientation. This integrative approach complements the practice orientations of various mental health professionals.

The second chapter discusses strategies for reading the case studies. Included is a pictorial representation featuring the biological, psychological, and social factors in the client's life. This visual summary is intended to serve as a pedagogical tool to help you practice integrating the competency-based assessment with the *DSM* when diagnosing mental illness in the subsequent chapters.

Chapters 3 through 12 are organized around selected diagnostic categories found in the *DSM-IV-TR* but there are some omissions. This was done to provide a more extensive review of the mental disorders that you will typically encounter in your clinical practice. Each chapter begins with an overview of a specific disorder followed by a conceptual map that serves as a way to systematically outline the diagnostic features of a specific classification. This map provides a reference point for formulating your differential assessment for each of the case studies. These cases are not listed in any particular order so you will have the opportunity to practice sorting through diagnostic criteria in order to arrive at an accurate assessment.

At the end of each chapter, you will also find a series of practical applications intended to sensitize you to the practicalities of formulating a differential diagnosis. Following Bloom's (1956) cognitive taxonomy, some of the activities will tap into beginning levels of knowledge about the different disorders. Others will speak to the advanced levels of synthesis and evaluation. That is, they will provide a series of activities ranging from knowing the signs and symptoms of a particular disorder to the more advanced levels of being able to think critically about the specific diagnostic categories. To illustrate knowledge of a specific diagnostic category, for example, you might be asked to determine when the symptoms supporting the presence of a specific disorder become evident in one of the case studies. You might also be asked to consider if there are behaviors that may warrant another diagnosis or if there is enough evidence to support a provisional diagnosis.

To use the book effectively, you need to be familiar with the knowledge and values that guide professionally accountable practices, be attuned to the information in the *DSM*, and be willing to critique your work. The intent of this book is to provide opportunities to think about and practice formulating an assessment. A key advantage is that this takes place with case illustrations of actual situations rather than experimenting on a real client. Hopefully you will be more comfortable making mistakes and then applying this new learning to actual practice situations. Each chapter focusing on a particular diagnostic classification is designed to be freestanding and autonomous. When using this book, it is helpful to keep in mind that it is organized to be practical and hands on. The conceptual map provided for each clinical disorder helps you to formulate a differential diagnosis and also to prepare for tests in courses related to psychopathology or human growth and development. In addition, the map is a useful tool as you study for credentialing tests after graduation such as licensure exams or certification.

LOOKING TO OUR OWN COMPETENCIES

The book's organization supports a competency orientation to education. Many professions have generated a list of competencies or measurable practice behaviors that encompass the essential knowledge, values, and skills that define that profession. Although this has been the norm in medicine, dentistry, and nursing, it can now be seen in the counseling professions. For example, the Council on Social Work Education revised its Educational Policy and Accreditation Standards (EPAS) in 2008 to move away from content-based curriculum requirements to a competency-focused curriculum (Council on Social Work Education, 2008). Another example can be found in the work of the American Association for Marriage and Family Therapy (AAMFT) that established a set of core competencies where practitioners can now clearly define what marriage and family therapists should be able to accomplish in their work with clients (Nelson et al., 2007).

The emphasis on competencies has changed how we teach professional skills by shifting the curricular focus to what we do in practice or an outcomes performance orientation. Educators are challenged to answer the question, "What do our students need to be able to do or to know at the end of their educational program?" Sternberg et al. (2000) described competencies in the language of tacit knowledge where they are distinguished as action-oriented, have a value base made up of beliefs and ideas, are cognitive and technical with both know-how and skill, and have a social dimension, which is comprised of working with others. This perspective makes a case for educational practices that link theory and action (Saleebey & Scanlon, 2005). Learning is no longer considered to be a passive activity where students memorize or analyze information but involves applying ideas to real-life situations. Academic coursework becomes the foundation for real-world skills. This book, with its emphasis on practicing the assessment situated in real-life case examples, supports this orientation.

PROPOSED MARKET

It is anticipated that this book will be a resource for practitioners with different levels of professional development ranging from students in graduate social work, mental health counseling, marriage and family therapy, or psychology programs to experienced practitioners and clinical supervisors. It is hoped that the case studies and practical applications will stimulate thinking whether they are assigned as a part of specific course work or to foster discussion between supervisors and their supervisees. The case examples are drawn from actual practice so they provide realistic opportunities to prepare for the realities of the assessment process. Through the drama found in a real client's story, the cases are intended to make the content come alive and hold your interest in what can be seen as boring and abstract material. You will find the diversity that characterizes contemporary mental health practice illustrated in a number of these case studies. Additionally, instructors and supervisors may ask you to complete the book's practice applications as part of a homework assignment, to supplement lectures, or to provide evidence of your understanding of the assessment process in practice. Some of the professional jargon will be demystified through the book's straightforward and readable style.

This book can be used as a primary or supplementary text in a range of courses such as psychopathology, direct practice methods, and human growth and development. The practice applications can be used to stimulate discussion in related courses about counseling theories and methods, ethics, or social policy. The book can also be used by educators in the field practicum experience who prepare student interns for working with clients. Professionals who want to refresh their diagnostic skills or have moved into the field of mental health from another practice specialty may also find the book a useful resource tool.

Acknowledgments

As the work on this book comes to a close and I look back on what has been accomplished, I realize that none of this could have been possible without the encouragement of so many who have been behind the scenes throughout this process. I take this opportunity to thank each and every one of you for your help over the past year and a half. The idea for this book came from listening to my students' struggles to apply abstract and complicated concepts about psychopathology to their work with real clients. Thank you for this inspiration. You have reminded me that learning the basic information necessary to assess clients is no easy task and assigning a diagnosis to someone can be intimidating. You kept me in the real world of practice when you brought your tough cases to our forum discussions in the classroom. I hope that I heard all of your concerns and translated them into this book. The successes and challenges that you uncovered in your work with clients led me to the competency-based assessment.

I will miss my first editor, Lisa Gebo, who took a medical leave shortly after I came on board with John Wiley & Sons, Inc. Regretfully, she died after a long struggle with cancer. Rachel Livsey gracefully stepped into the picture as my new senior editor. Her commitment to this project was clearly evident by her excellent suggestions and attention to detail. She was easy to work with, extremely supportive, and always available. In addition, her wry sense of humor added a lighthearted touch to our work. I still smile when I remember our conversations at length about the length of the manuscript. I would also like to acknowledge Peggy Alexander's hands-on efforts to keep the work moving forward until Rachel came aboard. I would like to thank Kara Borbely, senior editorial assistant, for managing the myriad details of the manuscript and seeing it through the publication process. I know there are a number of people who worked behind the scenes with her to make this book a reality such as Kate Lindsay, senior production editor, Rose Sullivan, senior production manager, and Marilyn Matos, production assistant. I hope you all know how much I appreciate your efforts.

I value the comments of the reviewers who took the time to look over the preliminary manuscript. You offered extremely helpful feedback and suggestions. I would especially like to acknowledge Agathi Glezakos, PhD, full-time lecturer, California State University, Long Beach, in the Department of Social Work who provided detailed and comprehensive feedback. I would also like to recognize the contributions from the remaining reviewers from the other universities around the country whose keen observations clearly reflected their interest in this book: Jeffrey S. Bedwell, PhD, University of Central Florida; Robin Bonifas, PhD, Arizona State University; Kurt Organista, PhD, University of California, Berkeley.

I would like to acknowledge my former dean, Debra McPhee, and the current interim acting dean, Phyllis Scott. Both promote the kind of organizational climate where efforts like this can be accomplished. I appreciate the assistance of my former doctoral student and now colleague Janet Courtney, and master's graduate student Tamika Strachan. Both helped in the early stages of the manuscript. Robert Nolan, a recognized agency director who specializes in working with children, contributed valuable remarks on the chapter devoted to the disorders in infancy, childhood, and adolescence.

Ultimately, I would like to tell my husband, Kenneth, how much I appreciate him. His confidence in me is very special. He has seen me through the writing of several books and still does not seem to mind when we turn down an invitation to socialize with friends because I have work to do. Nor does he mind when we have dinner at late hours or grab some fast food instead of a delicious home-cooked dinner. Although he claims to know nothing about my profession as a social worker, he always manages to find the right thing to say when I'm stuck and somehow manages to find words of encouragement when I find myself having so much to do and in so little time. Once again, I want him to know how grateful I am for his continuing love, patience, and support. His faith in me is a constant.

About the Author

Dr. Susan W. Gray is a professor in the School of Social Work at Barry University, Miami Shores, Florida. She has doctoral degrees in social work and education. Having taught and supervised students for 30 years, she is known as an energetic, fun, and yet challenging instructor. In addition to her current text, she co-authored *Psychopathology: A Competency-Based Assessment Model for Social Workers*, now in its second edition, and co-authored *Psychopathology: A Competency-Based Treatment Model for Social Workers*. Her most recent contribution includes *Advanced Social Work Practice in Clinical Social Work* for the Council on Social Work Education, delineating advanced practice level standards for the 2008 Educational Policy and Accreditation Standards. She has also written extensively on clinical supervision, professional regulation and licensure, rural practice, bereavement groups, intergenerational family assessment tools, the brief solution-focused model of practice, methods of classroom teaching, and aspects of cultural diversity. She is an active leader in state and national professional organizations. Additionally, she is involved in the professional community and continues her work with a community mental health center, hospice, nursing association, senior citizens foundation, marine institute, and the Florida Keys Area Health Education Center. Recognized as an engaging and informative speaker, she has presented numerous papers and workshops at the local, state, national, and international levels.

1

An Introduction to the Competency-Based Assessment

Imagine for a moment that a former client of yours, we'll call her Ellen King, calls you about her daughter, Carol. You had seen Ellen a few years ago for supportive counseling after her divorce from her husband, Gerald. She now asks if you could see Carol because, "She's driving me crazy." You schedule an appointment for the next afternoon.

Carol is currently enrolled in the 11th grade and wants to go to college after she graduates. However, her grades could be much better. Carol admits that she's "only failing a couple of classes." After introductions, Carol settles comfortably in your office and you ask, "What do you think has happened that your mother made an appointment for you to come here to see me?" Carol has a puzzled look on her face at this point. She confides that she does not know what the problem could be and adds with almost too much intensity, "I feel just fine." Carol thought that since her parents' divorce her mother had nothing better to do than to worry about her. "She thinks I'm a mental case. Just because I don't sleep as much as she does she gets all bent out of shape. Heck! Sleeping is for old people like her. I'm young and I have a lot to do. I can catch up on my sleep later," adds Carol.

You notice that Carol's speech is pressured as she goes on to describe those times when she's "on top of the world" and then a few days later when "I'm totally down." Carol denies any history of drugs or alcohol and this is corroborated by her mother.

What do you think is going on with Carol?

PERSPECTIVES ON THE ASSESSMENT

The assessment is an ongoing process of data collection that sets the stage for learning more about our clients. There are a number of methods to collect and evaluate information from a range of sources, including, for example, face-to-face interviews, direct observations of behavior, talking with those close to the client, a review of written documents or prior evaluations, and the use of measurement instruments. In the field of mental health, the most widely used categorical system to consider behavioral patterns is the *Diagnostic and Statistical Manual of Mental Disorders* or *DSM* (American Psychiatric Association, 2000). The diagnostic categories are supported by field investigations and the manual describes symptoms and related characteristics such as age at onset, predisposing factors, and prevalence. Specific criteria are also provided and include key symptoms, the duration of dysfunction, social and occupational impairment, and considerations for differentiating the diagnosis from other closely related syndromes. The *DSM* is organized around a multiaxial system geared to take into account the presenting problem as well as related issues, but it does not promote a specific theoretical orientation.

This book introduces the competency-based assessment that expands the *DSM's* focus by incorporating a parallel assessment of strengths and resilience. The competency-based assessment provides a framework for clarifying the client's competence, the "goodness of fit" between the client and his or her environment, *and* a consideration of the impact of mental illness. This approach to the assessment encompasses finding ways to support the client's coping and adaptation (Saleebey, 2008). "In this perspective, clients are regarded as active, striving human beings who are capable of organizing their lives and realizing their potentialities, as long as they have appropriate family, community, social, and environmental resources" (Compton & Galaway, 1999, pp. 354–355).

We need to be knowledgeable about many factors related to the client's presenting issues. This includes familiarity with the diagnoses spelled out in the *DSM* and the ability to apply them correctly. However, an assessment that is grounded in strengths and possibilities provides a more comprehensive picture of the person's "story." In this way, the diagnosis does not define the individual but becomes but one aspect of the multiple dimensions of a person's life. The dual focus of the competency-based assessment on problems *and* competencies helps to understand a client's diagnosis and to consider the experience of what it's like to live with mental illness (Gray, 2006, 2008). This approach to the assessment extends the understanding of the multiple contributors to mental illness; for example, the stressors in a person's life, the family's well-being, housing, income security, and community or the sense of belonging somewhere.

It has become increasingly common to encounter clients whose backgrounds differ from our own. Many times when our clients come to see us they are not at their best. In order to be effective, it is helpful to know about the many dimensions of a client's life including diversity and difference and how the client can potentially influence the assessment process. Sometimes differences can be interpreted as barriers. Integral to the competency-based assessment is an exploration of the multiple influences of diversity, which are an integral part of one's identity and their interplay with mental illness (Voss, Douville, Little Soldier, & Twiss, 1999). By exploring the full range of the client's experiences with mental illness these events can be transformed into opportunities for growth and change. For the remainder of this book, the competency-based assessment sets the stage for the evaluation of mental illness. Many of the client stories in this book include examples of diversity in order to highlight the ways in which the various dimensions of diversity affect a person's explanations of illness, help-seeking behaviors, and healing practices.

This chapter begins with an overview of the essential components of how the *DSM* is organized followed by an exploration of the theoretical foundations and perspectives that support the competency-based assessment; in particular, the biopsychosocial framework, systems theory, and the ecological perspective. Client competence is a major theme of the competency-based orientation to the assessment and contributions from the strengths perspective, empowerment, and resilience are accentuated. Integrating the *DSM* with the competency-based assessment provides a framework to focus on diagnosing mental illness balanced by simultaneous attention to the many ways that people cope when living with a diagnosis. This paradigm shift moves the assessment process from a perspective of helplessness to one characterized by hopefulness.

We now turn to an overview of the *DSM*.

OVERVIEW OF THE *DIAGNOSTIC AND STATISTICAL MANUAL OF MENTAL DISORDERS*

The *DSM* is regarded as the standard for classifying mental disorders in the United States and in varying degrees internationally. Beginning in the mid-19th century with various systems to collect census and mental health statistics and from a manual used by the U.S. Army, the *DSM* evolved over time to its current format that embodies an extensive scope of psychiatric or psychological issues and conditions. There have been numerous revisions and the *DSM* is currently in consultation, planning, and preparation for yet another edition. This section of our discussion begins with an introduction to the role of the American Psychiatric Association's (APA) role in the *DSM* followed by a review of the numerous subsequent editions highlighting how the manual has changed over time. The challenges and contributions facing the *DSM* are noted and the section ends with a look at the major features.

Introduction

The APA is considered the major professional organization for psychiatrists in the United States. The association publishes various journals, informational pamphlets, and the *DSM*. The *DSM* (APA, 2000) is used by psychiatrists and other professionals such as social workers, psychologists, counselors, and marriage and family therapists who can be found working in a range of settings. The *DSM* is widely recognized as the accepted diagnostic language in the field of mental health, insurance companies, and the pharmaceutical industry (Kutchins & Kirk, 1997). It is universally understood and facilitates the ability to understand the client's symptom picture. From the client's perspective, the extent to which he or she is heard and understood helps to reduce their anxiety (Bentley, 2002). The classification system of the *DSM* helps to sort through what may seem like a confusing array of problems and symptoms.

It is equally important to remember that not every client who comes to see you has a mental disorder. Many times clients who need help are struggling with difficult life circumstances and events and a *DSM* diagnosis may be unnecessary. In this case, the *DSM* provides a classification system for conditions that are not the focus of clinical attention, commonly referred to as V codes. These codes refer to the problems that people encounter in life that might prompt them to seek assistance but are not considered mental illness. For example, you might be working in a hospice setting and encounter someone who is grieving the loss of a loved one but the associated sadness is not to the extent where a diagnosis of major depression is warranted.

We now turn to an overview of some of the outstanding historical events that have contributed to the development of the current *DSM* and conclude with a summary of its major features.

The Evolution of the *DSM*

Starting with the thinking passed down by the Greeks that mental illness was the result of an imbalance of humors or body fluids, ideas about mental health in the United States were primarily influenced by concepts that had evolved in Europe (Katz, 1985). Up until the seventeenth century, physicians used a person's horoscope to diagnose mental disorders (Labruzza, 1994). Medieval doctors looked to four humors to explain differences in the person's personality. More specifically, blood accounted for a happy temperament, choler explained a fiery and competitive temperament, phlegm resulted in a cold, delicate disposition, and bile appeared to cause melancholy.

During the American colonial era, most people with a mental disorder were kept at home and cared for by family. Those suffering from mental illness were referred to as lunatics—a term derived from the root word *lunar* referring to the influence of the moon. The prevailing belief at the time was that a mental illness was caused by a full moon when a baby was born or by the infant sleeping under the light of a full moon. The lunatic was considered to be possessed by the devil. More often than not, the family member with a mental illness was confined to the attic or cellar and kept locked up in chains. Alternative arrangements included placement in settings referred to as madhouses that were run by physicians in their homes (Leiby, 1978). People who could not afford this type of care and had no relatives to look after them were confined to workhouses or almshouses where harsh treatment tended to prevail. Those who were homeless were most likely to end up in jail. Some led a solitary existence by camping out in the woods.

Beginning with the 19th century Dorothea Dix, an avid social work reformer, led the efforts to improve the treatment of the insane (Kreisler & Lieberman, 1986; Marshall, 1937). She advocated for placing those with a mental illness in what was called asylums where a more humane approach to care was provided. Unfortunately this backfired when the asylums became overcrowded from the influx of immigrants and the admission of those who were violent. Treatment approaches became harsher as staff attempted to control the large numbers of patients. The asylums ultimately became warehouses for the unmanageable.

Unfortunately, mental illness continued to remain poorly understood during this era. The science of phrenology was used to explain mental illness where the shape of the skull was studied in order to arrive at a diagnosis. During the mid-1800s, the American psychiatrist John P. Grey postulated that insanity was due to physical causes (Bockoven, 1963). Mental illness was considered to be caused by brain pathology and seen as incurable (Barlow & Durand, 2005). In 1882, Wilheim Greisinger wrote *Mental Pathology and Therapeutics* where he advanced the idea of mental disorders as diseases of the brain (Marx, 1972). Around this same time Emil Kraeplin began keeping statistical records of the symptoms people exhibited, the overall course of their disease, and their outcomes (Compton & Guze, 1995). Kraeplin's classification system for mental illness, particularly schizophrenia, helped to set the stage for the early foundations of the DSM. During the latter half of the 19th century and into the 20th century Adolph Meyer regarded mental illness as a reaction to a combination of psychosocial stressors and biological factors or influences (Winters, 1950). This perspective gained popularity when returning World War I veterans appeared to break down under the stress of combat.

The genesis of the DSM as we know it today can be traced back to the 1840s when the United States Bureau of the Census attempted for the first time to count the number of patients in mental hospitals. The Association of Medical Superintendents of American Institutions for the Insane or AMSAII, the precursor organization of the American Psychiatric Association, attempted to develop a uniform system for naming, classifying and recording cases of mental illness (Labruzza, 1997). The AMSAII continued to evolve over the years and in 1921 the name was officially changed to the present American Psychiatric Association. More than 25 years later a small task force was formed to create a new standardized psychiatric classification system that resulted in the 1952 publication of the first *DSM*. The goal was to encourage consistency in communication among clinicians. Known as the *DSM-I*, the manual was 130 pages long and listed a total of 106 mental disorders (Grob, 1991). Borrowing from Meyer's ideas about mental illness as a person's response to a combination of psychosocial stressors, many of the disorders in this edition were termed "reactions." The task of compiling mental hospital statistics was ultimately assumed by the newly formed National Institute of Mental Health in 1949. The *DSM* has been significantly updated five times: in 1968, 1980, 1987, 1994, and 2000.

The 1968 *DSM* Revisions

Drawn from a task force of 10 people, a revision of the *DSM-I*, called the *DSM-II*, was published in 1968. The revised manual listed 182 disorders and slightly increased to 134 pages in length. This edition represented the first attempt to coordinate with the World Health Organization's (WHO) *International Classification of Diseases Eighth Revision* or *ICD-8*. The *ICD* is the official coding system used by the United States to track the morbidity and mortality of diseases. Unfortunately symptoms for the disorders were not specified in detail. Psychiatrists would make different diagnoses based on the same symptoms thereby making the manual unreliable and the integrity of psychiatry as a field of practice was challenged (Mayes & Horwitz, 2005).

The media started to pay attention to the possibility that the treatment of those with a mental disorder was harsh and punitive. One example is the 1975 award winning movie *One Flew Over the Cuckoo's Nest* based on the 1962 novel of the same title. This was the first film to receive all five major Academy Awards (Best Picture, Actor in a Lead Role, Actress in a Lead Role, Director, Screenplay) since 1934. Filmed at Oregon State Hospital, the protagonist, Randle Patrick McMurphy (played by Jack Nicholson), was transferred to a mental institution in lieu of serving a sentence on a prison farm for statutory rape. While he had a history of violence, McMurphy showed no signs of mental illness. Once on the hospital's ward, he encounters Nurse Mildred "Big Nurse" Ratched (played by Louise Fletcher) who used a combination of subtle humiliation in group therapy, monotonous daily routines, and punishment thinly disguised as unpleasant medical treatments. McMurphy soon learns that most of the patients were more focused on their fear of nurse Ratched than on working toward becoming functional in the outside world. McMurphy instigates a series of events where the patients rebel against staff. As the movie moves toward its conclusion, a helpless McMurphy is seen being led to his bed by hospital staff. He has just had a lobotomy and the camera captures his unresponsive face and dull, lifeless eyes.

Long after the publication of the *DSM-II*, Clifford Beers highlighted the abusive treatment in institutions with an autobiographical account of his experiences when he was hospitalized for delusions, attempted suicide, depression, and mania in his 1980 book, *A Mind That Found Itself*. Beers described being restrained for days at a time leaving him completely helpless and in pain.

The 1980 and 1987 DSM Revisions

After 6 years of preparatory work, the next revision, the *DSM-III*, was published in 1980. It was a major departure from the earlier editions and more than tripled in size increasing to 494 pages. The *DSM-III* (APA, 1980) included "such features as diagnostic criteria, a multiaxial approach to evaluation, much expanded descriptions of the disorders and many additional categories" (p. 7). In total there were now 265 disorders. Every subsequent edition of the manual has been an expansion or refinement of the *DSM-III*. The introduction of the multiaxial system facilitated a more comprehensive evaluation with better attention to the different types of disorders, aspects of the person's environment and areas of function that could potentially be overlooked if the focus were limited to a single presenting problem. The description of the disorders was more explicit and the manual used more of a medical research-oriented model of disease. These descriptions had operational criteria that allowed them to be measured statistically and shifted the focus of the diagnostic process on behaviors that could be observed. Terms and theories associated with hypothetical or explanatory concepts such as references to unconscious motives found in the earlier editions were removed in this edition. The *DSM-III* also lined up with the newer version of the *ICD* or *ICD-9*.

In 1987, the *DSM-III* was revised and the *DSM-III-R* (or revised edition) was published. The *DSM-III-R* (APA, 1987) acknowledged that "the impact of the *DSM-III* has been remarkable" (p. xviii). Efforts to be more rigorous and precise were extended. Diagnostic categories were renamed and reorganized and significant changes in criteria were made. The manual expanded to 567 pages and now contained 292 diagnoses. The reliability of making the diagnosis was enhanced by providing a series of symptoms for a particular disorder and the patient only needed to show several of them but not all of them. Another departure from the previous manuals gave the flexibility to assign more than one diagnosis if the person met the criteria for more than one disorder. In prior editions, one usually had to choose the diagnosis that was the most obvious or urgent. The shift toward an empirical base for the diagnoses continued.

The 1994 DSM Revisions and the 2000 Update

The *DSM-IV* was published in 1994 listing 297 disorders and grew to 886 pages in length. A steering committee of 27 physicians who contributed to the revisions was introduced and was expanded to include four psychologists and one social worker,

Janet B. W. Williams, DSW. Increasing interdisciplinary input was a beginning step toward enlarging perspectives on the etiology of psychiatric problems is seen but interest in increasing the range of other professionals to work on the task force for reviewing the upcoming manual still remains. For example, the executive director of the National Association of Social Workers, Elizabeth J. Clark, wrote to American Psychiatric Association President Jay Scully in September 2008 asking for the inclusion of more social workers in the development of the *Diagnostic and Statistical Manual of Mental Disorders, Fifth Edition (DSM-5)* (NASW, 2009). She contended that a broad representation of mental health professions working on manual revisions would create opportunities to be inclusive of the biological, genetic, psychological, and the social and cultural aspects of psychiatric problems.

The steering committee for the *DSM-IV* created work groups of 5 to 16 members. The revisions were completed through a three-step process (Frances, Mack, Ross, & First, 2000). First, each group conducted an extensive literature review of the diagnoses assigned to them. This served to inform their final decisions and to document the process and the reasons for those decisions. The work groups subsequently asked for data from researchers to determine which criteria needed change. Finally, field trials were conducted to study the effects of the changes that were being considered; these field trials were funded by the National Institute of Mental Health (NIMH), the National Institute on Drug Abuse (NIDA) and the National Institute on Alcohol Abuse and Alcoholism (NIAAA). The literature review, reports on the analyses of data from researchers, and the field trials related to diagnoses can be found in a series of four edited volumes published in 1994, 1996, 1997, and 1998 by the American Psychiatric Association entitled *DSM-IV Sourcebook*. A major change from previous versions of the manual was to include a clinical significance criterion to almost half of all the diagnostic categories; for example, symptoms that cause clinically significant distress or impairment in social, occupational, or other important areas of functioning.

A text revision of the *DSM-IV*, known as *DSM-IV-TR* was published in 2000. The majority of the specific criteria for a diagnosis were unchanged but the language was refined. It included 100 additional pages of text focusing on the increased enumeration of criteria and specifiers. Care was taken in the text discussion and criteria to avoid the use of phrases such as "alcoholic" or "schizophrenic" emphasizing the classification system as descriptions of mental disorders rather than to have the disorder characterize the person. As such, the manual refers to the *person with* alcohol dependence or a *person with* schizophrenia. This change was intended to avoid the implication that all people with a particular diagnosis are the same. In addition, reference to individuals as patients was omitted. To facilitate the use of the *DSM-IV-TR* by a range of mental health practitioners, the terms *physician* and *psychiatrist* are not used. Instead, readers will find reference to terms such as *clinicians* and *mental health professionals*. Sexist language was eliminated. The information on each diagnosis was updated as well as some of the diagnostic codes in order to stay consistent with the *ICD*. A glossary of technical terms was included as well as a discussion of the highlights of changes from the *DSM-IV*. At this point the *DSM-IV-TR* has been translated into 22 languages extending its influence beyond the United States.

Development of the *DSM-5*

In 1999, initiatives were set in place to set the research priorities for the next edition of the *DSM*. In July 2007, the American Psychiatric Association announced the task force members who will oversee the development of the *DSM-5*. The new manual is recommending revisions in a number of diagnostic categories and adding dimensional assessments that would enable practitioners to evaluate the severity of symptoms as well as take into account the cross cutting of symptoms that exist across a number of different diagnostic categories. In addition, the proposed new edition is looking carefully at how race, gender, and ethnicity may influence the diagnosis. As with prior editions of the *DSM*, these efforts are not without criticism. David Kupfer, who is instrumental in the *DSM*'s revision, is reported to have said in a newspaper report, "One of the raps against psychiatry is that you and I are the only two people in the U.S. without a psychiatric diagnosis" (Grossman, 2008).

Challenges

Despite its stature in the mental health field, the *DSM* and its publisher, the American Psychiatric Association, have not avoided controversy and criticism over the years. For example the American Psychiatric Association's earlier classification of homosexuality as a mental illness led to its removal in 1973 as a diagnostic category in the sixth printing of the *DSM-II*. However, controversy remains over the category of sexual disorder not otherwise specified, which includes discussion about a state of distress about one's sexual orientation, as well as the diagnosis of gender identity disorder, seen (in adults) as discomfort with one's sex or sense of inappropriateness in the gender role of that sex (Hausman, 2003).

Another challenge to the *DSM* surfaced in 2003 when activists from MindFreedom International staged a hunger strike protesting what it believed to be an unjustified biomedical focus on mental disorders. The American Psychiatric Association was confronted to provide evidence of the claim that mental disorders are due to chemical imbalances in the brain. In response, the American Psychiatric Association published its position statement, *Diagnosis and Treatment of Mental Disorders*, on September 25, 2003, and encouraged an exchange of perspectives between the two organizations. The American Psychiatric Association became the center of yet another challenge when it was learned that psychiatrists from the United States were helping interrogators in Guantanamo and other detention facilities. Here, too, the American Psychiatric Association released a position statement, *Barring Psychiatric Participation in Interrogation of Detainees*, on May 22, 2006. In essence, the association took the position that psychiatrists should not take a direct role in the interrogation of particular prisoners but could offer general advice on the possible medical and psychological effects of techniques and conditions of the interrogation.

In 2008, the American Psychiatric Association generated criticism around questions about the influence of the pharmaceutical industry over its actions. A 2006 congressional investigation revealed that 30% of the association's financing, or approximately $62.5 million, came from the drug industry; half through drug advertisements in its journals and meeting exhibits, and the other half sponsoring fellowships, conference and industry symposiums at its annual meeting (Carey & Harris, 2008). In his role as president elect, Alan Schatzberg was criticized after it was discovered that he was a principal investigator on a federal study into a drug being developed by a private company, Corcept Therapeutics, that he had himself set up and in which he had several millions of dollars worth of stock (Chronicle of Higher Education, 2008).

Despite efforts to refine diagnoses, a number of critics suggest that the *DSM* format fails to provide convincing evidence for both the reliability and validity of diagnostic criteria (Kutchins & Kirk, 1997; Wakefield, 1992). S. J. Wolin and Wolin (1993) observe that the ever-expanding definitions of disorders create diagnostic avenues for a person's bad habits or annoying traits to be categorized as mental disorders (Widiger & Sankis, 2000). One example is the diagnosis of acute stress disorder (ASD) that was included in the *DSM-IV* without extensive research (Munson, 2001). Bryant and Harvey (2000) and others (see, for example, Bryant, 2000; Harvey & Bryant, 2002; Marshall, Spitzer, & Liebowitz, 2000) questioned whether the diagnostic criteria for ASD are essentially expected reactions that surface within the first month after a person experiences a traumatic event. According to Tavris (1992), the *DSM* has a long-standing history of developing diagnostic categories unfavorable to women and to members of some racial groups. There is also concern about unfairness to the elderly. First and foremost, the *DSM* focuses on diagnosis while the client's problems in living and the influence of their social context on mental health issues receives secondary attention. Despite the controversy and criticism over the years, the *DSM* has made significant contributions to the field of mental health (Bentley, 2002).

Contributions

As early as 1980, the *DSM-III* recognized that it was "only one frame in the ongoing process of attempting to better understand mental disorders," (APA, p. 12). While efforts to refine the diagnostic categories continue, the *DSM* is considered to be the gold standard for diagnoses in the field. The current improvements and ongoing refinements of the definitions of mental disorders have facilitated important advances in clinical research aimed at fostering an even better understanding of them. For example, the specificity of the diagnostic criteria has made it possible for researchers to select groups of subjects that are more homogeneous diagnostically and to pay particular attention to diagnostic variables. The inclusion of the multiaxial and specified diagnostic criteria based on the most up-to-date empirical research and clinical experience enhance the comprehensiveness of evaluations as well as making the assessment process more efficient (Bentley, 2002). This carries over to clinical practice. For example, identifying the problem helps the client to have some control over it and contributes to more effective psychotherapeutic and pharmacological treatment planning.

The *DSM* has turned out to be a major tool to organize observations and information about one or more troubling aspects of the client's life. The increased reliability and validity of the data that contributed to defining the various mental disorders in the *DSM-IV-TR* also helps to establish a clearer relationship between diagnosis and more effective treatment planning (Thyer & Wodarski, 2007). As well, insurance companies rely on its diagnoses for reimbursing clinicians. The manual remains popular in the United States and around the world. It continues to be regarded as a universal language to communicate with other professionals about a client's status (Williams, 2008).

Major Features

The *DSM* provides a categorical classification system that divides mental disorders into different types based on criteria sets with defining features. The official codes and diagnostic categories are listed, followed by the diagnostic criteria for each of the disorders together with descriptive text. The explicit statements of the constructs embodied in the diagnostic criteria have led to the *DSM*'s acceptance as a clinical, research, and educational tool for psychopathology. The diagnostic categories, supportive criteria, and descriptions of each disorder are not intended to be used in a cookbook fashion. Each person's experience with the same mental illness is different. Therefore, the diagnostic criteria are intended as guidelines.

Due to the heterogeneity of each person's clinical presentation, the *DSM* allows for diagnostic flexibility by including a number of criteria sets where the person only needs to show a subset of behaviors from a longer list of symptoms. For instance, someone who is struggling with borderline personality disorder only needs to present five out of a list of nine symptoms. The *DSM* also includes a discussion of the cultural variations found in a number of disorders in order to be aware of the influence of diversity on the diagnostic process. This parallels the increased awareness of the influence of diversity on the diagnostic process found in counseling schools and programs throughout the United States. For example, the Educational Policy and Accreditation Standards

(EPAS) of the Council on Social Work Education require accredited schools of social work to include curriculum content about diversity. It goes without saying that being unfamiliar with a person's cultural frame of reference runs the risk of incorrectly judging behaviors as pathology rather than seeing them as normal variations in the actions, beliefs, or experiences particular to the individual's background. The *DSM* also offers a description of culture-bound syndromes in an appendix that are not a part of the classification system.

The *DSM* classification system and criteria sets are regarded as prototypes and the client who closely resembles the description is considered to have the disorder. Less attention is given to isolated and noncriterion symptoms that do not support a specific diagnosis. This format helps to sort through a particular client's symptom picture and guides the process of making a differential diagnosis. Each category of specific disorders is given a number code. The numeric codes are generally used for administrative purposes such as medical record keeping, compiling statistical data, and/or reporting data to interested third parties such as governmental agencies, private insurers, and the World Health Organization. As an example, the *DSM* diagnostic codes have been mandated by the Health Care Financing Administration (HCFA) for reimbursement under the federal Medicare system.

Assigning the Diagnostic Code

When the disorder meets the descriptive criteria found in the manual it is given a numeric code and a name. The diagnostic codes are usually applied to the person's current symptom presentation. The code has three digit numbers followed by a decimal point and then one or two additional digit numbers. The last two numbers in the code provide for a more accurate recording of the diagnosis and are used to increase diagnostic specificity. The numbers also provide opportunities to classify a more homogeneous subgrouping of persons with the same disorder who share certain features. The fifth digit is sometimes assigned to code subtypes, severity, the course of the disorder, and specifiers.

The Diagnostic Code's Fifth Digit

The fifth digit is generally used to identify:

- Subtypes
- Severity
- Course of the disorder
- Specifiers

Subtypes

The subtype indicates the predominant symptom presentation within a specific diagnosis. For example, a person may be struggling with schizophrenia (coded as 298) but there are five distinct subtypes: Paranoid Type, Disorganized Type, Catatonic Type, Undifferentiated Type, and Residual Type. The digits following the decimal are used to indicate the subtype.

✍ Indicating Diagnostic Subtype for Schizophrenia: An Example

Schizophrenia	298
Schizophrenia, Paranoid Type	298.30
Schizophrenia, Disorganized Type	298.10
Schizophrenia, Catatonic Type	298.20
Schizophrenia, Undifferentiated Type	298.90
Schizophrenia, Residual Type	298.60

Not every subtype is assigned a number and may simply be indicated after the code and name of the disorder. For example, a person may be struggling with delusions. The diagnosis is coded as 297.1 and named as "Delusional Disorder," but there are seven distinct subtypes: Erotomanic Type, Grandiose Type, Jealous Type, Persecutory Type, Somatic Type, Mixed Type, and Unspecified Type. When a coded number is not used, the *DSM* instructs the practitioner to "specify type." In this instance, an example of the specific diagnosis would look like the following: "297.1 Delusional Disorder, Erotomanic Type."

Severity and Course of the Disorder

Severity indicates the intensity of the signs and symptoms and the degree to which the person's functioning is impaired. When appropriate, you may also be asked to apply severity criteria when formulating the *DSM* diagnosis. These criteria are generally required for mood, substance abuse, mental retardation, and conduct disorders. They are:

- Mild—Used when the client meets minimum criteria.
- Moderate—Considered an intermediate level, between the designations of mild and severe.
- Severe—This designation is made when the client meets many more symptoms than minimum criteria, some symptoms are especially severe, and social functioning is especially compromised.

The course of the disorder refers to the status of remission and may be indicated as:

- In partial remission—When the client previously met full criteria and some symptoms remain but there are too few to fulfill criteria currently.
- In full remission—This designation is used when the client has been symptom-free for a period of time that seems clinically relevant.
- Prior history—This applies when the client appears to have recovered, and the practitioner believes that it is important to mention it.

Using the mood disorders to illustrate coding for severity and course of the illness, if the person shows the symptoms of a major depressive episode, the diagnosis would be assigned the code of 296 and called "Major Depressive Disorder." If the person has been depressed only once, the first number added after the decimal point would be a 2, indicating a single episode. However, if the person has been depressed more than once, then the number after the decimal point would be a 3, indicating recurrent episodes. If the depressive episode occurs only once and is characterized as mild, the code would be recorded as 296.21. The number 296.22 indicates moderate severity, 296.23 represents severe but the person does not show any psychotic features. A 296.24 means severe and with psychotic features. As the person begins a course of recovery, a code of 296.25 indicates that the person is in partial remission. If the person has recovered or is in full remission, the code assigned would be 296.26.

The course of the disorder is usually indicated as "In Partial Remission" when the person meets some of the criteria for the disorder but is no longer showing the full criteria that were present when the original diagnosis was made. "In Full Remission" specifies that all the signs and symptoms of the disorder have disappeared but the diagnosis is clinically significant at the present time. Table 1.1 summarizes the assessment guidelines for indicating severity and course of a disorder.

An Example of Diagnostic Codes Indicating Severity and Course for Major Depression

Major Depressive Disorder, Single Episode	296.2
Major Depressive Disorder, Single Episode, Mild	296.21
Major Depressive Disorder, Single Episode, Moderate	296.22
Major Depressive Disorder, Single Episode, Severe Without Psychotic Features	296.23
Major Depressive Disorder, Single Episode, Severe With Psychotic Features	296.24
Major Depressive Disorder, Single Episode, In Partial Remission	296.25
Major Depressive Disorder, Single Episode, In Full Remission	296.26

Table 1.1 Guidelines for Severity and Course of the Disorder

Mild	The person shows few symptoms, if any, in excess of those needed to make the diagnosis and symptoms result in no more than a minor impairment to the person's social or occupational functioning.
Moderate	Symptoms or functional impairment in social or occupational functioning are between "mild" and "severe."
Severe	Many symptoms in excess of those needed to make the diagnosis are present or several symptoms that are particularly severe are present or the person shows marked impairment in social or occupational functioning.
In Partial Remission	The full criteria needed to diagnose the person's disorder have been previously met and currently only some of the symptoms or signs of the disorder remain.
In Full Remission	The person no longer shows any signs or symptoms of the disorder but it is still clinically significant to note the disorder; after a period of time, the practitioner may determine that the person is fully recovered and no longer codes the disorder as a current diagnosis.

Specifiers

In some instances, the *DSM* designates "specify if" as a part of making the diagnosis. These are specifiers that indicate if there are certain factors present in a person's particular diagnosis; for example, if someone is struggling with the somatoform disorder of "Pain Disorder Associated With Psychological Factors" it is coded as 307.80. You may further be asked to "specify if" the pain disorder is acute or chronic.

Specifiers may also indicate if the diagnosis is a past condition or the reason for the visit. The assigned diagnosis customarily represents a present condition. However, there may be instances when a person's past history of a particular diagnosis is useful to know. In this instance, a past diagnosis is modified with the phrase, "Prior History"; for example "308.3 Acute Stress Disorder, Prior History." If a person meets criteria for more than one disorder, then all of them are listed. The primary diagnosis is recorded first followed by "Reason for Visit" in outpatient settings or "Principal Diagnosis" in inpatient settings. The other diagnoses are subsequently listed in order of importance. The primary diagnosis is generally found on Axis I.

Including Diagnostic Specificity

Specifier for specific factors present	Specify if
Past history	Prior history of the diagnosis
Reason for visit	Reason for visit, or principal diagnosis
Severity	Mild, moderate, severe
Course	Partial remission, full remission

If there is some degree of doubt about a diagnosis, the term *provisional* may be used. In prior versions of the *DSM*, this was commonly referred to by the phrase "rule out" (APA, 1994; Munson, 2001). The term *rule out* has since been replaced by the designation of a provisional diagnosis. While there may not be enough information available to make a firm diagnosis (on Axis I or Axis II), you might have a strong supposition that the full criteria will ultimately be met. In this instance, the lack of clarity about the diagnosis is indicated by recording the diagnostic code, the suspected name of the syndrome, and followed by the term *provisional* after it. A specific diagnosis may be deferred in those instances when you have insufficient information to make a diagnosis all together. In this instance, the *DSM* diagnostic code 799.9 is assigned.

The designation "Not Otherwise Specified" is used for the times when the person comes to your attention with a mixed picture of behaviors showing symptoms that might suggest several different disorders. There may be a range of symptoms but they do not meet the full criteria for any particular disorder as described in the *DSM*. The person's symptoms may be due to medications, the person's culture, stress, or there may simply be limited information to support the diagnosis. All of the major classes of disorders allow for this situation with a category of "Not Otherwise Specified" or NOS.

Let's take the example of schizophrenia and the other psychotic disorders. This is a complex syndrome and there may be times when you do not have enough information to make a definitive diagnosis. In this situation, the code 799.9 is assigned to indicate the diagnosis is deferred. Sometimes you may have enough information to ascertain the presence of a psychotic disorder but you cannot further specify the type of psychotic disorder. When this occurs, a "psychotic disorder not otherwise specified" (coded as 298.9) is applied. If you are able to eliminate the possibility of a psychotic disorder all together but the client presents a symptom picture of an unspecified mental disorder, then the designation "unspecified mental disorder" (coded as 300.9) is applied. If you have enough information to determine a particular class of disorder but are unable to be any more specific than that, then you indicate the class of disorder followed by the designation "not otherwise specified." Examples of the diagnostic codes are summarized as follows:

Diagnosis deferred (*DSM* code 799.9)	Used on Axis I and Axis II, the practitioner has inadequate information to make any judgment about a diagnosis.
Psychotic disorder not otherwise specified (*DSM* code 298.9)	The practitioner has enough information to ascertain the presence of a psychotic disorder but unable to further specify the diagnosis.
Unspecified mental disorder (*DSM* code 300.9)	A psychotic disorder is ruled out but further specification is not possible.
Note the class of the disorder followed by "Not otherwise specified"	Assessment data indicates the specific class of disorder but further specification is not possible due to insufficient information or the clinical features of the disorder do not meet criteria for any of the specific categories in that class.

Organization of the Manual

The *DSM-IV-TR* disorders are grouped into 16 major diagnostic classes and one additional section entitled, "Other Conditions That May Be a Focus of Clinical Attention." The descriptive text discussion describes each disorder under the following headings: diagnostic features; subtypes and/or specifiers; recording procedures; associated features and disorders; specific culture, age, and gender features; prevalence; course; familial pattern; and differential diagnosis. A section may be left out when there is no information available. If specific disorders share common features, this information is incorporated in a general introduction to the group of disorders. A summary of the specific content of each section of the descriptive text discussion is summarized on Table 1.2.

Table 1.2 Descriptive Text Discussion in the DSM-IV-TR

Diagnostic features	Diagnostic information is clarified and illustrative examples frequently provided.
Subtypes and specifiers	Definitions of the subtypes and specifiers applicable to the specific diagnostic category.
Recording procedures	Guidelines for reporting the name of the disorder and instructions for applying any appropriate subtypes and/or specifiers along with selecting and recording the appropriate *ICD*.
Associated features and disorders	This section is divided into three parts:
	1. *Associated descriptive features and mental disorders*—Includes a discussion of features frequently associated with the disorder; other mental disorders associated with the disorder; disorders that may precede, co-occur with, or are consequences of the disorder in question; and predisposing factors and complications (if available).
	2. *Associated laboratory findings*—Reviews laboratory findings associated with the disorder such as (a) those considered to be "diagnostic" of the disorder, (b) findings noted to be abnormal in groups of individuals with the disorder, and (c) laboratory findings associated with complications of a disorder.
	3. *Associated physical examination findings and general medical conditions*—Information about symptoms (elicited by history or during a physical exam) that may be significant but are not essential to the diagnosis; also includes medical conditions that may precede, co-occur with, or is a consequence of a disorder; and includes those disorders coded outside the "Mental and Behavioural Disorders" chapter of the *ICD* that are associated with the disorder being discussed.

(continued)

Table 1.2 (continued)

Specific culture, age, and gender features	Variations in the presentation of the disorder attributed to the person's culture, developmental stage, or gender; as well as prevalence rates (related to culture, age, and gender).
Prevalence	Data on lifetime prevalence, incidence rates and lifetime risk for the disorder and, when known, data for different settings (such as community, primary care, outpatient mental health clinics, and inpatient settings).
Course	Typical lifetime patterns of symptom presentation and the evolution of the disorder: for example, age of onset and manner of onset of the disorder; episodic versus a continuous course; single episode versus recurrent; duration; typical length of the illness (and episodes); and progression over time, such as stable, worsening, or improving.
Familial pattern	Frequency of the disorder among first-degree biological relatives compared to frequency in the general population; indicates other disorders that tend to occur more frequently in family members of those with the disorder; information about heritability (for example, data from twin studies or known genetic transmission patterns).
Differential diagnosis	How to differentiate the disorder from other similar disorders.

The Multiaxial Assessment

The *DSM-IV-TR* organizes each diagnosis on five different axes; each relating to different aspects of the disorder. Each axis gives different information about the person, which may help plan treatment and predict outcome. The diagnoses of specific disorders are only recorded on Axes I and II. The diagnoses recorded on each of these axes have both names and numbers; the numbers commonly used for insurance and billing purposes. Table 1.3 outlines the information coded on each axis.

Axis I—Clinical Disorders

The reason the person comes to your attention or the primary diagnosis is generally recorded on Axis I. If more than one diagnosis is considered, then the one that is most responsible for the current assessment (or what brought the client to your attention) is listed first. All diagnoses are listed but the primary diagnosis is followed by the qualifying phrase, "Principal Diagnosis" or "Reason for Visit." If these phrases are not included, the assumption is that the primary diagnosis is recorded on Axis I. However, if there is no diagnosis to be coded on Axis I, V71.09 is recorded. This notation ensures that consideration of a diagnosis for Axis I has not been overlooked or forgotten. The following lists the disorders that are coded on Axis I.

Axis I—Clinical Disorders

Disorders Usually First Diagnosed in Infancy, Childhood, or Adolescence

Delirium, Dementia, and Amnestic and Other Cognitive Disorders

Mental Disorders Due to a General Medical Condition

Substance-Related Disorders

Schizophrenia and Other Psychotic Disorders

Mood Disorders

Anxiety Disorders

Somatoform Disorders

Factitious Disorders

Dissociative Disorders

Sexual and Gender Identity Disorders

Eating Disorders

Sleep Disorders

Impulse-Control Disorders Not Elsewhere Classified

Adjustment Disorders

Other Conditions That May Be a Focus of Clinical Attention

Table 1.3 The Multiaxial Assessment

Axis I—Clinical Disorders	Clinical symptoms causing significant impairment:
	• All clinical syndromes listed in the *DSM-IV-TR* except personality disorders and mental retardation.
	• Other conditions that might be a focus of clinical attention.
	• V71.09—Or no diagnosis on Axis I.
	• 799.9—Provisional diagnosis (or too little information to establish a diagnosis).
Axis II—Personality Disorders and Mental Retardation	The long-term problems:
	• Personality disorders.
	• Mental retardation.
Axis III—General Medical Conditions	Medical conditions that may influence or worsen Axis I and Axis II disorders:
	• All general medical conditions.
	• *ICD* codes can be used.
	• None (or no medical conditions).

(continued)

Table 1.3 (continued)

Axis IV—Psychosocial and Environmental Problems	Any social or environment problems that may impact Axis I or Axis II:
	Psychosocial and/or environmental problems.
Axis V—Global Assessment of Functioning (GAF) Scale	Indication of the client's overall level of functioning: Using a number between 1 (indicating persistent danger of hurting self or others) to 100 (indicating superior functioning) that shows the person's current level of functioning.

Axis II—Personality Disorders and Mental Retardation

Axis II is used to code the longer-lasting personality disorders and mental retardation. This separation ensures that relevant personality factors are part of the entire diagnostic picture. It also separates mental retardation from the other categories. Of all the disorders listed, mental retardation (and also the learning disorders that are listed on Axis I) requires diagnostic testing before the diagnosis can be made. If the person struggles with more than one personality disorder, all are listed and coded on Axis II. If you are aware of a person's defense mechanisms or maladaptive personality traits, these can also be included but they have no code number.

Similar to Axis I, if there is no diagnosis for Axis II the code V71.09 is assigned to denote that this category has not been overlooked or ignored. If you need more time or information to make a definitive diagnosis, the code 799.9 is used. In addition to Mental Retardation, there are 11 personality disorders that can be recorded on Axis II and they are as follows:

Axis II—Personality Disorders (and Mental Retardation)

Paranoid Personality Disorder

Schizoid Personality Disorder

Schizotypal Personality Disorder

Antisocial Personality Disorder

Borderline Personality Disorder

Histrionic Personality Disorder

Narcissistic Personality Disorder

Avoidant Personality Disorder

Dependent Personality Disorder

Obsessive-Compulsive Personality Disorder

Personality Disorder Not Otherwise Specified

Axis III—General Medical Conditions

Persons struggling with a mental disorder may have a related general medical condition that can play a role in treatment-planning and outcomes. Knowing the medical condition can help to better understand the person's situation and Axis III is where this information is recorded. In some situations, the medical condition has caused the mental disorder and in others the person may be taking medications that could affect the disorder. If the medical condition has caused the disorder, it is recorded on Axis I with the phrase "due to"; for example, the Axis I designation might be recorded as "Mood Disorder, Due to Hypothyroidism, With Depressive Features" and coded as 293.83. The Axis III designation would be "Hypothyroidism" and coded as 244.9. If there is no medical condition, "None" is recorded.

Axis IV—Psychosocial and Environmental Problems

Axis IV is reserved for any psychosocial stressors and/or environmental problems that impact on the conditions recorded on Axis I, II, and III. In general, only those that are considered to be relevant and have been present during the past year are noted. A positive event that causes stress, such as a job promotion, is included if it has caused difficulties for the client. More than one problem may be listed. Although you can be particularly attentive to events that have happened to the person over the last year, there may be some stressors that have happened a number of years ago that still exert an influence over the current diagnosis. As an example, someone might have a current Axis I diagnosis of Posttraumatic Stress Disorder (coded as 309.81). By history, you might have learned that this person was a veteran of the 1991 Desert Storm and this past war experience is a major contributor to the current symptoms of posttraumatic stress. Following is a listing of psychosocial and environmental events commonly recorded on Axis IV. It is recommended that you identify the relevant category and then detail the specific problems encountered by the client. Note that some have a "V code" designation.

Axis IV—Psychosocial and Environmental Problems

Problems with primary support group
    Childhood (V61.9)
    Adult (V61.9)
    Parent-child (V61.20)
Problems related to the social environment (V62.4)
Educational problems (V62.3)
Occupational problems (V62.2)

(continued)

Housing problems

Economic problems

Problems with access to health-care services

Problems related to interaction with the legal system/crime

Other psychosocial and environmental problems

The description "other psychosocial and environmental problems" is used for any stressor that does not fit into the listed categories. For instance, this category might be used to record natural disasters and catastrophes such as hurricanes, tornadoes, floods, or earthquakes. Again, keep in mind that there may be positive events in the person's life that may be stressful such as the birth of a child. However, these events are not recorded on Axis IV unless they create significant problems for the person. It is not uncommon for clients to present with a number of problems and following is a list of examples for these categories.

Primary support group	Death or illness of a relative, a divorce or separation, remarriage of a parent, abuse, or conflicts with relatives.
Social environment	Death or loss of a friend, acculturation problems, discrimination, retirement, or living alone.
Education	Academic problems, conflicts with classmates or teachers, illiteracy, or a poor school environment.
Occupation	Problems may include stressful work conditions, changing jobs, disagreements with coworkers or the boss, or unemployment.
Housing	Difficulties revolving around poor housing, living in a dangerous neighborhood, or not getting along with the landlord or neighbors.
Economic	Poverty, debt, credit problems, inadequate welfare or child support.
Access to health care	Inadequate health services, insufficient health insurance, no transportation to health services.
Interaction with the legal system/crime	Being arrested, incarceration, suing or being sued, being a victim of a crime.
Other psychosocial and environmental problems	Conflicts with human service professionals such as a psychologist, social worker, marriage and family therapist, or mental health counselor, exposure to war, other hostilities, natural disasters, or catastrophes.

Axis V—Global Assessment of Functioning (GAF) Scale

Axis V, or the Global Assessment of Functioning (GAF) scale, is used to assess the person's overall psychological, occupational, and social functioning (Frances, First, & Pincus, 1995). Scores can be assigned at the time of admission and/or at the time the person ends treatment. It can also be used at other times a person is receiving care; for example, over the course of the client's highest level of functioning during the past six months. In practice, the scores tend to vary due to the subjective assessment of the client's level of functioning and situation. Despite this drawback, it is considered the accepted measure of a person's level of functioning. Dziegielewski (personal communication, June 7, 2007), suggests that one way to reduce the element of subjectivity when recording a client's GAF score is to have agency staff meet together, perhaps through an in-service training, and develop a uniform understanding of threshold behaviors for assigning a particular score.

The number given on Axis V ranges from 1 to 100. A zero indicates that there has not been enough time to adequately assess a person's functioning. The complete GAF scale can be found in the *DSM-IV-TR* (APA, 2000, p. 34). The scale is divided into segments of 10 points. Ninety-one to 100 is the highest score. This reflects superior functioning in a wide range of activities, life's problems are seen as never getting out of hand, and the person is sought out by others because of his or her many positive qualities. In contrast, the span of 10 to 1 is the lowest level of functioning. Here, the person poses a persistent danger of severely hurting him- or herself or others or they have a persistent inability to maintain minimal personal hygiene or show serious suicidal acts with a clear expectation of death as the outcome. The range is summarized as follows.

Range of Global Assessment of Functioning Scale Scores

100—Superior functioning

90—Absent or minimal symptoms

80—Transient symptoms seen as expectable reactions to psychosocial stressors

70—Mild symptoms

60—Moderate symptoms

50—Serious symptoms

40—Some impairment in reality testing or communication

30—Behavior considerably influenced by delusions or hallucinations *or* serious impairment in communication or judgment

20—Some danger of hurting self or others *or* occasionally fails to maintain minimal hygiene

10—Persistent danger of severely hurting self or others *or* persistent inability to maintain minimal personal hygiene *or* serious suicidal act with clear expectation of death

0—Inadequate information

From practice experience, most individuals who require inpatient hospitalization usually have a GAF score of 50 or less.

SETTING THE STAGE FOR COMPETENCY-BASED ASSESSMENTS

In summary, the multiaxial system gathers a range of information that complements the competency-based assessment (Gray, 2008). That is, the competency-based assessment provides a framework to explore aspects of a person's life that go beyond the diagnostic signs and symptoms outlined in the DSM. Clients do not exist in a vacuum and there is more to a person's life story than a description of the features of a particular diagnosis. Merging the competency-based assessment with the DSM classification format individualizes each person's experience with a mental disorder and considers the many ways that people cope with life challenges and the factors that influence their struggles. More precisely, a person is not summed up by a diagnosis but instead is seen as a unique individual who also happens to be struggling with a mental illness. Once you begin to individualize patterns of mental illness as outlined in the DSM, the diagnosis does not become the defining feature of a person's life.

Mayer (2006) characterizes the DSM as a medical-diagnostic document that accentuates psychological behavioral syndromes that cause distress or disability. In keeping with this orientation, the DSM stresses the assessment of pathology while the client's problems in living with a diagnosis receive secondary attention. Observes O'Gorman (2000), ". . . one could argue that this is part of what we are paid to do, as every insurance company requests a DSM-IV diagnosis of what is 'wrong' with our client" (p. 15). While clients may struggle with a particular diagnosis they also have abilities as well as resources that can be found in the family, community, and culture

THE COMPETENCY-BASED ASSESSMENT

The competency-based assessment reconciles the attention to pathology by emphasizing strengths. By highlighting competence, the focus shifts toward helping people to achieve their potential and on understanding the stresses and demands that environmental transactions place on those who are struggling with mental illness. People are seen as growing, changing, learning, and in continuous interaction with their environment. Combining this approach with the DSM format decenters the problem-focused orientation by highlighting coping and adaptation (Gray, 2006). While clients may struggle with a particular diagnosis, the competency-based perspective moves toward awareness that they also have resources and abilities. The impact of family, community, and cultural values becomes a part of diagnostic consideration along with biological and psychological factors. The practitioner attempts to make sense of the clients' problems, tries to understand their worldview and considers what to do next with that information. The client's context is seen as an important part of understanding how the person's phenomenological presentation of self has developed not only over time but through interpersonal influences. The competency-based assessment offers an integrative and multidimensional framework for assessing mental disorders.

The distinguishing feature of the competency-based assessment is the parallel consideration of diagnostic features found in the *DSM* along with an appraisal of a person's unique experiences with mental illness. From this perspective, understanding the signs and symptoms of the mental disorders is advanced when the ways that people cope with a particular diagnosis or diagnoses are taken into account. This discussion begins with an overview of the concepts and theories supporting a competency-based orientation followed by a review of the partnership with strengths, empowerment, and resilience.

Introduction

Competence is a major theme for the competency-based assessment and includes three key components: the person's biological capacities, the psychological realm, and social or environmental qualities. Competence is further explicated by the strengths, empowerment, and resilience in a person's life. Figure 1.1 represents a graphic illustration of the relationship of the biological, psychological, social or environmental aspects and competencies in the client's life. By looking at the intersection of these dimensions, we

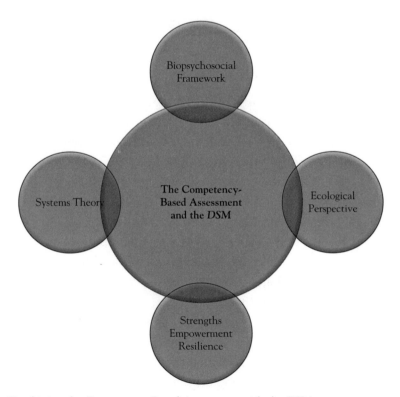

Figure 1.1   Combining the Competency-Based Assessment with the *DSM*

gain a more complete understanding of the client. The biological dimension addresses relationships among factors that include normal biology, disease processes (including metabolic), and genetic influences. The psychological aspects include thoughts, feelings, perceptions, motivation, reactions to "illness," behavior, and developmental considerations. The social component examines culture, ethnicity, environmental influences, family, peers, and social networks. Competencies are the client's strengths, empowerment, resilience, and available supports.

The *DSM* helps to sort through the signs and symptoms of mental illness and pathology. The manual's classification system determines whether deviations observed in a person's thought, mood, or behavior are seen as consistent with an established diagnostic category in the *DSM*. However, living with a mental illness is a different matter. The competency-based assessment provides a framework to learn about the client's competence as he or she struggles with a particular diagnosis. This individualizes the assessment of pathology by looking at each client's response to living with mental illness and considers his or her specific life circumstances. The foundations of the competency-based assessment model are drawn from a biopsychosocial framework together with elements of systems theory, the ecological perspective and strengths, empowerment, and resilience. Individuals and their environment are seen as interacting systems that extend from the biochemical to the psychological and social realms.

We turn to an overview of concepts from the biopsychosocial framework that supports the competency-based assessment.

The Biopsychosocial Framework

Individuals and their environments represent multiple systems that extend from the biochemical or biological to the psychological to the social realm. No single factor can be considered responsible for causing a behavioral response. The biopsychosocial framework, introduced by psychiatrist George L. Engel (1977) at the University of Rochester, posits that biological (including genetic influences), psychological (thoughts, emotions, and behaviors) and social factors (consisting of the family and groups, the neighborhood, the cultural setting, and the larger context of society) all play a role in a person's behavioral response to the circumstances of "disease" or mental illness. The biological component of the biopsychosocial framework addresses relationships among normal biology, disease processes, and genetic influences making a connection with each person's biological functioning. The psychological element looks for potential psychological contributors such as thoughts, feelings, perceptions, motivation, and reactions to "illness." The social aspect of the biopsychosocial framework investigates how different social factors such as cultural, environmental, and familial influences such as socioeconomic status, culture, poverty, and religion can influence health.

Because people are complex, understanding the dynamic interactions among biological, psychological, and social factors as they function within their environments provides a more complete clinical picture and highlights competencies that may be built upon. Consider, for example, an adult who is addicted to alcohol—we'll call him George. According to the *DSM*, George's diagnosis would be "Alcohol Dependence" and the related code is 303.90. However, the assigned diagnosis is only part of the behavioral picture. The biological, psychological, and social aspects of George's life all play a role in his drinking behaviors. Biologically, he does not eat well and begins to lose a great deal of weight. He runs the risk of developing other medical complications such as cirrhosis of the liver. In the short run, George has come to accept the associated hangover and headaches as the "price to pay" for his drinking but they leave him feeling disgusted with himself. This psychological reaction prompts George to make a "promise" that he will never drink again but he gives in and the very next day stops at a local bar for a "few beers" on his way home from work. George subsequently feels ashamed and disappointed in himself that he cannot "control" his drinking. Socially, his friends are limited to those he meets at the bar. The artificial sense of camaraderie he feels shores up his low self-esteem. However, George is able to continue working and supporting his family. His wife, who was his high school sweetheart, is worried about him.

The biopsychosocial framework supports the competency-based assessment in several ways. First, it organizes the exploration of the multiple systems that affect clients; the biological, psychological, social, and cultural aspects. Second, the competency-based assessment emphasizes understanding the client's present functioning and its relationship to past events. This underscores the importance of fully understanding each client's distinctive life history. The relationship between behavior and surrounding events is explored; that is, those events that can either elicit, maintain, or ameliorate problematic behaviors. Third, we become attentive to the signs and symptoms of a particular diagnostic category while at the same time paying attention to strengths. As shown in the example of "George," the environment plays a role in his behavior and enhances our understanding of the multiple effects of living with a diagnosis of alcohol dependence.

The overview of systems theory helps to explain the interactions between individuals and the various systems in their environments. Systems theory makes up a broad category of these symbolic representations.

Systems Theory Concepts

Barker (2003) defines systems theory as the concepts that emphasize reciprocal relationships among the elements that constitute a whole. Emphasized are the relationships among individuals, groups, organizations, or communities, and mutually influencing factors in the environment. A systems perspective focuses on the connectedness and the interrelation and interdependence of all the elements. Some would argue that systems theory is not actually a "theory" per se but a rather high level of abstraction. Bertalanffy (1962) sees it as "a working hypothesis, the main function of which is to provide a theoretical model for explaining, predicting, and controlling phenomena" (p. 17). Systems theory focuses attention on the diverse systems in which any complex living entity participates. Each system is an organized whole comprised of component parts that interact in a distinct way over time. For example, a social system is made up of individuals, each interrelated to constitute a whole. The limits of a social system are defined by established or arbitrary boundaries. It is these boundaries that give a social system its focus and identity as distinct from other social systems with which it interacts. A system's environment is, by definition, outside the system boundaries. An illustration of a person's social system might look like Figure 1.2.

Figure 1.2 portrays the dynamic interactions of an individual with other systems in the social environment. In this example, the person is placed at the center of the overlapping circles and involved in multiple systems consisting of family, work, and church.

As shown in this illustration, the individual is a part of many systems. According to systems theory, the person is affected by these systems and may also influence the systems.

The life of the social system is more than the sum of its members' activities and can be studied as a network of unique interlocking relationships with identifiable structural and communication patterns. A high degree of organization and interdependence exists among members of a particular social system. All systems are also subsystems of larger systems. There is interdependence and interaction between and among social systems. Systems have an equilibrium that is essentially fluid and even chaotic at times. Whether a specific system will be adaptive or not is its degree of openness. Open systems have permeable boundaries and this allows for an active interchange with their environments.

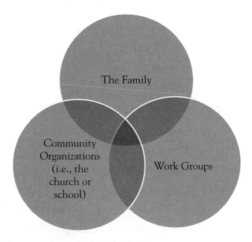

Figure 1.2   The Multiple Systems in an Individual's Life

Because systems are in dynamic interchange, a change in one part of the system will have consequences for other related systems. Problems arise when there is a "misfit" between individuals and the systems of which they are a part. As shown on Figure 1.2, the different systems in an individual's life could be the family, church, or work. Belonging to these different systems has an effect on the individual; for example, having a supportive family, seeing meaning in life by going to church, and earning a living in order to strive for a better existence could bring to bear a positive influence on someone living with mental illness. Ultimately this person may function at a higher level than someone who does not have the support of their family, does not go to church, or is unable to work.

The contribution of systems theory to the competency-based assessment is that it shifts the focus away from an essentially medical and linear model of causation and includes a consideration of the complex and diverse factors that can influence any specific human behavior; for example, living with mental illness. Systems theory organizes this attention to the many factors that have some bearing on a person's behavior and provides a broader, circular, more holistic orientation in order to understand fully the dynamics involved in a person's life. The contributions of different systems in facilitating or inhibiting behaviors are highlighted. Finally, systems theory allows for the recognition that social systems can change and adapt to their environment thus accentuating the many ways that people strive to cope and adapt. These systems terms are referred to as "structuring," "destructuring," and "restructuring" (Buckley, 1968).

We now review the ecological perspective, seen as an orientation that emphasizes understanding people and their environment and the nature of their transactions (Barker, 2003).

Aspects of the Ecological Perspective

The ecological perspective includes concepts borrowed from the field of ecology and compliments systems theory. According to Carol Germain (1991, p. 15), "ecology is the science that studies the relations between organisms and their environments." Used metaphorically, ecological concepts emphasize the reciprocity of person:environment exchanges in which each shapes and influences the other over time. The use of the colon in this configuration rather than a hyphen is deliberate. It underscores the transactional nature of the person or situation and the environment. The ecological perspective maintains a simultaneous focus on people and their environments and their reciprocal relationships; including, for example, families, groups, and communities (Gitterman & Germain, 2008). A person's coping behavior is understood in relation to the quality of his or her environment. When there is a good "fit" between a person and his or her environment they experience "adaptedness" (Dubos, 1968). Conversely, a poor fit generates stress.

Some of the major ideas the ecological perspective takes into consideration are (Germain, 1973, 1991, 1994; Gitterman & Germain, 2008; Hearn, 1979):

- *Social environment* refers to the conditions, circumstances and interactions that people have in order to survive. This includes the actual physical setting or social environment that society or culture provides; for example, the type of home a person lives in, the work he or she does, or the laws and social rules that govern one's behavior.
- *Habitat and niche* describe the nature of the person's physical and social environments. The physical habitat may include the physical settings, for example, residential dwellings, school settings, or the workplace to list a few. Human habitats are the spatial and temporal behaviors that help shape the person: environment transactions and regulate social distance, intimacy, privacy and/ or other interpersonal processes in the family, groups, community, and organizations. Niche refers to the status held by an individual, family, or group in the social structure of the community. It is possible to hold a stigmatized and destructive niche; for example, when someone is characterized as a "crazy" or a "drug addict."
- *Transactions* are the interactions that people have to communicate and interact with others in their environments. Considered a dynamic process, transactions can be positive or negative.
- *Energy* is the power of active involvement between people. It can take the form of input or output. Input is the energy coming into a person's life and adding to that life. Output is a form of energy going out of a person's life and taking something away from it.
- *Interface* denotes the exact point at which the interaction between a person and his or her environment takes place.
- *Adaptation* refers to the capacity to adjust to the surrounding environmental conditions. It is seen as the continuous, change-oriented, cognitive, sensory-perceptual, and behavioral processes people use to sustain or improve the "fit" between themselves and their environment. A person must change or adapt to new conditions and circumstances in order to continue functioning effectively. In the process of adaptation, people are affected by their environments but environments are also affected by people.
- *Coping* is a form of adaptation that implies a struggle to overcome problems; in particular, the way people deal with the negative experiences they encounter.
- *Life course* signifies the pathways of development that each person takes beginning from conception and birth through old age.

- *Life stressors* are usually externally generated and include difficult social or developmental transitions, traumatic life events or other conditions that disturb the existing fit between the person and his or her environments. Stress is the response to life stressors and it is characterized by troubled emotional or physiological states or both.
- *Interdependence* refers to the mutual reliance of each person on every other person (or/and groups of individuals in the social environment).

In summary, the ecological perspective advances understanding of the lack of "fit" between the person and his or her environment where both the practitioner and client work together to explore opportunities to mobilize strengths, locate empowering resources, and move toward a more optimistic view of coping abilities. When added to the competency-based assessment, the focus on understanding pathology is countered by a consideration of the client's context and resources. The ecological perspective extends our understanding of the dynamics within a person's social environments and facilitates a better understanding of why people behave the way they do. People are seen as influenced by their environments as well as able to influence the environment. Each person's unique experience with a particular disorder is considered. This supports the competency-based assessment by making the assessment process more individualized. Additionally, the dual focus of looking at the person *and* his or her environmental transactions helps to set the stage to work collaboratively with clients.

Strengths, empowerment, and resilience are fundamental to the effectiveness of the competency-based assessment.

THE PARTNERSHIP WITH STRENGTHS, EMPOWERMENT, AND RESILIENCE

The strengths perspective has been used with a variety of populations and problems such as substance use (Siegel et al., 1995), the elderly (Chapin & Cox, 2001; Perkins & Tice, 1999; Yip, 2005) domestic violence (Bell, 2003), families (Allison et al., 2003; Early & GlenMaye, 2000; Werrbach, 1996), and adolescents (Yip, 2006), but this discussion focuses on its connections to the field of mental health.

Strengths

Instead of focusing on problems and deficits, the strengths perspective shifts toward an exploration of clients' abilities, talents, and resources (Brun & Rapp, 2001; Saleebey, 2008). The client's problems are not ignored but rather than looking only at pathology and incompetence, the strengths perspective includes a consideration of talents, skills, possibilities, and hopes. The *DSM* establishes the basis for understanding the signs and symptoms of a particular diagnosis. As we attempt to diagnose the client's problem, this focus on illness and pathology runs the risk of seeing only deficits or flaws in our clients. The orientation to strengths expands the assessment by looking at resources, and positive qualities that can be put to use to help people to solve their problems and pursue positive change (Sheafor & Horjesi, 2003). The client's cultural and personal "stories," along with family and community resources, are explored (deJong & Berg, 2002). The strengths perspective, in conjunction with the medical model represented by *DSM*, provides a way to balance out the focus on problems.

A basic premise of the strengths perspective is that all persons are considered to have talents and skills and recognizes that there is something positive to be gained from difficulties and struggles. Saleebey (2008) identifies six guiding principles that can be found in the strengths perspective:

1. *Every individual, family, group, and community has strengths*—Focusing on pathology may prevent the recognition that people also have a number of strengths; for example, he or she may have graduated from high school, has a supportive family, is able to continue working, and is surrounded by a network of friends and neighbors.

2. *Serious problems such as mental and/or physical illness, trauma, or abuse may be injurious but they may also be sources of challenge and opportunity*—Although clients may have experienced trauma, they are not seen as helpless victims who are damaged beyond repair. Serious problems may open up other and perhaps better opportunities.

3. *Assume that you do not know the upper limits of the client's capacity to grow and change*—It goes without saying that the future is uncertain. However, it is important to appreciate the strengths that people do have. The practitioner does not hinder their clients' potentials for growth and the ability to take hold of opportunities as they present themselves.

4. *The practitioner strives to collaborate with clients*—We are not the expert in a client's life and it is important to acknowledge that we do not have all the answers to a client's problems. Instead, we should engage clients in a collaborative relationship.

5. *Every environment is considered to have resources*—People do strive to cope with adversity. Every community is seen as having something to offer. Resources such as formal counseling services or mutual support networks can

be a source of great strengths and help people to empower themselves and improve their lives.

6. *Recognize the value of caring for each other*—The strengths perspective acknowledges the importance of community and the value of including all of its members in society. Caring for each other and working for social justice is considered to be a basic form of civic participation.

Empowerment also focuses on strengths and environmental resources and shares many of the same features as the strengths perspective (Chapin & Cox, 2001).

Empowerment

In 1976, social worker Barbara Solomon introduced empowerment as a paradigm for practice in oppressed communities. Her model saw empowerment as a way to facilitate the client's own efforts to gain the resources needed to increase mastery over life situations or events. During the ensuing years other professions began researching empowerment as a multidimensional concept encompassing the personal, as well as the interpersonal and community aspects of a person's life (see Cox & Parsons, 2000, or Parsons, 2002, for a summary of this literature). At the personal level, empowerment is seen as self-efficacy or the perception of the ability to actively manage one's life challenges and develop a positive sense of self. The second dimension or interpersonal level of empowerment encourages clients to overcome obstacles through the development of social support systems or networking with others such as family and/or friends. The third dimension is described as the community or "sociopolitical" level. This dimension looks to those actions geared to influencing the social institutions that can facilitate (or get in the way of) self-help and mutual aid. This may consist of a person's participation in collective actions to advocate for rights, improve programs, and/or influence governmental decisions (Kruger, 2000; Stromwall & Hurdle, 2003). Parsons (2008) observes that empowerment is particularly beneficial to disempowered populations who are stigmatized groups in society such as people with mental illness. Instead of focusing on pathology, empowerment fosters a dialogue of possibilities by looking at problems through sociopolitical lenses, considering the client's experiences of power in the helping relationship, and highlighting strengths.

Barker (2003) summarizes the various dimensions of empowerment as "the process of helping individuals, families, groups, and communities to increase personal, interpersonal, sociopolitical strength and to develop influence toward improving their circumstances" (p. 120). Empowerment shifts the clients' participation in the relationships with us from passively receiving services to actively making decisions affecting their own lives and collaborating with their social networks. Rather than deciding what is "wrong" with the client, the relationship is based on mutuality and facilitating a two-way process that identifies choices and options.

Being a part of stigmatized groups, having negative experiences in interactions with the environment, and with larger environmental systems leads to learned helplessness, negative self-evaluation, and alienation. Empowerment is seen as a counter to this sense of powerlessness. It is anchored in the connection between the personal and the political and shifts from the notion of learned helplessness to one of learned hopefulness. Social justice is an aspect of empowerment. For example, a person with severe mental illness is often negatively labeled according to his or her symptoms. The empowerment perspective sets the stage for clients, other professionals, and lay people (including family members and others) to join forces with us to challenge these negative stereotypes. In this way, a more complete picture of the person with mental illness is portrayed rather than being seen as just another diagnostic label. Empowerment aspires to enhance the power and control that one has over his or her destiny or the "process of increasing personal, interpersonal, or political power so that individuals can take action to improve their life situations" (Gutierrez, 2001, p. 210). Throughout the assessment, it is helpful to emphasize, develop, and nurture strengths and positive qualities whenever possible in order to empower people.

Self-awareness is also a feature of empowerment. Self-awareness brings a deeper level of understanding to the struggles associated with having a mental illness. Formulating an assessment of another human being is subjective and experiential. When you are assessing others, you are also looking at yourself. To understand the subjective human experience, both yours and the client's, you need to develop a keen sense of self-awareness. That is, you must be continuously aware of biases and beliefs that may influence clinical judgment (Gardner, 2001). By developing self-awareness, you are better able to discern differences between your own interpretations and those of the client. It is essential that you do not force your reality or values on a client as this will ultimately lead to misunderstanding and interfere with the assessment process.

Notwithstanding the struggles of living with a particular mental disorder, your clients deal with many of the same feelings, issues, and problems that you do. Recognizing your own strengths when you are confronted with a problem is just as important as recognizing them in others. Directing your attention to client strengths as a part of the assessment process reduces defensiveness while allowing you to interact empathetically (Clark, 2001). The clients' strengths might include educational background, work history, problem-solving skills, and/or resources as well as having a positive attitude despite the challenges of mental illness. Using strengths to pursue empowerment can be located in the different levels in the client's life; for example on the individual, family or group, organizational and community levels (Saleebey, 2008). Throughout the assessment, strengths and positive attributes are identified in order to empower people.

Resilience

Building on an ecological perspective, resilience looks at how people attempt to maintain well-being despite adversity (Greene, 2002, 2007). Masten (1994) defines resilience as "a pattern over time, characterized by good eventual adaptation despite developmental risks, acute stressors, or chronic adversity" (p. 5). According to Gitterman (2001), resilience is the ability of an individual (and/or his or her family) to bounce back from adversity and resume functioning even when facing the serious difficulties, confusion, or hardships often found in mental illness. Resilience revolves around the idea that people will tend to use positive adaptive strategies to overcome adverse situations (Greene, 2007). Resilience can be seen as the internal strengths a person draws on in times of stress while protective factors represent those resources that facilitate resilience. Additionally, protective factors buffer, moderate, and protect a person against risk factors. Protective factors can include interpersonal relationships and the social context or support networks in the person's life.

Researchers have increasingly found support for the idea that people have the capacity to overcome adverse events in their lives (Garmezy, 1993; Lifton, 1999; Masten, 1994; Rutter, 1987). In other words, people are seen as often surviving and thriving despite the risk factors found in various types of problems and situations. The assumption is that people have the potential to recover, adapt, and rebound from adversity. This capacity to recover can also be found in multiple systems levels including individual, family, and groups, and communities and organizations.

Resilience provides a more optimistic view of a person's ability to cope. When combined with the competency-based assessment, new directions for tapping into a client's natural propensity to overcome adversity are offered. Gutheil and Congress (2000) note that the central theme of the strengths perspective is the focus on "capabilities, assets, and positive attributes rather than problems and pathologies" (p. 41) whereas resilience emphasizes the use of those strengths to cope with adversity and to survive despite difficulties. We are consistently striving to ascertain how a person who is struggling with mental illness manages to survive and regenerate.

The competency-based assessment assumes that all people have strengths and resources and our job is to look for those factors in all aspects of the client's life; for example, the personal, family, group, organizational, and community levels. The focus on competence emphasizes strengths, empowerment, and resilience. While investigating the signs and symptoms of a particular disorder, understanding clients in terms of competence and abilities is simultaneously attempted. The following questions guide the exploration of client competence.

Competency-Based Assessment Strengths, Empowerment, and Resilience

Personal

- What are your client's best qualities?
- How does your client describe his positive "qualities"?
- How would you characterize your client's sense of worth?
- What skills and potential does your client possess; for example, artistic or athletic talents, technological expertise, leadership, capacity for work?
- What are the indicators of resilience in your client; for example, the attributes of intelligence, sense of humor, optimism, creativity?
- What helps your client get through the day?
- Does your client have any hopes or dreams for his or her future and if so does he or she make specific plans to pursue them?
- Does your client have a positive relationship with you and is able to accept your offer to help?

Family

- To what degree is the family of origin, current family, spouse, or significant other available to provide support for your client?
- What type of support, resources, or assistance does the client's family (or current family, spouse, or significant other) provide for your client?
- Is your client's family psychologically healthy, communicative, stable, and supportive?
- Is your client's family resilient; for example, have affirming belief systems, facilitative organizational patterns, and positive communication processes?
- Does your client have a caring and supportive intimate partner relationship?

Group

- Are there friends, neighbors, coworkers, or fellow students available to help and/or support your client?
- Does your client have any positive peer relationships?
- Does your client belong to supportive groups; for example, social clubs, recreational or counseling groups?
- If your client is involved in group opportunities, does he or she find them pleasurable and self-fulfilling?
- Does your client benefit from his or her group affiliations?

Organizations

- Does your client belong to any organizations that are sources of strength and/or support; for example, a church, synagogue, social service agency, counseling center?
- Are there appropriate services and resources available to assist your client?

- Does your client see the organizations involved in his or her life as a resource?
- What specific benefits (and support) does your client receive?
- Does your client receive any special benefits; for example, financial help, advising, counseling, mutual aid support?
- If your client is working or going to school, does he or she perform well?

Community

- Does your client have adequate environmental resources; for example, housing, transportation, food?
- Does your client know how to access help?
- Does your client have a network of community relationships?
- Does your client feel positive about his or her community affiliations?
- What ethnic/cultural opportunities are available in your client's community?

SUMMARY

This chapter introduced the competency-based assessment and provided a description of the major elements of the model. The advantages of a parallel assessment of client "strengths" or competence and the behavioral syndromes found in the *Diagnostic and Statistical Manual of Mental Disorders* were elaborated. When combined with the DSM, the competency-based assessment helps to understand the information found in the manual while balancing the tensions inherent in a focus on pathology. At the same time, the assessment is individualized by recognizing each person's unique experience with a particular disorder. The chapter reviewed the major components of the DSM. Following is a summary of the key elements of the manual.

Key Components of the *Diagnostic and Statistical Manual*

Axis I	Refers to clinical disorders and other conditions that may be a focus of clinical attention and includes V codes.
Axis II	Records personality disorders and mental retardation and the V code (V 62.89) of borderline intellectual functioning.
Axis III	Reserved for general medical conditions relevant to Axis I and Axis II.
Axis IV	Psychosocial and environmental problems.
Axis V	Global Assessment of Functioning (GAF) Scale

The competency-based assessment looks at all aspects of a person's life and experience. This includes an exploration of the biological, psychological, and social dimensions in order to examine the possible etiology and explanations of the client's functioning. The key components supporting the competency-based assessment are summarized as follows:

☞ Key Components of the Competency-Based Assessment Model

Biopsychosocial framework	Validates the potential importance of biogenetic, psychological, social, and environmental factors in understanding a person's behaviors.
Systems theory	Advances the understanding of the interconnectedness of the different aspects of a person's life.
Ecological perspective	Pays attention to the multiple interactions that people have with their surroundings.
Strengths perspective	Decenters the focus on individual pathology and moves toward a consideration of client abilities and internal and external resources.
Empowerment	Focuses on the client's own endeavors to gain the resources that will enhance mastery.
Resilience	Understands how people maintain well-being despite adversity.

Chapter 2 introduces strategies for formulating the assessment. By making the diagnoses based on the cases found in this book along with the practical applications you will become more skilled at navigating the *DSM*. The clinical vignettes are designed to help you to become familiar with salient points about the signs and symptoms of a particular disorder and to practice formulating a competency-based assessment. It is anticipated that by the time you reach the last chapter, you will be familiar with the intricacies of the diagnostic categories and more sensitive to what it is like for someone to live with a mental illness.

Formulating the Competency-Based Assessment

Some Basics

INTRODUCTION

The methods and thoroughness of your assessment revolve around listening to a client's life story, analyzing pertinent case data, and formulating a specific diagnosis. This chapter provides tips and strategies for effectively reading and analyzing the case studies presented in this book. Not all of the syndromes listed in the *DSM-IV-TR* will be found and your task, much like what happens in actual practice, is to sort through the client's symptom picture in order to ascertain the appropriate diagnosis. The competency-based assessment framework helps to summarize, prioritize, and classify the information found in the *DSM* into an assessment format more familiar to mental health practitioners. Each person's experience with a mental illness is different even though the person may share the same diagnosis with others. There are many factors that complicate a client's presentation of a mental illness. As you attempt to understand a person's complex symptom picture, the competency-based assessment along with familiarity with the diagnostic categories found in the *DSM* advances your ability to interpret them correctly.

A Definition of Terms

In practice, it is common to use the terms diagnosis and assessment interchangeably. A diagnosis is distinguished in this book as the process of identifying the client's mental problem or problems, including related social and medical issues and the underlying causes. A differential diagnosis refers to the process of identifying the markers of one disorder versus another in order to reach an accurate diagnosis. Because of the medical connotation associated with the word *diagnosis*, many practitioners prefer to use the term *assessment*. Similarly, the assessment can be seen as the process of determining an understanding of the client's problem or problems. This may include a formal mental health diagnosis according to the *DSM* as well as a consideration of stressful life circumstances or events along with an understanding of what causes them. The competency-based assessment differs because it organizes a review of the individual's level of functioning as well as other relevant systems in the client's life such as family, community, or the environment. The competency-based assessment is a framework for understanding human behavior that includes intrapersonal or personal factors and also social influences. From this perspective, the practitioner seeks to understand a person's behavior from a multidimensional and dynamic ecological systems perspective with the goal of identifying strengths and resilience (Gray, 2006, 2008). This approach to the assessment process fosters a thorough understanding of the client's problems, which helps to demystify formulating a diagnosis and provides clinical insight into what seems to be a complicated symptom picture.

Reading the Cases

There are many ways to read case data and to interpret case findings, and in some instances you might even disagree with the diagnostic formulation. Rather than emphasizing what should be considered the right or wrong answer, from the very first reading you can maximize your learning through active, purposeful engagement with the case material.

The main purpose for presenting case studies is to demonstrate a logical and commonsense approach to the assessment process. With practice, you can discern the kind of information needed to complete the most accurate competency-based assessment possible drawing on the diagnostic categories of *DSM-IV-TR* (American Psychiatric Association, 2000). The purpose of the *DSM* is to, "provide clear descriptions of diagnostic categories in order to enable clinicians and investigators to diagnose, communicate about, study, and treat people with various mental disorders" (APA, 2000, p. xi). Clearly, an accurate diagnosis is the first step to identifying those behaviors that interfere with the individual client's social and occupational functioning. The competency-based assessment provides a framework for a comprehensive overview of the person's social history and pays attention to those factors that foster coping and adaptation along with understanding presenting symptoms. It also sets the stage for effective, evidence-based interventions. This book offers opportunities for you to conduct a careful analysis and to refine your diagnostic skills.

UNDERSTANDING THE CASE STUDIES

The primary purpose of the case studies is to give you an opportunity to practice constructing a competency-based assessment with a variety of mental health diagnoses. Be prepared to be both challenged and have a lot of fun with the scenarios. The discussion begins with suggestions for reading the case, getting started with formulating the competency-based assessment, and how to use the conceptual map to organize symptomatic features.

Getting Started

When you read the case studies in this book for the first time, look carefully for what seems to be troubling the client but be cautious about looking for data to support a premature assessment. Begin by reviewing the entire case without taking notes to get an overall sense of key symptomatic features. Focus on the bigger picture and not on specific details; in other words, appreciate the client's entire story and try not to become distracted by the specifics. If you listen to everything and focus on nothing, it can be more difficult to come to inaccurate conclusions, so take your time gathering information. Remember, the overall goal is to obtain accurate and relevant data needed to support your assessment.

Read the case and try to get a sense of the story from the client's point of view. This orientation is intended to develop your awareness of the client's perspective of the situation and to empathize with his or her struggles. In those instances where the client cannot accurately tell his or her story—often referred to as a poor historian—pay careful attention to what those who are close to the client have to share. At this point, it may be helpful to imagine that you have been assigned to the case or that you have been asked to be a consultant to the practitioner in the case. Start focusing your analysis with an initial statement of the problem that brought this client to your attention. Be careful, though, about simply accepting the presenting problem at face value without considering that this may actually be the initial representation of a larger symptom picture. In practice, defining and refining the initial presenting problem is the most difficult task. As sometimes happens, there you may not have enough information to make an accurate assessment. In those instances, defer making a diagnosis but ask yourself what specific information is needed to support a particular diagnostic category and what additional information is needed to fully understand the client's struggle.

Reread a case several times to get a better sense of the client's story. Once you are familiar with the case vignette, you are ready to begin a more deliberate analysis. At this stage of your review, it may be useful to tentatively develop a working hypothesis for yourself as a method for structuring your thinking about the specific details found in the case study. In the process, validate your preliminary appraisal as suggested by the symptoms illustrated in the vignette. A differential diagnosis will list all possible diagnoses for a client. When considering the specific *DSM* diagnosis, arrange these possibilities in order of the likelihood of the most probable diagnosis listed first.

Starting the Competency-Based Assessment Process

Although formulating an accurate diagnosis is the end result of a good assessment process, it only tells part of the client's story. As illustrated in Figure 2.1, the competency-based assessment goes further. It moves the individual into the forefront so that the diagnosis of a particular mental illness does not define the person but becomes only one part of the client's life story.

In this way, the competency-based assessment expands the focus of the assessment process and takes into account the full range of the client's life including those factors that both maintain or ameliorate a particular diagnosis. Notes Gray (2008), "The competency-based assessment reviews and understands an individual's past in order to distinguish among and interpret presenting concerns" (p. 10). Taken together, the competency-based assessment becomes a process of clarifying the client's history by considering the unique features of the client's personal and social systems, including strengths and the capacity for resilience, evaluating the goodness of fit between the client and his or her environment, and distinguishing the influence of a diagnosis of mental illness.

Figure 2.2 illustrates a conceptual map organized around the *DSM* classification system that begins with attempts to understand a person's diagnosis. It is a graphic tool

Figure 2.1   The Full Range of the Client's Life Story

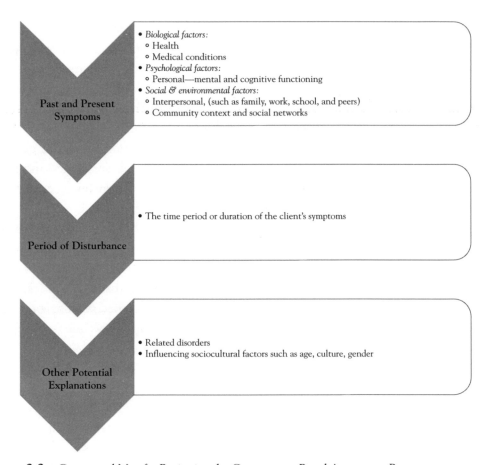

Figure 2.2   Conceptual Map for Beginning the Competency-Based Assessment Process

that helps you to navigate the client's symptoms picture and sets the stage for formulating the competency-based assessment.

The DSM Diagnosis

   Axis I—Clinical Disorders and other conditions that may be a focus of attention

   Axis II—Personality disorders and mental retardation

   Axis III—General medical conditions

   Axis IV—Psychosocial and environmental problems

   Axis V—Global Assessment of Functioning (GAF)

The Conceptual Map

The conceptual map begins with the connections among the past and present symptoms; for example, biological, psychological (including cognitive), and social functioning. The biological domain highlights information about the client's general physical health or medical condition. The psychological domain notes mental and cognitive functioning. This includes an exploration of personal issues and interpersonal concerns such as how the client's occupational and social functioning may be affected. The extent of impairment in one or more important areas of functioning or the increased risks for disability or even death is evaluated. Explored are: the nature of the presenting problem; the client's current life situation, including personal abilities; interpersonal concerns such as family, work, or school, and peers, and social support networks; and relevant historical data. Significant patterns or a set of symptoms that are associated with the client's present distress are brought to light.

Next, the period of the disturbance or duration of the client's symptoms is taken into account and sheds light on the extent of the client's struggle. Finally, other potential explanations for a particular set of symptoms or patterns found in the client's life are reviewed. The client's behavioral picture against other diagnostic categories and/or what might be considered to be expected and culturally sanctioned responses to a particular event are assessed; for example, the client's sad mood may be a response to the death of a loved one and not indicative of a major depressive episode.

The Next Steps

One of the most challenging aspects of practice is formulating a diagnosis using the *DSM*, so each chapter offers opportunities to explore a client's symptomatic features for specific diagnostic classifications. The conceptual map provides a road map to navigate the client's emerging symptom picture. It is a pedagogical feature repeated throughout the book to help you to evaluate the signs and symptoms of a particular disorder while also taking into account the broader picture of what it is like to live with a diagnosis. You might want to make a copy of this map and use it to help you to formulate your diagnosis for each of the cases in the book.

Become familiar with the *DSM-IV-TR* diagnostic criteria to help distinguish symptom patterns for particular disorders and to recognize their defining features. Initial use of the *DSM-IV-TR* can be confusing and can be compared to learning a foreign language. At first nothing makes sense but with practice you become more fluent. In the same way, learning the *DSM* terminology can be a daunting task. To help you to make the most of the conceptual map, each chapter provides an overview of the elements of each diagnostic category.

Clients often have many symptoms and these can suggest a number of different disorders. Reviewing case data provides opportunities to practice sifting through a client's history, attending to relevant data, determining which is the most likely accurate diagnosis (or diagnoses), and ultimately discovering strengths and competence characteristics of the competency-based assessment.

The Value of Practice

If particular cases seem irrelevant to your current practice, you can still gain valuable practice understanding a client's behavioral symptoms and formulating a cohesive diagnostic picture. Sort through a client's story and relate the symptom picture to a particular syndrome, and you will start to develop a systematic way of thinking about situations that can transfer from one job to the next (Leenders, Mauffette-Leenders, & Earskine, 2001). You will gain valuable practice opportunities by learning how to conduct a competency-based assessment, which includes the consideration of a psychiatric diagnosis by going through the cases presented in this book rather than simply memorizing a list of signs and symptoms. The *DSM* is a complex manual and it takes good appraisal skills to use it effectively. With practice, you will be able to see how the disorders are defined and make connections to each client's symptom picture. At the end of each chapter that describes a particular diagnostic classification, a series of practical applications are included to help you to further refine your skills.

THE COMPETENCY-BASED ASSESSMENT

The competency-based assessment assumes a strengths perspective. That is, when confronted with the diagnosis of a mental illness, people attempt to cope and adapt by drawing on personal resiliences as well as the protective factors and buffers in their lives. Empowerment encourages the client's active involvement in the assessment process. This outlook on the competency-based assessment process is shown in Figure 2.3, which illustrates the connection between the *DSM* diagnosis (or diagnoses) and the competency-based assessment.

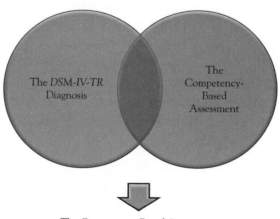

The Competency-Based Assessment

Figure 2.3   The Relationship Between the *DSM-IV-TR* and the Competency-Based Assessment

The competency-based assessment establishes the foundation that helps you to understand how a particular diagnosis develops for an individual in the context of his or her own life history. These elements, taken together, forge the unique aspect of each person's experiences with a mental illness or psychiatric diagnosis. This orientation to assessment is intended to organize the data illustrated in the case vignettes found in the following chapters. The competency-based assessment is a multidimensional framework that includes physical, psychological, cognitive, family, and community systems that adds breadth and depth to understanding the client's unique life experiences, found in the case vignettes.

From this perspective, clients are seen as "active, striving human beings who are capable of organizing their lives and realizing their potentialities as long as they have appropriate family, community, societal, and environmental resources" (Compton & Galaway, 1999, pp. 354–355). People who are confronted with the risks associated with a diagnosis of mental illness somehow try to deal with life's challenges as best as they can. Throughout the book the case illustrations focus on the specific disorder under discussion while challenging you to consider the competencies in a client's life. You get a fuller picture of assessing for competence that considers the client's unique experience with mental disorders.

Dziegielewski (2002) underscores the importance of the multidimensional aspects of the competency-based assessment framework through one of her experiences with a client who was diagnosed with schizophrenia. This client showed up at a local hospital emergency room with his jaw drenched with blood because he had been trying to pull his teeth out. He was hallucinating and claimed to have demons in his head. This young man was immediately admitted to the psychiatric unit of the hospital and antipsychotic medications were administered. Despite this intervention, he continued to struggle to remove his teeth. Several days later, a complete medical workup revealed that this client had a severe sinus infection that was causing a great deal of head pain. Unfortunately, by looking only at the hallucinations the client showed on admission, preliminary treatment efforts focused on psychiatric symptoms to the exclusion of a possible medical explanation for his behavior. Only later were other dimensions of this client's life considered. In retrospect, the hallucinations about demons may have been the client's way to draw attention to the inexorable pain he was experiencing as a result of his medical condition. The competency-based assessment guides the consideration of the full range of a person's life, including the multiple interactions between behaviors and surrounding events; that is, those events that either elicit or maintain problematic behaviors.

FORMULATING THE COMPETENCY-BASED ASSESSMENT

Although the client is the primary source of data, information should also be obtained from secondary sources such as written reports, medical documents, history and physical exams, prior clinical assessments, laboratory tests, and other clinical and diagnostic methods. Collateral information from family members, friends, or other health-care providers who know the client can also augment the client's history. Another source of useful information can be drawn from your observations of the client's verbal and physical behaviors, as well as interactions with others. In most cases, the consideration of the client's history and emotional status in order to determine which diagnosis is most likely. Historical information helps to assess the severity of the client's problems and current functioning. For example, if your client has consistently struggled with being able to distinguish the accuracy of his own perceptions and thoughts from external reality for the past 10 years and still struggling, you would probably consider the diagnosis of schizophrenia. In contrast, if the client has been ill for less than six months, you might consider assigning a diagnosis such as schizophreniform disorder.

Recent history is often more informative than ancient history. According to Meyer (1993), the assessment should also ask, "What's the matter?" (p. 2). Consider why the client has decided to seek help now or how he or she has come to your attention. People change and often the evolving symptoms will help to better understand the client. For instance, a diagnosis that seemed appropriate eight years ago might seem unreasonable in light of more recent symptoms.

At the outset, considering the multiple influences in a person's life may sound like a daunting task. There is so much data to consider! The *DSM* has a great deal of information about numerous diagnostic categories and the criteria frequently seem to be so subjective (Corcoran & Walsh, 2006; Dziegielewski, 2002; Thyer & Wodarski, 2007). You are cautioned against formulating any diagnosis based on subjective judgment rather than an objective appraisal of the client's behavior. For instance, although it may seem like a "crazy thing to do" if a client goes out on a shopping spree and buys $1,000 worth of shoes from the Payless discount shoe store, making the diagnosis of schizophrenia, seen as a severe psychotic disorder, would be unwarranted. More than likely the behavior is more symptomatic of bipolar I disorder. With practice, sorting through the client's story like those featured in this book and listening for pertinent details will gradually become easier.

Judgments about clients are also guided by ethical and legal considerations. It is beyond the scope of this book to outline all the legal requirements in the field of mental health and related problems, but you should be well versed in the Code of Ethics. One way to demonstrate professional accountability is to record a diagnostic assessment based on objective data that considers all aspects of a client's life and to refrain from using subjective data to support more subjective interpretations about a client's behavior.

Let's illustrate the competency-based assessment process. After reading the following brief case vignette, the conceptual map will be completed and then you can take a closer look at the multiple systems in the client's life to uncover strengths and competence. Here goes!

Augustine Absinthe has been in this country for 10 years. She emigrated from Haiti, adjusted well, and since coming to the United States prefers to use the name Agnes. Currently 32 years of age, Agnes works part-time as a housekeeper to help support her family. "With my salary we can buy 'extras' for my kids. Their job is to do well in school and I'll take care of the rest" she points out. The family she has worked for over the past several years admires her value of hard work and has become quite fond of her. Unfortunately, Agnes has a dark secret that she has not shared with anybody until now. "We are a very private people, you know. We have a saying. It goes, 'You do not wash your dirty laundry in public.' That means it is hard for us to talk about our troubles with strangers," states Agnes. She is terrified of thunderstorms. For years she has struggled with her fears, keeping her problem to herself.

It all started when Agnes was a child. She lived near the coast in Cap Haitian "or Le Cap as we Haitians call it." One day her father and grandfather had gone out fishing when a huge storm came up off the coast. When they didn't come back Agnes was terrified that they had died. They ultimately returned two days later, but her fears remained. They got a little better when she was a teenager but over the years her fear gradually started up again. During a storm, Agnes is afraid that the worst will happen and this scares her. Her anxiety increases even when the sky becomes overcast or bad weather is predicted.

During a storm, Agnes tries to ignore her fears but nothing seems to work so she just stays home and buries her face under the covers, staying far away from the windows so she doesn't have to hear the rain. Agnes knows it's silly to be afraid like that but she just can't stop herself. Her employers seem to understand and graciously give her the day off. If her husband is away from home, he calls her on his cell phone just to check-in until the storm has passed. The way he explains it, "My Agnes just has a little trembling in her feelings when we have a big storm. I think maybe this is something on her mother's side of the family. It's not like she has an evil spell over her or something like that." Agnes denies any panic attacks or other unusual incapacitating fears. Her history is unremarkable; no health problems or substance abuse . . . except for this fear of storms.

The conceptual map outlining Agnes Absinthe's symptoms is shown in Figure 2.4.

Case Review

I live in an area of the country known for its hurricanes and can understand that some people might feel uncomfortable during a storm, but Agnes Absinthe's persistent fear is clearly excessive. When there is a storm, her normal routine is interrupted and she cannot go outside to get to work. Instead, she hides inside the house away from the windows. Fortunately her longtime employers understand and simply give her the day off. Her husband seems supportive and calls to check up on her during a storm. Agnes is Haitian. She explains that people in her culture do not

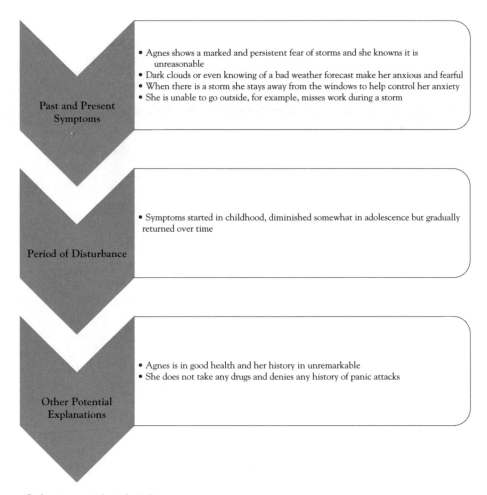

Past and Present Symptoms

- Agnes shows a marked and persistent fear of storms and she knowns it is unreasonable
- Dark clouds or even knowing of a bad weather forecast make her anxious and fearful
- When there is a storm she stays away from the windows to help control her anxiety
- She is unable to go outside, for example, misses work during a storm

Period of Disturbance

- Symptoms started in childhood, diminished somewhat in adolescence but gradually returned over time

Other Potential Explanations

- Agnes is in good health and her history in unremarkable
- She does not take any drugs and denies any history of panic attacks

Figure 2.4 Agnes Absinthe's Symptoms

talk about their problems to strangers, but there seems to be no cultural explanation for Agnes's persistent fear of storms. Although she stays inside during a storm, Agnes shows no signs of a panic attack or an embarrassing symptom when she is alone or in public places as would be found in the diagnosis of agoraphobia without history of panic disorder. Her fear of storms is not associated with any embarrassment or humiliation in situations that would characterize the diagnosis of social phobia diagnosis. Agnes seems to be able to function when there are no storms and she does not obsess over them as would be found in obsessive compulsive disorder. There is no medical history or use of substances that would better explain her symptoms.

Agnes Absinthe's competency-based assessment is shown in Figure 2.5.

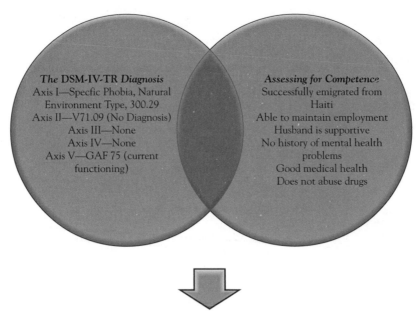

The DSM-IV-TR *Diagnosis*
Axis I—Specfic Phobia, Natural
Environment Type, 300.29
Axis II—V71.09 (No Diagnosis)
Axis III—None
Axis IV—None
Axis V—GAF 75 (current
functioning)

Assessing for Competence
Successfully emigrated from
Haiti
Able to maintain employment
Husband is supportive
No history of mental health
problems
Good medical health
Does not abuse drugs

Figure 2.5   The Competency-Based Assessment for Agnes Absinthe

THE COMPETENCY-BASED ASSESSMENT
FOR AGNES ABSINTHE

The defining feature of a specific phobia is the intense and irrational fear of some-thing that poses little or no actual danger. As you read Agnes's "story" at what point did you begin to think about a *DSM* diagnosis? When did her symptoms first emerge? Typically, fears usually appear in late childhood or adolescence. Agnes had a child-hood experience where her father and grandfather were lost in a storm and she was afraid they had died. At what point did you consider Agnes's fears were more intense than would be normally expected? Although her father and grandfather returned, Agnes subsequently made every effort to avoid exposure to storms and these fears per-sisted into adulthood.

Competencies exist side-by-side with the symptoms of a specific phobia in Agnes's life. She successfully emigrated, was able to continue working, had a good relation-ship with her employers, and her husband was supportive. In fact, he seemed to normalize her reaction to storms by explaining it as "a little trembling of her fears." If the feared object can be avoided, the person usually does not seek help and there was no mention of Agnes seeking professional assistance. Cultural factors may have influenced some of this reluctance to seek help or perhaps family support mitigated the impact of her symptoms. When the signs and symptoms of a specific phobia are taken into account along with the strengths and resilience in Agnes's life we are able to formulate a competency-based assessment and better understand her unique struggle with a mental illness.

ASSESSMENT GUIDELINES

We now turn to a discussion of general guidelines for using the *DSM* to consider a person's diagnosis and a series of principles guiding the competency-based assessment.

General Guidelines for the *DSM*

A mental disorder, as defined by the American Psychiatric Association (2000), is seen as a "significant behavioral or psychological syndrome or pattern that occurs in an individual and that is associated with present distress (e.g., a painful symptom) or disability (i.e., impairment in one or more important areas of functioning) or with significantly increased risk of suffering death, pain, disability, or an important loss of freedom" (p. xxxi). These behaviors or patterns are not intended to be seen as expected or culturally sanctioned responses to a particular event. There are several general guidelines for evaluating diagnostic information (APA, 2000) and the first step is to investigate the client's past and present symptoms. As you begin to sort through the diagnostic picture, a process of ruling out other disorders can be helpful.

Most of the *DSM-IV-TR* disorders contain diagnostic criteria to rule out other conditions, and they are referred to as exclusion criteria (APA, 2000). The two most common exclusion criteria are related to ruling out general medical conditions or the effects of substances as a cause of the disorder. A mental disorder due to a general medical condition is distinguished from a primary mental disorder. When a client has a mental disorder due to a general medical condition, the diagnostic picture is characterized by the presence of mental symptoms that are considered to be the result of the medical condition. For example, if a client has been diagnosed with chronic lymphocytic leukemia, is undergoing a course of chemotherapy, experiences anemia and this causes an episode of delirium, the diagnosis (on Axis I) would be "delirium due to chemotherapy." The person's chronic lymphocytic leukemia and anemia would be listed again on Axis III. You then begin to look for three essential exclusionary criteria:

1. Evidence from the client's history, physical exam, or laboratory findings that the disturbance is the direct consequence of a medical condition.
2. The disturbance is not better accounted for by another mental disorder.
3. The disturbance does not occur during the course of a delirium episode (but considered to be the cause of the delirium).

The substance-related disorders are considered when the client takes a drug of abuse (including alcohol), experiences the side effects of a medication, or/and is exposed to toxins. For example, a person may be on a speed run (a high dose of an amphetamine) and subsequently crashes (withdrawal). In this instance, the diagnosis would be "amphetamine withdrawal." However, there are a number of mental disturbances that may be brought on by the individual's substance use such as delirium, persisting dementia, amnestic disorder, psychotic disorder, mood disorder, anxiety disorder, sexual dysfunction, or sleep disorder. In those instances, the practitioner refers to the substance-related disorders for substance-specific codes.

Other factors to consider during the assessment process of ruling out other disorders include a consideration for the factitious or malingering disorders. A factitious disorder "is not real, genuine or natural" (Thomas, 1997, p. 559). The key feature of the factitious disorder is that the person displays physical and psychological symptoms that are intentionally produced, are completely under the person's voluntary control, and are deliberately used to assume the sick role. Individuals with this disorder often have multiple records of hospitalizations, medical appointments, and complaints of being sick; all of which may impair relationships and/or job performance. Persons with factitious disorder often have a distorted perception of justice as well as a sense of entitlement, which seems to further justify their sick role. They may also show feelings of victimization (Bellamy, 1997). Malingering involves a pattern of behavior similar to that seen in someone who has a genuine medical disorder but instead of having an actual medical problem, the person deliberately and consciously pretends to be suffering from "something" that is nonexistent. These intentional symptoms are produced with external incentives in mind such as in order to arouse sympathy, avoid criminal prosecution or military duty, obtain drugs, or receive financial rewards. A good example would be someone injured on the job and who pretends to be making a slow recovery in order to continue receiving benefits from workmen's compensation or an insurance settlement. It tends to occur more frequently in men but women can also be affected.

Factitious disorder is often confused with malingering and the most notable difference between the two is the incentive for maintaining symptoms. In factitious disorder external incentives to continue symptoms are not present but the person maintains the sick role (APA, 2000). In malingering, there is an external motivation for the person to continue to have symptoms. The person who malingers deliberately and intentionally produces symptoms in order to obtain appreciable rewards or incentives. Persons with malingering disorder are able to stop their symptoms when they are no longer profitable or when the danger of being discovered becomes too great. Malingering may be considered to be adaptive under certain circumstances, but a factitious disorder always implies psychopathology.

Additional factors to take into account in the rule-out process include the influence of culture, behaviors that could be considered as age-appropriate, and other conditions that may be a focus of clinical attention; for example, physical abuse, sexual abuse, and neglect. Culture plays a role when looking at the impact of a person's cultural context and how this may influence the expression of symptoms and dysfunction. Additionally, the cultural background of both the client and the practitioner may affect their relationship and ultimately how symptoms are understood and interpreted. Age-appropriate behaviors apply to the client's chronological age and his or her sociocultural context. Abuse and neglect issues might potentially place the person at higher risk for mental disorders but there are several different ways in which they can be considered. For example, a person with a history of sexual abuse may not meet the criteria for a specific mental disorder and the abuse will be the primary focus of treatment. Another way of evaluating the impact of abuse is that the person may have a mental disorder, such as alcohol dependence, but it is unrelated to the individual's history of sexual abuse. Alternatively, the person may have a mental disorder such as borderline personality disorder, which is related to the problem of sexual abuse. Figure 2.6 summarizes the exclusion criteria considered when making the diagnosis.

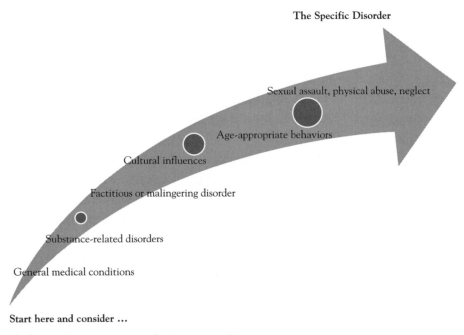

Figure 2.6   Exclusion Criteria in the Assessment Process

Hierarchic principles are also a part of determining the diagnosis. For example, disorders due to a general medical condition (such as a client who experiences a panic attack due to hypoglycemia, diagnosed as anxiety disorder due to hypoglycemia with panic attacks) and substance-induced disorders (the client who experiences a psychotic episode while binging on amphetamine diagnosed as amphetamine-induced psychotic disorder with delusions) preempt a diagnosis of any other disorder that could produce the same symptoms.

Another application of the hierarchic principle is when a more pervasive disorder, such as schizophrenia, has essential or associated symptoms that are defining symptoms of a less pervasive disorder, for example dysthymia. In this instance, the more pervasive disorder is diagnosed, if diagnostic criteria are met. In other words, if a client has the symptoms of dysthymia and the symptoms of schizophrenia are also present, then only the schizophrenia is diagnosed.

Principles Guiding the Competency-Based Assessment

Making a diagnosis is not as simple as comparing a list of client symptoms to a set of criteria. In the case vignettes in the following chapters, clients often have many symptoms that suggest a number of different disorders. In most cases, the practitioner carefully sifts through the client history to determine which diagnosis is most likely. Formulating the competency-based assessment is more than relying on intuition. Effective judgments concerning clients are grounded in empirical observations and documentation of client characteristics. As you read the case vignettes, keep in mind the following assessment guidelines (Jordan & Franklin, 2003):

- *Focus on the client's history.* The psychosocial history offers historical information that will help determine the appropriate diagnostic assessment. For example, if the client claims to be hearing voices but has been ill for less than six months, the diagnosis of schizophreniform disorder may be considered (as opposed to schizophrenia).
- *Carefully consider the client's recent history.* Illnesses develop sequentially. Clients change and often the newly evolving symptoms of an illness will be more informative. For example, a client may have had a prior diagnosis of a major depressive disorder, single episode. The client's history reveals an ongoing struggle with depression, but two years later, he comes to the practitioner with symptoms of an abnormally elevated or euphoric mood. In this instance, the diagnosis would be changed to bipolar I disorder, most recent episode manic.
- *Practitioner observations may be more accurate than client "complaints."* The signs of a mental illness, or what you observe about the client's behavior, may be less

distorted by symptoms, or the client's. For example, a client may complain about anxiety but you might see a series of needle tracks on his arm that may more accurately be a sign of substance use.

- *Objective assessments are more reliable than subjective assessments*. Although it may seem obvious to focus on systematically gathering data to support or refute a diagnosis, this tip adds a note of caution to relying on intuition about a specific disorder. Seasoned practitioners, for example, who have seen a number of clients over the years, may have a hunch early on in the interview about a client's diagnosis. Given this intuition, one runs the risk of attending only to those symptoms supporting a particular diagnosis, and may overlook important diagnostic information. A multimethod approach to the assessment avoids the temptation to diagnose first and then ask questions to support this clinical picture. The assessment may include both quantitative and qualitative measures. The quantitative methods allow for operationally defining a client's problems; for example, a scale that provides a numerical score of the client's depression. Qualitative approaches describe the complexity of the client's problems in more detail.

- *Carefully consider data generated by the client in crisis*. How a person responds to a crisis situation may provide useful information but it may not reveal much about day-to-day behavior. Relying on observations of clients under stress may distort your assessment. Consider the ecstatic person who just found out that she won the "Dream Home" on HGTV and who has forgotten about the misery caused by her divorce.

- *Consider the "rule of parsimony."* Clients may present with several symptoms that could warrant a number of different diagnoses. Rather than assigning multiple diagnoses, look for data to support a single diagnosis that could potentially explain all of the symptoms. For example, a client may report feelings of sadness that could support a diagnosis of dysthymia and a major depressive disorder. The specific symptoms of each classification are closely related. However, when considering assigning the diagnosis, the classification of a major depressive disorder, recurrent would encompass the entire range of the client's symptoms thus reducing the need to assign several diagnoses.

The case histories presented in the remaining chapters provide opportunities for you to try out your diagnostic skills with a variety of client situations that are most often encountered in the mental health field. The case content requires you to separate facts from opinions and develop a competency-based assessment that integrates the specific language of the *DSM-IV-TR* classification system.

Competency-Based Assessment Guidelines

1. Focus on the client's history.
2. Carefully consider the client's recent history.
3. Practitioner observations are more accurate than client "complaints."
4. Objective assessments may be more reliable than subjective assessments.
5. Carefully consider data generated by the client in crisis.
6. Consider the "rule of parsimony."

SUMMARY

This chapter reviewed a number of tips and strategies for effectively reading and analyzing the case studies presented in this book. The discussion began with highlighting the importance of an accurate assessment as the first step toward identifying those behaviors that interfere with the individual client's social and occupational functioning as well as those that foster coping and adaptation. Suggestions for how to read the case vignettes were outlined; for example, completing a preliminary reading of the vignette to get a sense of the big picture and then rereading the case study to get a better sense of the client's story. A conceptual map that serves as a graphic tool to look at past and present symptoms, the period of disturbance, and other potential explanations that inform the competency-based assessment was highlighted. The chapter provided a number of tactics aimed at helping you to rule out other disorders and prioritize the most serious concern using hierarchic principles. The chapter concluded with a series of overarching principles to guide the competency-based assessment process.

We now turn our attention to the specific diagnostic classifications beginning with the disorders commonly found in infancy, childhood, and adolescence outlined in the next chapter.

Disorders in Infancy, Childhood, or Adolescence

INTRODUCTION

Disorders in infancy, childhood, or adolescence were largely excluded in earlier editions of the *Diagnostic and Statistical Manual of Mental Disorders* (DSM). Initially, most childhood disorders were relegated to the adult diagnostic categories with the exception of mental retardation and schizophrenia, childhood type (Cass & Thomas, 1979). Diagnostic refinements have continued over the years and in 1968 a specific section devoted to children was incorporated. Subsequent editions of the *DSM* have facilitated efforts to examine the complex behavioral problems found in children by systematically grouping behavioral disorders in infancy, childhood, and adolescence.

There are a number of factors that affect the assessment of mental illness in a child. Unlike the adult who generally seeks help for problems on his or her own, children are usually brought to clinical attention by their parents or teachers. In many instances the very young child may not completely understand the assessment process and all the related diagnostic questions that we take for granted. This highlights the importance of including parents (or the primary caretaker) when attempting to get a clear picture of the child's symptoms. In addition, children tend to have more difficulty expressing themselves in words. A very young child may have only a rudimentary understanding of verbal communication. For that reason, you might want to consider trying to communicate with the child through the use of toys and play materials. It is beyond the scope of this chapter to provide an in-depth discussion of the communication methods that are user-friendly to children, so you may want to review additional sources of information such as Gary Landreth's *Play Therapy* (2002) or Nancy Boyd Webb's *Social Work Practice with Children* (2003). The competency-based assessment, with its emphasis on the various systems in a client's life, supports including multiple informants as ancillary sources of information to ensure a successful evaluation of the child. You might consider asking the child's parents (or legal guardians) for consent to obtain information from additional family members, teachers, day care staff, and others who play a role in the child's life.

Cultural Considerations

The broader community and ethnic or cultural environment affecting the child are also a part of the assessment process (Pederson, 2008). The definition of what is considered to be acceptable behavior or what is seen as deviant is influenced by one's environment and can also play a role formulating an accurate diagnosis. If your background differs and the parents and/or child do not believe that you fully understand their specific customs or traditions, then the risk for misinterpreting symptoms increases (Canino & Spurlock, 2000). Consider the child who is exposed to poverty or discrimination and has problems assimilating into the larger culture; being raised with a strong history of inequity may make this family suspicious of the outsider. This is the youngster who may be hesitant to cooperate fully with you as you attempt to evaluate his or her behavior. On the surface this might look like resistance, but it may really be a reluctance to trust a stranger.

The *DSM* has made great strides toward taking the influence of diversity into account but relevant data about behavioral and developmental differences due to culture, ethnicity, and/or socioeconomic status remains largely unexamined (Lum, 2007; Paniagua, 2005). Obviously, broad generalizations are to be avoided. The comprehensive approach to the competency-based assessment provides a framework to examine disorders from an integrated perspective that acknowledges social and cultural influences and their implications for symptom development.

Developmental Considerations

The child's developmental stage is also a factor in the assessment process. Development can be understood as periods of transition or a lifelong process of growth, maturation, and change (Carter et al., 2005). Children and adolescents are affected almost daily by these changes. The child's developmental stage helps to determine whether behavior is normal or problematic. Understanding normal child developmental milestones helps to accurately evaluate the significance of problem behaviors; that is, behaviors considered typical at one age may be problematic at another age or developmental level. Those of us who are parents are all too familiar with the developmental stage popularly called the terrible twos (Ostrander, 2004). For example, oppositional behavior and temper tantrums are not seen as major problems for the 2-year-old but they may be considered significant difficulties for the 11-year-old.

As the child moves through various developmental stages their thought processes become increasingly sophisticated. Cognitive development refers to the child's thinking skills. A child with impaired cognitive abilities cannot be expected to function in the same way as a child of normal intelligence across all stages of development. Consider the child who struggles with cognitive problems such as a reading disorder or a developmental delay that interferes with learning. In addition, he or she may show behavioral problems as a way to distract from their inability to learn like other children. These performance difficulties may lead to a negative sense of self, which may influence later developmental stages.

Psychosocial development refers to the attitudes and skills needed to become a productive member of society (Ashford, LeCroy, & Lortie, 2005). Throughout the child's development his or her interactions with the world—beginning with the ability to form attachments to family members—affect health and other aspects of life. Mental health is influenced by the complex interactions within the child (or biological, psychological, and genetic), the child's environment (that is, parents, siblings, family relations, peers as well as neighborhood, school, and community), and the way these factors interact with one another. Children with developmental delays are more than likely to show a number of behavior problems such as dropping out of school or ending up in the juvenile justice system. They are also at a higher risk for developing a mental disorder (Baker et al., 2003). Mash and Wolfe (2010) observe that while psychological disorders in children have a different set of symptoms, all share the commonality of being an indication of adaptational failure or the lack of meeting the challenges associated with a particular developmental milestone. This is the child who is in some way different from other children of the same age. The competency-based assessment takes into account the struggles that play a role in the developmental course along with a parallel evaluation of the child's strengths. From this assessment perspective, issues pertaining to specific age groups as well as the strengths affecting developmental pathways are highlighted.

OVERVIEW OF THE MAJOR CHARACTERISTICS OF THE DIAGNOSTIC CLASSIFICATIONS

How do we determine if a child has a particular mental disorder that requires professional attention or whether this is something that the youngster will simply outgrow or overcome on his or her own? One place to start is being able to describe the features that make up a particular disorder and how it is classified in order to come to a decision about a particular diagnosis. Differentiating between normal child development and specific childhood syndromes will more than likely result in a better understanding (Kazdin, 2000). For diagnostic convenience, the *DSM* provides a separate section

A Child's Behavioral Warning Signs

Withdrawn or social problems:

> Prefers to be alone
>
> Secretive
>
> Sulks a lot
>
> Lacks energy
>
> Unhappy
>
> Overly dependent on others
>
> Prefers to play with younger children

Attention or thought problems:

> Unable to concentrate
>
> Cannot sit still
>
> Acts without thinking
>
> Too nervous to concentrate
>
> Performs poorly on school work
>
> Cannot get his or her mind off certain thoughts

Delinquency or aggression:

> Associates with other children who get into trouble
>
> Lies and cheats
>
> Argues a lot
>
> Mean to others
>
> Demands attention
>
> Destroys other people's property
>
> Disobeys at home and at school
>
> Stubborn and moody
>
> Talks too much
>
> Teases others
>
> Explosive temper

Anxiety or depression:

> Lonely
>
> Numerous fears and worries
>
> Needs to be perfect
>
> Feels unloved, nervous, sad, and depressed

for disorders usually diagnosed in infancy, childhood, or adolescence (American Psychiatric Association, 2000).

Many disorders have an onset during childhood or adolescence but may not be formally diagnosed until adulthood so there is not always a clear distinction between childhood and adult disorders. A child with a major psychiatric disorder is affected in several areas of his or her life. These may include emotions, social or intellectual abilities, or the use of language. When you consider a potential diagnosis, Webb (2003) suggests looking into the following groupings of problems to better distinguish some of the warning signs to look for (or to ask the child's parents). It is not the magnitude of changes in a child's life but the consistency that is significant.

The specific diagnosis assigned to a child's set of symptoms will usually depend on a combination of characteristics listed above and/or the severity of the illness. The disorders for infants, children, and adolescents can be primarily organized into two main groups: disorders of undercontrolled behavior and disorders of overcontrolled behavior.

Distinguishing the Disorders

The DSM diagnoses represent undercontrolled behavior or when the child lacks or has insufficient control over his or her behavior as compared to what can normally be expected of a child of a similar age. These disorders include the pervasive developmental disorders (PDD) or autism spectrum disorders (ASD) followed by the more common attention deficit and disruptive behavior disorders.

The diagnoses of autism, Asperger's, and pervasive developmental disorder not otherwise specified (PDD-NOS) are commonly called ASDs or sometimes simply referred to as the autistic disorders (Freitag, 2007). The DSM goes beyond this subset of the broader autism phenotype and distinguishes the PDDs by including a discussion of the rarer Rett's disorder and childhood disintegrative disorder. The latter two disorders are extremely rare and because you will probably not see them in your clinical practice, they are not emphasized in this chapter. ASD and PDD are often used interchangeably.

The second group of disorders consists of overcontrolled behaviors or the types of disorders that usually create more problems for the child themselves than for others. These are the youngsters who will report feelings of shyness or unhappiness. We address selective mutism and separation anxiety, one of the anxiety disorders that apply exclusively to children and adolescents who have experienced some kind of life stress or trauma such as relocation or divorce.

To increase your diagnostic understanding, we address the tic disorders of Tourette's and chronic motor or vocal tic disorder. Since the elimination disorders are usually seen as symptomatic expressions of other problems, encopresis and enuresis are reviewed.

A Note on Mental Retardation

Noble, Maluccio, Whittaker, and Jones (2008) make a distinction that intellectual disability is a physical and mental condition rather than a psychiatric disorder. Intellectual disabilities, or mental retardation, can be traced to a number of sources including biological factors, prenatal damage due to toxins, deprivation of nurturance or stimulation, fetal malnutrition, premature birth, viral infections during pregnancy, and childhood infections, injuries, or poisonings (APA, 2000). The definitive diagnosis of mental retardation is generally made by other professionals such as physicians, so this *DSM* category is not addressed here. Keep in mind that these children, in addition to impaired development, may also exhibit a number of other disorders such as anxiety, or conduct disorder.

INCIDENCE AND PREVALENCE

Approximately 73.5 million children under 18 years of age live in the United States and that number is expected to grow to 85.7 million by the year 2030 (Child Trends Data Bank, 2007). It is anticipated that from 12% to 22% of all children under age 18 will need some type of services for mental, emotional, or behavioral problems. Approximately 1 out of every 50 children already receives mental health services (Latest Findings in Children's Mental Health, 2004).

Looking at the Specific Disorders

The prevalence of the PDDs is four to five times higher for boys than for girls, with the average age for the earliest PDD diagnosis of 30 to 36 months. The PDDs are linked to toxins such as environmental pollutants and fetal alcohol syndrome. Early onset may occur at 8 to 10 months of age (Werner, Dawson, Osterling, & Dinno, 2000). Estimates from the Centers for Disease Control (2010) show that between 1 and 80 and 1 in 240 children, or an average of 1 in 110 children, have a PDD diagnosis.

The main diagnostic category for the PDDs is autistic disorder (AD). Yeargin-Allsopp and colleagues (2003) estimated that approximately 3 of every 1,000 children ages 3 to 10 years old have autism and it seems to be more common than some of the well-known disorders such as diabetes, spina bifida, or Down's syndrome. The diagnosis of autism is usually made by age 3. The prevalence rates of Asperger's disorder, another of the PDDs, range from 0.03 to 4.83 per 1,000 children (Fombonne & Tidmarsh, 2003). Boys seem to be more likely to have Asperger's than girls (Mattila et al., 2007).

Attention deficit/hyperactivity disorder is one of the most common disorders of childhood affecting approximately 3% to 5% of children worldwide (Nair, Ehimare, Beitman, Nair, & Lavin, 2006). Approximately 30% to 50% of those with ADHD will continue to have symptoms into adulthood (Stern, H. & Stern, T., 2002). It is diagnosed two to four times more frequently in boys than in girls (Sciutto, Nolfi, & Bluhm, 2004). A large community-based study conducted by Kurlan and colleagues (2001) found that more than 19% of school-age children have tic disorders and those with attention deficit hyperactivity disorder (ADHD) show higher overall rates than other children. On average, ADHD will manifest two and a half years before the tics appear (Bruun & Budman, 2005).

Other disorders. Transient tic disorder occurs in approximately 4% to 24% of school children (Fahn, 2005). It is the mildest form of tic disorder, and may be underreported because of its temporary nature. Tourette's is a more prevalent tic disorder occurring in 10 per 10,000 of the U.S. general population (Bagheri, Kerbeshian, & Burd, 1999). Soiling seems to correspond to stress-induced disruptive or distressed (dysregulated) behaviors but the U.S. prevalence rates for encopresis are less evident. However, Mellon, Whiteside, and Friedrich (2007) studied three comparison groups of 4- to 12-year-olds with fecal soiling and noticed a relationship to dysregulated behavior, finding a little more than 10% of the study population had a history of sexual abuse and another 10% were referred primarily for other types of psychiatric problems. Exploring prevalence rates for enuresis, Shreeram and colleagues (2009) found an overall 12-month occurrence of 4.45% based on a nationally representative sample of 8- to 11-year-old children in the United States who participated in the 2001 to 2004 National Health and Nutrition Examination Surveys. The prevalence of selective mutism is about 7 per 1,000 children or an incidence rate of a little more than 1% (Lindsey, Piacentini, & McCracken, 2002).

One of the most common childhood anxiety disorders is separation anxiety. Based on data from the 2001 to 2003 National Comorbidity Survey Replication (NCS-R), a nationally representative survey of U.S. households, the lifetime prevalence estimates of childhood separation anxiety disorders were estimated at 4.1% (Shear, Jin, Ruscio, Walters, & Kessler, 2006). Approximately one-third of the respondents who were diagnosed in childhood (36.1%) had symptoms that persisted into adulthood thus highlighting the importance of recognizing separation anxiety disorder in childhood.

THE PERVASIVE DEVELOPMENTAL DISORDERS

Have you ever had a parent tell you that their child always seemed a little odd? They are usually the first to notice when something is unusual and generally by the first two years of the child's life (Myers, Johnson, & Council on Children with Disabilities, 2007). For example, their infant might be babbling at one moment and then suddenly become silent, withdrawn, self-abusive, or indifferent to others around them.

The PDDs are a constellation of symptoms characterized by a triad of atypical communication, social impairments, including atypical social interactions, and atypical responses to social and perceptual stimuli in the environment (Harris, 2000). Some of the earliest signs to look for when considering a PDD is the child's failure in the development of the paralinguistic signaling system (or nonverbal communications) characterized by poor eye contact, failure to develop a protodeclarative point (or pointing to show something such as when a child points his finger to show his dad an airplane), and the lack of facial affect that demonstrates reciprocal engagement or shared attention.

The Major Symptoms of PDD

Communication. Language delays are the most common reasons that bring children with PDD to the professional's attention. Speech may consist of repeating phrases spoken to them (echolalia), using phrases in unusual ways, saying the same phrases over and over again (perseveration), and reversing pronouns (for example, saying something like "You want cookie" when it is the child who wants the cookie).

Social interactions. The child's problems with social interactions stem from an impaired ability to perceive events around them and to accurately interpret communications from others. The child may show unusual and unexpected responses, including a tendency to interact less with others. This is the youngster who may make less eye contact, including when spoken to, or may avoid eye contact all together. He or she may seem to have less interest in sharing with others, show little emotion, and prefer to focus on an object rather than to show it to the parent. There is an overall less reciprocal giving and taking of objects. These difficulties with social interaction make it easier to misunderstand the child. That is, simple requests from a parent may not produce the expected response making the child seem stubborn.

Restricted behaviors. Unlike most children of the same age, the child with PDD may have unusual interests and his or her play may appear to be less imaginative and more repetitive. For instance, rather than playing with a toy car, the child may be more interested in simply spinning the wheels over and over. They might show an attachment to odd items, such as being attached to a plastic cup and keeping it nearby instead of behaving like most children who form attachments to a favorite blanket or soft cuddly toy. Other unusual behaviors that might be seen are sitting in a "w" position (similar to sitting on his or her legs, the child sits on the floor with knees bent so that the feet are out to either side of the hips shaping the legs into a "w") rather than with legs extended (or folded) in front of them, hand flapping, repetitive spinning, walking on toes or other movements that appear to have no purpose.

Cognitive abilities may also be affected. Many children with PDD may have some degree of mental retardation and a small number of children (with autism or Asperger's disorder) may show exceptional talents in areas such as math or art. This is referred to as splinter abilities (Melvin, 2002). Perhaps the most popular example of this

Major Characteristics of the Pervasive Developmental Disorders

Communication	This is the first noticed symptom.
	The most pervasive is a failure to make compensatory use of gestural communication in the absence of spoken capacity.
Social interactions	Unable to develop the types of social relationships expected for the child's age.
Restricted behaviors, interests, and activities	A preoccupation with restricted and narrow interests as well as preoccupation with (sensory) parts of objects.

savant category can be found in the 1988 movie entitled *Rain Man*. The protagonist, portrayed in the Academy Award–winning performance by actor Dustin Hoffman, was a character called Raymond who could instantly determine the day of the week for distant dates and multiply extremely large numbers in his head.

The PDDs are described as occurring on a continuum because of the wide variability of impact they have on the child's everyday functioning. On one end of the continuum is autistic disorder, which is seen as the more severe diagnosis, and extending to the milder Asperger's disorder at the other end of the continuum. There is a common set of symptoms comprising the diagnostic criteria for the autistic disorder, Asperger's, and PDD-NOS. The symptoms will be reviewed with respect to how each is associated with altered perception or the processing of specific types of social or environmental stimuli.

We now turn our attention to autistic disorder, or autism, where children behave in bizarre, unusual, and often puzzling ways. Every aspect of the child's world is affected. It is almost as if the child never successfully entered reality because of such serious disturbances in his or her development (Rutter, 2000).

BEGINNING WITH AUTISTIC DISORDER

Put yourself in the place of a parent with an infant or young toddler who will not cuddle, look into your eyes, nor respond to affection or even to a gentle touch. Unlike other children, those with autism seem incapable of forming normal relationships or communicating with anyone. As the child grows older he rarely speaks or when he does, he talks in an unusual way. This is the child who does not use facial expressions or gestures to communicate his needs or to tell you how he feels. There is no smile, no nods, no holding up toys for you to look at. Over the years, the child becomes more and more isolated and caught up in his own world of rituals and interests. If interrupted, the child becomes extremely upset.

Past and Present Symptoms

- Impaired social interaction (at least two):
  - Markedly deficient regulation of social interaction through multiple nonverbal behaviors (eye contact, facial expression, body posture, gestures)
  - Lack of peer relationships appropriate to development level
  - Absence of seeking to share achievements, interests, or pleasure with others
  - Absence of social or emotional reciprocity
- Impaired communication (at least one):
  - Delayed (or absent) development of spoken language—the child does not try to compensate with gestures
  - For those who can speak, notable deficiency in ability to begin or sustain a conversation
  - Repetitive, stereotyped, or idiosyncratic language
  - Appropriate to the developmental stage, absence of social imitative play or spontaneous make-believe play
- Activities, behaviors, or interests that are repetitive, restricted, and stereotyped (at least one):
- Abnormal (in focus/intensity) preoccupation with interests that are restricted and stereotyped
  - Rigid routines or rituals with no function
  - Repetitive stereotyped motor mannerisms
  - Persistent absorption with parts of objects

Period of Disturbance

- Onset must be before age 3 with delays or abnormal functioning in either social interaction, language as used in social communication, or symbolic or imaginative play

Other Potential Explanations

- The child's symptoms are not better explained by childhood disintegrative disorder

Figure 3.1   Conceptual Map for Autism

The Clinical Picture

Autism is distinguished by serious abnormalities in communication and language, social impairments, and restrictive and repetitive behaviors and interest beginning before the child is 3 years of age. Every aspect of the child's interaction with his or her world is affected. These are children who do not develop the types of social relationships expected for their age. It is believed that information processing in the child's brain is affected by how the nerve cells and their synapses connect and organize (Levy, Mandell, & Shultz, 2009). Onset is usually gradual but some children may seem to develop normally and then regress (Stefanatos, 2008).

Autism is considered to be a spectrum disorder; that is, symptom patterns, range of abilities, and the child's characteristics are expressed in many different combinations and in varying degrees of severity (Lord, Cook, Leventhal, & Amaral, 2000). In other words, children with this diagnosis are vastly different from one another. For example, one child may be severely impaired by being silent, mentally disabled, and constantly hand flapping and rocking in contrast to another higher functioning child who may have distinctly odd social approaches, narrowly focused interests, but talkative and somewhat dogmatic.

The child displays 6 or more of 12 symptoms of impairment across all three of the major symptom areas. Figure 3.1 is a conceptual map that charts the signs of autism.

AUTISTIC DISORDER

The conceptual map summarizes the characteristic triad of symptoms of autistic disorder: impairments in social interaction; impairments in communication; and restricted interests and repetitive behavior. Autism is distinguished from the other childhood developmental disorders by the child's social deficits. Children with autism may have other co-occurring symptoms that are independent of the diagnosis but can affect the individual and the family. We now turn to a review of these co-occurring symptoms.

Other Co-Occurring Symptoms

Sensory abnormalities are one of the most common symptoms occurring in more than 90% of those with autism (Geschwind, 2009). For example, sights, sounds, smells, or textures that do not seem to bother most children can be painful or confusing for the child with autism. In addition, studies show that 60% to 80% of these individuals show motor signs that include poor muscle tone, poor motor planning, and walking on toes. Although motor deficits are pervasive across the PDDs, it seems to occur more frequently for those with autism. Approximately three-quarters of children with autism may also show unusual eating behaviors with being selective about what's eaten as the most common problem. Additionally, eating rituals and refusing food can occur (Dominick, Davis, Lainhart, Tager-Flushberg, & Folstein, 2007). However, atypical eating patterns are not essential for the diagnosis of autism.

It should come as no surprise that parents of children with autism have higher levels of stress (Montes & Halterman, 2007). Interestingly, siblings report less conflict but are at a greater risk for developing poorer sibling relationships as adults (Orsmond & Seltzer, 2007).

Differential Assessment

The disorders that most often co-occur with autism are mental retardation and epilepsy. The child may also show symptoms of hyperactivity, anxieties and fears, and mood problems (Kim, Szatmari, Bryson, Streiner, & Wilson, 2000). Selective mutism is differentiated from autism by the child's appropriate communication skills in certain contexts but impaired social interaction and restricted patterns of behavior are not shown.

Of the five PDDs, Asperger's disorder is closest to autistic disorder in symptoms and likely causes.

BEGINNING WITH ASPERGER'S DISORDER

A colleague of mine shared one of her experiences working with the mother of a child with Asperger's. This mother was scolding her child for talking to her in what could best be described as a bombastic and overblown manner. She told him to stop backtalking to her. My colleague vividly remembered the child's response. He said, "Sorry Mom, from now on I'll talk to your front." Unlike autism, those with Asperger's have no substantial delay in language development but show difficulty in understanding appropriate social communication by literally and concretely understanding messages.

The Clinical Picture

In many ways, Asperger's disorder (AD) and autism are similar. However, AD is set apart by the child's major difficulties in social interaction and unusual patterns of interest and behavior while cognitive and communication skills remain relatively intact (Klin, Volkmar, & Sparrow, 2000). These children show the same kinds of social impairments and restricted, stereotyped interests found in children with autism but not the general delays in language, cognitive development of age-appropriate self-help skills, adaptive behavior (other than social interaction), or curiosity about the environment. Delayed motor milestones and motor clumsiness are commonly reported but not an essential diagnostic feature.

Overall, a child with AD comes across as a little eccentric; that is, the child tends to be socially inept, egocentric (or an excessive preoccupation with oneself), and preoccupied with abstract, narrow interests. For instance, you might be wearing your favorite perfume when meeting a child with a diagnosis of Asperger's for the first time and he or she might state bluntly, "Somebody around here stinks. I think it's you, Miss Gray.

Yes, Miss Gray you definitely stink." The child is unable to recognize the effect of his or her actions on others. It is unclear if AD is a distinct disorder or should be considered as the extreme on a continuum of social behavior (Baron-Cohen, 2000). There is some debate whether AD is a variation of autism or simply describes higher-functioning children with autism (Volkmar & Klin, 2000).

Figure 3.2 is a conceptual map that charts the symptom course of Asperger's.

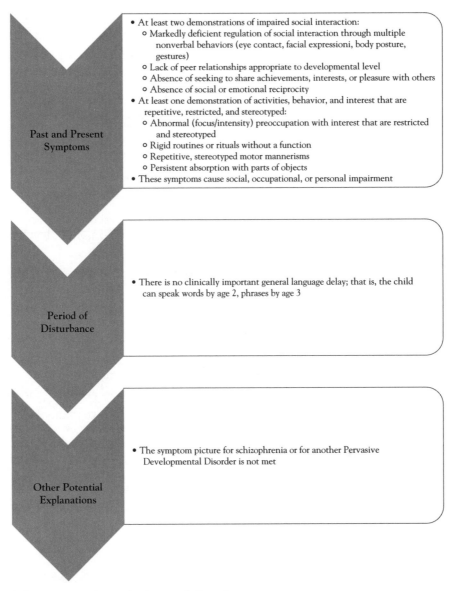

Figure 3.2   Conceptual Map for Asperger's Disorder

ASPERGER'S DISORDER

In summary, Asperger's is regarded as a part of the autism spectrum but it is distinguished by significant difficulties in social interaction along with restricted and repetitive patterns of behavior and interests. The key diagnostic distinction is the child's relative preservation of linguistic and cognitive development. A review of the other pervasive developmental disorders follows.

The Other PDDs

Rett's disorder. Retts disorder is a rare and severe neurological developmental disorder that has been seen only in females although some variations have been described in males (Christen & Hanefeld, 1995). Specifically, girls with this disorder have a normal head circumference at birth. Following a period of what looks to be normal prenatal and early development for the first 6 months to a year, they begin to display a specific pattern of deficits and they are summarized as (APA, 2000):

- Deceleration of head growth between ages 5 and 48 months.
- Loss of previously acquired purposeful hand skills (between 5 and 30 months) with the subsequent development of stereotyped hand movements (such as wringing hands).
- Loss of social engagement early on though social interaction often develops later.
- Appearance of poorly coordinated gait or trunk movements.
- Severely impaired expressive and receptive language development with severe psychomotor retardation.

Childhood disintegrative disorder. Childhood disintegrative disorder describes a child who shows a significant loss of previously acquired skills before the age of 10 years. This loss follows a period of what looks to be normal development in verbal and nonverbal communication, social relationships, play, and adaptive behavior for the first two years of life. The child shows losses in at least two of the following areas:

- Expressive or receptive language.
- Social skills or adaptive behavior.
- Bowel or bladder control.
- Play.
- Motor skills.

In addition, the child shows abnormalities in two of the following areas of functioning (APA, 2000):

- Qualitative impairment in social interaction (such as an inability to develop peer relationships or a lack in social or emotional reciprocity).
- Qualitative impairments in communication (such as a delay of spoken language or lack of make-believe play).
- Restricted, repetitive, and stereotyped patterns of behavior, interests, and activities (including motor stereotypes and mannerisms).

Pervasive developmental disorder, not otherwise specified (NOS). Pervasive developmental disorder NOS, also called atypical autism, is considered a subthreshold condition; that is, some but not all features of autism or another explicitly identified PDD are seen. No specific guidelines for diagnosis are provided and it is used when the criteria are not met for a more specific PDD disorder.

THE ATTENTION DEFICIT AND DISRUPTIVE BEHAVIOR DISORDERS

The attention deficit and disruptive behavior disorders are another series of disorders found in childhood. They are typically found in children who have difficulties in maintaining attention, keeping focused, completing work, being impulsive, or repeatedly engaging in antisocial behaviors such as lying or cheating. Because of the similarities among symptoms, there are a number of disorders in this category grouped together. Following is a review of each syndrome.

Beginning With Attention Deficit/Hyperactivity Disorder

Attention deficit/hyperactivity disorder elicits the most frequent referral for professional help (Erk, 2008). Usually referred to by its initials of either ADHD or ADD, it is a controversial disorder with debate primarily centering on how it is diagnosed and treated (Schonwald & Lechner, 2006). Environmental toxins, drug exposure in utero, and a history of child abuse and multiple foster care placements are related to ADHD (Harvard Mental Health Letter, 2004). Hyperactive children can get into minor difficulties because of their activity level, but they are not bad children per se. It is their behavior that tends to overwhelm others, leading to friction in their interpersonal relationships. This is the child who has poor concentration and is disorganized or is a "motormouth" who endlessly talks about everything and anything to anyone who will listen. He or she does not pay attention, is in constant motion, and simply cannot wait for his or her turn. In school the child fails to complete assignments and forgets chores at home. This is not in defiance of authority but a consequence of forgetfulness and disorganization.

The Clinical Picture

ADHD is characterized by the key behaviors of inattention, and hyperactivity/impulsivity. This diagnosis represents two distinctly different problems, although they appear to be linked together. Many of the symptoms of ADHD occur from time to time in just about everyone but to make the diagnosis it is the frequency of these symptoms (six months or more) and the significant impairment they cause in at least two types of situations in the child's life: for example, at school (in the classroom or on the playground), or social life (at home, in the community, or in social settings). If you see a child who is active on the playground but not elsewhere, then the problem might not be ADHD.

Children with ADHD are different from one another and as a result there are three subtypes to classify those with a common set of symptoms (see table below):

Figure 3.3 is a conceptual map of the symptom course for attention deficit/hyperactivity disorder. The specifier in partial remission is included for those whose current symptoms do not fulfill diagnostic criteria.

ADHD Subtypes

Predominantly inattentive type (ADHD-PI)	Describes the child who has problems mainly with the symptoms of inattention.
	Children with this subtype are less likely to act out or have difficulties getting along with other children. They can be easily overlooked because they can sit quietly, seem dreamy, spacey, or in a fog, and they are not paying attention to what they are doing.
Predominantly hyperactive-impulsive type (ADHD-HI)	Describes the child who has problems mainly with symptoms of hyperactivity-impulsivity.
	This subtype is easier to identify because the child is all over the place and rarely sits still for long. The child may be aggressive, defiant, oppositional, and rejected by his or her peers. Placement in special education classes or suspension is common.
Combined type (ADHD-C)	Describes the child who has problems with both symptoms of inattention and hyperactivity-impulsivity.
	Most children have the combined type.

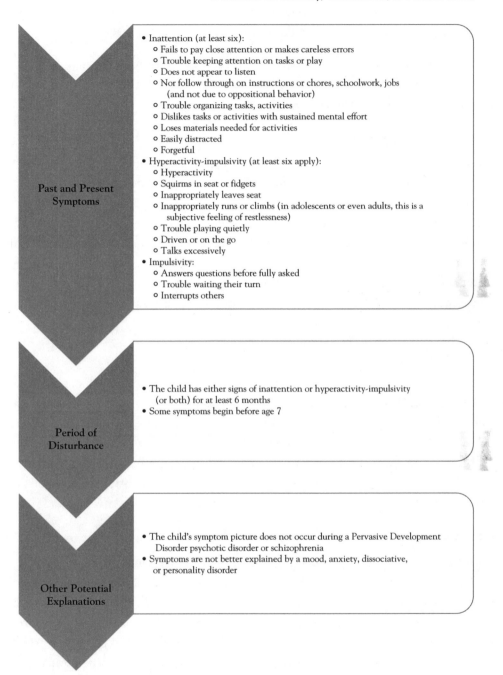

Past and Present Symptoms

- Inattention (at least six):
  - Fails to pay close attention or makes careless errors
  - Trouble keeping attention on tasks or play
  - Does not appear to listen
  - Nor follow through on instructions or chores, schoolwork, jobs (and not due to oppositional behavior)
  - Trouble organizing tasks, activities
  - Dislikes tasks or activities with sustained mental effort
  - Loses materials needed for activities
  - Easily distracted
  - Forgetful
- Hyperactivity-impulsivity (at least six apply):
  - Hyperactivity
  - Squirms in seat or fidgets
  - Inappropriately leaves seat
  - Inappropriately runs or climbs (in adolescents or even adults, this is a subjective feeling of restlessness)
  - Trouble playing quietly
  - Driven or on the go
  - Talks excessively
- Impulsivity:
  - Answers questions before fully asked
  - Trouble waiting their turn
  - Interrupts others

Period of Disturbance

- The child has either signs of inattention or hyperactivity-impulsivity (or both) for at least 6 months
- Some symptoms begin before age 7

Other Potential Explanations

- The child's symptom picture does not occur during a Pervasive Development Disorder psychotic disorder or schizophrenia
- Symptoms are not better explained by a mood, anxiety, dissociative, or personality disorder

Figure 3.3   Conceptual Map for Attention Deficit/Hyperactivity Disorder

ATTENTION DEFICIT/HYPERACTIVITY DISORDER

Attention deficit hyperactivity disorder is the most commonly diagnosed disorder in childhood. The child struggling with this disorder often has other problems and they are reviewed in the following discussion.

Associated Characteristics

Children with ADHD usually display other problems, including cognitive deficits, speech and language impairments, and/or interpersonal difficulties. You can expect to see a child in your practice with a learning disorder or speech patterns that are difficult to understand. Relationships with adults can be conflicted because the child might be argumentative, unpredictable, and explosive. Tasks and situational factors can also be problematic. For example, children with ADHD struggle to attend to tasks, regulate their activity levels, and control impulsive behaviors in order to work consistently. Situations that are complex or boring or that have many distractions are also challenging for the child.

Differential Assessment

Almost 80% of children with ADHD have a co-occurring disorder that complicates the assessment (Pliszka, 2003). The most common of these are oppositional defiant and conduct disorder, anxiety, and depression. Tourette's is found in 50% of those with ADHD (Evidente, 2000). Some forms of epilepsy can cause symptoms resembling ADHD. Other medical conditions to be excluded are hypothyroidism, anemia, lead poisoning, chronic illness, hearing or vision impairment, medication side effects, and sleep impairment.

Other Attention Deficit and Disruptive Behavior Disorders

Conduct disorder. About 30% to 50% of children with ADHD will ultimately develop a conduct disorder (Barkley, 1998). These are the children who violate societal rules and who are at a risk of getting into serious trouble at school or with the police. Expect to see a child who may fight, cheat, steal, and set fires, destroy property, or use illicit drugs.

When considering a conduct disorder, explore whether the child has repeatedly violated rules, age-appropriate societal norms, or the rights of others for the past 12 months or more. This is shown by at least three or more symptoms of aggression against people or animals, property destruction, lying or theft, or serious rule violation that has occurred in the prior six months.

There are a number of specifiers associated with the diagnosis of conduct disorder and they are mild, moderate, and severe. Subtypes indicate onset, such as childhood, adolescent, or unspecified.

Behaviors Seen in Conduct Disorder

Aggression against people or animals:

Frequent bullying or threatening

Often starts fights

Has used a weapon that could cause serious injury (a gun, knife, club)

Shown physical cruelty to people, animals

Engaged in theft with confrontation (robbery, extortion, mugging, purse snatching)

Forced sex on someone

Property destruction:

Deliberately sets fires to cause damage

Destroyed the property of others

Lying or theft:

Broken into building, car, or house of another

Frequently lies or breaks promises for gain ("conning")

Stolen valuables without confrontation (forgery, shoplifting)

Serious rule violation:

Starting at age 13, frequently stays out at night against parents' wishes

Runs away overnight twice or more

Beginning at age 13, engages in truancy

Oppositional defiant disorder. Oppositional defiant disorder (ODD) is more prevalent in children who have had a succession of different caregivers or live in families with harsh, inconsistent, and/or neglectful child-rearing practices (APA, 2000). About 50% of children with ADHD, primarily boys, will meet criteria for ODD by seven years of age or later (Barkley & Benton, 1998). This disorder is characterized by an ongoing pattern of disobedient, hostile, and defiant behavior toward authority figures, which goes beyond the bounds of normal childhood behavior. This is the child who appears to be stubborn.

Specific features distinguish ODD. First, the child's defiance must interfere with the ability to function in school, home, or the community. Second, the defiance cannot be the result of another disorder such as the more serious conduct disorder, depression, anxiety, or a sleep disorder. Lastly, the child's problems must have been going on for at least six months. The behavioral pattern may include the following behaviors.

Behaviors Seen in Oppositional Defiant Disorder

Losing temper

Arguing with adults

Defying or refusing to carry out the rules or requests of adults

Deliberately doing things that annoy others

Blaming others for own mistakes or misbehavior

Being touchy or easily annoyed

Being angry and resentful

Being spiteful or vindictive

Disruptive behavior disorder NOS. Sometimes you might be aware of situations where the child's behavior is clearly disruptive to the extent where problems are occurring but there are not enough symptoms present to consider a conduct disorder or oppositional defiant disorder. Alternatively, you may not have enough information to make a definitive diagnosis or the child's circumstances are unique. For example, this might be the child who is not in a good foster care placement, has been physically or sexually abused, or is raised in a home where the mother is abused or living in poverty. Disruptive behavior NOS is seen as a kind of catchall diagnosis for disruptive behavior problems in children. Typically the child demonstrates significantly impaired interpersonal or family relationships and/or disturbed school functioning. The NOS diagnosis provides an avenue to document that problems are occurring but to do so in a tentative manner. In this way, the child's symptom picture can be clarified in greater detail over time as more information becomes available.

TIC DISORDERS

Tic disorders are sudden, repetitive, nonrhythmic motor movements or phonic productions such as eye blinking, facial grimacing, and throat clearing, grunting, or whistling to the repetition of complete words or phrases. The more complex motor tics involve multiple, sequenced movements, and can include behaviors such as twirling in place, tapping a certain number of times, or stooping to touch the ground. The most common are facial tics (Kesaree, 2003).

Tics seem to worsen during adolescence and the symptoms become more unpredictable from day to day. Coprolalia (a tic made up of obscene, inappropriate, or aggressive words or statements such as "giving the finger") often appears first in adolescence causing considerable distress. Tics increase in frequency in stressful situations, even if they are of a positive nature such as being keyed up about going on vacation. Some people's tics are most obvious in relaxed conditions, such as quietly watching television. Tics tend to diminish in a new or highly structured setting, for example at the doctor's office.

The Clinical Picture

The diagnostic criteria for all tic disorders specify that the symptoms must appear before the age of 18 and that they cannot result from ingestion of such substances as stimulants or from such general medical conditions as Huntington's disease. Tic disorders can be seen as occurring along a continuum of least to most severe in terms of disruption and impairment, with transient tic disorder at one end and Tourette's disorder, seen as the most severe, at the other.

The disorders can be summarized as follows:

✍ The Tic Disorders

Transient tic	Consists of multiple motor and/or phonic tics lasting at least four weeks but less than 12 months.
Chronic tic	Either single or multiple motor or phonic tics, but not both, and are present for more than one year.
Tuourette's	Both motor and phonic tics are present for more than a year.
Tic disorder NOS	Assessed when tics are present but do not meet criteria for any specific tic disorder.

Differential Assessment

Children and adults with tic disorders are at increased risk for depression and other mood disorders, as well as anxiety disorders. This comorbidity may be due to the burden of dealing with a chronic, disruptive, and often stigmatizing disorder. The energy and watchfulness required to suppress tic symptoms may contribute to social anxiety, social withdrawal, self-preoccupation, and fatigue. Low self-esteem and feelings of hopelessness are common in patients diagnosed with tic disorders. Behaviors of obsessive compulsive disorder (OCD) have been noted in as many as 80% of individuals with tic disorders, but only 30% actually meet the full criteria for OCD (O'Connor, 2001). Distinguishing complex tics from simple compulsions can be difficult. Touching compulsions appear to be characteristic of the tic-related type of OCD. Increasing numbers of children with tic disorders are also diagnosed with a conduct disorder.

THE ELIMINATION DISORDERS

The elimination disorders can be summarized as follows:

☞ The Elimination Disorders

Encopresis	When the child accidentally (or on purpose) repeatedly passes feces in inappropriate places.
	This behavior is not caused solely by the use of substances (laxatives, for example) or from a general medical condition.
Enuresis	Accidentally (or on purpose) the child repeatedly urinates into clothing or the bed.
	A medical condition (for instance diabetes, seizures, spina bifida) or the use of substances (such as a diuretic) does not cause behaviors.

Looking at Encopresis

Jonathan smelled so bad that his foster parents complained to their social worker that they did not think they could continue to care for him. Jonathan really didn't seem to care and he acted as if there was nothing wrong at home. He would laugh when someone told him he smelled. Encopresis is the clinical term used for children 4 years old or older who have chronic (long-term) constipation and they usually do not have control over the leakage of stool.

Encopresis refers to the child who cannot control his or her bowel movements so they pass bowel movements in their underwear; soiling or fecal incontinence are terms used for the same thing. In most cases encopresis develops as a result of long-standing constipation. With constipation, children have fewer bowel movements than normal, and the bowel movements they do have can be hard, dry, and difficult to pass. Once a child becomes constipated, a vicious cycle can develop. Over a long period of time the large intestine slowly fills with stool and stretches out of shape. As the large intestine stretches larger and larger, liquid stool from the small intestine begins to "leak" around the more formed stool in the colon. In the beginning, this leakage is usually small amounts that streak or stain the underwear and most parents just assume their child isn't wiping him or herself very well.

As the intestine stretches further, the amount of leakage increases so that eventually these children begin to have accidents; that is, they pass whole bowel movements in their underwear. Because the accidents consist of stool that is leaking through the intestine and not getting completely digested, they are usually very dark and sticky, smell very bad, and have to be scraped off the skin and clothing.

The emotional aspects. Encopresis can cause both physical and related emotional problems. Children with this disorder can certainly feel upset by the accidents they have when they soil their clothes. For example, the child's self-esteem and interactions with other people can be adversely affected. They may avoid going to school, playing with friends, or spending the night away from home. Parents may feel guilt, shame, anger, or distaste by the problem. They may punish their child for his or her encopretic behaviors, often out of anger and frustration over the "disgusting" situation. In turn, the child will often be aware of a parent's feelings and become even more emotionally affected. The symptoms of encopresis may resemble other conditions or medical problems, so an examination by a health-care provider or physician is central to making a definitive diagnosis.

Common Symptoms of Encopresis

Loose, watery stools

Involuntary stooling or needing to have a bowel movement with little or no warning, which may soil underwear when a child cannot get to the bathroom in time

Scratching or rubbing the anal area due to irritation by watery stools

Withdrawal from friends, school, and/or family

Hiding underwear

When diagnosing encopresis according to the *DSM*, there are two specific types: with constipation and overflow incontinence, and without constipation and overflow incontinence.

Looking at Enuresis

Characterized as the involuntary discharge of urine during the day or at night, enuresis is a common disorder among children in the United States. Most of the time the child cannot control the discharge but in some instances it may be intentional. Similar to encopresis, it is stressful for both parents and the child. It is considered more common at younger ages and among black youth. Boys are more often affected than girls especially among younger school-age children. Enuresis declines with maturity and most children will eventually stop bed-wetting on their own.

The *DSM* distinguishes three subtypes of enuresis (APA, 2000).

Subtypes of Enuresis

Nocturnal only	Considered the most common, in which the child wets only during sleep at night.
Diurnal only	The passage of urine during waking hours and most often during the early afternoon on school days.
Nocturnal and diurnal	The combination of nocturnal and diurnal patterns.

OTHER DISORDERS

As children grow up they often go through periods of shyness or they may be anxious around others. However, the disorders of selective mutism and separation anxiety go beyond these expected and temporary behaviors. We now turn to a review of these syndromes, which may be seen in your practice primarily because of the associated problems they generate for the child and his or her family.

BEGINNING WITH SELECTIVE MUTISM

Considered a rare disorder, selective mutism (SM), formerly called elective mutism, can best be characterized as a childhood social communication anxiety disorder. This is not a child who is unwilling to speak but one who simply fails to speak in particular situations. SM seems to be overrepresented among immigrant children who are adjusting to a new culture and/or a new language (Zelenko & Shaw, 2000). Typically, the child is exposed to one language at home and another in school.

Past and Present Symptoms
- Despite speaking in other situations, the child consistently does not speak in social situations where speech is expected (for example at school)
- This behavior interferes with educational or occupational achievement or with social communication
- The child's behavior does not occur solely during a Pervasive Developmental Disorder or by any psychotic disorder

Period of Disturbance
- The child's speech patterns have lasted at least one month (excluding the first month of school)

Other Potential Explanations
- The child's speech behavior is not caused by unfamiliarity (or discomfort) with the spoken language needed in the social situation
- Additionally, the speech behavior is not better explained by a communication disorder; for example, stuttering

Figure 3.4   Conceptual Map for Selective Mutism

The Clinical Picture

An essential feature of SM is the child's failure to speak in some social situations despite talking in other settings such as with family at home. It occurs before a child is 5 years old and is first noticed when he or she starts school. SM may be an extreme form of social phobia (Kristensen, 2000). The *DSM* emphasizes the relationship between SM and the anxiety disorders (APA, 2000). Figure 3.4 is the conceptual map that serves as a guide to the symptoms of selective mutism.

Selective Mutism

The distinguishing feature of selective mutism is the failure to talk in social situations where there is an expectation for talking. The child has the ability to speak and understand language but nevertheless does not speak. Interestingly, most children who struggle with selective mutism can function normally in other aspects of their lives.

Differential Assessment

Children with SM may struggle with excessive shyness, a fear of being embarrassed, or social isolation and withdrawal. Anxiety appears to be a key problem, which can cause avoidance but not to the extent found in social anxiety disorder. SM can be confused with a PDD, especially if the child is withdrawn. However, if the child is simply not talking in social situations, then the presence of a PDD can be ruled out. Selective mutism is not part of a developmental disorder nor is it a communications disorder. Children with SM are at a higher risk for also developing encopresis and enuresis (Manassis, 2009). It is helpful to include a speech-language pathologist and pediatrician when making a definitive diagnosis.

Separation Anxiety Disorder

All children experience an occasional worry at one time or another but separation anxiety disorder (SAD) is set apart by excessive worries that can overwhelm a child. This is different from the normative fear of strangers or stranger anxiety that typically develops when the child is 8 to 10 months of age. Separation anxiety disorder is evident when leaving or even the thought of leaving a parent, another caregiver, or the home causes significant distress. Even a temporary separation such as having to go to school is upsetting. The child's fears may appear to be irrational and typically he or she will go to great extremes to avoid being apart from the parent. For instance, the child may cry or scream if the parent leaves. In rare instances the child may even threaten suicide. Physical complaints such as having a stomachache or feeling nauseous are common.

The Clinical Picture

Children with SAD are recognized by age-inappropriate, excessive and disabling anxiety about being apart from their parents or away from home. Young children may have nightmares with separation themes and older children may have difficulty being alone in a room by day, or even sleeping alone. SAD usually occurs after the child has experienced a major stressful event such as moving, going to a new school, or having lost a family member to death, military deployment, incarceration, or illness.

Figure 3.5 is the conceptual map that charts the child's anxiety about being separated.

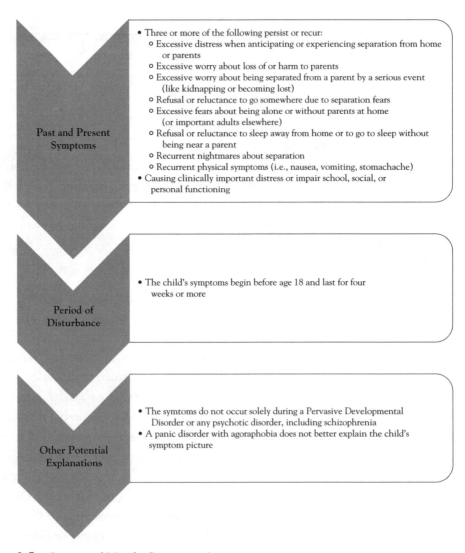

Figure 3.5   Conceptual Map for Separation Anxiety

SEPARATION ANXIETY

Although children may lose friends as a consequence of a repeated refusal to participate in activities away from home, they remain reasonably socially skilled and are generally able to get along with others. Unfortunately, school performance may suffer due to frequent absences.

FINAL THOUGHTS

Key features of the disorders of infancy, childhood, and adolescence discussed in this chapter:

Autism is a severe disorder with an onset before the age of three that is characterized by abnormalities in social functioning, language, and communication, and by unusual interests and behaviors. Considered a spectrum disorder, the symptoms and characteristics of autism are expressed in several different combinations and in degree of severity.

Asperger's disorder is characterized by significant difficulties in social interaction and by unusual patterns of interest and behavior in children who show relatively intact cognitive and communication skills.

Rett's disorder is a severe neurological developmental disorder found, to date, only in girls.

Childhood disintegrative disorder is where the child is apparently moving through normal development and then shows a significant loss of the previously acquired language, social skills, and adaptive behavior occurring before the age of 10.

Pervasive developmental disorder NOS is when the child shows the social, communication, and behavioral impairments associated with PDD but do not fully meet criteria for the other PDDs, schizophrenia, or other disorders.

Attention deficit/hyperactivity is distinguished by two lists of symptoms. The first includes inattention, poor concentration, and disorganization, and the second includes symptoms of hyperactivity and behavioral impulsivity.

Conduct disorder is marked by a pattern of repetitive behavior where the rights of others or social norms are violated.

Oppositional defiant disorder is diagnosed when children and adolescents usually show a pattern of defiant and disobedient behavior including resistance to authority figures. This symptom pattern is not as severe as conduct disorder.

Disruptive behavior NOS is used when you may not have enough information to make a definitive diagnosis for ADHD. It is considered to be a kind of catchall diagnosis for disruptive behavior problems in children.

The tic disorder of Tourette's is assessed when both motor and phonic tics are present for more than a year.

The elimination disorders consist of encopresis, which is the passage of feces into inappropriate places such as in clothing or on the floor, and enuresis characterized as the involuntary discharge of urine either during the day or night.

Selective mutism is diagnosed when the child fails to talk in specific social situations even though they may speak loudly and frequently at home or in other settings.

Separation anxiety disorder, a common anxiety disorder in children, is shown when developmentally inappropriate, excessive, and disabling anxiety about being apart from parents or away from home are displayed.

PRACTICING THE COMPETENCY-BASED ASSESSMENT

There are a number of disorders that are initially seen in children or young adolescents such as anorexia nervosa, depression, or schizophrenia that continue to cause problems as the child progresses into adulthood. The disorders highlighted in this chapter are those organized in the *DSM* under the category of those usually first diagnosed in infancy, childhood, or adolescence and serve as the focus of our practical applications. Notice that the assessment process includes ancillary sources of information such as the child's parents, or a medical report.

Case Illustrations

As seen in the following case illustrations, working with children can be both demanding and rewarding. In my own practice experience, one of the major elements is to love the work. Hopefully, you will also notice the practitioner's ability to communicate on the child's level in these scenarios along with patience, perseverance, and good communication skills. We now turn to the stories of Anthony Moretti and Paulie Merkel.

The Case of Anthony Moretti

This was my first visit with 6-year-old Anthony Moretti, so I invited his mother to accompany him into my office. He and his family were referred to the Children's Counseling Center by his pediatrician. Prior to meeting with Anthony, I spoke with Mrs. Moretti about preparing him for our session and how to describe to him why I would be seeing him. At this point, I had obtained background information from Anthony's parents and his pediatrician.

Anthony's medical history showed that he was in good overall health. The pediatrician's report indicated that when Anthony was 2-and-a-half years old, he had presented with vague complaints of nausea accompanied by a high fever. Further tests revealed nothing definitive. The fever cleared but Anthony had subsequently become constipated. Several months later, he had impacted feces and was prescribed laxatives and suppositories. Anthony's symptoms improved but following this he would experience alternating periods of constipation where he would not go to the toilet for several days and had runny diarrhea. He would soil his pants several times a day accompanied by what was described as foul smelling and sticky feces. By age 4, Anthony was taking laxatives regularly and his stool became softer and more regular. On the pediatrician's current examination, there was a palpable fecal mass in his lower abdomen and soft feces could be felt in the rectum.

Background history obtained from both parents, Vinnie and Maria Moretti, indicated that Anthony is the youngest child having two older sisters ages 9 and 12. His birth was uncomplicated and he was not constipated as an infant. Mrs. Moretti observed that Anthony seemed to develop at a slower pace than his sisters but she was not alarmed. She and her husband described Anthony as a happy little boy. "We come from a large Italian family," said Mrs. Moretti, "and Anthony would love to give hugs and kisses to all our relatives, especially his grandmothers. He is their only grandson and they dote on him."

Toilet training was seen as the biggest problem. Mrs. Moretti attempted to toilet train Anthony when he was about age 4. She stated, "I tried not to get stressed out but Anthony would have to sit on that potty for hours. He would usually manage to produce a little something but rarely a normal stool. It was so hard for me to keep from losing my patience with him because he looked like he was trying so hard." After he was done, Anthony continued to soil his pants frequently during the day. Sometimes Mrs. Moretti would change his pants only to have them soiled again half an hour later.

"It's like my Anthony could never get it together," she continued. Anthony was also wetting the bed at night but was able to stay dry during the day. "I tried getting him up at night but that didn't work. He's 6 now and I still put him in diapers before he goes to bed," related Mrs. Moretti.

I commented that this must be hard for the family and both Mr. and Mrs. Moretti agreed. "Anthony is my only boy and I want to be out there playing baseball with him just like my father did with me. But no, the kid's inside playing dolls with his sisters. That's not normal," said Mr. Moretti. "But he does play the dad and wants to be a police officer when he grows up," interjected Mrs. Moretti. Mr. Moretti shifted in his chair so he could look directly at his wife and replied, "Maria, we've been over this a thousand times. You know that I'm afraid that he'll. . . ." He gave me a furtive glance and continued, "Grow up being the kind of man who likes other men." "Vinnie, Anthony doesn't play with the other boys because he's afraid he'll have an accident. When he does, they tease him something awful. He can't go on sleepovers because he still wets the bed, so he plays with his sisters. Once we solve his problems, I just know he'll be okay. I'm sure of it," said Mrs. Moretti. I could sense the tension between the couple at this point.

When Anthony turned 5, it looked like Mr. Moretti might lose his job as a high school history teacher and the extra pay he received as a football coach was cut. Mrs. Moretti went back to work in order to supplement the family's income. Mr. Moretti shared that as far as he was concerned seeking help for his son was a bigger problem for him than their financial situation. He commented, "I work with kids all day and here I can't get my own son to sh--t in the pot!" He turned to me with an apologetic look and continued, "Excuse me for the language ma'am but I wonder if Anthony doesn't get better, what will happen to him when he gets to high school? We've tried everything and we're at our wits end. We've read all the books, tried everyone's advice . . . and still no success."

Mrs. Moretti's return to work was a difficult adjustment for Anthony. At first, he cried when his mother dropped him off at school. In after care, he was described by the staff as anxious and would repeatedly ask if his mother was okay. He needed constant reassurance that nothing bad had happened at home. If Mrs. Moretti was a little late to pick up Anthony he would anxiously stare at the door. Anthony also started to have nightmares. The Morettis had to leave a nightlight on in his room. He could not sleep with them because of his soiling and wetting. After several weeks, Anthony started making friends and his teachers reported a positive adjustment. Anthony's favorite subject was reading, especially history stories.

When I met with Anthony, I noticed that he was of average size and seemed a little shy. The most striking feature was his expressive dark brown eyes. He entered my office holding his mother's hand. He sat close to her and his eyes roamed all around the room as his mother and I exchanged greetings. Anthony did consent to having his mother leave and seemed willing to engage with me.

Nodding in the direction of my play corner, I asked Anthony if anything looked interesting to him. He went over to the doll house and started playing with the family figures. I said, "Let's tell a story about this family. What are these people like? Are they nice? Mean? Scary?" He explained each one to me indicating that everybody in the family was "nice." We continued this discussion for a while and then I introduced the problem by commenting. "It's time for the little boy to go to the bathroom. What should he do?" Anthony then put the little boy doll on the toilet. I asked, "What is the little boy doing?" Anthony replied, "He's going poopy." "What are the mom and dad doing?" I inquired. "They're watching TV," replied Anthony. "Okay," I said and asked, "How is the boy doing in the bathroom?" Anthony replied nonchalantly, "He's fine." I began to think about what Anthony was trying to tell me through his story.

How would you formulate your competency-based assessment for Anthony Moretti?

The Case of Paulie Merkel

I first met Paulie the summer before he was to start the seventh grade. The intake report indicated that during the previous school year he had struggled with focus, especially in his math class. I remembered some of my own experiences with math and thought that's probably what motivated me to go into the counseling field. In this profession, I don't have to use figures all that much. Math is so cumulative that missing a single class or even spacing out for a few minutes can make a student feel totally lost.

Paulie is now 12 years old and currently lives with his maternal grandparents, Roger and Jamima Duval. He was brought to the clinic by his grandmother at the suggestion of his sixth grade teacher who seemed to take a special interest in him. His grandparents always thought that Paulie was smart, but felt he was an underachiever in most subjects at school. According to Mrs. Duval, his grades have consistently suffered from severe distractibility and a lack of organizational skills. Paulie's past report cards describe him as disruptive and oppositional in class. In addition, he shows difficulty paying attention during structured and unstructured activities.

I asked his grandmother for her perspective on Paulie's struggles in school and at home. His grandmother responded, "We tried a lot of things, like taking him swimming to tire him out for example but Paulie is like a whirlwind. He's a Duracell bunny. He just keeps going and going. Sometimes I simply cannot control his energy. It's like he can't keep still." She continued, "It is not just my Paulie that is affected by his behavior, it's everybody in that classroom. He cannot deal with a classroom situation."

Mrs. Duval shared that her grandson often lies about his school work, which then creates problems at home. "I can't tell you how many times my husband and I have been up all night doing a project because Paulie 'forgot' when it was due. In fact," she added, "Paulie has always had problems with inattention, easy distractibility, daydreaming, and poor organization." She paused and added with emphasis, "and in that order! My husband and I just don't know what to do with him anymore. Right from the start in school, it took him longer than others to complete homework and examinations."

Mrs. Duval went on to say that her husband had a medical appointment and could not come in for today's appointment. She added, "My husband tried to change his doctor's appointment so he could come in today but it's just impossible dealing with those people at the clinic. He's okay and all but just needed his heart checked. He promised me he would come in next time if you need to see him."

She continued, "Paulie became the first kindergartner I have ever heard of to be suspended from school for trashing the classroom. It seems that Paulie had returned to the room after school had let out and turned it upside down, upending chairs, ripping posters off walls, emptying out the cabinets. Books and papers were everywhere. When my husband went to pick him up, Paulie came clean about what he had done. As he told us what happened, he claimed that the mess had been caused by a monster. After all these years, I can still remember the look in his eyes when he admitted that he was the monster. He was so remorseful."

Paulie has been living with his grandparents since he was a toddler. Mrs. Duval shared that her daughter struggles with substance abuse and has drifted in and out of Paulie's life. "Even when he lived with his mother, he was seen as rebellious," she stated. His father had virtually abandoned him from birth and his mother, overwhelmed by the task of raising him alone, relapsed into drug and alcohol abuse. She was frequently drunk and around Paulie she was moody and volatile. Mrs. Duval added, "Paulie ran wild. He refused to obey her and had no bedtime routine. Usually he would watch TV until he fell asleep on the couch. He never had any rules to follow and no structure. I just knew my daughter needed help so we offered to step in and care for Paulie. The rest is history."

Paulie's psychiatric history is unremarkable. His father is reportedly very similar to Paulie and remembered as someone who would get frustrated easily. However, his father has never been diagnosed. Paulie's medical history is also unremarkable, and he is not taking any medications.

In the past, school administrators had contacted Mr. and Mrs. Duval and recommended that Paulie be evaluated by his pediatrician for medication. Even though Paulie has always attended good schools, his grandparents doubted the wisdom of placing their grandson on drugs. They thought it would only compound his problems. Mrs. Duval was concerned about Paulie's potential for developing a substance abuse problem like his mother.

I asked about Paulie's developmental history and Mrs. Duval indicated that Paulie did not crawl. Instead, he was a bottom shuffler. "Almost from the very first," shared his grandmother, "he struggled to concentrate, and would respond aggressively by biting when frustrated." Mrs. Duval drew a deep breath and said, "Paulie has had behavioral problems almost all of his short life."

She continued, "By age 2, Paulie's inability to follow directions, sit still, keep out of dangerous situations, and learn from his mistakes had gone far beyond what we know as the 'terrible twos.' In preschool, he would take those little plastic balls out of the toy chest, but wouldn't put them back when asked. When his teachers sang, 'Clean up, clean up, everybody everywhere. Clean up, clean up, everybody do your share,' he would not do his share. My husband and I simply assumed that he had a rebellious streak, what with his father being gone and all. Paulie couldn't focus enough to finish simple tasks at home either, like putting away the pieces of a really simple puzzle. I remember that one of us would have to get down on the floor with him and show him how to do it, one piece at a time. Paulie could not go to sleep easily either. It was like his mind would not shut down. Sometimes I couldn't help but feel that the real problem was that my husband and I simply didn't know how to parent a highly spirited child. After all, we're the grandparents and to be honest we're a little old to be raising kids again at our age. I believed, or I guess I wanted to believe that the only thing wrong with Paulie was that he was just a boundary-testing pain-in-the-neck."

I then met with Paulie alone. He is small for his age and upon initial evaluation, I found him so hyperactive that he could only sit for a short period of time. He was fidgety, appeared slightly anxious, and frequently looked around my office. His speech was characterized by increased content but normal delivery. During the interview Paulie occasionally became distracted and he would lose track of what he was talking about, but was redirected easily. He required redirection to stay focused.

During the interview, Paulie described himself as dumb, but cool. He admitted that he hung out with older, rebellious students like himself to compensate for his feelings of inadequacy. He loved his mother but was struggling to maintain a relationship with her. He indicated that he hated his father and wanted nothing to do with him. He had a solid and positive relationship with his grandparents, and he especially respected his grandfather.

I asked Paulie about school and he responded, "I'm 12 years old and for as long as I can remember, I've had opposite sides to myself. I'm told that I'm 'gifted' . . . very smart and creative. But I also have to work really, really hard at things that seem much easier for other kids, like paying attention and memorization. Here's an example. In math or science I'm quicker at figuring things out than other kids. Like when my teacher tells us a new way to divide with fractions. It seems obvious to me and not to other kids but when I'm trying to listen to someone talking or lecturing, my mind starts to wander. I remember once when we were talking about plants in science. It made me think about my grandmother's garden and what she was going to plant next year. And that made me think about a new kind of tomato." Paulie paused and looked distracted so after a moment I redirected him. He resumed, "Oh yeah, I think it was one of those heirloom tomatoes. I wanted to grow them from seeds and plant some for my grandfather because he likes vegetables. And then that made me think about the food he likes to eat. My mind is sort of like branches on a tree, and pretty soon I don't know what the discussion is about any more. Sometimes this is good when I'm talking to someone, because it helps me branch out on our conversation. If I'm in class, it helps me bring up new ideas that no one else has thought of. But it also hurts me because I don't always fully get what the teacher is saying. Sometimes I have complicated ideas that I can't seem to explain to others. That's really frustrating."

Paulie continued, "When I'm doing something that's hard for me, like writing, I drift off and end up doing a quick job so I can do something else that I'm better at. But then I don't get a very good grade on my paper and I feel bad. The problem is, there are so many interesting things that I would rather be doing that I think are just as educational as writing. I'd rather watch the History Channel or movies. Don't get me wrong, I love school, but I hate it that homework takes away time from doing the things I really like." As our session concluded, I thanked Paulie for talking with me. He awkwardly smiled. As he got up to leave, he turned back and said, "Any time. You're really cool."

How would you formulate your competency-based assessment for Paulie Merkel?

PRACTICAL APPLICATIONS

Childhood is a vulnerable time and after reviewing the disorders discussed in this chapter we can better understand that for some children growing up is a challenge. As we have seen, various factors influence the developmental path and the competency-based assessment offers a framework to examine the broad array of activities and events that affect the child's well-being. Understanding family, social, and cultural variables of childhood provides insight into opportunities to create an environment where the child can thrive.

1. Ideally childhood is a time to enjoy life with all the time in the world to play, learn, and imagine a great future ahead. Are things getting easier for the children of today's generation? For instance, a child may have a parent who is incarcerated, unemployed, or struggling with a drug or alcohol problem. Parents may have separated due to a divorce and the child now lives either with grandparents or is placed in foster care. All of these developments have implications for mental health practice and the diagnoses mentioned in this chapter. Identify the challenges you believe confront children today. Once done, debate with a colleague or with your supervisor whether children today have it easier than in past generations.

2. The diagnosis of ADHD has been controversial for almost 40 years (Parrillo, 2008). Although children from all social classes have been affected, we know that slightly more children with ADHD are found in lower socioeconomic groups than in higher ones. Perhaps this can be attributed for by the co-occurring conduct problems seen in children with ADHD. Conduct problems are known to be associated with the ecological conditions associated with low socioeconomic status such as family adversity and stress. Based on your practice experience, list those factors in practice that may make the diagnosis of ADHD for youngsters from underprivileged backgrounds more prevalent. If your practice is limited in this area, interview another professional who primarily works with children with this diagnosis.

   We also know that ADHD is seen more frequently in boys than in girls. In addition, hyperactive behavior may be related to cultural differences. Think of what you can do to be attentive to the influence of gender and culture in the assessment process. In addition, ask a respected colleague to reflect on this same issue and then compare your responses.

3. Take a look at the CBS news feature of Tim Howard, an American who is diagnosed with Tourette's. He is the starting goalkeeper for England's soccer team, Manchester United. His story can be retrieved from: http://www .cbsnews.com/stories/2005/01/13/60minutes/main666797.shtml.

   Compare his experiences with one of your clients who struggles with this disorder. If you have not worked with someone like this, what insights can you gain from what he has gone through?

Appendix

Competency-Based Assessments for Chapter 3 Case Examples: Listing of Case Diagnoses

Figures 3A.1 through 3A.4 provide the diagnostic assessment for each of the cases illustrated. They are organized in the order that they appear in each chapter.

CASE REVIEW FOR ANTHONY MORETTI

Anthony's symptoms support the diagnosis of encopresis. He has had a medical checkup and apparently his fecal incontinence is associated with constipation and overflow incontinence. This is included in Anthony's *DSM* diagnosis.

In addition, Anthony continues to wet the bed and so an additional diagnosis of enuresis was made. The specifier, nocturnal only, is added.

When Mrs. Moretti returned to work, Anthony showed a brief period of separation anxiety; he worried about his mother, cried upon separation, and started having nightmares. However, after several weeks, he began to adjust to school and after care and so a diagnosis of separation anxiety is not warranted.

The consequences of additional psychological problems associated with Anthony's symptom picture are evident in the stresses felt by his parents along with the tension between the couple. His father worries about his son's future. Mr. Moretti is afraid that Anthony may "like other men" or develop a homosexual orientation when he grows up. Though stated less directly, Mrs. Moretti's frustration and sense of failure could be heard.

Figure 3A.1   The Conceptual Map for Anthony Moretti

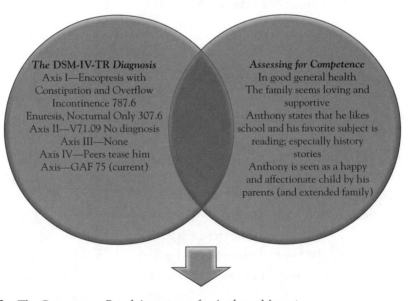

Figure 3A.2   The Competency-Based Assessment for Anthony Moretti

The competency-based assessment includes a parallel look at the strengths found in a client's life. The Moretti family, though at their wits end, are an intact family and both parents (and extended family such as the grandmothers) seem to love Anthony despite his encopresis and enuresis. Anthony is described as a happy and affectionate little boy. When he engages with the practitioner, he seems to have a sense of his struggle. He also seems to have a solution when he suggests through play with the dollhouse figures that his parents should be watching TV or perhaps place less of an emphasis on his toileting. Anthony's interest in reading, especially history stories, bears a strong likeness to his father's job as a history teacher.

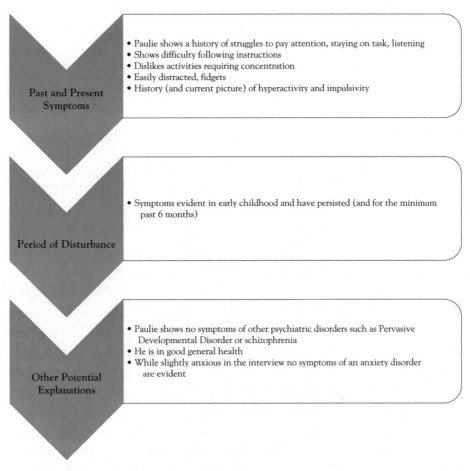

Figure 3A.3   The Conceptual Map for Paulie Merkel

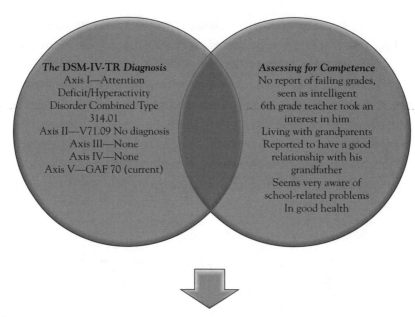

The DSM-IV-TR Diagnosis
Axis I—Attention
Deficit/Hyperactivity
Disorder Combined Type
314.01
Axis II—V71.09 No diagnosis
Axis III—None
Axis IV—None
Axis V—GAF 70 (current)

Assessing for Competence
No report of failing grades,
seen as intelligent
6th grade teacher took an
interest in him
Living with grandparents
Reported to have a good
relationship with his
grandfather
Seems very aware of
school-related problems
In good health

Figure 3A.4   The Competency-Based Assessment for Paulie Merkel

CASE REVIEW FOR PAULIE MERKEL

Each child is different and the competency-based assessment provides a framework to explore the unique features of each child and their experiences with ADHD. In Paulie's situation, despite his struggles in school, he had a sixth-grade teacher who took a special interest in him. Paulie has been in his grandparent's care since he was a toddler. Although his symptom picture challenges his elderly grandparents, they seem to care for him and tolerate Paulie's hyperactive and inattentive behaviors. They have not expressed any intentions of giving up on their grandson or for him to live elsewhere; for example, his grandmother reports staying up late to help Paulie to complete "forgotten" projects or helping him to learn how to pick up after himself as a young child.

Paulie's mother currently struggles with substance abuse and has been in and out of his life. His father has been out of the picture since he was an infant. Paulie is reported to have much respect for his grandfather. His grandmother's description of his behavior supports criteria for both inattention and hyperactivity-impulsivity traced to at least when he was 2 years of age, and these behaviors continue up to the present time. Though his grandparents are elderly, they clearly remember problems with Paulie's level of hyperactivity; he is described as the "Duracell bunny" or a whirlwind.

His grandmother shares an incident when Paulie trashed his kindergarten class. Unlike conduct disorder or oppositional defiant disorder, Paulie is clearly remorseful. Mrs. Duval vividly recalls the look in his eyes when he admitted to being the monster that tore up the classroom. Paulie currently keeps friends who are described as rebellious. However, the motivation seems to stem from a sense of inadequacy or low self-esteem rather than from a defiance of adult authority. Paulie's developmental history indicates he did not crawl like other children and supports a long pattern of struggles with concentration, impulsivity, and an inability to follow directions.

Though Paulie has had problems with his attention span and his grades are reported to have suffered, he is considered to be a bright youngster. Paulie seems to have good insight into his behavior. He describes his ability to grasp ideas quickly but goes on to talk about what gets in his way of memorizing ideas or following lectures. Clearly, he has no interest in subjects that require concentration. If mental retardation were present, Paulie would probably show a picture of learning slowly and may perhaps be overactive and impulsive. In contrast, once Paulie's attention is captured he seems able to learn. Unlike a child with autistic disorder, Paulie seems to engage with the practitioner.

4

The Cognitive Disorders

Delirium and Dementia

INTRODUCTION

Cognition involves the mental processing of information. Memory and thought combine to store, retrieve, and manipulate this information. Yet have you ever walked into a room and then could not remember why you went there in the first place? Do you find yourself making a shopping list before going to the grocery store to make sure you will not forget something? Absentmindedness and difficulty concentrating are signs of aging that most people experience as they grow older. In contrast to the normal processes of "forgetfulness" that happens at one time or another in our lives, the cognitive disorders happen when something goes wrong, very wrong. For example, it's considered normal if you misplace your keys but if you cannot remember what your keys are for, then there is a problem. The principal symptoms of the cognitive disorders include significant negative changes in the way a person thinks, and/or remembers information.

This chapter reviews the major classes of the cognitive disorders you will commonly encounter in practice. They are delirium and dementia. You will probably not see amnestic disorder but distinguishing its symptoms from delirium and dementia is important for making an accurate competency-based assessment. For that reason, it is included in this chapter.

Delirium represents a change in consciousness that develops over a short period of time, typically a few hours to days. Individuals find it difficult to pay attention or to think clearly and have a diminished awareness of their environments. Dementia is a progressive deterioration of brain function that is marked by impairment of memory, confusion, and an inability to concentrate. It is helpful to keep in mind that these disorders have either a medical- or substance-related cause or a combination of these factors.

INCIDENCE AND PREVALENCE

Delirium. How often delirium occurs in the general population is unknown. However, it is more frequently observed in at least 10% and up to 50% of general medical patients after surgery and particularly in intensive care units (Gleason, 2003). Overall, it seems that the sick and elderly are at a higher risk for the diagnosis of delirium. For example, at the time of admission to the hospital, it is estimated that 10% to 22% of elderly patients are delirious and the prevalence is even higher in certain subgroups. For example, in 28% to 48% of patients with advanced cancer on admission to the hospital or hospice, approximately 90% of these patients will more than likely experience delirium in the hours to days before death (Lawlor et al., 2000). Delirium can also be found in 60% of nursing home residents older than 75 years of age (Fann, 2000). Delirium equally affects males and females (American Psychiatric Association, 2000).

Dementia. The elderly are also at a higher risk for dementia and the prevalence for all types of this diagnosis is about 2% to 4% of persons after the age of 65 with the rate of occurrence increasing to 20% after age 85 (Smith, 2000). Age is also a factor for dementia of the Alzheimer's type. Approximately 1.4% to 1.6% of persons between the ages of 65 and 69 years of age are diagnosed with Alzheimer's disease and the frequency increases to 16% to 25% for those over 85 years (APA, 2000). The percentage of adult Americans who were 75 years or older increased from 5.60% in 1990 to 6.89% in 2000 (Smith, 2000). This represents a 2% increase in just 10 years and this trend is expected to continue (Mokdad et al., 2004). The growing number and proportion of older Americans underscores the importance of being able to accurately assess for dementia. People with severe dementia often need to be cared for in nursing homes or in long-term care institutions and approximately one-third to one-half of those with this diagnosis are living in these settings (Rockwood & MacKnight, 2001). There seem to be no adequate studies to report the incidence of amnestic disorders (B. Sadock & Sadock, 2007).

OVERVIEW OF THE MAJOR CHARACTERISTICS OF THE DIAGNOSTIC CLASSIFICATIONS

There are a number of other *DSM* disorders that can include cognitive difficulties such as the anxiety or mood disorders. The competency-based assessment, which looks at a range of factors in a person's life, encompasses an exploration of the multiple factors that can lead to the cognitive disorders. We begin with a discussion of delirium.

DELIRIUM

Delirium is seen as a state of disturbed consciousness and cognition or perception that develops acutely, fluctuates during the course of the day, and is attributable to a physical disorder. It is characterized by an acute change or fluctuation in mental status plus inattention, and either disorganized thinking or an altered level of consciousness. It is difficult for a person to pay attention or to think clearly if he or she has a reduced awareness of his or her environment. This altered mental state is characterized by a sudden deterioration in cognitive functions (such as memory, orientation, speech, and language) and the inability to sustain attention. This causes the individual to become disconnected from his or her immediate surroundings and to misinterpret reality. Delirium is a syndrome with many causes and often is produced by a combination of medically related factors; for example, age-related reactions to medications, high levels of medication or drug use, and imbalances in neurotransmitters.

☜ Central Features of Delirium

Disturbed consciousness
Impaired ability to attend to the environment
Underlying medical condition or drug intoxication/withdrawal

Delirium is often found in older people in nursing homes and in hospitals, especially frail older adults who take several medications to treat a number of conditions (Ely et al., 2001; Ely et al., 2004; McNicoll et al., 2003). People who experience complications such as pressure sores, falls, fractures, infections, or urinary incontinence are at an even greater risk. A preexisting diagnosis of dementia can also predispose a person to a diagnosis of delirium. Delirium is categorized by its etiology due to general medical conditions, substance-related conditions, or it is multifactorial in origin. Drugs may be the most frequent single cause of delirium and it is helpful to have some familiarity with how they can affect someone. Table 4.1 summarizes the most common general medical and substance-related causes of delirium.

The metabolic abnormalities most frequently associated with delirium include hyponatremia (or an electrolyte disturbance of low sodium in the blood), hypoxia (or a deficiency in the amount of oxygen reaching body tissues), hypercapnia (or a condition marked by an unusually high concentration of carbon dioxide in the blood as a result of hypoventilation), hypoglycemia (or an abnormally low level of glucose in the blood), and hypercalcemia (or an abnormally high concentration of calcium in the blood). Although delirium may be precipitated by virtually any drug, the common substance-induced causes of delirium are alcohol or benzodiazepine withdrawal and benzodiazepine

Table 4.1 Common Causes of Delirium

General Medical	Substance-Related
Infectious	*Intoxication*
Urinary tract infections	Alcohol
Meningitis	Hallucinogens
Pneumonia	Opiods
Sepsis	Marijuana
	Stimulants
Metabolic	Sedatives
Hyponatremia	
Hepatic encephalopathy	*Withdrawal*
Hypoxia	Alcohol
Hypercarbia/hypercapnia	Benzodiazepines
Hypoglycemia	Barbiturates
Fluid imbalance	
Uremia	*Medication-induced*
Hypercalcemia	Anesthetics
	Anticholinergics
Postsurgical	Meperdine
Hyper/hypothyroidism	Antibiotics
Ictal/postictal	
Head trauma	*Toxins*
	Carbon monoxide
Miscellaneous	Organophosphates
Fat emboli syndrome	
Thiamine deficiency	
Anemia	

and anticholinergic drug toxicity (the anticholinergic agent is the substance that blocks the neurotransmitter acetylcholine in the central and peripheral nervous system).

The Clinical Picture

The symptoms of delirium include a constellation of physical, biological, and psychological disturbances where impaired attention is considered the core cognitive disturbance (APA, 2000; Morrison, 2007; B. Sadock & V. Sadock, 2007). The delirious person presents with a wide variety of symptoms. Individuals will have different clinical profiles, but most will experience disturbances of memory, orientation, language skills, mood, thinking, perception, motor behavior, and the sleep-wake cycle. Delirium may be of a hyperactive variety manifested by "positive" symptoms of

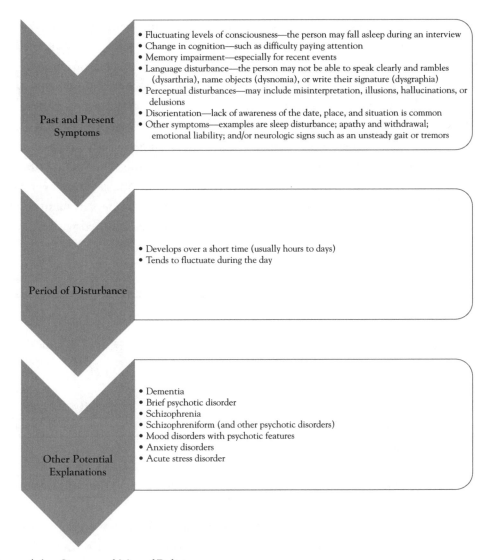

Figure 4.1   Conceptual Map of Delirium

agitation or combativeness, or it may be of a hypoactive variety (often referred to as "quiet" delirium) manifested by "negative" symptoms such as inability to converse or focus attention or follow commands. Hallucinations, anxiety, agitation, and insomnia are the most common behaviors. When assessing the diagnostic picture of delirium, the following conceptual map in Figure 4.1 helps navigate the client's behavioral terrain.

A Closer Look at Delirium

Although individual symptoms of delirium are nonspecific, their patterns are highly characteristic; that is, there is an acute onset (sometimes abruptly, but often over hours or days), a fluctuating course (symptoms tend to wax and wane over any 24-hour period and typically worsen at night), and transient nature (in most cases, delirium resolves within days or weeks). Delirium also frequently involves a prodromal phase over two to three days, seen as malaise, restlessness, poor concentration, anxiety, irritability, sleep-disturbance, and nightmares. When you take the person's history, it is helpful to pay particular attention to the time course in the development of the delirium. The competency-based assessment explores underlying causative factors as well as the person's social environment in order to fully evaluate the symptom picture. The person may not be lucid at the time they come to your attention, so interviewing close family members or friends can provide valuable insights into changes in mental status. Without a comprehensive assessment, delirium can easily be confused with a number of other disorders; for example dementia, depression, or psychosis.

Delirium Diagnosed if (a) + (b) + one of either (c) or (d)

(a) *Acute onset and fluctuating course*
Evidence of an acute change in mental status from the person's baseline that changes in severity during the day.

(b) *Inattention*
The person has difficulty focusing attention; for example, is easily distractible or has difficulty keeping track of conversation.

(c) *Disorganized thinking*
The person's thinking is disorganized or incoherent, as evidenced by rambling or irrelevant conversation and unclear or illogical flow of ideas.

(d) *Altered consciousness*
A rating of the person's level of consciousness as other than alert (normal); for example, vigilant or hyperalert, lethargic or drowsy, stuporous or comatose.

Diagnosing delirium is complicated by the fact that there are no definitive tests for it, but a physical examination and laboratory tests aimed at identifying the most likely etiologies found in general medical and substance-related causes can provide useful data to support the diagnosis. As a rule these tests include a urinalysis, complete chemistry panel, complete blood count, and oxygen saturation. Additional tests may include a chest X-ray, arterial blood gas (ABG), neuroimaging (techniques such as magnetic resonance or MRI used to visualize the shapes and sizes of brain regions and to observe evidence of brain activity), or an electroencephalogram (often referred to as an EEG, which is a method of recording the brain's electrical activity by means of electrodes attached to the scalp).

Differential Assessment

Delirium shares many of the clinical features of dementia and someone with a diagnosis of dementia is considered to be at a higher risk for delirium. In addition, it is not unusual for both disorders to co-occur (APA, 2000). Although the two syndromes may overlap and be present at the same time, delirium is not the same as the confusion found in dementia. Persons with delirium may display periods of complete lucidity interspersed with periods of confusion in contrast to dementia where the cognitive deficits are generally more stable; that is, the diagnosis of dementia requires a chronic impairment and the symptom picture is characterized by a generally progressive and irreversible cognitive and psychosocial decline in function.

Dementia is usually not associated with a change in the level of consciousness found in delirium. However, with both there may be nocturnal worsening of symptoms with increased agitation and confusion referred to as "sundowning." Typically, the person is relatively lucid in the mornings with maximum disturbance at night. A key difference between delirium and dementia is cognitive improvement.

Delirium should also be differentiated from the psychotic disorders, especially the symptoms of manic disorganization. Delirium may share many of the same features of other clinical disorders, but the key differentiating factor is symptom duration. It is helpful to ask the question, "What is the time course for the development of the person's change in mental status?" As a corollary, a differential assessment of delirium cannot accurately be made without knowing the affected person's baseline level of cognitive function.

Key Points

Delirium is a disorder of attention and cognition.

It has an abrupt onset.

It has an identifiable medical or substance-related precipitant.

Delirium can masquerade as chronic dementia or functional psychosis and obscure the underlying physical or substance-related causes (Murphy, 2000). The hallucinations and apparent confusion found in schizophrenia can resemble delirium but the person does not have the disorientation, memory loss, and sleep disturbance seen in delirium. Persons with generalized anxiety disorder may experience agitation, but it is without the disorientation, confusion, and memory loss found in delirium. When you consider the diagnosis of delirium, remember the most common causes such as a change in or addition to a person's prescribed medications, a withdrawal from alcohol or other sedative-hypnotic drugs, an infection or a sudden change in neurologic, cardiac, pulmonary, or metabolic state. The specific coding noted in the *DSM* determines these distinctions:

- Due to a General Medical Condition—List/indicate the general medical condition.
- Substance Intoxication Delirium—The diagnosis is coded based on the substance used and specifically references the substance-related disorders for substance codes; for example code 291.0 refers to Alcohol Intoxication Delirium.
- Substance Withdrawal Delirium—This diagnosis is coded on the substance used.
- Delirium Due to Multiple Etiologies—The diagnosis codes each of the specific etiologies.
- Delirium Not Otherwise Specified (NOS)—Used when the person does not meet a definitive diagnostic category.

Diagnostic Tips

Has the person experienced a change in his or her mental status?
Can a medical and/or substance-related contributor be identified?
Are there risk factors that predispose someone for the diagnosis of delirium; for example, old age, recent surgery, fractures, a preexisting diagnosis of dementia?

BEGINNING WITH DEMENTIA

Dementia is distinguished by progressive memory impairment in the presence of other cognitive defects and describes an acquired, persistent, global impairment of a person's cognitive/intellectual processes severe enough to interfere with social or occupational functioning. Dementia, like delirium, is recognized as a syndrome but the diagnosis itself does not shed light on the cause. For example, dementia has a number of causes such as Alzheimer's disease or HIV infection (APA, 2000). Although dementia is age-related, it is distinct from the normal aging of the brain. In general, the etiology of dementia is a brain neuronal loss (or loss of neuron points in the brain) that may be due to neuronal degeneration or to cell death secondary to trauma, infarction (a condition in which brain tissue dies because the arterial blood supply is blocked), hypoxia (a deficiency in the amount of oxygen reaching body tissues), infection, or hydrocephalus (excessive accumulation of fluid in the brain). Unfortunately, the definitive cause of dementia may not be determined until an autopsy can be performed after the person has died. Table 4.2 lists the specific diseases associated with dementia. Each shares a common symptom presentation for dementia but the diagnosis is differentiated based

Table 4.2 Specific Diseases Associated with Dementia

Disease	Description
Alzheimer's	This is the most common cause of dementia and accounts for greater than 50% of all cases. Persons with a family history of Alzheimer's are at higher risk. Down's syndrome, a prior head trauma, increasing age also place the person at a higher risk for Alzheimer's. The course is progressive and death generally occurs about 8 to 10 years after onset.
Vascular	This is the second most common cause of dementia. Risk factors are the presence of cardiovascular and cerebrovascular disease. The course can show either a rapid onset or progress more slowly. The cognitive deficits are not reversible, but progression can be halted with the appropriate treatment of the vascular disease.
HIV	The diagnosis of dementia is limited to those who are affected by the direct action of HIV on the brain. Associated illnesses such as meningitis, lymphoma, or toxoplasmosis producing dementia are categorized under dementia due to general medical conditions.
Head Trauma	The extent of dementia is determined by the degree of brain damage (usually at a younger age) and men are most commonly affected.
Parkinson's	Dementia occurs in 20% to 60% of those diagnosed with Parkinson's Disease, a slow and progressive neurological condition characterized by tremors, rigidity, involuntary and rhythmic movements of the extremities, motor restlessness, and posturing instability. The most common symptom is bradyphrenia (or slowed thinking).
Huntington's	Persons with a family history of Huntington's are at higher risk for the disease characterized by a degenerative course that includes difficulties in cognition, emotion, and movement. The most prominent symptom is emotional lability.
Pick's	Onset of this disease generally occurs between the ages of 50 to 60. This form of dementia has a degenerative course distinguished by impairments in memory, concentration, abstract thinking, and speech along with disorientation and apathy. Individuals respond poorly to psychotropic medications.
Creutzfeldt-Jakob	A rare illness due to slow viruses or prions, where onset generally occurs between the ages of 40 to 60 with a rapid progression of the dementia. Persons lose mental alertness, experience memory loss, and are disoriented along with the distinctive feature of myoclonus (a shock-like contraction of muscles). Ten percent of cases are familial.

on etiology (APA, 2000). For example, if a person experienced a head trauma severe enough to impair his or her memory then the diagnosis would be recorded as "dementia due to head trauma."

The Clinical Picture

Dementia is considered when a person's cognitive defects cannot be better explained by another diagnosis. The presence of memory loss is required, in addition to one or more cognitive defects in the categories of *aphasia* (a language disturbance that can affect a person's ability to use and understand spoken or written words), *apraxia* (loss of the ability to execute or carry out skilled movements and gestures, despite having the desire and the physical ability to perform them), *agnosia* (an inability to recognize and identify objects or family and friends), and *a disturbance in executive function* (or difficulty in making decisions) must be present (APA, 2000; Gray, 2008; Morrison, 2007; B. Sadock & V. Sadock, 2007). Although many people find that as they get older their memory is not as good as it once was, this does not imply dementia unless the memory loss impairs job performance or social roles. For example, the person may no longer be able to handle his or her finances and may need help balancing a checkbook or even signing a check. I still remember the husband of a client in a nursing home who would visit every day just to dress his wife. Without assistance, she would put her clothes on backward or inside out. On some days, she would "forget" to dress at all. His wife was oblivious to how she looked, so she was generally uncooperative when her husband tried to help her. Dressing became an ordeal that would take hours but her husband did not seem to mind, insisting that he had nothing better to do with his time. He remembered his wife as someone who was meticulous about her appearance and he just could not bear to see her try to dress herself on her own.

A chronic and persistent course generally distinguishes dementia from delirium. Although delirium typically comes on acutely and resolves quickly the acute onset does not always definitively rule out the diagnosis of dementia. For example, the dementia seen following stroke or a head trauma can begin suddenly. Similarly, there are other dementias, particularly Creutzfeldt-Jakob disease (a disease of the central nervous system known to cause degenerative, progressive brain deterioration precipitated by an infectious organism known as a prion or an infectious particle) that seems to come on almost out of the blue. There are some dementias that can have prolonged periods of plateau such as the dementia following a stroke, most follow a characteristic pattern of a progressive decline where the person's memory gets worse over time; that is, dementia usually has an insidious course and can develop over weeks to years.

Key Points

Dementia is a disorder of memory impairment coupled with other cognitive defects, notably aphasia, apraxia, agnosia, and loss of executive function.
It can have a gradual or acute onset and shows a progressive course.
It may be caused by a variety of illnesses—Alzheimer's is the most common, followed by vascular dementia.

The signs of dementia may be stable over brief periods of time while the person experiences a nocturnal worsening of symptoms (or sundowning). Memory impairment is often greatest for short-term memory. The person often struggles to recall names or recognize familiar objects. The executive functions of organization and the ability to plan may be lost. An ominous response to your attempts to explore someone's history is when he or she looks blankly at you and then turns to face his or her spouse; as if looking for an answer; this is a characteristic sometimes called the head-turning sign (Rockwood & MacKnight, 2001). There are also personality quirks that signal dementia and paranoia, hallucinations, and delusions are often present. Eventually in the advanced stages of dementia the person becomes mute, incontinent, and bedridden. When looking for dementia in the client's story, Figure 4.2, a conceptual map, helps navigate the client landscape.

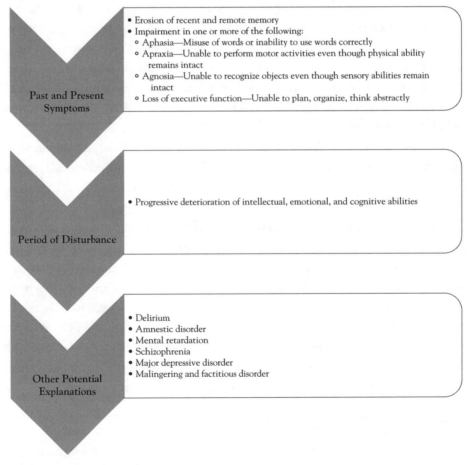

Figure 4.2   Conceptual Map for Dementia

DEMENTIA

As distinguished on the conceptual map, dementia represents a serious loss of cognitive ability far beyond what could be expected from the normal aging process. A person's cognitive abilities, memory, attention, language, and problem solving are seriously affected. In the later stages, the individual may be disoriented in time and not know the day or the week or month, or even be unaware of where they are.

Differential Assessment

In the main, dementia is differentiated from delirium, which has a rapid onset, fluctuations in and out of a confusional state, and difficulty attending to surroundings. Delirium is usually caused by a physical condition, such as an infection, and so the underlying causes need immediate attention. In contrast, the presence of a progressive memory loss is an essential feature of dementia. It is possible that delirium can be superimposed on dementia, particularly in hospitalized elderly individuals (Fick & Foreman, 2000; Meagher, 2001); for example, a person who is already diagnosed with dementia may develop a high fever, which causes delirium. At this point, because the effects of delirium are so similar to the features of dementia (disorientation and memory loss) the dementia is usually not assessed until after the delirium clears. Dementia increases the risk of delirium. It should be noted that the combination of being elderly and chronically cognitively impaired leads to a higher risk of delirium (Lindesay, Rockwood, & Macdonald, 2002).

Dementia should also be distinguished from other disorders where impaired cognition may be a part of the symptom picture, such as mental retardation. Dementia is often seen in the face of depression and differentiating dementia from the symptoms of depression can be difficult. For example, persons with a diagnosis of major depression can appear to have cognitive impairment that looks like dementia or pseudodementia. However, in pseudodementia persons may complain extensively of memory problems but their mood symptoms are more prominent. These individuals sometimes respond to your questions with a bland response such as, "I don't know." However, when pressed for an answer they are able to come back with a correct response. Elderly persons in particular may appear to have dementia when they are actually suffering from depression. The behaviors of those struggling with a psychotic disorder can also resemble the symptoms of dementia. Consider the diagnosis of dementia only if the person's cognitive deficits cannot be fully attributed to the primary psychiatric disorder.

Alzheimer's-Type Dementia

Alzheimer's is the most common form of dementia and accounts for approximately two-thirds of all dementia diagnoses seen in the older population (B. Sadock & V. Sadock,

2007). Currently 4.5 million Americans have the disease and prevalence rates double every five years beyond age 65 (Lynch & Pocinki, 2007). If current trends continue and prevention is still not possible, an estimated 13.2 million people in the United States will have Alzheimer's-type dementia by 2050 (Herbert, Scherr, Bienias, Bennett, & Evans, 2003). Alzheimer's is expected to increase in the population of older adults as a result of the "baby boomers" who are entering the ranks of the elderly (Herbert et al., 2003). A 2005 Census Bureau report on aging in the United States notes that the population age 65 and older is projected to double in size to about 72 million within the next 25 years (He, Sengupta, Welkoff, & DeBarros, 2005). The 85 and older age group is now the fastest growing segment of the population. According to the National Institute on Aging (2005), nearly half of those 85 years of age and older may already have Alzheimer's. Early onset is a subtype of Alzheimer's disease. It is less prevalent and can occur at a much earlier age (or in people aged 30 to 60). Late onset is diagnosed in people over age 65 (Lindesay, Rockwood, & Macdonald, 2002). It is estimated that 26.6 million people worldwide had Alzheimer's in 2006, and it is anticipated this number may quadruple by the year 2050 (Brookmeyer, Johnson, Ziegler-Graham, & Arrighi, 2007; United Nations, 2007).

Alzheimer's is an age-related and irreversible brain disorder that occurs gradually resulting in memory loss, behavior and personality changes, and a decline in thinking abilities. On average, a person with Alzheimer's disease can live for 8 to 10 years after diagnosis though the disease can last for up to 20 years, making it the "longest good-bye" (Gray, 2008). It ultimately destroys a person's ability to remember, reason, and execute simple tasks. A certain number of changes in the way the brain functions can be expected in the normal aging process, but Alzheimer's happens when the nerve cells in the brain begin to lose their ability to function. When these specialized brain cells are no longer able to communicate or coordinate with each other, they begin to die. Eventually, when enough of these nerves and their connections are lost, the ability to remember and to use language is also gone. As nerve cells stop working properly, the person's memory fails. For example, a person with Alzheimer's may not only forget a word like "shoe" but is also unable to remember what it is used for. Personality changes may also occur over time. For example, a normally easygoing person may become paranoid and accuse someone of stealing money or that his or her spouse is having an illicit affair. When frustrated or tired, the individual may become uncharacteristically angry. The person may put things in odd places. For example, a purse may end up in the freezer or clothes may go into the dishwasher. As the disease continues its course, the person may start to wander or become agitated. Eventually other areas of the brain shrink and lose function. At this point, the person needs help with all their daily needs.

The course of the disease is different for each person as well as the rate of decline. More than 25 years ago, Dr. Barry Reisberg (1984) was the first to develop a functional assessment of Alzheimer's disease that has generally been categorized into mild, moderate, and severe stages. Individuals vary in the length of time spent in each stage and in which stage the signs and symptoms will appear. Because the stages overlap, it is difficult to definitively place someone in a particular stage. However, the progression is always in the direction of the worsening of symptoms. The focus of early-stage or mild Alzheimer's is cognitive decline. Memory and concentration problems are evident and communication issues surface. The person undergoes changes in personality and a few idiosyncratic behaviors start to show up. Mid-stage or moderate Alzheimer's is exemplified by a decline in the functioning of many bodily systems and an increasing reliance on caregivers for activities of daily living. The cognitive problems of the mild stage continue to get worse and new ones emerge. Memory and cognition problems become severe, communication is distorted, and the individual's personality changes. In late-stage or severe Alzheimer's disease the personality deteriorates completely. Cognitive symptoms become worse and physical symptoms become profound. The loss of brain cells in all parts of the brain leads to a lack of functioning in all systems of the body. The behaviors of the earlier stages are replaced by a dulling of the mind and erosion of the body. Table 4.3 summarizes the stages of Alzheimer's-type dementia and provides examples of behavior for the practitioner to look for in each of the phases.

In the early or mild stage, the person may undergo a memory loss mistakenly attributed to age or stress such as difficulty in remembering recently learned facts. At this point, the Alzheimer's disease is not fully apparent and may go undiagnosed for years. This stage is typified by mild cognitive impairment (Small, Gagnon, & Robinson, 2007). After a while, small memory lapses appear and then grow more serious. It is the increasing loss of memory that eventually leads to the definitive diagnosis of Alzheimer's but all aspects of the person's memory are not affected equally. For instance, the older memories about what happened in the person's life (episodic memory), facts learned (semantic memory), and implicit memory (the memory of the body on how to do things such as using a knife to cut up food) are affected to a lesser degree than those newly learned facts. For a small number of individuals, difficulties with language, executive functions, perception (agnosia), or the execution of movements (apraxia) are more prominent than memory problems (Forstl & Kurz, 1999). Language problems become more evident as vocabulary shrinks and word fluency diminishes. It is common for people to substitute or make up words that sound like or mean something like the forgotten word. However, these individuals are still able to communicate basic ideas. At this early mild stage, the individual may politely chat about superficial topics such as the weather or avoid talking just to keep from making mistakes. Performing fine motor tasks such as signing a check or buttoning a shirt and certain movement, coordination, and planning difficulties (apraxia) may be present. The person often looks clumsy.

Table 4.3 The Main Stages of Alzheimer's-Type Dementia

Early-Stage Alzheimer's (Mild)	Mid-Stage Alzheimer's (Moderate)	Late-Stage Alzheimer's (Severe)
Memory or other cognitive deficits are noticeable The person can compensate for them Functions independently	Mental abilities decline Personality changes occur Physical problems develop The person becomes more dependent on caregivers	Complete deterioration of the person's personality Loss of control over bodily functions Totally dependent on others
Sample Behaviors • Word- or name-finding becomes noticeable to others. • Decreased ability to remember names when introduced to new people. • Decreased knowledge of recent events. • Decreased ability to perform complex tasks such as planning dinner for guests. • May seem subdued or withdrawn especially in socially or mentally challenging situations.	**Sample Behaviors** • Unable to recall important details, such as current address, telephone number. • Becomes confused about where they are or about the date, day of the week, or season. • Trouble with less challenging mental arithmetic such as counting backward from 40 by 4s or from 20 by 2s. • Needs help choosing clothing for the season or the occasion. • Forgets the name of their spouse or primary caregiver. • Needs help getting dressed properly and without supervision may make errors such as putting pajamas over daytime clothes or shoes on the wrong feet. • Needs help with toileting such as flushing the toilet, wiping, and disposing of tissue properly. • Increasing episodes of incontinence. • Personality changes such as suspiciousness or compulsive repetitive behaviors. • Tends to wander and become lost.	**Sample Behaviors** • Loss of capacity for recognizable speech (although words or phrases may occasionally be uttered). • Needs help with eating and toileting and there is general incontinence. • Loses the ability to walk without assistance, the ability to sit without support, and the ability to hold their head up. • Reflexes become abnormal; swallowing is impaired.

In the moderate stage of Alzheimer's, progressive deterioration eventually hinders the person's independence to the point where they are not safe on their own. They lose the ability to follow written instructions and often need help choosing the right kind of clothing for the season or occasion. Eventually the person needs help getting dressed because confusion may cause them to put their pajamas over daytime clothes or shoes on the wrong feet. Speech difficulties become more apparent and the person is unable to recall vocabulary or incorrectly substitute words (paraphasias). Most individuals are no longer aware that they are not communicating coherently or do not remember things. During this stage the person starts having problems recognizing family members and friends. They may mix up identities such as thinking that a son is a brother or that the spouse is a stranger. They become unable to recall their addresses or phone numbers. The persons can be confused about where they are and what day, season, or year it is. Reading and writing skills become compromised or lost completely. These individuals lack judgment and may tend to wander. They may become restless and exhibit repetitive movements or continually repeat certain stories, words, or motions such as shredding a tissue. Personality changes become more evident leading to a variety of challenging behaviors; for example, agitation, frustration, or anger may lead to incidents of cursing, kicking, hitting, biting, screaming, or grabbing. Episodes of urinary or fecal incontinence may also occur.

Over time, these individuals become increasingly confused, irritable, or aggressive. In the last or severe stage of Alzheimer's, they require help with all of their daily needs. They may experience mood swings, language breakdown, and long-term memory loss. As their senses decline, they withdraw from others (Waldemar et al., 2007). They lose the ability to walk without assistance and then become unable to sit up without support. At this stage, they are usually incontinent and may no longer speak coherently. Family members are rarely recognized. Swallowing difficulties can cause them to choke and they may refuse to eat. Gradually bodily functions are lost ultimately leading to death.

There are several ways to code Alzheimer's-type dementia based on the person's age at onset. For example, "with late onset" is used when the onset of dementia is after the age of 65 years. Early onset refers to persons 65 years of age or younger. The various signs and symptoms are also included, such as "without behavioral disturbance, with delusions" or "with depressed mood."

BEGINNING WITH AMNESTIC DISORDER (AMNESIA)

Amnestic disorder is relatively uncommon and characterized by isolated disturbances of memory without impairment of the person's other cognitive functions. This disorder may be due to a general medical condition or substance-related. Some of the more common medical conditions include head trauma, hypoxia (a shortage of oxygen in the body), herpes simplex encephalitis (a rare form of herpes simplex virus–I affecting the brain where the person experiences "flu-like" symptoms followed by neurological deterioration), and posterior cerebral artery infarction (also known as a posterior cerebral artery stroke occurring when blood cannot flow to cerebral structures in the brain).

Amnestic disorder is often associated with specific structures in the brain; for example, damage of the mammillary bodies (two small, spherical masses of gray matter at the base of the brain in the space between the hypophysis and oculomotor nerve that receive and relay olfactory impulses), fornix (a C-shaped bundle of fibers or axons in the brain that carries signals from the hippocampus to the mammillary bodies), and hippocampus (a part of the inner brain that involves learning and memory). Bilateral damage to these structures produces the most severe deficits. The substance-related causes may be due to the persisting effects of substance abuse, prescribed, or over-the-counter medications, or an accidental exposure to toxins. Alcohol abuse is the leading cause of the substance-related amnestic disorder. The persistent use of alcohol may induce Wernicke-Korsakoff syndrome or Wernicke's encephalopathy (caused by a thiamine deficiency along with other deficiencies in many other vitamins and minerals as a result of chronic, heavy alcohol use). This disorder is characterized by the person's striking inability to form new memories, with subsequent "blank spots" often filled in with confabulation (a tactic where the person makes up false answers or stories in an attempt to hide memory losses) (Gray, 2008; Morrison, 2007; B. Sadock & V. Sadock, 2007).

Key Points

Memory alone is affected when the person cannot recall previously learned information or past events.
Causes are by identifiable participants and they are often medical- or substance-related.
Can be reversible in some cases.

The Clinical Picture

The amnestic disorder presentation is one of deficits in memory; that is, the person's cognitive defect must be limited to memory alone. The ability to learn and recall new information is always affected while the inability to recall previously learned information varies depending on the specific areas of brain damage (APA, 2000; B. Sadock & Sadock, 2007). The person often remembers things from the remote past better than what has happened more recently. Memory problems are most apparent on tasks that require spontaneous recall. As a part of the clinical picture you may see a number of personality changes in the person including confusion and disorientation (APA, 2000). With amnesia, there is usually a disorientation to time and often to place but rarely to self. Some individuals do well in familiar environments, but can be lost in a new place. Those with a severe amnestic disorder may lack insight into their memory problems and vehemently deny impairment despite evidence to the contrary. Others might acknowledge that they have a problem but seem unconcerned by it. Sometimes, early in the illness, the person will try to hide a memory loss by making up experiences (confabulation). You might also observe apathy, a lack of initiative, or emotional blandness in the person. Other individuals may seem to be friendly or agreeable but have a superficial range of emotional expression. A person can recover from amnestic

Figure 4.3   Conceptual Map for Amnestic Disorder

disorder, but chronicity is usually the rule. There are multiple amnestic syndromes (i.e., due to a general medical condition such as hypoxia, stroke, head trauma, or herpes simplex encephalitis or substance-induced), but the differences among them revolve mainly around what a person can and cannot remember. The most frequent cause of amnestic disorder is chronic alcohol use with a vitamin B1 (thiamine) deficiency, typically known as substance-induced persisting amnestic disorder or Wernicke-Korsakoff's syndrome. When recording the diagnosis, the practitioner indicates the specific medical condition, such as due to a stroke or the substance, such as alcohol. Figure 4.3 is a conceptual map for amnestic disorder.

AMNESTIC DISORDER

As seen on the conceptual map, there are a number of symptoms associated with amnestic disorder. This disorder primarily involves the loss of memories previously established, a loss of the person's ability to create new memories, or the loss of the ability to learn new information. In addition, the person struggling with an amnestic disorder may be disoriented with respect to time and space. In other words, this is the person who does not know the day of the week. If pressed for details, the individual will more than likely deny that anything is wrong despite evidence to the contrary. Others may be able to admit to a problem but show no emotion. Still others may undergo a personality change and it is almost as if distinctive personality features have vanished.

Differential Assessment

Like the other cognitive disorders, memory problems are a part of the symptom picture for amnestic disorders. Consider the diagnosis of delirium if memory dysfunction occurs in association with impaired consciousness with diminished abilities to focus, sustain, or shift attention. For dementia, memory impairment is accompanied by multiple cognitive deficits; for example, aphasia, apraxia, agnosia, or a disturbance in executive functioning. Amnesia may occur in the context of the dissociative disorders but the amnestic disorders are differentiated, by definition, due to the effects of a general medical condition or substance use.

FINAL THOUGHTS

The cognitive disorders are "a clinically significant change from a previous level of functioning" (APA, 2000, p. 135). This chapter reviewed the disorders commonly encountered by the practitioner; that is, delirium and dementia and the most frequently seen Alzheimer's-type dementia. In their most severe forms, they can produce deficits in thinking, reasoning, and problem solving. Amnestic disorder, less commonly seen, was reviewed to help you to formulate a careful assessment of a person's functioning. The competency-based assessment calls attention to the importance of exploring the biological, psychological, and social influences in the person's life. Delirium highlights biological contributors as it is caused by a brain injury that accompanies metabolic or toxic brain disturbances. In contrast, dementia is the consequence of strokes, certain serious infections and brain tumors, brain injury, and chronic progressive brain diseases. Expect to encounter families struggling with caring for their loved one at home. The impact on the family as the person struggles with symptoms of dementia, especially of the Alzheimer's type highlighted in this chapter, can be devastating. The competency-based assessment helps both clients and their families to understand the eventual physical and "personality changes" that will occur over the course of the illness.

Table 4.4 provides a summary of the features of these disorders. Each person's experience with mental illness is different and as the client tells you his or her "story" a great deal of information may be shared. The challenge is to be able to listen attentively for symptoms in order to come to an accurate conclusion about the diagnosis and to keep in mind the other aspects of the client's life that may influence onset, the course of the mental illness, and prognosis.

Table 4.4 Summary of the Features of Delirium, Dementia, and Amnestic Disorders

Features	Delirium	Dementia	Amnestic Disorder
Onset	Hours to days	Weeks to years	Acute or insidious
Course/duration	Fluctuates within a day	Stable within a day	Variable (transient or permanent) depending on the etiology, often medical or substance use condition
	May last hours to weeks (though the *DSM* does not specify a limit)	May be permanent, reversible, or progressive over weeks to years	
Attention	Impaired	May be impaired	
Cognition	Impaired memory, orientation, language	Impaired memory, orientation, language, executive function	Impaired memory and usually for recent memories
Perception	Hallucinations, delusions, misinterpretations	Hallucinations, delusions	Disoriented with respect to time and space (rarely to self), may lack insight into the memory loss
Sleep/wake	Disturbed, may have complete day/night reversal	Disturbed, may have no pattern	
Mood/emotion	Labile affect	Labile affect, mood disturbances	Varies from no apparent emotional reaction to the memory loss to an apparent personality change where the person may appear apathetic, bland, or not their former self
Identified precipitant	Likely precipitant is present	Identifiable precipitant is not required	Identifiable precipitant
Shared characteristics	Memory loss	Memory loss	Memory loss
	Confusion	Confusion	Confusion
	Decreased alertness and orientation	Decreased alertness and orientation	Decreased orientation
	Problem with perception, mood, and behavior	Problem with perception, mood, and behavior	Problem with perception, mood, and behavior (in select cases)

To complete the picture of the cognitive disorders, a summary of the diagnostic categories is listed in Table 4.5. Keep in mind that each disorder is characterized by memory impairment but the symptom picture differs. The most important aspect of a differential assessment is to look carefully at the extent of the person's memory impairment, how it begins, and the extent social and occupational functioning has been impaired.

Table 4.5 Summary of the Three Main Types of Cognitive Disorders

Delirium

This disorder is characterized by a disturbance of consciousness and a change in a person's cognition (i.e., memory deficit, disorientation, language disturbance of the development of a perceptual disturbance that cannot be better explained by a preexisting, established, or evolving dementia) that develops over a short period of time (usually hours to days). The diagnosis is made according to etiology:

- Delirium due to a general medical condition.
- Substance-induced delirium (due to drug abuse, medication, or toxin exposure).
- Delirium due to multiple etiologies.
- Delirium not otherwise specified (NOS).

Delirium is a rapidly developing fluctuating state of reduced awareness where the person has trouble shifting or focusing attention. At least one defect of memory, orientation, perception, or language is present and the symptoms are not better explained by dementia. Inattention is usually the first symptom and this can be seen by the practitioner as drowsiness or somnolence (the state of near-sleep). Many people will be clearer in the morning and worse in the evening (or sundowning). Delirium can develop into dementia and the two conditions can potentially co-exist. The underlying cause of delirium is usually a disease process that lies outside of the central nervous system.

Dementia

Dementia is characterized by acquired losses of cognitive and emotional abilities severe enough to interfere with daily functioning and the person's quality of life. The person has a decline from a previous level of functioning and must have at least one of the following cognitive deficits: aphasia, apraxia, agnosia, or a disturbance in executive functioning. The dementias are also classified according to presumed etiology:

- Dementia of the Alzheimer's type.
- Vascular dementia.
- Dementia due to other general medical conditions (i.e., human immunodeficiency virus [HIV] disease, head trauma, Parkinson's disease, Huntington's disease).
- Substance-induced persisting dementia (i.e., due to drug abuse, medication, or toxin exposure).

Although the potential for this diagnosis can occur as early as age 3 or 4, dementia is found primarily in older adults. Alzheimer's disease, the most common form of dementia, is progressive memory impairment and predominantly the loss of short-term memory. The person's ability to focus attention and recall remote events may at first be subtly impaired and always worsens with time. Full recovery can occur with certain types of dementia (i.e., hypothyroidism, subdural hematoma). Dementia involves damage to the person's central nervous system.

(continued)

Table 4.5 (continued)

Amnestic Disorder

This diagnostic classification is distinguished by memory impairment that is affected far more than any other function. There is no requirement for a reduced ability to focus or shift attention. Sometimes a person can forget a conversation held a few minutes before or they may confabulate experiences to hide a memory loss. The amnestic disorders are coded according to presumed causes:

- Amnestic disorder due to a general medical condition.
- Substance-induced persisting amnestic disorder.
- Amnestic disorder not otherwise specified (NOS).

It is possible for a person to recover but the disorder usually has a chronic course. The amnestic disorders are distinguished by isolated disturbances of memory without impairment of the person's other cognitive functions.

Cognitive Disorder Not Otherwise Specified (NOS)

This diagnosis is set apart for a symptom picture characterized by cognitive dysfunction presumed to be due to either a general medical condition or substance use that does not meet criteria for the other cognitive disorders.

Delirium. The person's specific signs and symptoms distinguish each diagnostic category. Those with delirium are commonly not oriented to time (for example, they do not know the day of the week) or to place (they will not know where they are). Their attention span is short and they are unable to focus. Thinking is disconnected and the person is often preoccupied with imaginary experiences, or hallucinations. Typically, the person is restless, agitated, and constantly moving around aimlessly.

Dementia. Those with dementia show a comprehensive deterioration of intelligence, and emotional and cognitive abilities. Personality changes are common and the person struggles with once familiar tasks.

Amnestic disorder. The primary cognitive symptoms found in amnestic disorder are in remembering and perceiving. As a rule, the person struggles with both short- and long-term memory. Very remote events are remembered better than those that took place a few weeks or months ago. In contrast to the normal aging process and the absent-mindedness that we all experience at one time or another, the cognitive disorders are chronic and irreversible.

We now turn to a series of case illustrations of the cognitive disorders intended to provide opportunities to refine assessment skills.

PRACTICING THE COMPETENCY-BASED ASSESSMENT

The following case illustrations provide an opportunity to practice the competency-based assessment by testing your ability to differentiate among the different cognitive disorders. Cognition and memory are key aspects of the cognitive disorders, so information is drawn not only from the client but also from a number of ancillary sources such as interviews with family or friends who know the individual, and/or results from a physical exam or laboratory tests. Integral to competency-based practice, the challenge is to listen to the client's entire "story" and discern its interplay with diagnostic criteria found in the *DSM*.

Case Illustrations

Each case offers a systematic way of looking at the events in a client's life in order to discern the onset of symptoms of a cognitive disorder, analyze pertinent information, and arrive at the correct diagnosis. Since each case is anchored in a real life context I anticipate that you will gain a sharpened understanding of the cognitive disorders and what might become important to look for more carefully in future cases in your practice. We begin with Myrna Joy Bilbus's story.

The Case of Myrna Joy Bilbus

Dementia - mid stage alz. [handwritten annotation]

As a part of her job at Bay Pines Community Center, Mary Tredway gave presentations to her local community about the services and programs the center offered for the elderly. She primarily spoke to different church groups, at health fairs, and sometimes even went to the schools. Mary loved this part of her job because it gave her a chance to meet all kinds of people. Sometimes these presentations brought new clients to the center. That's how she met Harry Bilbus. He had approached her after one of her talks saying, "I'm a little concerned about my wife, Myrna Joy, and would like your opinion. Well, maybe a second opinion. You see, I'm planning on taking her back to our doctor because she just isn't herself anymore. I was hoping that she was going through some kind of phase or something and she would get better. It doesn't look like that's happening. I'm sure he'll prescribe vitamin pills or something like that just to make her more like my old Myrna Joy. So even though I'm looking for a second opinion, I guess I'm really asking you first." According to Mr. Bilbus, Myrna Joy's last physical checkup by her internist who specialized in geriatrics revealed no evidence of physical illness or any neurological problems. Mary sensed that Mr. Bilbus was genuinely worried about his wife so she invited him to come to her office at Bay Pines the next day to tell her more.

Mr. Bilbus looked down, shifted his weight from one foot to another and said, "You see I'm a very private person and talking about my wife to a stranger is really hard . . . but you seem to know so much about those old people and the services that can help them solve their problems. I'm thinking maybe, just maybe you would know a little something about what's bothering my Myrna Joy. She just isn't herself anymore." With a determined look he added, "I'll be in to see you tomorrow, first thing."

As promised, Mr. Bilbus showed up for his appointment. He arrived a little early and looked uncomfortable in the waiting room. When he saw Mary, he brightened and seemed eager to talk with her. "May I call you . . . ," Mary started to ask. Mr. Bilbus interrupted, "Oh, Just call me Harry. Everybody does." Mary responded, "Great! Most folks around here call me Mary." "Okay," responded Harry, "Miss Mary it is." Once settled in Mary's office, he blurted out, "You see, it's my wife's memory. It's just not as good as it once was. Lately I've been feeling like I lost my best friend. You see, Myrna Joy and I have been together a long time. We married over 50 years ago. When we first met, it was like they say on that TV commercial for the computer dating service. When I looked into her eyes, my heart melted. Really! We've been soul mates ever since. You know what they say about married people. After you live with someone for so long that you finish each other's sentences. Well that's how it is for me and my Myrna Joy. Well, it used to be that way but lately it's different. Now, she doesn't talk much and when she does, she usually forgets a word or two and then looks at me to fill her in." Drawing in his breath, he added, "I guess age is finally starting to catch up with us." Mr. Bilbus shifted in his chair, tightened his hands together in a nervous gesture and continued. "It seems to be getting worse."

Harry looked lost in thought for a moment and then continued, "We have two wonderful sons. Our oldest is Tim. He's some kind of 'big shot' in an investment company. He makes good money, lives in a big house out in California and is doing really well. He married his college sweetheart and we're waiting on grandchildren. I'm afraid we're probably going to have to give up in that department. He calls us every weekend, rain or shine. Our youngest, Mike, is in sales. He lives about eight hours away and calls as much as he can. They're pregnant with our third grandchild. Here, let me show you pictures." Mr. Bilbus fumbles in his pocket and pulls out his wallet. Right on the very top was a well worn photo of two young boys. "You couldn't ask for two greater kids. They're really smart, just like their father. The new one is going to be a girl. We're so proud." Ms. Tredway commented on the photos and encouraged Mr. Bilbus to go on. "What was I talking about? Oh, yeah. When the boys call, Myrna Joy says a nice hello and then hands the phone over to me. In the old days, she would be on the phone with them for hours. You know how mothers are. They want to know everything . . . what they're eating . . . how things are on the job . . . the latest girlfriend and on and on. Myrna Joy never seemed to run out of questions when it came to her boys! She would remember every minute detail about their lives."

Mr. Bilbus added, "That reminds me of something else that just happened." He looked to Mary and asked, "Do you have time? I can see this center is a busy place. You must have other important things to do around here." Mary responded, "No, Harry. You are my most important priority right now. Take all the time you need." Harry looked relieved at this point. "Myrna Joy took on a complete personality change the other week. I just couldn't believe it. The boys were starting to get worried about her and planned a vacation to see us. I'm thinking they really wanted to see firsthand what was up with their mother. Well, when Myrna Joy got wind of their trip, she just went berserk! She's normally pleasant and easygoing but this time she started yelling and screaming that they weren't going to be snooping on her. She even took the rolling pin and chased me outside. Now that's not my usual Myrna Joy! And there have been other changes, too. Are you sure, Miss Mary that you don't have something else to do?" Mary Tredway sensed that Mr. Bilbus was uncomfortable so she asked if he would like a tour of the center but he declined. This appeared to be a fragile moment in their conversation. Mary Tredway explained that their conversation would be kept confidential and added that she met a number of people who had worries a lot like what Mr. Bilbus was going through. He looked relieved. "We don't need therapy or anything like that," he said and continued, "My Myrna Joy has always kept a neat house. Why you could even eat off the floor! Lately, it hasn't been like that. I opened the refrigerator yesterday and guess what I found?" A brief silence elapses. "Well, right there on the front shelf was an iron. Don't ask me why Myrna Joy put it in there. Another time I found a frying pan. When I asked about it, she just smiled. I'm beginning to wonder if my Myrna Joy even remembers what an iron is for. To top it off, we spent days looking for that iron. Turned the whole apartment upside down. Her cooking is not so good anymore either. She forgets about food left cooking on the stove. I don't know how many times I've found pots burning and Myrna Joy seems oblivious to it all." Mr. Bilbus took another deep breath, "I'm glad to know all this is just between us 'cause her hygiene is not so good anymore either. I don't know how many times I've had to flush the toilet because she forgot and she's always been so careful about hygiene and how she looks." Mr. Bilbus went on to describe how Myrna Joy wakes up in the middle of the night and wanders around the house. "I've taken to locking all the doors after one night when the nice neighbor who lives upstairs in our condo called to tell me that she saw Myrna Joy wandering around the tennis courts. My wife has never played tennis a day in her life! When I asked her about it, she didn't remember a thing. She doesn't drink alcohol and has never taken drugs, so I really can't understand her crazy behavior. I'm hoping you can help."

"It sounds like you've had a lot on your mind worrying about your wife," stated Ms. Tredway. Mr. Bilbus nodded his head in agreement. "Now that you look back on it, when were you first aware that something was, well, not quite right with Myrna Joy," asked Mary Tredway. He responded that it seemed really gradual, adding "It's really hard to pinpoint it to a specific day." She then invited Mr. Bilbus to come back to the center for their afternoon hot lunch program and suggested that he bring Myrna Joy. He agreed to return the following week after her doctor's appointment. "I'll make all the arrangements with the kitchen so they will be expecting you. Just drop by my office after you have lunch so I can meet Myrna Joy."

Ms. Tredway was happy to see Mr. Bilbus when he returned with Myrna Joy. After eating lunch, Mr. Bilbus introduced his wife to Ms. Tredway. She observed that Myrna Joy looked much younger than her 74 years. Her appearance was clean and, at first glance, Myrna Joy looked neatly dressed wearing an attractive black sweater set and slacks. However, Ms. Tredway noticed that Myrna Joy's sweater was backward and the cardigan was inside out. It also looked like Myrna Joy's zipper on her slacks was open. Although Mary Tredway couldn't be sure, she wondered if Myrna Joy was even wearing any underwear. Throughout the interview, Myrna Joy maintained good eye contact and seemed to pay attention to the conversation. She smiled continuously and asked her husband several times when they were going to have lunch. "I'm hungry," she asserted (despite having already just eaten lunch at the center). Repeatedly, Mr. Bilbus would patiently respond, "In a minute, honey. Let's talk for a little bit longer to this nice lady." Ms. Tredway began the conversation by sharing that Mr. Bilbus had come in earlier and talked about their children and grandchildren. She replied, "Okee-dokey smokey. That's nice of you to ask about us."

Ms. Tredway then asked Myrna Joy for the names of her grandchildren. Mrs. Bilbus looked out the window for a moment and responded, "Okee-dokey smokey, but they're rotten little bastards you know." Mr. Bilbus looked embarrassed and gently stroked his wife's hand much as one would do with an upset child. "Now come on honey, I know you know their names. I'm sure they will come to you in a minute. Just concentrate a little harder," he prodded. After what seemed like a very long minute, he added, "Our oldest is Chris and the youngest is Scott. You remember now, don't you?" His wife simply smiled and nodded her head.

Mary Tredway commented to Myrna Joy, "It sounds like you're upset." She replied, "Okee-dokey smokey, but I couldn't be happier. I'm tired and I just don't feel like helping you anymore." She then turned to her husband and again asked when they were going to have lunch. Mary Tredway suggested they return to the cafeteria for a snack.

On their way to the cafeteria, Mr. Bilbus shared that the doctor's appointment went well. "Myrna Joy is in good health but the doctor wants to do some more tests and take pictures of her brain, just to check her out. Funny that he would want to take a look at her brain since she never had any head injury. Well, I guess he knows what he's doing." Ms. Tredway invited Mr. Bilbus to join their free hot lunch program and bring his wife along so he could have a break in the middle of the day. He agreed to return with his wife.

How would you formulate your competency-based assessment for Myrna Joy Bilbus?

The Case of Mary James

Mary James is 70 years of age, never married, and lives alone. She has an active social life consisting of Sunday dinner with her niece, Beatrice Herren, and their family. She also plays Mah Jong with friends every Thursday. One afternoon Mary heard her phone ring and jumped up to answer it. One of her flip-flops caught on the edge of the rug and she fell. Unable to get up, Mary crawled over to the phone, which had long stopped ringing by now. She called 911. The emergency medical squad took her to the emergency room of a nearby hospital where X-rays showed a hip fracture.

Beatrice Herren was called and she met her aunt at the hospital. Mary wore a health alert bracelet and her medical history noted that she has diabetes, which is treated with metformin (Glucophage) twice daily. At the time of her hospitalization, Mary's vital signs were normal. Considering that she was facing surgery, the physician on call in the emergency department asked Beatrice if her aunt was acting normally. The physician then asked Mary a few questions. She responded clearly, was socially appropriate, and concisely described how she came to be hospitalized. She also shared details of her past. Mary was oriented to time and place and told the physician her age and birth date. She expressed concern for taking up so much of her niece's time at the hospital. Mary even joked with the physician asking, "How many doctors does it take to change a light bulb?" "I don't know," replied the physician while her niece just smiled. "Well, it depends on whether it has health insurance!" Mary chuckled. She then asked about her impending surgery. The physician explained, "The hip is basically a ball and socket joint. The area just below the ball is known as the femoral neck or interochanteric region. That's where your fracture occurred when you fell. We'll wait for the X-rays to be sure but I'm confident you have what's called an interochanteric fracture." He added, "This is a very common type of hip fracture." The physician then asked, "On a scale of 0 to 10 with 10 being the highest level, how would you rate your pain right now?" Mary responded that she was at a "7." After confirming that Mary has no history of drug allergies, the physician prescribed hydromorphone (Dilaudid) for pain and methocarbamol (Robaxin) for spasms.

Mary was admitted and transferred to the orthopedic floor. When Beatrice saw her aunt she immediately became worried about her behavior and called for the nurse on the unit. Beatrice told the nurse that she saw a distinct change in her aunt since she came into the hospital. The nurse went over to Mary's bedside, introduced herself, and explained, "Sometimes your brain can be affected by surgery and we need to monitor how well your brain is working. If it's okay, I'd like to ask you a few questions." Mary responded, "What am I doing here? It's Thursday and I'll be late for Mah Jong with my friends." "Ms. James, would you like your niece to stay in the room while we talk?" asked the nurse. "She should stay!" Mary replied. Turning to Beatrice, the nurse stated,

"You are welcome to stay but please, don't help your aunt to answer any questions. We'll get better information if she does this on her own." Beatrice nodded in agreement and stepped toward the door and out of her aunt's sight. The nurse continued, "Ms. James, can you spell the word 'world' backward for me?" Mary started but became distracted by the magazines on her bedside table. The nurse went on, "Ms. James, do you know what today's date is?" Mary seemed confused by the question and again, talked about playing cards with her friends. Mary looked anxious at this point in the conversation. The nurse continued, "Mary, tests reveal that you have a slight urinary tract infection, which is being treated with antibiotics. Looking over your chart, you seem to be responding well to the medication the doctor prescribed." Both the Dilaudid and Robaxin were discontinued and Mary remained comfortable with acetaminophen.

Within 24 hours of the change in her medications, Mary had her surgery without complication. Once Beatrice saw her aunt back in her hospital room she found her to be just like she was when she was first admitted. Even Mary's sense of humor had returned. When a nurse came in to take her vital signs, Mary asked, "How many nurses does it take to change a light bulb?" Beatrice just rolled her eyes and smiled. Mary was already up, walking short distances and plans were being made for a discharge to a rehabilitation facility. When Beatrice saw the nurse who had questioned Mary earlier she commented, "I was really worried that maybe my aunt was crazy when I left the hospital the other day." The nurse responded, "I think she's going to be just fine." After two weeks of rehabilitation Mary returned home with home care services.

How would you formulate your competency-based assessment for Mary James?

PRACTICAL APPLICATIONS

To heighten awareness of the cognitive disorders and the impact they can have on a person's family, a series of practical applications follow.

1. Think back on the cases of Myrna Joy Bilbus and Mary James illustrated in this chapter. Use each as a backdrop to answer the following:
   a. At what point did you begin to suspect the presence of a cognitive disorder?
   b. Were any of the diagnostic criteria questionable?
   c. At what point in the case discussion were you able to definitively consider a specific diagnosis?
   d. Was there any information that you would have liked to have had? If so, explain why this would be important.
2. Identify some of the ethical issues related to formulating a diagnosis for someone with a cognitive disorder. Are there any relevant cultural issues to consider?

3. Another way to learn about the cognitive disorders is to participate in real-life situations. Interview someone you know who is at least 70 years old or older (for example, aging grandparents, other relatives, neighbors, friends).

   a. Ask them how they have dealt with the aging process and the losses that they have encountered as a part of aging; encourage as much specificity as you can.

   b. Inquire about what kind of community services they think would be helpful for somebody that they know and would they use them; explain why or why not.

   c. Have they (or do they know of anyone who has) actually used a particular service targeting the elderly and what was their experience?

Appendix

Competency-Based Assessments for Chapter 4 Case Examples: Listing of Case Diagnoses

Figures 4A.1 through 4A.4 provide the diagnostic assessment for each of the cases illustrated. They are organized in the order that they appear in each chapter.

CASE REVIEW FOR MYRNA JOY BILBUS

Harry Bilbus, Myrna Joy's husband of 50 years, approached the practitioner at a local elderly day center, Bay Pines, asking for "advice" about his wife. He shares that he has noticed gradual changes in her and she does not seem like herself anymore. Mr. Bilbus goes on to describe the typical symptoms supporting a diagnosis of Alzheimer's disease. Myrna Joy is seen as less communicative and when she does talk she forgets certain words. He fills them in for her and goes on to say that Myrna Joy's speech pattern only seems to be getting worse. In addition, her personality seems to be changing; for example, though she loves her sons, she became upset at the thought of an impending visit from them. Myrna Joy's forgetfulness is to the extent that she does not seem to remember the use for familiar household items. She also gets up at night and on one occasion wandered out the door not knowing her way back home. On interview, Myrna Joy was not well kempt; her clothes were on backward and the practitioner was unsure if

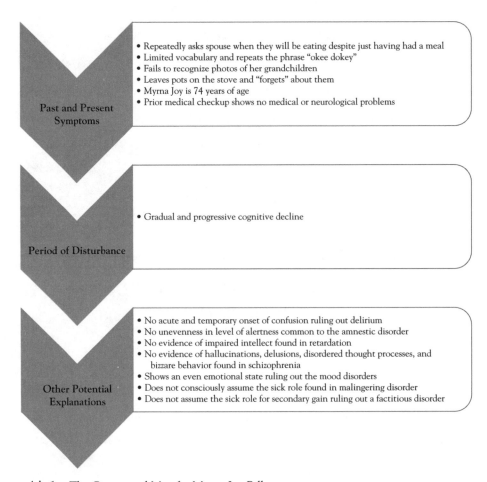

Past and Present Symptoms
- Repeatedly asks spouse when they will be eating despite just having had a meal
- Limited vocabulary and repeats the phrase "okee dokey"
- Fails to recognize photos of her grandchildren
- Leaves pots on the stove and "forgets" about them
- Myrna Joy is 74 years of age
- Prior medical checkup shows no medical or neurological problems

Period of Disturbance
- Gradual and progressive cognitive decline

Other Potential Explanations
- No acute and temporary onset of confusion ruling out delirium
- No unevenness in level of alertness common to the amnestic disorder
- No evidence of impaired intellect found in retardation
- No evidence of hallucinations, delusions, disordered thought processes, and bizarre behavior found in schizophrenia
- Shows an even emotional state ruling out the mood disorders
- Does not consciously assume the sick role found in malingering disorder
- Does not assume the sick role for secondary gain ruling out a factitious disorder

Figure 4A.1   The Conceptual Map for Myrna Joy Bilbus

her pants were zipped and closed. Conversation appeared stereotypic and she "forgot" important details.

The couple has two sons. Although they do not live nearby (the closest is eight hours away), they do stay in regular contact with their parents. Mr. Bilbus is clearly devoted to his wife and reaches out for help and "advice" about her condition. He is her primary caretaker and apparently in good health. A recent checkup for Myrna Joy also reveals no medical problems. Despite Myrna Joy's symptom picture, her husband agrees to take her to the elder center and seems to normalize her day as much as possible at this point in time. Though the prognosis is poor for Myrna Joy's functioning, the competency-based assessment identifies a number of positives to build on in facing future challenges in Myrna Joy's life with the diagnosis of Alzheimer's disease.

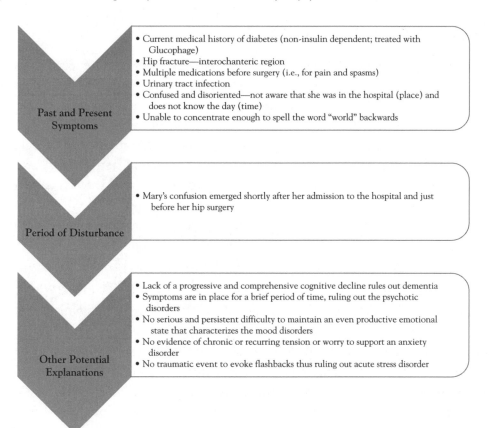

The DSM-IV-TR *Diagnosis*
Axis I—Dementia of the
Alzheimer's Type with Late
Onset without Behavioral
Disturbance 294.10
Axis II—V71.09 No diagnosis
Axis III—Alzheimer's disease
331.0
Axis IV—None
Axis V—GAF 35 (current)

Assessing for Competence
Spouse, Harry, is loving and
supportive
Mr. Bilbus has reached out for
help
Two children who stay in
regular contact with their
parents
Myrna Joy is pleasant and
cooperative
Her husband, her caretaker
and spouse for 50 years, is in
good overall health

Figure 4A.2   The Competency-Based Assessment for Myrna Joy Bilbus

Past and Present Symptoms
- Current medical history of diabetes (non-insulin dependent; treated with Glucophage)
- Hip fracture—interochanteric region
- Multiple medications before surgery (i.e., for pain and spasms)
- Urinary tract infection
- Confused and disoriented—not aware that she was in the hospital (place) and does not know the day (time)
- Unable to concentrate enough to spell the word "world" backwards

Period of Disturbance
- Mary's confusion emerged shortly after her admission to the hospital and just before her hip surgery

Other Potential Explanations
- Lack of a progressive and comprehensive cognitive decline rules out dementia
- Symptoms are in place for a brief period of time, ruling out the psychotic disorders
- No serious and persistent difficulty to maintain an even productive emotional state that characterizes the mood disorders
- No evidence of chronic or recurring tension or worry to support an anxiety disorder
- No traumatic event to evoke flashbacks thus ruling out acute stress disorder

Figure 4A.3   The Conceptual Map for Mary James

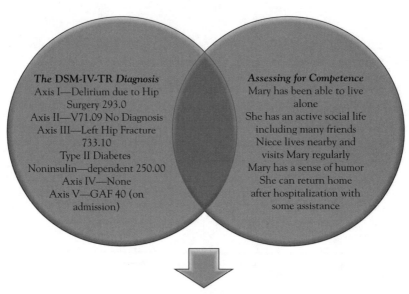

The DSM-IV-TR *Diagnosis*
Axis I—Delirium due to Hip
Surgery 293.0
Axis II—V71.09 No Diagnosis
Axis III—Left Hip Fracture
733.10
Type II Diabetes
Noninsulin—dependent 250.00
Axis IV—None
Axis V—GAF 40 (on
admission)

Assessing for Competence
Mary has been able to live
alone
She has an active social life
including many friends
Niece lives nearby and
visits Mary regularly
Mary has a sense of humor
She can return home
after hospitalization with
some assistance

Figure 4A.4   The Competency-Based Assessment for Mary James

CASE REVIEW FOR MARY JAMES

The competency-based assessment is attentive to each person's unique experience with a diagnosis. In this situation, we see an elderly woman, Mary James, who is 70 and lives alone, has many friends and a niece who lives nearby and visits regularly. However, a simple accident, like falling at home, illustrates the fragility of Mary's life and how quickly it can change. She is hospitalized and experiences an episode of delirium. Mary's symptoms are: an acute change occurred in her mental status shortly after she was hospitalized; she was not lucid for a brief period of time; and she was back to her "old self" on discharge or her confusion was transient in nature.

We also see her resilience and humor as she recovers from her hip surgery. Her niece noticed that her aunt was back to telling jokes with the hospital staff. Overall, Mary James can be described as a bright and engaging woman who is able to return back home from the hospital with after-care assistance. No further problems with memory are found thus supporting her *DSM* diagnosis of delirium due to hip surgery.

The Substance-Related Disorders

INTRODUCTION

How many of you start your day with a cup of coffee? Perhaps you enjoy a sip of wine or other alcoholic drink with friends at the end of the day to relax and catch up on the latest news. Most of us have used psychoactive substances that alter mood and/or behavior at one time or another in our lives. We figure these habits are all right as long as they do not interfere with our job, social life, or relationships with others. Most of us do not abuse substances but when that happens, it is considered a substance-related disorder. According to the Substance Abuse and Mental Health Services Administration (SAMHSA) (2009), in 2008, an estimated 22.2 million persons or 8.9% of the population aged 12 or older were classified with substance dependence or abuse in the past year based on criteria specified in the *DSM*. Add to that estimate the reality that between 20% and 50% of all hospital admissions are related to the effects of alcohol abuse and/or addiction (Greenfield & Hennessy, 2004). Wilens (2006) suggests that between 10% and 30% of adults in the United States have a substance-use disorder. That makes alcohol and drugs a part of the lives of many people.

We now turn to an overview of the incidence and prevalence of the substance-related disorders.

INCIDENCE AND PREVALENCE

Of the estimated 22.2 million persons with substance dependence or abuse, 3.1 million were classified with dependence on or abuse of both alcohol and illicit drugs, 3.9 million were dependent on or abused illicit drugs but not alcohol, and 15.2 million were dependent on or abused alcohol but not illicit drugs (SAMHSA, 2009).

Alcohol use. Looking at estimates of alcohol consumption in the U.S. general population, slightly more than half of Americans aged 12 or older reported being current drinkers of alcohol in the 2008 survey or 51.6% (SAMHSA, 2009). This translates to an estimated 129.0 million people, which was similar to the 2007 estimate of 126.8 million people (51.1%). Past month alcohol use rates by age show a decline between 2002 and 2008. For example, the rates for those aged 12 or 13 were estimated at 4.3% to 3.4%, 14 or 15 years of age at 16.6% to 13.1%, 16 or 17 years of age at 32.6% to 26.2%, and 18- to 20-year-olds at 51.0% to 48.7%. However, the rate of current alcohol use among youths aged 12 to 17 was 14.6% in 2008. This estimated rate is lower than the 2007 reported rate of 15.9%. Youth binge and heavy drinking rates in 2008 were 8.8% (lower than the 9.7% rate in 2007) and 2.0%, respectively.

There is also some variation of current alcohol use rates across various racial and ethnic groups. For instance, among persons aged 12 to 20, past month alcohol use rates in 2008 were 17.2% among Asians, 19.0% among blacks, 22.9% among those reporting two or more races, 23.1% among Hispanics, 26.4% among American Indians or Alaska Natives, and 30.1% among whites.

Further, in 2008, an estimated 12.4% of persons aged 12 or older drove under the influence of alcohol at least once in the past year. As a parallel, in 2008, 10.0 million persons aged 12 or older reported driving under the influence of illicit drugs during the past year. This corresponds to 4.0% of the population aged 12 or older, the same as the rate in 2007 (4.0%), but lower than the rate in 2002 (4.7%). In 2008, the rate was highest among young adults aged 18 to 25 or 12.3%. This percentage has dropped since 2002, when it was reported at 14.2% (SAMHSA, 2003).

Illicit drug use. In 2008, an estimated 20.1 million Americans aged 12 or older were current (past month) illicit drug users, meaning they had used an illicit drug during the month prior to the survey interview. This estimate represents 8.0% of the population aged 12 years old or older. The illicit drugs included marijuana/hashish, cocaine (including crack), heroin, hallucinogens, inhalants, or prescription-type psychotherapeutics used nonmedically. The rate of current illicit drug use among persons aged 12 or older seems to have stabilized. Specifically, in 2008, estimated use was at 8.0%, which is the same estimate reported in 2007. Among those aged 50 to 59, the rate of past month illicit drug use increased from 2.7% in 2002 to 4.6% in 2008. This trend may partially reflect the aging into this age group of the baby boom cohort, whose lifetime rate of illicit drug use is higher than those of older cohorts.

Among youths aged 12 to 17, the current illicit drug use rate remained stable from 2007 (9.5%) to 2008 (9.3%). Between 2002 and 2008, youth rates declined significantly for illicit drugs in general (from 11.6% to 9.3%) and for marijuana (8.2% to

6.7%), cocaine (0.6% to 0.4%), prescription-type drugs used nonmedically (4.0% to 2.9%), pain relievers (3.2% to 2.3%), stimulants (0.8% to 0.5%), and methamphetamine (0.3% to 0.1%).

It is hard to get a clear picture of the consumption of drugs due to their illicit nature and covert use. However, estimates show that marijuana was the most commonly used illicit drug (15.2 million past month users) in 2008 (SAMHSA, 2009). Among persons aged 12 or older, the rate of past month marijuana use in 2008 (6.1%) was similar to the rate in 2007 (5.8%). The usage rates for other drugs vary over time. For example, in 2008, there were 1.9 million current cocaine users aged 12 or older, comprising 0.7% of the population. These estimates were similar to the number and rate in 2007 (2.1 million or 0.8%), but lower than the estimates in 2006 (2.4 million or 1.0%). Hallucinogens were used in the past month by 1.1 million persons (0.4%) aged 12 or older in 2008, including 555,000 (0.2%) who had used Ecstasy. These estimates were similar to the corresponding estimates for 2007. The number of past month methamphetamine users decreased by more than half between 2006 and 2008. The numbers were 731,000 in 2006, 529,000 in 2007, and 314,000 in 2008. From 2002 to 2008, there was an increase among young adults aged 18 to 25 in the rate of current nonmedical use of prescription pain relievers (from 4.1% to 4.6%) and in LSD (from 0.1% to 0.3%). There were decreases in the use of inhalants (from 0.5% to 0.3%) and methamphetamine (from 0.6% to 0.2%).

Tobacco products use. The rate of current use of any tobacco product among persons aged 12 or older remained steady from 2007 to 2008 (28.6% and 28.4%, respectively). Rates of current use of cigarettes, smokeless tobacco, cigars, and pipe tobacco also did not change significantly over that period. However, between 2002 and 2008, past month use of any tobacco product decreased from 30.4% to 28.4%, and past month cigarette use declined from 26.0% to 23.9%. Rates of past month use of cigars, smokeless tobacco, and pipe tobacco in 2008 were similar to corresponding rates in 2002. The rate of past month cigarette use among 12- to 17-year-olds declined from 9.8% in 2007 to 9.1% in 2008, continuing a decline since 2002 when the rate was 13.0%. However, past month smokeless tobacco use did not decline over this period (2.0% in 2002 and 2.2% in 2008).

OVERVIEW OF THE MAJOR CHARACTERISTICS OF THE DIAGNOSTIC CLASSIFICATIONS

A substance disorder is diagnosed when a substance is judged to be etiologically related to the person's symptom picture. The *DSM-IV-TR* (American Psychiatric Association, 2000) section that provides an overview of the substance use disorders is structured differently from the rest of the manual. To reflect this, you will notice that this chapter is organized in a different way from the other chapters in this book. Essentially, the disorders are first divided on the basis of the nature of the disorder; that is, problems that arise from substance *use* or are *induced* by the substance. For those disorders related to *use* of a substance, there are two descriptive categories to choose from when making the diagnosis: dependence or abuse. When considering those disorders *induced* by use of a substance there are also two categories to describe the effects and they are intoxication or withdrawal.

Substance use disorders. Looking at the substance use disorders, the generic criteria for dependence and abuse look like the following.

Diagnostic Criteria for Dependence and Abuse

Substance Dependence: The person's maladaptive pattern of substance use leads to clinically significant distress or impairment in a single 12-month period by three or more of:

Tolerance shown by either of:
- Marked increased intake of the substance is needed to achieve the same effect.
- With continued use, the same amount of the substance has less of an effect.

Withdrawal as shown by either of:
- The substance's characteristic withdrawal syndrome is experienced.
- The substance (or one closely related) is used to avoid or relieve withdrawal symptoms.

The *amount or duration* of use is often greater than intended.

Tries repeatedly to *control or reduce* substance use.

Spends a lot of *time* using the substance, recovering from its effects or to obtain the substance.

Important social, work, or recreational activities are *given up or reduced* because of substance use.

Use is *continued* despite knowing problems have been caused or exacerbated.

Substance Abuse: The person's maladaptive substance use pattern causes clinically significant distress or impairment in a single 12-month period by one or more of:

- Because of repeated use, the person *fails to carry out* major work, home, or school obligations.
- The person continues to use substances even when it is physically *dangerous* to do so.
- Repeatedly has *legal problems* resulting from substance use.

Despite knowing substance use has *caused (or worsened) social or interpersonal problems*, the person continues to use the substance.

- Keep in mind the person has never met criteria for substance dependence.

Notice that the symptoms listed in the *DSM* for dependence or abuse do not address the subjective reasons of why users will prefer a particular substance. Though you may hear terms like "denial" or "craving" in your practice, they are not a part of the *DSM* diagnostic criteria because these conditions are considered to be difficult to evaluate. This leaves the question of whether a substance use disorder is a primary disorder or a symptom of another underlying issue unaddressed.

Substance-induced disorders. Looking at the substance-induced disorders, the generic criteria for intoxication and withdrawal can be summarized as follows.

Diagnostic Criteria for Substance Intoxication and Withdrawal

Substance Intoxication:

The person develops a *reversible syndrome* due to recent use of (or exposure to) a substance that affects the central nervous system.

During (or shortly after) using the substance, the person *develops clinically important behavioral or psychological changes* that are maladaptive.

This condition is *not the result* of a general medical condition nor better explained by another mental disorder.

Substance Withdrawal:

A syndrome specific to a substance develops when the person who has used it frequently (and for a long time) *suddenly stops* or markedly reduces its intake.

Causes *clinically important distress* or impairs work, social, or other functioning.

This syndrome is *not the result* of a general medical condition nor better explained by another mental disorder.

There are also a number of other classifications of mental disorders with features of the substance-induced disorders. For example, these include substance-induced delirium, persisting dementia, persisting amnestic disorder, substance-induced psychotic disorder, substance-induced mood disorder, substance-induced anxiety disorder, substance-induced sexual dysfunction, and substance-induced sleep disorder. To facilitate a differential diagnosis, it is helpful to be familiar with the diagnostic criteria for each of these different classifications of mental disorders and then to be able to recognize that they can also include symptoms of intoxication, withdrawal, or as a longer lasting consequence of the misuse of a substance. By definition, these disorders are directly caused by the effects of various substances including alcohol, medications, or toxins (see Table 5.1).

Grouping the substances. In order to classify the specific substances, the *DSM* uses 11 groupings (plus the designation not otherwise specified). There are similarities among these groupings of substances, and they are:

☞ Similarities Found Among the Substances

Central nervous system depressants	Alcohol, and the sedatives, hypnotics, and anxiolytics
Central nervous system stimulants	Amphetamines, cocaine, nicotine, and caffeine
Opioids	Heroin, opium, codeine, and morphine
Hallucinogens	Marijuana/cannabis, LSD, and others
Other drugs	Inhalants and phencyclidine

On the face of it, the basic disorders are alcoholism and drug use so you might consider these groupings artificial. However, the *DSM*'s classification system represents an attempt to define the disorders related to all of the substances uniformly.

ADDING DIAGNOSTIC SPECIFICITY

Keep in mind that the *DSM* lists more than 100 numbered or coded substance-related disorders. When all the subcodes and specifiers are taken into account, you will find hundreds of ways to assign a specific diagnosis to your client. You might consider this a mix-and-match approach to the diagnostic process. In essence, for any substance-related disorder the diagnosis begins with the name of the substance(s) responsible, and the type of problem (such as dependence, abuse, intoxication, or withdrawal). For example, if a person were compulsively using cocaine to the point where it was causing significant problems at work or in social relationships then the diagnosis would be

Table 5.1 Summary of the Specific Substance Related Disorders Listed by Class of Substances and Diagnostic Codes

	Delirium	Dementia	Amnestic Disorder	Psychotic Disorders	Mood Disorder	Anxiety Disorder	Sexual Dysfunction	Sleep Disorder	Dependence	Abuse	Intoxication	Withdrawal
Alcohol	291.0 I/W	291.2	291.1	291.5/.3 I/W	291.8 I/W	291.8 I/W	291.8 I	291.8 I/W	303.90	305.00	303.00	291.8 PD
Amphetamines	292.81 I			292.11/.12 I	292.84 I/W	292.89 I	292.89 I	292.89 I/W	303.40	305.70	292.89 PD	292.0
Caffeine						292.89 I		292.89 I			305.90	
Cannabis	292.81 I			292.11/.12 I		292.89 I			304.30	305.20	292.89 PD	
Cocaine	292.81 I			292.11/.12 I	292.84 I/W	292.89 I/W	292.89 I	292.89 I/W	304.20	305.60	292.89 PD	292.0
Hallucinogens	292.81 I			292.11/.12 I and *	292.84 I	292.89 I			304.50	305.30	292.89	
Inhalants	292.81 I	292.82		292.11/.12 I	292.84 I	292.89 I			304.60	305.90	292.89	
Nicotine									305.10			292.0
Opioids	292.81 I			292.11/.12 I	292.84 I		292.89 I	292.89 I/W	304.00	305.50	292.89 PD	292.0
PCP	292.81 I			292.11/.12 I	292.84 I	292.89 I			304.90	305.90	292.89 PD	
Sedatives, Hypnotics, Anxiolytics	292.81 I/W	292.82	292.83	292.11/.12 I/W	292.84 I/W	292.89 W	292.89 I	292.89 I/W	304.10	305.40	292.89 PD	292.0 PD

Notes: I = Intoxication; W = Withdrawal; PD = Perceptual disturbances

*May include the hallucinogen-related Hallucinogen Persisting Perception Disorder, code 292.89 (or flashbacks)

cocaine dependence. In some situations the time relationship of substance use to the onset of the problem behavior may be specified. Going back to our example of the diagnosis of cocaine dependence, let us say that the person is now in the early stages of recovery but still has some lingering problems; that is, he or she used cocaine within the previous 12 months but has not recently used cocaine for at least two months. In that case, the specifier would be noted as early partial remission.

Including specifiers. Specifiers are included when coding for substance dependence. Until the person has experienced at least one month of partial (or full) remission, no course specifiers are added to the diagnosis of substance dependence.

Substance Dependence Specifiers

With physiological dependence/without physiological dependence	With physiological dependence is used when dependence is accompanied by evidence of tolerance (or marked increased amounts of the substance to achieve intoxication or there is a diminished effect with the same amount used).
	Without physiological dependence is used when there is no evidence of tolerance or withdrawal but the person instead shows a pattern of compulsive use (with three of the following features: taking larger amounts than intended; spends a lot of time to obtain the substance; important social, work, or recreational activities are given up or reduced because of substance use; or use is continued despite knowing problems have been caused or exacerbated).
Early full remission/early partial remission/sustained full remission/sustained partial remission	Early full remission is 2 through 12 months with no symptoms of dependence or abuse.
	Early partial remission is 2 through 12 months with at least one criterion for either dependence or abuse.
	Sustained full remission is 13 months or more with no symptoms of dependence or of abuse.
	Sustained partial remission is 13 months or more with meeting at least one criterion for either dependence or abuse.
In a controlled environment	Does *not apply* to nicotine.
	Not used during the first month.
	For those who live in an environment where it would be difficult to obtain the substance (such as a therapeutic community or hospital).
On Agonist therapy	Does *not apply* to cannabis, hallucinogens, inhalants.
	Taking medication to block the effects of the substance in question.

Methods of ingestion. A further diagnostic consideration is how a substance is ingested, in particular the rapidity of onset and excretion effect of the substance in question. For instance, if an individual rapidly absorbs a substance, such as by smoking, snorting, or injection, he or she will have a quicker onset of action and a much shorter duration of its effects. In this instance, a person will more than likely develop dependence or abuse. A longer half-life (or the time it takes for a person's body to eliminate half the remaining substance) extends the period in which the user will experience substance withdrawal, thus reducing the likelihood of withdrawal symptoms.

Polysubstance-related disorder. About 10 years ago, Staines and colleagues (2001) studied clients who were struggling with alcohol dependence and found that many of these individuals were using multiple substances instead of only one. Referred to in the *DSM* as polysubstance dependence, this is a pattern of abuse of three or more psychoactive substances, often used simultaneously, in which no one substance predominates (APA, 2000). A person with polysubstance dependence is psychologically addicted to being in a state of intoxication but because no one single drug predominates, the individual does not develop the symptoms of physical dependence (for example, tolerance or physical withdrawal when stopping a particular substance). In order to make this diagnosis, the person must be using (or abusing) at least three groups of substances (excluding caffeine and nicotine). In those situations where there is a pattern of problems associated with multiple drugs and criteria are met for more than one specific substance-related disorder, each diagnosis should be made. For example, if a person is abusing alcohol, cocaine, and diet pills (amphetamines), polysubstance dependence is coded (304.80 Poly Substance Dependence) and accompanied by a list of the substances abused. In our example it would be: 305.00 Alcohol Abuse, 305.60 Cocaine Abuse, and 304.70 Amphetamine Abuse. Unfortunately, little is known about how various substances interact with one another (Barrett, Darredeau, & Phil, 2006).

LOOKING AT THE SPECIFIC SUBSTANCES

Everyone is different and so it should come as no surprise that the effects of substances will vary as well. The substance-related disorders are unique in that they can create emotional problems in a person's life as well as for his or her family. More than likely someone with any one of the substance disorders will ask for help with a range of psychosocial problems and not just for substance use per se. This is the individual who may have legal problems, is not doing well in school or at work, or perhaps there is some tension with family or friends. It is often hard to admit that you are creating your own problems through substance use, so expect your client to be reluctant to volunteer information about his or her use of alcohol and/or other substances that may really be at the heart of their difficulties. This underscores the competency-based approach to the assessment that includes looking at a wide range of factors in a client's life, including how the person copes with life's challenges and adversity.

There are many ways substance use or induced effects can manifest themselves. Coupled with the specific classifications listed in the DSM, consider the following:

- *Route of administration*—Substances can be taken into the body in a number of ways. They include oral ingestion (swallowing), inhalation (breathing in), injection into the veins (shooting up), or depositing into the mucosa (moist skin) in the mouth or nose (snorting). How a substance is taken determines how quickly it will have an effect on someone. For example, the person who snorts cocaine will more quickly feel the impact of the drug (because it will absorb more rapidly into the bloodstream) than someone who swallows it.
- *Speed of onset within the class of substance*—Some substances are more fast-acting than others. For instance, diazepam (Valium), a tranquilizer prescribed for its anti-anxiety qualities, acts more quickly than a phenobarbital (Nembutol), a drug prescribed for its sedative qualities.
- *Duration of effects*—Some substances are short-acting and leave the body quickly while others might be longer-lasting and dissipate more slowly.
- *Interactivity of multiple substances*—Sometimes people will use multiple substances without knowing how they might interact together.
- *Associated mental disorders*—Substance-related disorders often co-occur with other mental disorders. How often have we heard a client's account of attempts to self-medicate the highs associated with bipolar disorder through the use of sedating drugs? The effects of each individual substance can also vary in the face of a co-occurring mental disorder.

We now turn our attention to the specific substances listed in the DSM, beginning with the alcohol-related disorders.

Alcohol-Related Disorders

Alcohol is a legal substance for anyone over the age of 21. The alcohol in beverages is absorbed into the human blood stream in about 5 to 10 minutes and can stay in the body for several hours. Although considered a depressant, the initial effect on the user is one of stimulation. Low doses, considered one or two drinks, can lower a person's inhibitions and make him or her feel more comfortable. For reasons not yet clearly understood, some individuals will become more aggressive than they would ordinarily be.

Alcohol sensitizes NMDA (N-methyl D-aspartate) receptors in the brain making them more responsive to the excitatory neurotransmitter glutamate boosting brain activity. These effects are most pronounced in the areas of the brain associated with thinking, memory, and pleasure. Continued drinking affects more areas of the brain, which further impedes the ability to function properly. This increased amount of alcohol desensitizes the same brain receptors and activates the inhibitory GABA (gamma-aminobutyric acid) system. GABA's task is to calm the central nervous system (CNS) and to promote sleep. Higher doses depress the CNS and initially produce a feeling of relaxation but then lead to intoxication commonly referred to as drunkenness. This is where the person has poor physical coordination (staggering), memory loss, cognitive impairment (confused), slurred speech, and blurred vision. Reaction time is slowed and the ability to make judgments is reduced. High doses can lead to vomiting, coma, and even death.

Alcohol dependence and abuse. Alcohol dependence meets the generic criteria for substance dependence and for most people takes on a progressive course. For instance, when tolerance and withdrawal symptoms are reported in early adulthood the person is at a higher risk for developing a later alcohol use disorder (O'Neill & Sher, 2000). There are three types of brain damage associated with long-term alcohol dependence. One is a degenerative disease of the brain characterized by abnormal eye movements, difficulties with muscle coordination, and confusion known as Wernicke's encephalopathy. Another condition is called Korsakoff's psychosis (or amnesic-confabulatory syndrome), which is a neurological condition involving impairment of memory and cognitive skills such as problem solving and learning. The third condition is alcoholic dementia, sometimes referred to as Wernicke-Korsakoff syndrome, where the person experiences problems with memory and cognitive skills.

Alcohol abuse is considered less severe than dependence and supported by generic substance use criteria but its course is more variable. Unfortunately, both abuse and dependence are often associated with using (or abusing) other substances such as cannabis, cocaine, heroin, the amphetamines, sedatives, or nicotine (Gossop, Marsden, & Stewart, 2002). This combination contributes to increased risks for suicide, accidents, or violence (Canapary, Bongar, & Cleary, 2002).

Alcohol intoxication. When making the diagnosis of alcohol intoxication, the person has recently been drinking and experiences clinically significant maladaptive behavioral or psychological changes such as mood liability, inappropriate sexual or aggressive behavior, impaired judgment, or problems in social or work interactions. Another mental disorder or medical condition does not account for symptoms. One or more of the symptoms shown in Figure 5.1 develop during or shortly after alcohol use.

There are some individuals who binge drink to achieve intoxication or consume a large amount of alcohol in a short period of time. For men this is five or more drinks at a time and for women the amount is usually four or more.

Alcohol withdrawal. A person can experience severe reactions to withdrawing from alcohol such as convulsions, tremors, and mental confusion also referred to as withdrawal

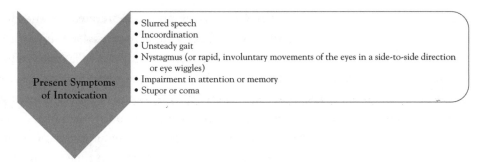

Figure 5.1   Alcohol Intoxication

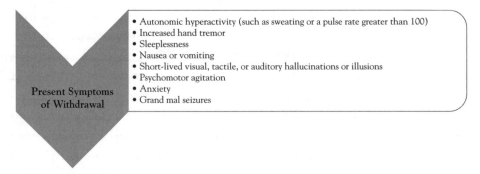

Figure 5.2   Alcohol Withdrawal

delirium or delirium tremens (the DTs). For these reasons, detoxification should take place in carefully monitored settings. The diagnostic criteria for withdrawal are stopping or reducing alcohol use that has been heavy and prolonged. Within several hours to a few days after, a person develops two or more of the symptoms in Figure 5.2.

In rare instances, the specifier "with perceptual disturbances" can be added when hallucinations with intact reality testing or auditory, visual, or tactile illusions occur in the absence of a delirium. The term *intact reality testing* means that the person knows that his or her hallucinations are induced by the substance and do not represent external reality.

Amphetamine- (or Amphetamine-Like) Related Disorders

The amphetamines are commonly referred to as speed or pep pills. They are CNS stimulants and synthetically manufactured, often illegally. They have been around for a long time. For instance, pilots in the military, especially the U.S. Air Force, would use amphetamines (Dexadrine) as stimulants to fight fatigue and increase alertness. They were called go-pills. Interestingly, despite the known dangers of this drug, 65% of the U.S. pilots in the Desert Storm campaign of 1991 were reported to have used an amphetamine compound at least once (Emonson & Vanderbeek, 1995).

The amphetamines are a class of synthetic drugs classified as a Schedule II drug, which means that they have a currently accepted medical use that is severely restricted. They also have a high potential for abuse. The amphetamines are available legally through a prescription by a medical doctor or through sources that illegally manufacture look-alike drugs. They may come in tablet or capsule form. The smokable form looks like shaved glass slivers or clear rock salt that can be swallowed (bomb), ingested through the nose (sniffed or snorted), or injected. A rare method involves rubbing the drug into the gums (dabbing).

Amphetamine dependence and abuse. When either smoked or injected, feelings of an intense sense of euphoria (a feeling of great happiness or well-being) often referred to as a rush or a flash begins quickly and lasts only a few minutes. Tolerance associated with dependence develops rapidly and the person will need larger doses to achieve the same effects. The diagnosis for amphetamine dependence meets the generic criteria for substance dependence. Similarly, the diagnosis for amphetamine abuse meets the generic criteria for substance abuse.

Amphetamine intoxication. Criteria for amphetamine intoxication is characterized by the presence of clinically significant behavioral or psychological changes that are maladaptive; for example, blunted affect (or a lack of emotional reactivity), hyper-vigilance, interpersonal sensitivity, anger, anxiety or tension, changes in sociability, stereotyped behaviors, impaired judgment, and impaired work or social functioning. Shortly after use, two or more of the symptoms in Figure 5.3 occur that cannot be better explained by a general medical condition or a different mental disorder.

Amphetamine withdrawal. When a person stops taking amphetamines, withdrawal symptoms occur. They can begin within a few hours to several days. The effects are the opposite of intoxication and include agitation, anxiety, depression, and exhaustion. The severity of withdrawal symptoms depends on the degree of use/abuse. Crashing

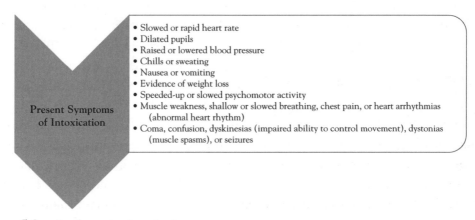

Figure 5.3   Amphetamine Intoxication

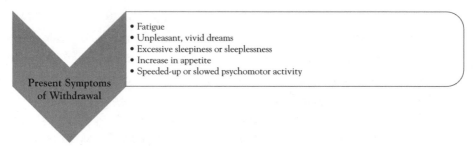

Figure 5.4   Amphetamine Withdrawal

(or a marked withdrawal) often follows an episode of intense high doses or speed runs. The person experiences an intense craving that may later diminish in the face of ensuing depression, fatigue, and insomnia (which strangely enough may be accompanied by a marked need for sleep). The person's fatigue and apathy worsen in the half day (and up to four days) following the crash. Suicide attempts may also result.

The criteria for withdrawal apply to the person who has been using an amphetamine or similar substance heavily and for a long time suddenly stops or markedly reduces his or her intake. Within a few hours (to several days) the person develops a dysphoric mood (a general feeling of unhappiness) and two or more of the symptoms in Figure 5.4 that are not better explained by a general medical condition or a different mental disorder.

Caffeine-Related Disorders

Caffeine is considered a drug because of its stimulating effects on the central nervous system. Although commonly related to coffee and coffee-based drinks like latte, it can be found in a number of beverages; for example soda, some teas, energy drinks, chocolate, and a number of over-the-counter medications like pep pills and cold and flu remedies. The effects of caffeine are to increase alertness, decrease fatigue, and improve muscle coordination.

Caffeine is similar in chemical structure to adenosine, another structure in our bodies whose function is to dilate the blood vessels in the head (among other things). Caffeine blocks this dilation causing a mild stimulating effect on the central nervous system. For that reason, caffeine is commonly found in headache and migraine medications. It also enhances the effects of aspirin.

Most of us have a cup of coffee in the morning just to get us started. Barlow and Durand (2008) estimate that somewhere around 90% of Americans regularly use caffeine in any given year. This substance is legal and generally considered safe, making it the most commonly used and least harmful of the psychoactive substances. It is readily available, generally inexpensive, and the need for the proverbial caffeine-fix does not lead to the compulsive drug-seeking behaviors found in the other substances. It is

Present Symptoms
of Intoxication

- Restlessness
- Nervousness
- Excitement
- Sleeplessness
- Red face
- Increased urination
- Gastrointestinal upset
- Muscle twitching
- Rambling speech
- Rapid or irregular heartbeat
- Periods of tiredlessness
- Speeded up motor activity

Figure 5.5   Caffeine Intoxication

possible to skip that cup of coffee in the morning but you might be left with some side effects like a headache later in the day. Juliano and Griffiths (2004) identified a number of other symptoms such as fatigue, decreased energy or activity, decreased alertness, drowsiness, decreased contentedness, depressed mood, difficulty concentrating, irritability, foggy or not clearheaded, and the flu-like symptoms of nausea, vomiting, and muscle pain or stiffness. Caffeine withdrawal is a diagnostic category listed in the *DSM-IV-TR* for further study (APA, 2000).

Caffeine intoxication. Although it is highly unlikely you will encounter someone in your practice asking for help with caffeine withdrawal (Griffiths, Juliano, & Chausmir, 2003), the *DSM* diagnostic guidelines propose that someone who has recently consumed 250 milligrams of caffeine or the equivalent of just 2½ cups of brewed coffee is eligible for this diagnosis (APA, 2000). Shortly after ingestion, the person experiences five or more of the symptoms in Figure 5.5 that are not better explained by another mental disorder or the result of a medical condition.

Cannabis-Related Disorders

Cannabis is considered the most routinely used illicit drug in the United States. It comes from the leaves, buds, flowers, and resin from the cannabis plant (*Cannabis sativa* or *Cannabis indica*). Native to Central Asia, these plants tend to grow wild and consequently are commonly referred to as weed. Another name is marijuana, which also goes by numerous street names; for example pot, grass, herb, Mary Jane, reefer, skunk, boom, gangster, kif, chronic, and ganga (or ganja).

The plants contain a number of psychoactive compounds (cannabinoids) that are believed to alter mood and behavior. The most potent is delta-9-tetrahydrocannabinol (THC). The THC latches onto specific receptors in the brain known to be involved with appetite regulation and the perception of pain. The most common form of ingestion

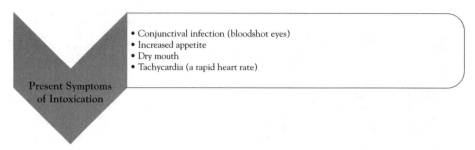

Figure 5.6   Cannabis Intoxication

is smoking, commonly called a joint. When made into a cigar it is referred to as a blunt. If eaten (for example, baked in food such as brownies), the resin has a hallucinogenic effect.

Cannabis dependence and abuse. The diagnostic criteria for cannabis dependence and cannabis abuse follow the generic criteria for substance use. Typically, people who use cannabis enjoy the feeling of relaxation, increased sensory awareness, and elevated mood the drug provides. Those who continuously use cannabis are often seen as passive, lacking ambition, and prone to depression, suspiciousness, panic or anxiety attacks, and impaired judgment.

Cannabis intoxication. When someone has recently ingested cannabis and shows clinically significant maladaptive behavior or psychological changes such as impaired motor coordination, euphoria, anxiety, a sensation of slowed time, impaired judgment, or social withdrawal, consider the diagnosis of intoxication. Two or more of the signs in Figure 5.6 develop within 2 hours that are not better explained by another mental disorder or medical condition.

The specifier "with perceptual disturbances" may be considered.

Cocaine-Related Disorders

Cocaine comes from the leaves of the coca plant (*Erythroxylon coca*), a native of the eastern slopes of the Andes. An addictive drug, it comes in two main forms. One is a white crystalline powder (cocaine hydrochloride) that can be snorted into the nostrils or dissolved in water and injected. Snorting may cause erosion of the membranes inside the nose. When that happens, look for someone with a runny nose, nose bleeds, loss of the sense of smell, hoarseness, and problems swallowing. The second form is crack cocaine hydrochloride that is processed with ammonia or baking soda and water into a freebase cocaine that can be smoked. It looks like chips, chunks, or rocks. When smoked, cocaine reaches the brain very quickly resulting in a rapid high.

Cocaine acts as a powerful stimulator of the CNS. It takes only about 50 to 100 milligrams, considered a typical dose, to rapidly induce feelings of self-confidence, exhilaration, and energy that can last for about 15 to 45 minutes before giving way to fatigue and melancholy. This drug also increases a person's heart rate and blood pressure and very high doses can potentially lead to cardiac arrest and respiratory failure. Cocaine blocks the re-uptake of dopamine, serotonin, and noradrenalin into the neurons leading to higher than normal levels of these neurotransmitters in the brain.

Cocaine dependence and abuse. Cocaine dependence and cocaine abuse follow the generic criteria for dependence and abuse for substance use. Extended use leads to anxiety, depression, suicidal ideation, weight loss, aggressiveness, sexual dysfunction, sleeping problems, and paranoid delusions and hallucinations (Barlow & Durand, 2008). A number of those who are chronic cocaine abusers will go on to develop a drug-induced psychosis that looks very much like paranoid schizophrenia, sometimes referred to as coke paranoia.

Cocaine intoxication. In order to consider cocaine intoxication, the person must have recently used cocaine and show clinically significant maladaptive behavioral changes such as euphoria or affective blunting, changes in sociability, hypervigilance, interpersonal sensitivity, anxiety, tension or anger, stereotyped behaviors, impaired judgment, or impaired social or occupational functioning. Similar to amphetamine intoxication, the person must show two or more of the symptoms in Figure 5.7 that are not better explained by another mental disorder or medical condition. Similarly, the specifier with perceptual disturbances may be considered.

Cocaine withdrawal. Cocaine withdrawal is seen when the person stops or reduces cocaine use that has been heavy and prolonged. The person has a dysphoric mood and shows two or more of the symptoms in Figure 5.8 that are not better explained by another mental disorder or medical condition.

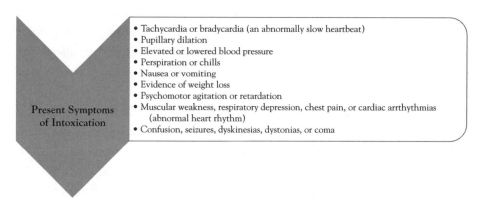

Figure 5.7   Cocaine Intoxication

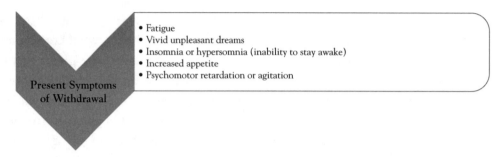

- Fatigue
- Vivid unpleasant dreams
- Insomnia or hypersomnia (inability to stay awake)
- Increased appetite
- Psychomotor retardation or agitation

Present Symptoms of Withdrawal

Figure 5.8   Cocaine Withdrawal

Hallucinogen-Related Disorders

The hallucinogens alter a person's perception and consciousness. The two most commonly used drugs of this class are LSD (acid) and MDMA or ecstasy, which acts as both a stimulant and a hallucinogen. MDMA causes the brain to dump large amounts of serotonin into the synapses and raises dopamine levels. It produces feelings of energy, empathy, openness, and a desire for physical contact, teeth clenching plus mild visual and auditory hallucinations. A number of users describe a hangover the following day characterized by feelings of fatigue, drowsiness, and sore jaw muscles (APA, 2000). MDMA is not considered toxic but can cause death due to overheating and dehydration. It also inhibits the production of urine and can lead to a fatal buildup of fluid in the tissues.

The most widely used hallucinogens are the LSD group. This includes LSD (lysergic acid), LSA (d-lysergic acid amide), mescaline (found in the peyote cactus plant), DMT (dimethyltryptamine, found in ayahuasca), and psilocybin (the main active ingredient found in certain species of mushrooms). The most common is LSD, referred to as acid, which is sold illegally in tablet form, capsules, and occasionally as a liquid (Barlow & Durand, 2008). The effects of the drug tend to peak at 2 to 4 hours and may last for half a day. Those taking the drug often refer to the experience as a trip and adverse reactions are known as a bad trip. A person may also experience flashbacks. The cause of flashbacks is unknown but they can develop weeks or months after the last use of LSD.

Hallucinogen-persisting perception disorder. Hallucinogen-persisting perception disorder, or flashbacks, can be diagnosed with the hallucinogen-related disorders. The essential feature is a transient recurrence of disturbances in a person's perception reminiscent of those experienced during one or more earlier episodes with the hallucinogenic. After stopping the use of a hallucinogen, the person goes on to reexperience one or more of the perceptual symptoms that were encountered while intoxicated with the hallucinogen.

✍ Examples of Perceptual Symptoms

Geometric hallucinations (for example, tunnels and funnels, spirals, lattices, including honeycombs and triangles, and cobwebs)

False perceptions of movement in the peripheral visual fields

Flashes of color

Intensified colors

Trails of images of moving objects

Positive afterimages

Halos around objects

Macropsia (visual perception that objects are larger than they actually are)

Micropsia (or the Alice in Wonderland syndrome where objects are smaller than in reality or what you see in a car's rearview mirror)

Hallucinogen-persisting perception disorder causes clinically significant distress or impairment in a person's social, work, or other important areas of functioning. These symptoms cannot be better accounted for by a general medical condition (such as anatomical lesions and infections of the brain) or by another mental disorder (such as delirium, dementia, schizophrenia) or hypnopompic hallucinations (or hallucinations upon wakening commonly seen in the neurologic sleep disturbance narcolepsy).

Hallucinogen dependence, abuse, and withdrawal. The criteria for hallucinogen dependence and hallucinogen abuse follow the generic criteria for substance use dependence and abuse. Because tolerance to LSD occurs rapidly, it is rarely used for more than once a week. More frequent use does not produce effects worth the trouble of taking the drug more often. The *DSM* does not define a withdrawal syndrome though some people are reported to crave LSD or other hallucinogens after stopping.

Hallucinogen intoxication. The first symptoms of hallucinogen intoxication a person usually experiences are somatic. They may include dizziness, tremor, weakness or numbness, and tingling of the extremities. Perceptual changes, usually illusions, may take place and could also include the apparent amplification of sounds and visual distortions (such as body image) as well as synesthesias (or where one type of sensory experience produces the sensation of another; for example, someone might comment, "Can't you just hear the changing colors on the trees?"). Other behavioral or psychological changes include depression or anxiety, ideas of reference (believing that causal events, remarks, and so forth refer to oneself), fear of becoming insane, persecutory ideas, impaired judgment, and impaired work or social functioning. The specific reactions are influenced by the setting and by the person's expectations. For example, some users find the drug experience pleasant in contrast to others who become anxious. Extremely negative reactions subside within 24 hours or the time it takes to excrete the drug. Shortly after use, two or more of the symptoms in Figure 5.9 occur.

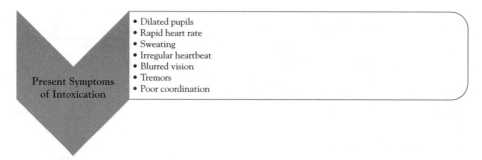

Figure 5.9   Hallucinogen Intoxication

Inhalant-Related Disorders

Inhalant users will breathe almost anything that evaporates or can be sprayed from a container to produce intoxication. These substances can be found in more than 1,000 ordinary household products. The most common are spray paint, paint thinner, gasoline, amyl nitrate (or poppers that are a small and usually brown bottle of solvents), nitrous oxide (laughing gas), nail polish remover, felt-tipped markers, airplane glue, contact cement, dry-cleaning fluid, and spot remover. The inhalants are readily available, inexpensive, and easy to conceal.

Most inhalants act directly on the CNS to produce psychoactive effects. The substances are inhaled and absorbed rapidly by the capillary surface of the lungs. This results in a rapid peak in blood levels. The substances enter the brain rapidly and produce an intensity that resembles the effects produced by an intravenous injection of other psychoactive drugs. The most common form of ingestion involves sniffing the inhalant directly from an open container (bagging) or from a rag soaked in the substance and held to the face (huffing). Either method can cause a high that can last for hours. Some users spray aerosols directly into the nose. Inhalants can cause brain, nerve, and liver damage to the user's body.

Inhalant dependence, abuse, and withdrawal. The criteria for inhalant dependence and abuse follow the generic criteria for substance use dependence and abuse. Heavy and sustained users can develop tolerance within several hours to days after use. Some people develop a rash around the nose and mouth from constant inhalation. Withdrawal is not included in the *DSM*.

Inhalant intoxication. Many of the symptoms of intoxication look like alcohol intoxication with initial excitation followed by drowsiness, disinhibition, lightheadedness, and agitation. Later symptoms include ataxia (unsteady movement and staggering gait), disorientation, and dizziness. More severe intoxication causes insomnia, weakness, trouble speaking, disruptive behavior, and occasionally hallucinations. When diagnosing intoxication, consider that the person has recently and intentionally used

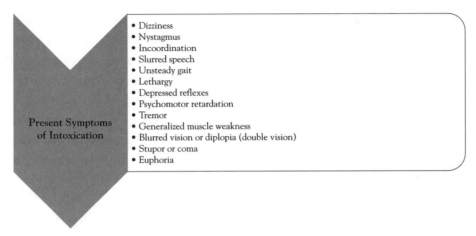

Present Symptoms of Intoxication

- Dizziness
- Nystagmus
- Incoordination
- Slurred speech
- Unsteady gait
- Lethargy
- Depressed reflexes
- Psychomotor retardation
- Tremor
- Generalized muscle weakness
- Blurred vision or diplopia (double vision)
- Stupor or coma
- Euphoria

Figure 5.10   Inhalant Intoxication

volatile inhalants or has had brief high-dose exposure to them. During this experience (or shortly after) the person develops clinically significant behavioral or psychological changes that are maladaptive; including, for example, apathy, assaultiveness or belligerence, impaired judgment, and impaired work or social functioning. The physical symptoms of intoxication that you might look for are two or more of the symptoms in Figure 5.10.

Nicotine-Related Disorders

Nicotine is a poisonous and oily liquid found in the nightshade family of plants called *Nicotiana tabacum*. Nicotine is ingested in various ways; that is, through the smoke in cigarettes, cigars and pipe tobacco, or though smokeless tobacco (chewing), and snuff (finely ground tobacco that is snuffed into the nose or dipped and held in the cheek or lower lip). Although these products contain other ingredients, it is the nicotine in tobacco that causes dependence.

Nicotine in tobacco smoke rides on small particles of tar. The smoke with the nicotine and tar mixture is absorbed by the lungs and within about 7 seconds reaches the smoker's brain. This is an efficient drug-delivery system because about 90% of inhaled nicotine is actually absorbed. The nicotine from smokeless tobacco is absorbed more slowly but more nicotine per dose is absorbed than from cigarettes. Consider that holding an average-size chew (or dip) in the mouth for 30 minutes will provide the user with as much nicotine as smoking four cigarettes. Also, the nicotine stays in the bloodstream for a longer time.

Neurochemical changes also occur in the brain, which suggests that a limited exposure to nicotine can initiate dependence in the user. Nicotine mimics the effect of acetylcholine (or the neurotransmitter in the brain that appears to be involved in learning and memory), causing the release of acetylcholine and norepinephrine. The user experiences a sense of release from stress and may even experience feelings of euphoria. Additional physical effects may involve an increase in blood pressure and heart rate, faster respiration, constriction of the arteries producing a cool, pale skin, and stimulation of the central nervous system. At high doses, a person may experience convulsions. Chronic use of nicotine can lead to changes in the brain and therefore in one's behavior. Nicotine is highly addictive as it provides almost immediate results from the neurochemical changes in the brain (National Institute on Drug Abuse, 2005).

Nicotine dependence. Some of the generic criteria for dependence that apply to nicotine require further explanation. Tolerance, for example, is shown by a more intense effect of nicotine the first time it is used during the day. Nicotine is not stored in the body so its effects last a short time. It metabolizes fairly quickly and disappears within a few minutes. As the day continues, nicotine has less of an effect causing the person to need to absorb more and more nicotine in order to be able to experience its effects.

Stopping the use of nicotine use produces a well-defined withdrawal syndrome and many people will take nicotine to relieve (or avoid) the unpleasant withdrawal symptoms as soon as they wake up in the morning. I remember the mother of one of my good friends would smoke her first cigarette while she was taking her morning shower. Another criterion, amount, or duration of use is greater than intended, can be seen when the person uses up his or her supply of cigarettes (or other nicotine products) faster than originally intended. Repeated efforts to control or reduce substance use is evident when the person who smokes talks about his or her desire to stop. Many actually do try to quit smoking but few are successful (Hughes, 2004). The symptom described as spending a great deal of time using the substance can best be characterized by chain smoking. People do not need to spend a great deal of time attempting to obtain nicotine. Like caffeine, nicotine is legal, easy to obtain, and relatively cheap compared to some of the other substances; heroin, for example. Giving up or reducing important social, work, or recreational activities can be seen when a person avoids going to places where smoking is restricted. Continued use despite knowing the problems the substance can cause is apparent when an individual continues to smoke despite having a tobacco-induced medical condition like bronchitis or chronic obstructive lung disease.

Nicotine withdrawal. The symptoms of withdrawal are the upshot of when a person tries to stop using nicotine. The diagnosis is made when someone who has used nicotine for at least several weeks abruptly stops using nicotine. Within 24 hours they show four or more of the symptoms in Figure 5.11.

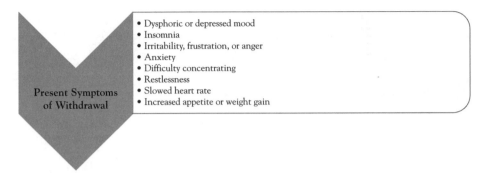

Figure 5.11   Nicotine Withdrawal

Opioid-Related Disorders

The opiates relax the user. You may have heard the expression, "going on the nod"; that is, the person goes back and forth from feeling alert to drowsy. The term *opioid* comes from *opium,* a narcotic resin extracted from the unripe seed pods of the opium poppy (*Papaver somniferum*). Widely used as pain relievers, the opioids are a class of drugs that depress the CNS. The opioids include naturally occurring alkaloids such as morphine and derivatives of these (such as heroin) and synthetic compounds (such as methadone). The prescription opiates include morphine, meperidine (Demerol), methadone, codeine, and various drugs for coughing and pain. They come in a variety of forms such as capsules, tablets, syrups, solutions, and suppositories. Illicit opioids include heroin, considered as the most devastating of the opioid drugs. Heroin is a white or brownish powder that is usually dissolved in water and then injected into a vein (mainlining) or into a muscle. More recent ingestion methods include smoking through a water pipe (or standard pipe), mixed in with a marijuana joint or cigarette, inhaled as smoke through a straw (called chasing the dragon), or inhaled as powder through the nose. Heroin has several times the power of morphine to produce euphoria and blunt the perception of pain. First-time opioid users often experience vomiting and dysphoria.

Opioid dependence and abuse. Opioid dependence follows the generic criteria for substance-use dependence. Tolerance makes it necessary for the person to use increasing doses of opioids in order to achieve the same effects. Regular use induces physical dependence that develops within the first few doses. A person's life quickly becomes dominated by the pursuit and use of the drug. Once addicted or hooked, a person will go to almost any length to obtain drugs. The generic criteria for abuse described for substance use are used to make the diagnosis of opioid abuse.

Opioid intoxication. When injected, the effects of an opioid are felt almost immediately (called a rush). Depending on the effects on an individual, this is rapidly followed

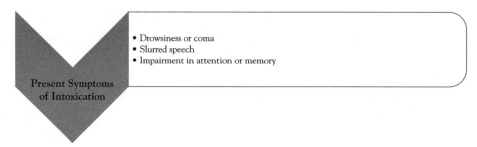

- Drowsiness or coma
- Slurred speech
- Impairment in attention or memory

Present Symptoms
of Intoxication

Figure 5.12   Opioid Intoxication

by a sense of euphoria, drowsiness, the perception of warmth, a dry mouth, and heaviness in the extremities. Some may experience a flushed face and itchy nose. Opioid intoxication is considered when the person has recently used an opioid and shows clinically maladaptive behavioral or psychological changes such as euphoria followed by apathy, dysphoria, psychomotor agitation (or retardation), impaired judgment, or impaired social or work functioning that developed during (or shortly after) opioid use. The person's pupils constrict or you might find papillary dilation due to anoxia (absence of oxygen supply to an organ or a tissue) from severe overdose. Opioid intoxication includes one or more of the symptoms in Figure 5.12 and are not better explained by another mental disorder or medical condition.

You might encounter a client who comes to an interview wearing dark glasses. For some people this might be a fashion statement but for the opioid user it is more than likely a strategy to hide their pupils. If you suspect that your client is an opioid user, ask the client to remove his or her glasses. Other physical signs might be scarring of the arms or other places where veins are prominent resulting from long-term injection use of heroin.

Phencyclidine- (or Phencyclidine-Like) Related Disorders

The phencyclidine-related disorders are a class of hallucinogens that produce feelings of depersonalization and a sense of detachment from reality. This is appealing to the occasional drug user who values escapism. Known as designer drugs, the chemical structure of the known drugs of abuse have been manipulated to produce a seemingly endless lineup of new drugs. The phencyclidines include phencyclidine (PCP, Sernylan) and ketamine (Ketalar, Ketaject), which is a derivative of cyclohexamine and phencyclidine. Another dissociative drug is dizocilpine (DZ, MK-108). However, because PCP is inexpensive and easy to produce (it literally can be mixed in a bathtub) it continues to be popular with those who value it for the euphoria that it produces.

PCP, a white crystalline powder with a distinctively bitter chemical taste, is a hallucinogen. Popularly called angel dust, at least 30 forms of the drug have been identified

(Doweiko, 2006). PCP comes in tablet, capsule, and colored powders and can be snorted, smoked, injected, or eaten. If smoked, symptoms begin within a few minutes and if swallowed, symptoms generally begin within an hour of use. It is a highly potent drug that can produce psychotic symptoms that are sometimes hard to distinguish from schizophrenia. PCP's addictive potential is pronounced.

Ketamine is a surgical anesthetic that surfaced as a recreational drug in the 1990s with the rave scene. Although it can be manufactured in illicit laboratories the process is difficult so most of the drug is diverted from human or veterinary supplies (Gahlinger, 2004). The drug comes in powdered form by drying ketamine in a stove. It is usually inhaled (snorted) but sometimes smoked by sprinkling the drug on tobacco or marijuana. Depending on the dose, effects begin within 30 to 45 minutes and can last for up to 2 hours. Because of its effect on memory, it is popular as a date-rape drug.

Dizocilpine is an anticonvulsant originally developed to treat traumatic brain injury and neurodegenerative diseases such as Huntington's, Alzheimer's, and amyotrophic lateral sclerosis (ALS) or Lou Gehrig's disease. The legal development of the drug was stopped when neurotoxic-like effects were seen in certain regions of the brain. Some recreational users report unpleasant experiences such as strong aural (or auditory) hallucinations.

Phencyclidine dependence and abuse. The generic criteria for substance-use dependence apply to dependence but some of the craving criteria do not apply. Although those who heavily use the drug report cravings, the symptoms of tolerance and withdrawal are not clearly demonstrated. Phencyclidine is easy to obtain and therefore a person might use the drug several times a day, spending a significant part of the day using the substance. In addition, the person might continue to use the drug despite psychological or medical problems. He or she might also get into situations, such as fighting, that could lead to legal problems.

Generic criteria for substance abuse apply to phencyclidine abuse. Although some individuals may use the drug less often than people with dependence, they may still encounter problems at home, work, or with relationships. Legal problems are common, such as driving while under the influence of the drug.

Phencyclidine intoxication. Intoxication is considered when a person experiences two or more of the symptoms in Figure 5.13 within an hour (if swallowed) or less (if smoked, snorted, or used intravenously). A medical condition or another medical condition does not better explain the symptom picture.

The person also shows clinically significant maladaptive behavioral changes such as belligerence, assaultiveness, impulsiveness, unpredictability, psychomotor agitation, impaired judgment, or impaired social or occupational functioning that developed during (or shortly after) phencyclidine use.

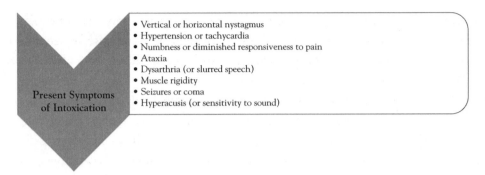

Figure 5.13   Phencyclidine Intoxication

Sedative-, Hypnotic-, or Anxiolytic-Related Disorders

Sedatives, hypnotics, and anxiolytics are used for different purposes. The sedatives have a calming effect, the hypnotics are sleep-inducing, and the anxiolytics are anxiety reducing. However, they all share the common symptoms of intoxication and withdrawal. The major drugs included in this class of substances are the benzodiazepines such as diazepam (Valium) and alprazolam (Xanax), and the barbiturates, such as pentobarbital (Nembutal). Other classes include the carbamates and the barbiturate-like hypnotics.

The benzodiazepines and the barbiturates are Schedule IV drugs under the Federal Controlled Substances Act, which means that they are considered to be accepted for medical use and must be prescribed by a physician, physician assistant, or nurse practitioner. They are used to reduce tension, irritability, agitation, and serious anxiety. Users value them for the disinhibition they produce, meaning that they induce a feeling of euphoria, reduce anxiety and guilt, and boost self-confidence and energy.

Sedative, hypnotic, or anxiolytic dependence and abuse. The generic criteria for substance-use dependence and abuse do not differ substantially for sedative, hypnotic, and anxiolytic abuse and dependence. Both dependence on sedatives, hypnotics, and anxiolytics and their abuse involve maladaptive behavioral changes, mood changes, impaired judgment, impaired social or occupational functioning, impaired speech, coordination problems, and an unsteady gait.

Abuse generally happens in two ways. Initially, some people may start with a prescription for insomnia or anxiety and then begin to increase the dose to varying degrees. Abuse may also occur in conjunction with the use of other substances, often to mitigate the undesired effects of other drugs. For example, a person might use an intoxicating dose of a benzodiazepine to come down from a cocaine high or ease the symptoms of heroin withdrawal.

Sedative, hypnotic, or anxiolytic intoxication and withdrawal. As with most drugs, the specific effects are dependent on the setting where they are consumed and the expectations of the user. Mood is often labile ranging from euphoria to hostility and depression. Loss of memory, similar to alcohol consumption, can also be seen. In fact, the diagnostic symptoms for sedative, hypnotic, and anxiolytic intoxication are exactly the same for alcohol intoxication.

Withdrawal can be seen when the person abruptly stops taking the drug. Here, too, the withdrawal symptoms for sedatives, hypnotics, and anxiolytics are identical to the symptoms for alcohol withdrawal. Once the person has stopped taking the drugs, the symptoms that originally led them to seek relief in the first place may reemerge; for example, anxiety, agitation, and insomnia. The diagnostic challenge is to distinguish this symptom picture from withdrawal symptoms. Paying attention to duration may be useful. That is, any symptoms that remain or newly emerge two to three weeks after the drug has been stopped are probably the old or original symptoms reemerging.

FINAL THOUGHTS

The mind-altering substances discussed in this chapter all yield four basic types of disorder and they are summarized as substance-use or substance-induced disorders. There are 11 classes of substances listed in the *DSM* and with few exceptions; all yield to these four basic types.

The *DSM* provides a listing of the specific diagnoses associated with the class of substances. I have adapted this format to summarize these substance-related disorders and list each by class of substances and diagnostic codes.

Substance-Use Disorders	Substance-Induced Disorders
Substance dependence—Seen as taking a substance frequently enough to produce clinically important distress or impaired functioning along with certain behavioral characteristics. It is seen in all classes of drugs *except* caffeine.	*Substance intoxication*—Considered an acute clinical condition that results from recent overuse of a substance. This designation applies to a person who uses a substance only once. All drugs *except* nicotine have a specific syndrome of intoxication.
Substance abuse—Considered a residual category where substance use produced problems for the person but symptoms do not meet criteria for substance dependence. It applies to all classes of substances *except* caffeine and nicotine.	*Substance withdrawal*—This is a collection of symptoms specific for the class of substance that develops when the person who has frequently used a substance stops or markedly reduces the amount used. It applies to all classes of substances *except* caffeine, cannabis, PCP, the hallucinogens, and the inhalants that have an officially recognized withdrawal syndrome.

PRACTICING THE COMPETENCY-BASED ASSESSMENT

The identification and assessment of the substance-related disorders poses a number of challenges for professionals. Conducting the competency-based assessment is more than learning how to apply the empirically supported diagnostic criteria found in the *DSM*. The following case illustrations provide a small glimpse into this challenge.

Case Illustrations

Case studies offer opportunities to put the competency-based assessment into action rather than memorize information about diagnostic criteria for each of the classes of substances. The following scenarios help to foster an appreciation of the interdependence of substances with the various aspects of the client's life and to apply knowledge about substance-use to realistic situations. We begin by turning our attention to Georgette Turnbull.

The Case of Georgette Turnbull

Georgette told the practitioner, "This is my benzo story. It all started with my accident a couple of years ago. I suppose you want to hear it from the beginning. Okay, here goes. It all started after my husband Frank retired from his career as a fireman and we moved to a small rural community in the foothills of the Appalachian mountains."

The setting was idyllic and at first the couple enjoyed the leisurely pace of small town life. Prior to her retirement, Georgette had worked as an office manager and did not miss her hectic schedule. She found that people in her new town were really nice and laid back. Georgette enjoyed the southern culture and the friendly small town atmosphere. Unfortunately, Frank felt confined and he soon became restless with all the free time that came with his retirement. After a few months he took a job as a carpenter's helper for a local contractor. This left Georgette with long hours alone in their house in the country. She didn't mind at all. It gave her the opportunity to work in her garden, a hobby she had always wanted to pursue. She also started canning and preserving what she had grown. Unfortunately, it turns out that being home alone was not such a good thing for Georgette after all.

One afternoon on her way into town to pick up some groceries, Georgette swerved her pickup truck to avoid some wild turkeys crossing the road. She lost control and hit a tree on the passenger's side. The accident left her with a crushed pelvis. After what seemed like a prolonged hospitalization and rehabilitation, Georgette gradually started getting around again with the use of a walker. Before he left for the day, Frank would put a bench out in the yard for Georgette to work in her garden. Things were finally getting back to normal, or so she thought. Her muscle spasms changed all that.

In retrospect, Georgette thought that the spasms were probably there all along but she didn't notice them until she started working in her garden again. "Maybe I put too much strain on myself," she said. One afternoon, Georgette remembered reaching over to pull an errant weed and felt excruciating cramps in the muscles of her lower back. She called Frank, who came home, took one look at her, and immediately rushed his wife to the emergency room. The emergency room doctor gave Georgette an injection of Valium to relax her muscles. "It was like heaven. The Valium worked like a charm. It calmed my nerves, my pain, and helped me rest," remembered Georgette.

Before the accident, Georgette always thought of herself as in good health. Her only hospitalizations were for the birth of her two children. She never drank alcohol or smoked and rarely even took an aspirin. "Mental illness is common in my family and my brother is schizophrenic. He was a heavy cannabis user so I was always afraid that I could possibly get addicted," Georgette told her doctor when she went to see him the following day. Her doctor said she was anemic and gave her several iron injections. He also prescribed Valium, 5 mg twice a day.

Georgette remembered thinking at the time, "Valium has to be the number one muscle relaxer out there, but highly addictive. I have to be very careful how I take it. I remember my mother was on barbiturates and that was horrible. But the doctor said it was okay."

For about three years everything was fine and the Valium was causing no problems, at least that Georgette knew of. She was sleeping well and eventually resumed all of her activities. "Then about a year or so ago, I remember starting to feel strange in the mornings. It was like I had this need to take more Valium, which I started to do," Georgette told her practitioner. "Funny, but it worked. I went through one bottle after another and when I went for my checkups, the doctor just asked me if I needed another refill. Somewhere along the way, I discovered the wonderful world of Internet drugs. I could get anything I wanted and overnight, too," she added. More and more of her time was taken up each week to obtain her supply.

"So here was my routine. I would take one pill first thing in the morning and then jump into the shower. Almost 15 minutes later, I would start to feel slower, drowsier, and more relaxed. It wasn't exactly an unpleasant feeling but there was nothing really great about it either. If I took two pills before lunch, I would lie down after eating a sandwich and watch TV. I could already feel them kick in. The intensity rapidly increased and it was hard to keep my eyes entirely open, but the funny thing is I didn't really feel the need to sleep either. This feeling of relaxation was intensified but movement would be increasingly difficult as time went by. I was glad to be home alone so Frank wouldn't notice the changes in me, though he did start to complain that I had changed. He said I had become moody and wasn't listening to him. It was as if I had trouble following a conversation. Now if I took five pills, I could feel the first effects right away. The usual wave of relaxation and calmness would overcome me then followed by extreme drowsiness. I could shake the drowsiness, though, but if I dropped my guard, sleep would come easily and quickly. Some days I would just sleep in front of the TV. My garden has been so neglected. It was hard to move steadily and I constantly stumbled around if I did move," said Georgette.

She continued, "I knew by this time that something was very wrong. I started to do some research on the Internet and realized that I was addicted to the Valium. By this time I was up to 30 mgs a day. I got scared and went to my doctor and told him what I was doing. He said what I needed to do was cut back. He also said I could come to see you . . . so here I am."

How would you formulate your competency-based assessment for Georgette Turnbull?

The Case of Frankie Singer

Frankie is a 16-year-old adolescent who was admitted to the detention center. His intake report indicated that he seemed reluctant to talk to anybody and that he answered questions reluctantly giving mostly yes or no responses. However, he did seem to relate to the counseling intern who was assigned to complete his psychosocial history. The intern, Mary Margaret Straughn, remembered her first encounter with Frankie. When she entered the admissions area, she thought she heard Frankie mumble something under his breath that sounded like, "Oh, sh__. Another f__kin 'do-gooder' therapist. Well, at least she can't remove me from my home 'cause that's already been done."

Before meeting with Frankie, the intern reviewed his file. Court records indicated that Frankie was currently enrolled in the ninth grade at a school located in what Mary Margaret recognized as one of the worst sections in town. The school report documented a long history of suspensions and truancies that started when he was about 9 years old. His grades are poor and it looked like he certainly had not been promoted on his academic success.

Frankie's behavior problems started when he was about 4 years old, the time he was initially placed in foster care. His mother was a well-known crack addict and the most recent home investigation indicated that her current live-in boyfriend had an extensive police record, mainly for assault and battery. Frankie's mother was seen as neglecting Frankie's two younger half-siblings by different fathers and they, too, were removed from her care. Apparently for the past 12 years, Frankie's mother had been in and out of a number of drug treatment programs as she struggled to stay sober. During that time, Frankie had been placed in a number of foster homes. Because of his behavior, his home placements usually did not last long. He was reported to be a youngster who often lost his temper and argued with his foster parents. An early psychological evaluation characterized Frankie as someone who is often angry and resentful. Frankie's had periods where his behavior seemed to improve and usually during the times he was reunited with his mother when she was able to stay sober. Unfortunately, Frankie's mother continued to relapse and Frankie was returned to the care of the state child welfare system.

This is Frankie's second admission to the detention center. His first occurred when he was 14 years old. At that time, Frankie was observed to have few friends and was characterized as a loner. Unfortunately, it was during that stay when he was introduced to the "Players," a local street gang. Subsequent court records documented a history of numerous charges for property destruction, breaking and entering into residential homes, and stealing radios and other valuable electronic equipment from cars. His most recent charge involved an armed robbery. During this admission, Frankie was charged with a felony theft and public intoxication. His school truancy and suspensions have continued.

After reading Frankie's record, the intern felt overwhelmed and rationalized to herself that working with Frankie would be a good learning experience. Mary Margaret wanted to specialize in working with adolescents after she graduated and was glad to have a really good supervisor here at the detention center. "How can I empathize with this kid's experiences," wondered Mary Margaret. She remembered that when she was growing up her father was in the military and she moved around frequently. "The only difference was that I had my family," reflected Mary Margaret. "And they loved and supported me. Here, I get the picture of a youngster whose father is not even mentioned and his mother has always struggled with problems of her own like substance abuse. Guess she had no energy left over to raise Frankie or his half-siblings. Surely this parental rejection and the constant series of unsuccessful foster care placements must have contributed to feelings of low self-esteem for Frankie. Poor academic performance and belonging to a gang sure didn't help either," she thought.

Undaunted, the intern approached Frankie and invited him to tell her his story. She was surprised by his candor about his affiliation with the Players. "I have some friends in here, you know," he added with a conspiratorial tone. "But don't ask me about my court charges. F__k, I guess it's safe to talk about my initiation. You see, when you drink, you're a man . . . and I'm the man. We have contests to see how much and how fast we can down the stuff," added Frankie. He continued in a condescending singsong voice, "Well, Miss Mary Margaret you look clueless. Let me explain. You see I was actin' the other night and that's when I got arrested. Know what I mean?" Mary Margaret started to have a sinking feeling at this point. She felt that Frankie was deliberately using slang as a way to make fun of her . . . and it was working. She guessed that Frankie was talking about binge drinking, but she was afraid to ask. Frankie was slumped in his chair and his hat shaded his eyes so it was hard for her to gauge how he was really feeling. He shifted slightly and continued, "So now I guess you're gonna ask me about LSD. They all do. That's in my record, too. Well, if you must know, me and my friends like to get fried. We like a little LSD every now and then. Doesn't everybody?" Frankie then sat up in his chair, and looked directly into Mary Margaret's eyes. She was sure he could see her embarrassment. He asked, "So Miss Counselor, what do you do for a good time?" Mary Margaret was starting to get annoyed at this point. Not only did she object to Frankie's foul language, she also didn't like the way the conversation was making her feel so inept. "Well, I guess this is what they call the resistant client," reflected Mary Margaret.

How would you formulate your competency-based assessment for Frankie Singer?

PRACTICAL APPLICATIONS

This chapter began with the suggestion that most of us have used psychoactive substances at one time or another. Beyond the legal drugs of alcohol, nicotine, or caffeine, some of you may have even had occasional experiences with illegal substances such as smoking grass (marijuana), snorting some candy (cocaine), or even swallowing a little black beauty (amphetamine). Most of us do not abuse drugs and simply rationalize occasional use by telling ourselves that it is okay as long as it does not interfere with our work or social relationships. Unfortunately, the substance-related disorders are one of the most prevalent mental health problems in the United States (Vuchinich, 2002). In keeping with the comprehensive framework of the competency-based assessment, the following three activities are intended to expand your understanding of the struggles that clients encounter with the substance-related disorders and the challenges they present.

1. Reflect back on the case of Frankie Singer. Imagine for a moment that he is one of your clients. What feelings do his behavior and pattern of substance abuse evoke for you?
   a. Describe how can you develop a relationship with this youngster and what might possibly get in your way of developing an empathic connection with him.
   b. Identify what you need to do to remain objective when conducting your competency-based assessment.
2. Many practitioners enter the counseling field based on personal life experiences with the substance-related disorders and related life problems. Reflect back on your own experiences related to substance use and identify how they might apply to your work in this area. Alternatively, find a colleague who you know has struggled with substances and ask this person about his feelings and reactions. How do they compare with your thoughts and ideas?
3. Case studies have often been used as a framework for discussion in classes about psychopathology, mental health, or human growth and development to list a few. Select one of the cases in this chapter and in a small group with fellow students challenge yourselves to think about the many issues involved in the problem of substance use. Develop a series of questions you would ask to formulate the competency-based assessment for the client's substance use. How could these assessment questions be generalized to other client situations?

Appendix

Competency-Based Assessments for Chapter 5 Case Examples: Listing of Case Diagnoses

Figures 5A.1 through 5A.4 provide the diagnostic assessment for each of the cases illustrated. They are organized in the order that they appear in each chapter.

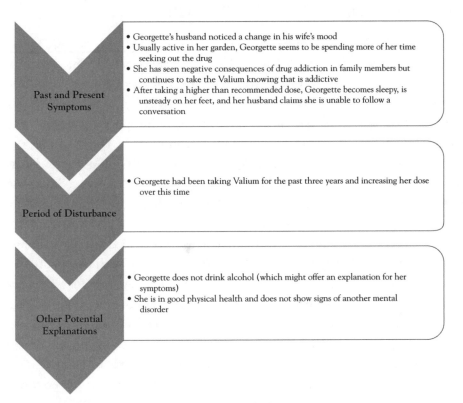

Past and Present Symptoms
- Georgette's husband noticed a change in his wife's mood
- Usually active in her garden, Georgette seems to be spending more of her time seeking out the drug
- She has seen negative consequences of drug addiction in family members but continues to take the Valium knowing that is addictive
- After taking a higher than recommended dose, Georgette becomes sleepy, is unsteady on her feet, and her husband claims she is unable to follow a conversation

Period of Disturbance
- Georgette had been taking Valium for the past three years and increasing her dose over this time

Other Potential Explanations
- Georgette does not drink alcohol (which might offer an explanation for her symptoms)
- She is in good physical health and does not show signs of another mental disorder

Figure 5A.1   The Conceptual Map for Georgette Turnbull

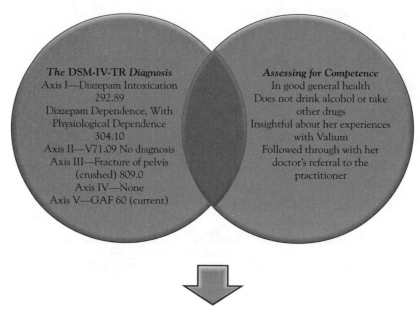

Figure 5A.2   The Competency-Based Assessment for Georgette Turnbull

CASE REVIEW FOR GEORGETTE TURNBULL

Georgette started taking Valium in order to relieve severe muscle spasms experienced after an auto accident that caused a crushed (fractured) pelvis. She had been taking the drug for several years. Georgette's husband started to notice a change in his wife's mood, which could be considered the psychological change found in diazepam intoxication. She was extremely drowsy and unsteady on her feet, as well. However Georgette shared that she does not drink so alcohol could be ruled out to better explain her reactions and behaviors. You might consider the presence of dependence because Georgette was taking more than the maximum recommended dose of Valium. She was also spending more and more time obtaining the drug. Although she was fearful of an addiction and had seen the negative consequences of barbiturate addiction in her mother and cocaine use in her brother, Georgette continued to take Valium.

Georgette describes her Valium experiences in some detail with the practitioner and seems motivated to work on her dependence on the drug. At her doctor's suggestion, she voluntarily followed through with the referral. Her husband is out of the house because of his job, but he did take his wife for emergency care when needed. Another aspect of competence in Georgette's story is that she seems to have good insight into her dependence on Valium and how it has impacted her life. In addition, having a brother who was described as both mentally ill and a heavy cannabis user contributed to her stated fear of becoming addicted to drugs.

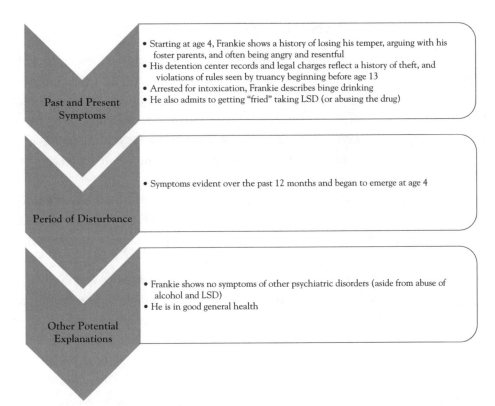

Figure 5A.3   The Conceptual Map for Frankie Singer

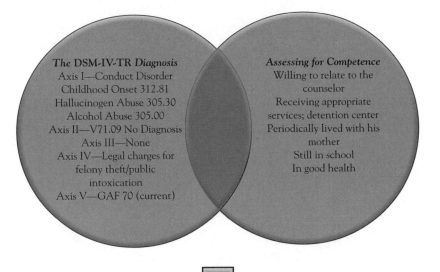

Figure 5A.4   The Competency-Based Assessment for Frankie Singer

CASE REVIEW FOR FRANKIE SINGER

Frankie's history reflects the main features of diagnostic criteria for conduct disorder beginning at a very early age. He is seen as argumentative, and has a history of aggression shown by stealing items. Unfortunately, his last charge reflects confronting his victim via an armed robbery. He clearly violates social rules with his long history of truancy and suspensions from school starting when he was about 9 years old. Psychological reports describe Frankie as angry and resentful. While in foster care he often lost his temper and argued with his foster parents.

This is Frankie's second admission to the detention center; during his first admission he was introduced into a local street gang. It is unclear when his substance abuse (alcohol and LSD) began, but one wonders whether this was part of gang membership and involvement because it is not mentioned earlier in his records.

The practitioner is hard-pressed to find strengths and competency in Frankie's story but it ought to be pointed out that he is in a detention center where presumably counseling and vocational services would be available. Though his prognosis with an early onset of conduct disorder is not particularly favorable, he is in a facility where assistance is available. Further, though he taunts his counselor, Frankie does on some level seem willing to engage with her. He is also in school, in good health, and does have somewhat of a relationship with his mother. Although we cannot predict Frankie's future, the elements to counterbalance a troubled history, low self-esteem, poor academic performance, delinquency, and associations with a deviant peer group (the Players gang) are in place.

6

Schizophrenia and Other Psychotic Disorders

INTRODUCTION

The psychotic disorders are a group of illnesses that primarily affect the mind. They are a category of severe mental disorders where the person's personality is seriously disorganized and contact with reality is impaired. The person becomes affected to a degree where he or she is unable to think clearly, make good judgments, respond emotionally, communicate effectively, understand reality, and behave appropriately. The person simply loses touch with reality. There are a number of notable examples of the psychotic disorders. One is John Forbes Nash Jr., the 1994 Nobel Prize winner in economics. A gifted mathematician who was obsessed with finding an original idea to ensure his legacy, John Nash spent years searching for secret messages in numbers. Though he was a promising graduate student, he succumbed to auditory hallucinations that contributed to his struggles to hold a job. His wife eventually divorced him after he became increasingly paranoid and started to behave erratically (though she steadfastly remained a source of support). The couple eventually remarried. Nash was ultimately able to live with and largely ignore his psychotic episodes. He went on to achieve success in his field of math and received the Nobel Prize. A popular movie based on a book with the same title by Sylvia Nasar was made in 2001 chronicling his experiences entitled *A Beautiful Mind*, starring the actor Russell Crowe.

Another well-known example is John Hinckley. In 1981 he made the news headlines when he attempted to assassinate President Ronald Reagan. He was obsessed with the award-winning actress Jodie Foster and believed that he could win her love by taking extreme measures to impress her. Both men were eventually diagnosed with schizophrenia.

During a psychotic episode, the person is confused about reality and often experiences delusions, hallucinations, bizarre behavior, incoherent or disorganized speech, and/or disorganized behavior. Symptoms vary from person to person and may change over time. The competency-based assessment provides a framework to consider the full range of the person's experience with the different types of psychotic disorders.

INCIDENCE AND PREVALENCE

The first signs of the psychotic disorders generally appear when a person is in his or her late teens, twenties, or thirties (B. Sadock & V. Sadock, 2007). A study by Goldner, Hsu, Waraich, and Somers (2002) reports the lifetime prevalence or the proportion of individuals expected to experience a psychotic disorder at 0.55%. Most psychotic disorders tend to occur equally for males and females but the onset for men seems earlier or at ages 20 to 28, as compared to women who are affected at ages 26 to 32 years. Childhood and middle or old age onset is considered rare (Hassett, Ames, & Chiu, 2005; Kumra, Shaw, Merka, Nakayama, & Augustin, 2001). In general, the earlier the onset of symptoms, the more severe the illness is for the person. The disorganized type of schizophrenia tends to start earlier or in adolescence or young adulthood. Paranoid-type schizophrenia tends to start later or at the age of 25 or 30 (American Psychiatric Association, 2000).

Schizophrenia. The lifetime prevalence of schizophrenia is approximately 0.4% to 0.6% of the entire population affecting a wide range of cultures and countries both developed and developing (Bhugra, 2006; Goldner, Hsu, Waraich, & Sommers, 2002). It is estimated that about 1.5 million people worldwide will be diagnosed annually (Murray & Jones, 2003) and appears to be the same for men and women up to age 60 years. About 20% to 40% of those with schizophrenia will experience their first psychotic symptoms before age 20. About 100,000 to 200,000 new cases are anticipated every year in the United States or 7.2 people per 1,000 (Moore & Jefferson, 2004). Schizophrenia is not a common diagnosis, but it is considered to be a serious and chronic disease.

There are a number of sociodemographic factors that have been linked with a greater risk for developing schizophrenia. For example, poverty and membership in a lower social class have long been associated with higher rates of schizophrenia (Mueser & McGurk, 2004; Mulvany, O'Callaghan, Takei, Byrne, & Fearon, 2001). It has been speculated that this association could be due to a lack of proper health care during fetal development or that symptoms are more visible than those of a more privileged social class due to delayed treatment. Those who live in urban areas are also more likely to develop schizophrenia than those living in rural areas (van Os, 2004; van Os, Krabbendam, Myin-Germeys, & Delespaul, 2005). Migration is also considered to be a contributor to a higher risk for schizophrenia especially as it relates to social adversity, racial discrimination, family dysfunction, unemployment or poor housing conditions

(Selten, Cantor-Graae, & Kahn, 2007). Abuse or trauma experienced in childhood is also seen as a risk factor for developing schizophrenia later in life (Janssen et al., 2004; Schenkel, Spaulding, Dilillo, & Silverstein, 2005).

OVERVIEW OF MAJOR SYMPTOMS

There are a number of warning signs associated with the psychotic disorders. The most prominent symptoms include delusions and hallucinations as well as bizarre behavior, strange incoherent or disorganized thinking/speech, social withdrawal as well as other symptoms such as difficulty remembering, maintaining a consistent attention span, ability for abstract thinking, and planning ahead or displaying strange movements.

Psychosis describes characteristics and behaviors that encompass delusions, hallucinations, disorganized (or catatonic behavior), incoherent or disorganized speech, aimless agitation or total immobility and a level of affect that ranges from apathy and

Major Symptoms of the Psychotic Disorders

Symptom	Definition	Example
Delusions	Delusions are false or fixed beliefs that are based on incorrect deductions or misrepresentations of reality. These beliefs are not normative within the person's cultural or religious group. These false beliefs persist despite incontrovertible, obvious proof of their falsity.	A person with schizophrenia may believe that he or she is the President of the United States. These persons may have delusions that the police are spying on them or believe that creatures from outer space have special devices that are able to control their thoughts.
Hallucinations	Hallucinations are experiences of sensory events in the absence of actual environmental stimulation. A person may feel, smell, taste, see, and/or hear things that are not really there. Auditory hallucinations are especially common in schizophrenia.	The persons may hear voices that command them to do something when no one else is around.
Disorganized or bizarre behavior	Bizarre behavior is a pattern of conduct or demeanor that is far removed from normal and expected experience. In some rare instances, the person may maintain a rigid, bizarre position for hours on end. Alternatively, the person may engage in constant and random or repetitive movements such as twirling a random lock of hair.	People with schizophrenia may talk to themselves, walk backward, laugh suddenly and without explanation, or make funny faces.

(continued)

Symptom	Definition	Example
Disorganized speech	Disorganized speech is a style of speaking that includes mimicking, disconnected or incoherent speech patterns, and/or the invention of new words. These persons may mimic speech patterns of those around them or copy the tone, words, or fragments of overheard conversations (echolalia). The person may condense or combine words or invent new words (neologism). Others may continuously repeat the same word or sentence (perseveration) or use rhyme or puns (clanging). Disorganized speech may also be seen when the person fails to answer specific questions (go off on a tangent) or arbitrarily jump from topic to topic (derailment). This nonsensical speech may suggest confused or disorganized thinking. The person may show poverty of speech where he or she talks less and more slowly than other people, not answer questions (or provide a brief response), or suddenly stop talking in the middle of a sentence.	To illustrate "clanging," when asked how they are doing, these people might respond with, "Click-tock, I smell a clock."
Social withdrawal	Social withdrawal is when the person may avoid others or act as though others do not exist. The person may exhibit decreased emotional expressiveness.	For example, the person may talk in a low and monotonous voice and avoid eye contact while showing a blank facial expression.
Other	Flat affect is the observable absence of (or minimal presence of) facial expression as if the person is unaffected by the contextual environment that surrounds him or her.	The person may look at you with "vacant eyes" and show little change in expression. The person may also laugh or cry at incongruous times.

withdrawal to rapid and abrupt shifts (Barlow & Durand, 2005). Although many of these features are a part of schizophrenia, they are not found in everyone with the diagnosis. Many persons with schizophrenia experience a number of common symptoms and yet each individual's course and outlook is different. This presentation underscores the value of the competency-based assessment that includes an examination of the extent of the person's social and occupational functioning, resources, capacity for interpersonal relationships, life stressors, and the impact of the social environment. Each variable plays an important part in the assessment process. A complex set of symptoms characterizes schizophrenia but there are specific patterns that tend to appear together (Hersen & Thomas, 2006). To refine our understanding of the psychotic disorders, we begin our discussion with schizophrenia and the five subtypes.

THE PATH OF SCHIZOPHRENIA

Perhaps more than any of the psychotic disorders, schizophrenia has a debilitating effect on those who struggle with the diagnosis. Schizophrenia has a chronic course and generally continues throughout the remainder of a person's life with varying degrees of intensity. If the onset is mild and promptly treated, the individual may not experience any further onset of symptoms. However, the typical course is an ongoing pattern of varying periods of relative recovery (or residual phases) and periods of active phase psychosis that substantially impair a broad range of social and occupational functioning. For example, the person's ability to work, go to school, or enjoy meaningful relationships with others or even to take care of themselves is seriously affected. Social problems such as long-term unemployment, poverty, and homelessness are common. The person struggles to tell the difference between real and unreal experiences, logical and illogical thoughts, or appropriate and inappropriate behavior. Those with schizophrenia most commonly experience auditory hallucinations, paranoid or bizarre delusions, or disorganized speech and thinking.

Schizophrenia often has comorbid (or co-occurring) disorders such as major depression, anxiety disorders, and substance use (Sim, Chua, Chan, Mahendran, & Chong, 2006). Commonly abused substances include alcohol, stimulants (such as cocaine and amphetamines), nicotine, cannabis, phencyclidine (or PCP), and LSD. Approximately 50% of those with schizophrenia have a substance-use disorder. Because of the high risk for substance use, it is important to distinguish between a psychosis triggered by drug use or alcohol from an episode of schizophrenia. For example, the assessment for an alcohol-induced psychotic disorder (with delusions or hallucinations) is confirmed if the psychosis ends when the person withdraws from drugs or alcohol and returns if the individual resumes alcohol or substance abuse.

The person may also experience symptoms of other mental disorders, especially depression, obsessive and compulsive symptoms, somatic complaints, dissociative symptoms, and other mood or anxiety symptoms. General medical conditions that may be etiologically related to (or produce) psychotic symptoms include cancer in the central nervous system, encephalitis, neurosyphilis, thyroid disorders, Alzheimer's disease, complex partial seizures, Huntington's disease, multiple sclerosis, stroke, Wilson's disease, some vitamin B deficiencies, and systemic lupus erythematosus. There are a number of medications that have mild to severe psychotic side effects and some can precipitate delusions and severe confusion. Those already assessed with the diagnosis of schizophrenia may be at a special risk for medical problems associated with poor self-care (such as hepatitis, tuberculosis, or emphysema).

Schizophrenia may develop abruptly but typically it has a gradual, insidious course that takes place over about five years (Hersen & Thomas, 2006). Although approximately 25% of people with the diagnosis become symptom-free (Muesser & Jeste, 2008), the disorder normally encompasses a progressive deterioration of functions, at least during the first few years. Three phases are indicative of the schizophrenic cycle; they are the prodromal phase, an active or acute phase, and a residual phase.

The Prodromal Phase

The prodromal (or precursor) phase of schizophrenia is the period of time before symptoms become fully apparent. It may last for only weeks or months but the average length of this phase is between two and five years. The prodromal phase is when the person's level of functioning begins to deteriorate but it is difficult to distinguish signs and symptoms in order to make an accurate assessment. The person experiences odd behaviors such as anxiety or restlessness. Hallucinations may begin to occur but not with full impact. There may be a gradual loss of reality. Nonspecific symptoms such as sleep disturbance, irritability, depressed mood, poor concentration, fatigue, and behavioral difficulties such as deterioration in role functioning and social withdrawal can also be seen during this phase. I remember one of my students talking about a client who shared feeling "out of sorts" with odd feelings and hearing troubling voices for several months before anyone else could see visible evidence of them. It was not until his strange behaviors became noticeable that the diagnosis of schizophrenia was considered. During the prodromal phase, the person's outward behaviors gradually begin to reflect these inner distortions.

The Active Phase

During the active phase, where the disorder persists for at least six months, psychotic features such as hallucinations, delusions, thought disorder, and grossly disorganized thinking, behavior, and speech characterize the person's behavioral picture. As these symptoms become more severe, the person is usually not able to care for him- or herself appropriately. The person may also show a flat affect (for at least one month) during the active phase (B. Sadock & Sadock, 2008). The period after recovery from a first (psychotic) episode and extending for up to the subsequent five years is commonly referred to as the "early course." People who experience their first episodes of psychosis have been found to be a danger to themselves or others and there is a higher than average rate of suicide associated with schizophrenia (Palmer, Pankratz, & Bostwick, 2005). If the person experiences a further deterioration of symptoms (and level of functioning) it is most likely to occur during the early course of his or her illness. This is seen as the "critical period." Most follow-up studies have shown that up to 80% of people will have experienced a relapse (Edwards, Harris, & Bapat, 2005). Before a relapse occurs, there is usually the prodromal period (or the less overt psychotic symptoms) followed by emotional disturbance and then the full-blown (often called florid) psychotic symptoms; developing over a period of about four weeks.

When the person shows truly odd and irrational behaviors, this is commonly characterized in lay terms as a "psychotic break" and practitioners have come to use this term to describe the first episode of psychosis. The onset of the first psychotic episode may be abrupt or insidious. It is these outward symptoms that are first noticed by family members and others close to the person. It is possible that the person's break with reality may have actually occurred prior to the time before people around them have noticed that something is seriously wrong. However, it is this symptom-rich period following the psychotic break that is regarded as the active phase of the illness. Though it is possible for the person to recover, the more typical pattern following the first break is one of varying periods of relative recovery (or the residual phases) and periods of new active phase symptoms that are expected to continue throughout the remainder of the person's life.

The Residual Phase

The residual phase follows, when the prevailing features are in remission. This is sometimes considered a "filler" category because the person may have improved to the point where he or she no longer has enough features to support the presence of schizophrenia (Barlow & Durand, 2005). Gray (2008) suggests the following metaphor to differentiate the active and residual phases. Imagine a full glass of milk. It can be easily identified as a glass of milk based on its color, texture, smell, and taste. This is analogous to the active phase of schizophrenia because the individual has all the attributes characteristic of schizophrenia. Further, imagine that glass of milk as now empty. However, enough of a residue remains so that one can still identify its prior content as milk. Extending the analogy of the empty glass of milk, the residual phase suggests that the person has some remaining features of schizophrenia but not to the extent that he or she could be fully assessed for the disorder.

Phases of Schizophrenia

Prodromal	Period of time before symptoms become fully apparent.	
Active	Period of active psychosis.	"Early course" or "critical period"—the five-year period after the first psychotic episode when relapse can occur.
Residual	Prevailing features are in remission.	

In real life, people with schizophrenia do not always follow these discrete phases or categories, thus causing some degree of ambiguity for an accurate assessment. When diagnosing schizophrenia, the disorder must persist for at least six months and include at least one month of the active phase symptoms (or less if they are successfully treated). This means two or more of the following symptoms are present: delusions, hallucinations, disorganized speech, grossly disorganized (or catatonic) behavior, negative symptoms (APA, 2000; Hersen & Thomas, 2006; B. Sadock & V. Sadock, 2007).

Positive and Negative Symptoms

Though schizophrenia is a complex syndrome, the professional can distinguish the diagnosis from other disorders based on the relative grouping of core clinical symptoms, known as positive and negative. A third category of "disorganized" has recently been considered as it is shown to be a dimension independent of the positive symptoms under which it was previously included (APA, 2000). Differentiating between the positive and negative symptoms can be confusing. Simply put, the positive symptoms are symptoms that are in excess of normal behaviors. These are symptoms that most people do not normally experience. Conversely, the negative symptoms are the loss or absence of normal traits. For example, the person with schizophrenia may have a flat affect or a restricted range of emotions (the deficit) when he or she should be vibrant and emotionally expressive (a feature present in people without schizophrenia).

Positive Symptoms—The Psychotic Dimension

The symptoms of delusions (or disturbances in thought content) and hallucinations (or distortions in perception) that are now classified as positive symptoms will be considered as manifestations of the "psychotic dimension" (APA, 2000, p. 766).

Delusions

A delusion is a false belief that cannot otherwise be explained by one's intelligence level, culture, or religious background. A key feature of the delusion is the extent to which the person is convinced that the belief is true. A person with a delusion is absolutely convinced that it is true and he or she will hold firmly to this belief regardless of evidence presented to the contrary. There are several different types of delusions and they vary widely. The delusions may be persecutory, referential (or about oneself), grandeur in nature, somatic (involving the body), religious, or erotomanic (involving sexuality). The delusions of persecution, referential, and grandeur are more common. They are summarized as follows:

> *Delusions of persecution*—This type of delusion involves the person's belief that they are being stalked, tricked, framed, or hunted. This is one of the most

common delusions and causes a sense of paranoia for the person. You may hear the person talk about an international spy ring that is after them.

Delusions of reference—Referential delusions are when the person attaches a special meaning to the actions of others or to various objects even when there is no information to confirm the experience. For instance, the person may believe that the popular CNN news anchor Anderson Cooper is sending special messages intended just for them. If the individual has some degree of insight that their referential delusions may not be entirely true, this is referred to as "ideas of reference."

Delusions of grandeur—Another common delusion is delusions of grandeur, which consist of the person's belief that they are a significant figure such as a movie star, rock singer, political leader, or someone incredibly powerful or wealthy. For example, the person may refer to himself as Elvis Presley, or President Obama. More commonly, the person believes that he or she has accomplished some great achievement for which they have not received sufficient recognition.

Somatic delusions—Somatic delusions usually revolve around the person believing that he or she has a terrible illness (and not schizophrenia but one of a more bizarre variety). For example, the person may be convinced that his body is infested with worms or that he is being sprayed with harmful cosmic rays.

Religious delusions—Religious delusions involve the belief that the person has a special relationship with God. The person may state that he is the incarnation of Gabriel the Archangel and placed on this earth to remove evil from the world. These may be combined with other delusions, such as delusions of grandeur (the belief that the "Archangel" [or person] was chosen by God, for instance), or delusions of control or delusions of guilt (a false feeling of remorse or fault). Claims that God is speaking directly to them or that they are God or God's chosen messenger are typical examples you can expect to encounter in practice. This mixing of delusions is not unusual but there is usually one theme that is more dominant. For example, the person's religious delusion that he is God may be more prominent than the grandiose or persecutory elements.

Erotomanic delusions—Erotomanic delusions involve false ideas and feelings about relationships that do not exist. Much like the experiences of John Hinckley described in the introduction to this chapter, these individuals may believe that a famous actor or actress is in love with them. Alternatively, they may believe that their spouse or partner has cheated on them when this is not in fact the case. They may go about gathering "evidence" to confront the spouse or partner about the affair. They may also believe that others they are not particularly fond of have a strong sexual attraction to them. In bizarre instances, they may imagine that people have their sexual organs in wrong places, such as breasts where a nose or an ear might be located.

Delusions of control—Delusions of control are where the person believes that another person, group of people, or external force controls their thoughts, feelings, impulses or actions. An example would be the person who talks about aliens who make him or her move in certain ways. Thought broadcasting (the false belief that the person's thoughts are heard out loud), thought insertion (thoughts are being inserted into someone's mind by someone else), and thought withdrawal (the belief that an outside force, person, or group of people is removing or extracting the person's thoughts) are also examples of delusions of control.

Unlike hallucinations that occur in sensory realms, delusions are fixed beliefs that misinterpret events and relationships. They are the most common of symptoms of schizophrenia. Some individuals may have a single delusion that seems to dominate their lives while others have many delusions. Like hallucinations, the delusions can be antagonistic and threatening. Those that are unbelievable or fantastic are referred to as "bizarre." The bizarre delusions are completely inconsistent with reality and it is highly unlikely that they will ever actually happen. For instance, although it is not unusual for a person to entertain the thought that his or her spouse or partner is having an affair, it is bizarre to think that the spouse or partner has cheated on him by having that affair with space aliens. The combination of delusions and hallucinations frequently go hand-in-hand. The interaction of these two symptoms creates mental chaos for the person and the loss of reality.

In addition to observing the person's behavior and/or talking with those close to him or her, there are a number of questions you may wish to ask your client in order to further explore the presence of delusions. They are:

Questions to Ask to Explore Delusions

- Do you sometimes feel like people are talking about you?
- Do you sometimes feel like people are purposefully trying to hurt you (or offend you or are against you)?
- Have you ever felt like you were receiving special messages intended just for you from the television, radio (magazines or the computer), or some other source?
- Do you sometimes feel that you have special powers (or exceptional talents or special abilities) that others don't have?

- Have you ever felt something or someone outside of yourself was controlling your behavior (thoughts or feelings) against your will?
- Have you ever found yourself thinking so intensely about something that others have been able to hear your thoughts?

Hallucinations

Hallucinations are internal sensory perceptions that are not actually present. They may occur within any sensory realm (sound, sight, taste, smell, and touch). Auditory hallucinations (or hearing voices when no one else is there) are the most common followed by visual hallucinations (or seeing the image of something that is not real). These voices have often been described as providing a running commentary of the person's behaviors and intentions or as commanding presences telling them to do (or not to do) certain things. A client known to one of my former students characterized the voices as a "tape playing inside my head." The tone of these voices is often highly negative and critical, and attempts to humiliate the person. Sometimes the experiences of these voices are so real that the person is convinced that a transmitting device has been planted inside of his or her body.

Here, too, you might want to ask your client a series of questions aimed at bettering the exploration of hallucinations, particularly auditory hallucinations. They are:

☜ Questions to Ask About Hallucinations

- Do you sometimes hear things that other people cannot hear?
- When this happens, what exactly do your hear?
- What were the voices saying?
- How often does this happen?

Positive Symptoms—The Disorganized Dimension

Introducing the proposed category of "disorganized," this dimension includes disorganized thought, rambling or chaotic speech, erratic behavior and inappropriate affect (Ho, Black, & Andreasen, 2003). The person's disorganized thinking becomes apparent in his or her speech patterns. For example, you might notice your client losing his or her train of thought during a conversation or jumping from one topic to another at random (loose association). Additionally, this individual may give an answer but it is totally unrelated to the question. Speech patterns may be highly circumstantial; that is, the person may talk continuously and provide numerous but irrelevant details while never really getting to the point. Occasionally a conversation may be so disorganized that it is completely jumbled or "word salad"; many meaningless words tumbled together in random order, much like a salad. Persons with a psychotic disorder must have at least one (or more) positive symptom.

Disorganized or erratic behavior may be seen in a range of behaviors from simply being unable to maintain personal hygiene to unpredictable and socially inappropriate outbursts. For example, you may notice that someone has completely removed all of his or her clothes and is wandering around naked in public. They might wear a heavy coat in the middle of the summer or put on odd or inappropriate makeup. Additionally, the individual may mutter to him- or herself or shout for no apparent reason.

Catatonic behaviors are seen with less frequency but are a form of disorganized behavior. The person may assume a rigid and uncomfortable looking posture for hours or days and resist efforts to move them. Waxy flexibility is when people will allow themselves to be moved into new positions but they do not move on their own.

Negative Symptoms—The Negative (Deficit) Dimension

Negative symptoms include features such as flat or blunted affect and emotion. The person may have poor eye contact, unresponsive facial expressions, and limited body language or movement. Despite the obvious appearance of blunted affect, there is often a normal or even heightened level of emotionality in persons with schizophrenia, especially in response to stressful events (Cohen & Docherty, 2004). Difficulty with speaking, poverty of speech, or speech disturbance is referred to as *alogia*. The person may have trouble choosing words and struggle to give brief answers to questions. The inability to experience pleasure is called anhedonia. Avolition refers to the lack of motivation or loss of goal directed behavior. Here, the person can sit for long periods of time and seem indifferent to what is going on around them. Those symptoms that appear to be secondary to depression, medication side effects, or hallucinations or delusions should not be included (APA, 2000). Overall, the negative symptoms severely diminish the unique characteristics of an individual's personality.

A summary of both positive and negative symptoms follows.

Positive Symptoms	Negative Symptoms
Delusions	Blunted affect
Hallucinations	Alogia or poverty of speech
Disorganized thought and speech	Anhedonia or the inability to experience pleasure
Disorganized behavior and catatonic behavior	Avolition or loss of motivation or goal directed behavior

The symptoms of schizophrenia are not permanent and they tend to change over time. However, a minimum number of two (or more) of both positive and/or negative symptoms must be present before the presence of schizophrenia can be considered. Once the formal diagnosis of schizophrenia has been made, it can continue to be applicable later on in the person's life even if that person has fewer than the minimum specified symptoms for the (earlier) diagnosis or they are no longer apparent.

Still confused about positive and negative symptoms? The *DSM* has proposed a three-dimensional model to describe symptoms based on studies that suggest that a person's symptoms appear to vary within one of three factors or dimensions rather than across them, (APA, 2000). This distinction may simplify the separation of positive and negative symptoms. The alternative proposed descriptors are the psychotic dimension, disorganized dimension, and the negative (deficit) dimension. For example, the psychotic dimension describes the degree to which hallucinations are present. If a person's delusions worsen, then hallucinations also tend to become more severe. Alternatively, the severity of disorganized or negative symptoms, the other two dimensions, is less related to the severity of the person's delusions and/or hallucinations. The three proposed dimensional descriptors are summarized as follows.

Proposed Dimensional Descriptors for Schizophrenia

Psychotic Dimension	Hallucinations
	Delusions
Disorganized Dimension	Disorganized speech
	Disorganized behavior
	Inappropriate affect
Negative (deficit) Dimension	Affective flattening
	Alogia
	Avolition

The Clinical Picture

Schizophrenia is diagnosed on the basis of symptom profiles. Because no single symptom is specific to schizophrenia, the assessment depends on a person having at least one active flare-up lasting a month or less that consists of two characteristic symptoms (such as delusions, hallucinations, evidence of disorganized thinking, and emotional unresponsiveness). A conceptual map of the pathway through the symptoms of schizophrenia looks like Figure 6.1.

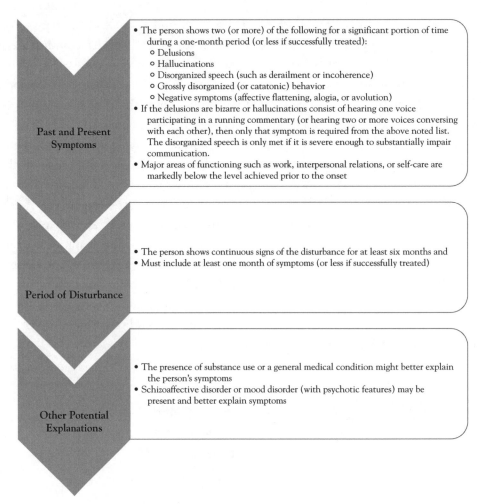

Figure 6.1   Conceptual Map for Schizophrenia

The following illustrates the symptoms to look for when considering the diagnosis of schizophrenia. They can be found in the "story" of Byron Mills.

Byron Mills is a 20-year-old single young man who is living at home with his parents. He is a part-time college student and currently unemployed although he was working in a fast-food restaurant up until about six months ago. Byron came to the practitioner's attention after he was brought to the local hospital emergency room by the police because he was destroying the furniture in his room. His parents became alarmed over his violent behavior and called the police. He was examined and admitted to the psychiatric unit for further observation. Byron's parents were worried about their son's increasingly "odd" behavior for the past six months.

Mr. and Mrs. Mills provided the following background information about their son. Growing up, Byron was described as a pleasant and cooperative little boy but somewhat "high strung." He never dated or showed any romantic interest in girls (or boys). After graduating high school, he started college as a part-time student taking about one or at the most three courses while working part-time in a fast-food restaurant. After Byron started college he took on what his parents characterized as "funny" beliefs about other people and even himself. For instance, after taking his college American history course he was convinced that President Truman was really Pocahontas reincarnated to save the western world. His parents described themselves as plain middle-class people and were surprised when Byron started talking about the idea that he was "chosen" to go to Washington, DC, to help the president start a "save the world's energy" campaign. Byron admitted that this was not as prestigious as saving the entire world but nevertheless felt that his assigned task was an exceptional honor. His parents were mystified about who "chose" their son for such special status.

At first, the Mills just dismissed their son's behavior as excitement about his status as a college student but his ideas became increasingly odd. He became more aloof and preferred to stay in his room for hours at a time. Mrs. Mills admitted to putting her ear to the door and hearing Byron talk when no one else was there. His "conversations" made little sense to her. Sometimes after hearing loud thuds like things being dropped, she would peek into Byron's room. She saw him becoming increasingly agitated as if he was responding to voices, but, again, no one was there. Byron was becoming increasingly isolated and started missing work. He was finally let go from his job at the fast-food restaurant.

For the past month, his parents could hear him pacing around in his room at night. It seemed that his personal hygiene was deteriorating, too. Byron would go for days without showering, changing his clothes, or shaving. (He refused to go for a haircut about three months ago.) It was about that time Mr. and Mrs. Mills heard Byron moving the furniture in his room around until the fateful night when he started destroying it. His parents reported that Byron was in good overall health and he did not have a history of drinking, smoking, or taking drugs.

The prodromal phase of Byron's illness is where he was characterized by his parents as a pleasant young man but a little "odd" or eccentric and withdrawn. The active phase begins when his symptoms become evident and Byron ultimately experiences his "first psychotic break"; this is where he is brought to the emergency room by the police. Over the past six months Mrs. Mills heard her son engage in conversations when no one was there; an example of auditory hallucinations. At times she observed that these conversations did not make sense; an example of disorganized speech. Byron's delusions become evident to his parents when he was convinced that he was "chosen" to help the president to save the world's energy. He was unable to continue working and going to school, and his personal hygiene deteriorated; an example of a decline in social and occupational functioning. The duration of Byron's active symptoms was for six months and he showed clear signs of his disturbance for at least one month. There was no evidence in Byron's history of a medical illness or substance use that could better explain his behavior.

Keep in mind that the specific *DSM* diagnostic code for schizophrenia is made according to the appropriate subtype. For diagnostic purposes, you would initially record the code number assigned to schizophrenia and then assign the specific subtype. After one year of the initial onset of the active phase symptoms, a specifier indicating the course of symptoms over time can then be added. For example, when a person shows active and primarily negative symptoms of disorganized type schizophrenia and he or she has clinically significant residual symptoms between episodes the notation on Axis I of the *DSM* would be coded as code 295.10 Schizophrenia, Disorganized Type, Episodic With Interepisode Residual Symptoms, With Prominent Negative Symptoms. Alternatively, if the person shows symptoms throughout all or most of the course of the struggle with the disorder (and the negative symptoms are also present), the Axis I designation would be 295.10 Schizophrenia, Disorganized Type, Continuous, With Prominent Negative Symptoms. Many people with schizophrenia also have an abnormal premorbid personality. This often takes the form of a schizoid or schizotypal personality disorder. You can expect to find a history of this set of symptoms in persons who later develop a diagnosis of schizophrenia.

Specifying the Course of Schizophrenia Symptoms over Time

Episodic With Interepisode Residual Symptoms	Clinically significant attenuated psychotic symptoms shown between episodes.
	If applicable, specify "With Prominent Negative Symptoms."
Episodic with No Interepisode Residual Symptoms	Between episodes, attenuated psychotic symptoms not shown.
Continuous	No remission of psychotic symptoms.
	If applicable, specify "With Prominent Negative Symptoms."
Single Episode In Partial Remission	One episode of psychotic symptoms and attenuated symptoms remain.
	If applicable, specify "With Prominent Negative Symptoms."
Single Episode In Full Remission	No psychotic symptoms remain.
Other or Unspecified Pattern	No specific or distinct symptom pattern.

In summary, a diagnosis for schizophrenia is made when two or more prominent symptoms consistent with the disorder are present for the better part of a month or more; for example, delusions, hallucinations, disorganized speech or behavior, and the negative symptoms such as blunted affect, alogia, anhedonia, avolition. Once the presence of schizophrenia is noted then the subtype of the illness is specified. According to the *DSM-IV-TR*, the subtypes of schizophrenia are defined by the predominant symptoms at the time of the most recent assessment and there is a possibility that may change over time. These subtypes include: paranoid type (which is characterized by the person's preoccupation with delusions or auditory hallucinations); disorganized type (where disorganized speech and behavior and flat or inappropriate affect are prominent); catatonic type (where characteristic motor symptoms are foremost); undifferentiated type (which is considered a nonspecific category and used when none of the other subtype features are prominent); and residual type (characterized by an absence of prominent positive symptoms but a continuing evidence of the disturbance is shown). The discussion of subtypes begins with a look at paranoid-type schizophrenia.

PARANOID-TYPE SCHIZOPHRENIA

Paranoid schizophrenia is considered to be the most common type of schizophrenia. The following discussion outlines a symptom picture that is dominated by relatively stable but paranoid delusions usually accompanied by auditory hallucinations (hearing voices) and disturbances of perception. Missing are disturbances of affect, avolition, and speech. In addition, catatonic symptoms are not prominent.

The Clinical Picture

The central characteristics of paranoid-type schizophrenia are delusions and hallucinations that wax and wane across recurrent psychotic episodes. Auditory hallucinations are the most common. Despite the psychotic ideation, these persons often appear to be the most "normal" among persons with schizophrenia regardless of the presence of obviously psychotic ideas. Their behaviors and physical appearances tend to remain relatively unaffected. They are also better able to take care of their own day-to-day needs. It is this level of social functioning that sets the person apart from the other subtypes of schizophrenia. The majority of individuals with schizophrenia experience the onset of symptoms in their early twenties, but those with paranoid-type schizophrenia start having symptoms at a later age; on the average, 35 years of age.

A key feature of this subtype is the combination of false beliefs (delusions) and the hearing of voices (auditory hallucinations) with more nearly "normal" emotions and cognitive functioning. The delusions usually involve thoughts of being persecuted or harmed by others. The person may have exaggerated opinions of his or her importance or reflect other themes of jealousy or excessive religiosity. The person may appear to be anxious, frightened, angry, aloof, and argumentative. They may also show a superior and patronizing manner and be rather formal (or extremely intense) in interactions

Figure 6.2   Conceptual Map for Paranoid-Type Schizophrenia

with others. Though there is no basis to support the delusions, they are typically organized around what seems to be a well-reasoned framework. Those with this subtype generally function at a higher level than the other subtypes. When looking for the paranoid type of schizophrenia, the conceptual map in Figure 6.2 helps you to find your way among the details of the client's life story.

Although it is not a common occurrence, the individual may be at a higher risk for suicidal or violent behavior toward self or others when under the influence of their delusions. It is usually the hallucinations that "command" the person to complete these behaviors.

Differential Assessment

Those with paranoid-type schizophrenia often seem to look the most "normal" despite the obviously psychotic ideas. Their behaviors and physical appearances are not affected to any degree and they can usually take care of their daily needs. Some individuals are able to work and perhaps even maintain social relationships. When considering the presence of paranoid-type schizophrenia, consider the presence of the symptoms of disorganized type; for example, is the person's speech incoherent or is their affect inappropriate? Also rule out the symptom picture for catatonic-type schizophrenia; that is, does the person have any abnormal or disorganized motor behaviors? As with any diagnostic consideration, look first for any other conditions that may better explain the person's symptom picture, such as a general medical condition, use of substances, or another diagnostic category.

The next subtype addressed is the disorganized-type schizophrenia.

DISORGANIZED-TYPE SCHIZOPHRENIA

Disorganized schizophrenia is seen as an extreme expression "disorganized" behavior and speech accompanied by flat or inappropriate emotion and affect. In contrast to paranoid-type schizophrenia, delusions and hallucinations are not the most prominent aspect of the symptom picture.

The Clinical Picture

Formerly referred to as "hebephrenic," the characteristics of the disorganized type of schizophrenia are disorganized speech, disorganized behavior, and flat (or inappropriate) affect coupled with inappropriate emotional responses to a situation. The person often deteriorates rapidly, talk's gibberish, and neglects his or her hygiene and appearance. An example of disorganized speech might be inappropriate laughter unrelated to the topic of conversation often described as "silly." Other features you might see include grimacing, strange mannerisms, and other oddities of behavior (APA, 2000). The person with this subtype may also withdraw socially and to an extreme extent.

These individuals are usually active but in an aimless and nonproductive fashion. Unfortunately, the person's problems are usually chronic (Hardy-Bale, Sarfati, & Passerieux, 2003). For a conceptual map of the typical characteristics of disorganized-type schizophrenia, see Figure 6.3.

Differential Assessment

Individuals with this subtype of schizophrenia show the most obviously psychotic symptoms when seen against the other subtypes. For instance, these individuals often deteriorate rapidly, talk "nonsense" or gibberish, and are unable to pay attention to his or her hygiene and appearance. You will often find a premorbid diagnosis of schizoid personality disorder in the person's history. When considering the presence of disorganized type, it is helpful to eliminate the features of the other forms of schizophrenia, in particular the catatonic-type schizophrenia. For example, does the person show any unusual or disorganized motor activities?

We now turn to a review of catatonic-type schizophrenia.

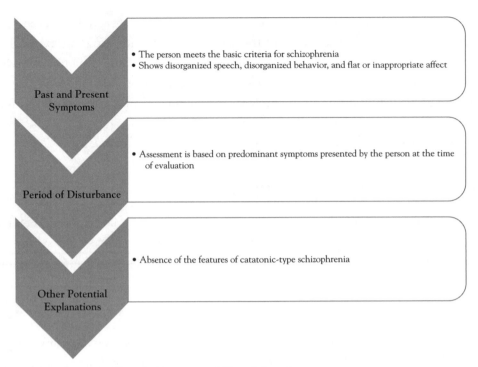

Past and Present Symptoms
- The person meets the basic criteria for schizophrenia
- Shows disorganized speech, disorganized behavior, and flat or inappropriate affect

Period of Disturbance
- Assessment is based on predominant symptoms presented by the person at the time of evaluation

Other Potential Explanations
- Absence of the features of catatonic-type schizophrenia

Figure 6.3   Conceptual Map for Disorganized-Type Schizophrenia

CATATONIC-TYPE SCHIZOPHRENIA

The discussion of catatonic-type schizophrenia introduces a number of key terms that are important to remember when considering an assessment.

Key Terms

Negativism	Demonstrated when the person refuses to follow instructions without an apparent motive or maintains a rigid posture despite attempts to move them.
Mutism	Refusal to talk.
Mannerisms	Unnecessary movements that are part of goal-directed behavior, such as the grand gesture of the pen when signing one's name.
Stereotypy	Behaviors that are not goal-directed, such as folding a crease in a piece of paper over and over until it eventually shreds.
Posturing	The person spontaneously poses or assumes a position that is bizarre or inappropriate.
Catalepsy	When the person poses or assumes a position that is bizarre or inappropriate and holds it for hours.
Waxy flexibility	When the person resists any attempts to change his or her (bizarre) position.

Hyperactivity	Behavior that has no apparent purpose and is not influenced by external stimuli.
Echolalia	Involuntary and meaningless repetitions of another's words.
Echopraxia	Mimicking the physical actions and movements of others.

The Clinical Picture

Catatonic-type schizophrenia is distinguished by the person's abnormal and striking physical movements or the complete lack of movements. The symptoms are disturbed movement (immobility or excessive motor activity), extreme negativism (such as an adamant refusal to follow any suggested course of action), somatic (body) and language symptoms. Sometimes the person assumes an odd and uncomfortable-looking pose and then holds it for hours (catalepsy). The person might look like one of those figures you see in a wax museum and this behavior is referred to as catatonic posturing. The catatonic symptoms take precedence over all of the other subtypes even if there are prominent negative or paranoid symptoms.

If you attempt to change the person's position, he or she may resist. At other times, the person will move his or her limbs but maintain the newly fixed position for hours or days; referred to as waxy flexibility. The person may move about quite freely demonstrating what looks like purposeless and undirected motor activity or imitating other people's movements. Echopraxia is the mimicking of the physical gestures and movements of others much like pantomime. The psychomotor disturbances, which alternate between extremes of excitement and stupor may cause injury. Sometimes the person may engage in seemingly purposeless repetitive movements such as crossing and uncrossing legs, and behaviors may commonly involve the whole body such as rocking back and forth (referred to as stereotypy or stereotyped behaviors). Individuals may be unable to eat or drink on their own and even their normal body elimination processes may require monitoring causing added sources of injury. In addition, the person may experience complications from untreated malnutrition, dehydration, electrolyte disturbances, or exhaustion. According to the *DSM*, "There are potential risks from malnutrition, exhaustion, hyperpyrexia (*sic* abnormally high fever), or self inflicted injury" (APA, 2000, p. 315).

Language symptoms may be evident when the person remains mute during these episodes, refusing to speak and/or make odd facial expressions. When the person is not mute, he or she may echo phrases in a parrot-like fashion that others have spoken to them (echolalia). The person might answer a question repeatedly until asked to stop (or perseveration). It should be noted that some people have developed a linguistic style that contains what is commonly referred to as "fillers." That is, the person may punctuate a statement with comments such as "like you know" or "sort of" or "I mean." This is not to be confused with perseveration. A conceptual map to chart the typical symptoms of catatonic type schizophrenia would look like Figure 6.4.

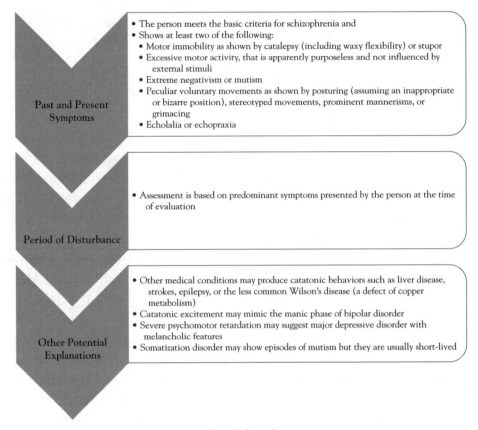

Past and Present Symptoms

- The person meets the basic criteria for schizophrenia and
- Shows at least two of the following:
  - Motor immobility as shown by catalepsy (including waxy flexibility) or stupor
  - Excessive motor activity, that is apparently purposeless and not influenced by external stimuli
  - Extreme negativism or mutism
  - Peculiar voluntary movements as shown by posturing (assuming an inappropriate or bizarre position), stereotyped movements, prominent mannerisms, or grimacing
  - Echolalia or echopraxia

Period of Disturbance

- Assessment is based on predominant symptoms presented by the person at the time of evaluation

Other Potential Explanations

- Other medical conditions may produce catatonic behaviors such as liver disease, strokes, epilepsy, or the less common Wilson's disease (a defect of copper metabolism)
- Catatonic excitement may mimic the manic phase of bipolar disorder
- Severe psychomotor retardation may suggest major depressive disorder with melancholic features
- Somatization disorder may show episodes of mutism but they are usually short-lived

Figure 6.4   Conceptual Map for Catatonic-Type Schizophrenia

Differential Assessment

Although the catatonic type of schizophrenia is considered as one of the most classic of the subtypes, you will probably not see it often in your practice. What sets the person with catatonic-type schizophrenia apart from the other subtypes is his or her abnormal physical movements; more typically slow and retarded often to the point of stupor. When considering this subtype, look for a medical condition that may be at the root of the person's abnormal physical behaviors. A mood disorder such as major depressive disorder with melancholic features may affect a person's psychomotor behaviors by slowing them down. Another mood disorder, bipolar disorder, may also look like the abnormal behaviors of catatonic-type schizophrenia; for instance, the symptoms of catatonic excitement are seen in the manic phase of the bipolar disorder. A person struggling with somatization disorder may occasionally be mute or have abnormal motor activity. However, these episodes are usually short-lived lasting for only a few hours or days and not years as seen in catatonic-type schizophrenia.

Following is a discussion of the undifferentiated type of schizophrenia.

UNDIFFERENTIATED-TYPE SCHIZOPHRENIA

Undifferentiated schizophrenia is a subtype characterized by a number of psychotic symptoms such as delusions, disorganized behavior, disorganized speech, flat affect, or hallucinations but they do not meet diagnostic criteria for paranoid, disorganized, or catatonic-type schizophrenia. In other words, the person has some of the symptoms seen in these other subtypes but not enough of any of them to determine a definitive diagnosis.

The Clinical Picture

The picture of undifferentiated-type schizophrenia shows a person who displays the positive and negative symptoms of schizophrenia but neither one dominates their presentation. Consider a classification based on symptoms that could be paranoid, disorganized, or catatonic. The characteristics are virtually indistinguishable from the other subtypes and the determination for undifferentiated type is made by exclusion rather than the presence of a clear symptom picture. This subtype is assigned when the person does not meet the specific criteria for paranoid, disorganized, or catatonic types of schizophrenia. Figure 6.5 is a conceptual map to guide your assessment of undifferentiated-type schizophrenia.

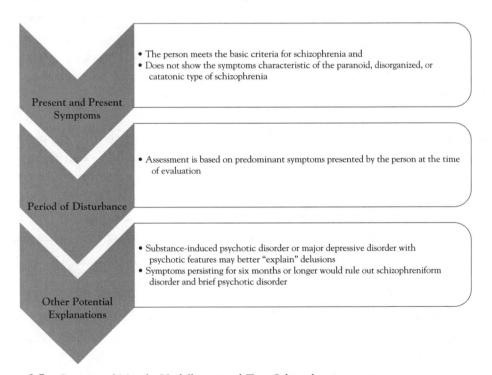

Figure 6.5   Conceptual Map for Undifferentiated-Type Schizophrenia

Differential Assessment

The differential assessment of undifferentiated type is one of exclusion. That is, if the person is actively psychotic and does not meet criteria for any of the other subtypes, then consider the undifferentiated type. Take into account alternative explanations for the person's symptoms; for example, a medical condition, substance use, or other disorders.

The last subtype of schizophrenia is the residual type.

RESIDUAL-TYPE SCHIZOPHRENIA

Residual-type schizophrenia is characterized by a person's past history showing at least one episode of schizophrenia but there are currently no positive symptoms present such as delusions, hallucinations, or disorganized speech or behavior. In essence, this subtype may represent a transition between a full-blown episode and complete remission or it may continue for years without any further psychotic episodes.

The Clinical Picture

Residual-type schizophrenia is considered when the person has had prior psychotic episodes (at least one or more) that would warrant the diagnosis of schizophrenia. Although the person does not currently display strong positive symptoms, he or she still exhibits remnants or "leftovers" of previous active disease. The person may have negative symptoms such as withdrawal from others, or flat affect or poverty of speech, but the symptoms are not as pronounced as they once were. This tends to indicate that the disorder has not completely resolved. The residual status may be in place for years or the individual may end up with new episodes of psychosis.

This diagnosis is essentially a "filler" category; that is, the person may have either been treated or spontaneously improved to the point of no longer having enough symptoms for an assessment of the active disorder of schizophrenia. Although seldom used in practice, you might encounter this diagnosis as a part of insurance-related or forensic evaluations. In reality it may be more helpful to use the diagnosis originally designated and use specifiers such as "Episodic with Interepisode Residual Symptoms" or "Single Episode in Partial Remission." A conceptual map charting residual-type schizophrenia would look like Figure 6.6.

Differential Assessment

In essence, this subtype is seen as a "filler" category because the person already has an established diagnosis of schizophrenia but has improved to the point of no longer having enough active symptoms to warrant a diagnosis of active disease. In practice this diagnostic category is more often used for insurance purposes or a forensic evaluation.

Past and Present
Symptoms

- The person at one time met criteria for schizophrenia—catatonic, disorganized, paranoid, or undifferentiated type
- Absence of prominent delusions, hallucinations, disorganized speech, and grossly disorganized (or catatonic) behavior but shows
- Continuing evidence of schizophrenia (the person is still ill) but symptoms are present in an attenuated form

Period of Disturbance

- Assessment is based on predominant symptoms presented by the person at the time of evaluation

Other Potential
Explanations

- The person shows enough of the behaviors to support the diagnosis for schizophrenia

Figure 6.6   Conceptual Map for Residual-Type Schizophrenia

THE OTHER PSYCHOTIC DISORDERS

There are a number of closely related psychotic disorders that do not meet the diagnostic criteria for schizophrenia and they are sometimes referred to as schizophrenia-spectrum disorders. These variations are classified as: schizophreniform disorder (characterized by experiences of schizophrenic symptoms for more than one month but fewer than six months); schizoaffective disorder (where the person shows symptoms of schizophrenia that are combined with either mania or severe depression); and the three less frequently seen disorders of delusional disorder (characterized by delusions that persist for at least one month); brief psychotic disorder (characterized by experiences of delusions, hallucinations, and/or disorganized speech and behavior lasting for at least one day); and shared psychotic disorder (where a person develops delusions after associating with one or more independently psychotic delusional people).

The Other Psychotic Disorders

Schizophreniform Disorder	Positive and negative symptoms lasting for at least six months and including at least one month of active phase symptoms.
Schizoaffective Disorder	Psychotic thought problems of schizophrenia and mood problems of depression or bipolar disorder.

(continued)

Delusional Disorder	Delusions persisting for at least one month.
Brief Psychotic Disorder	Delusions, hallucinations, and/or disorganized speech and behavior lasting for at least one day.
Shared Psychotic Disorder	A "healthy" person develops delusions after associating with one (or more) independently psychotic person (or people).

Schizophrenia can be thought of as a range of related conditions that share a common set of symptoms. From this perspective, schizophrenia can be located on a continuum ranging from "normal" (or no symptoms of schizophrenia) on one end and severe schizophrenia on the other with most symptomatic individuals with schizophrenia-spectrum disorders falling somewhere in the middle of both extremes. A key factor in the assessment process is the time duration of symptoms. We now turn to a closer look at these other psychotic disorders beginning with schizophreniform disorder.

Schizophreniform Disorder

Schizophreniform disorder is considered similar to schizophrenia but in a milder form; that is, symptoms (both positive and negative) last between one month and up to six months. Although the person may look to be struggling with schizophrenia, he or she may later recover completely with no residual effects. Social and occupational functioning is less impaired and the person may be able to function socially and work during this time. However, it goes without saying that most people who struggle with delusions and hallucinations for a month will probably have encountered some difficulties.

The symptoms for schizophreniform disorder are identical to those of schizophrenia, but the two diagnoses differ in terms of duration and the extent of the person's dysfunction. This diagnostic category helps to avoid coming to premature conclusions about a person's behaviors. When symptoms last for longer than six months, the assessment becomes one of schizophrenia. More than half of those who are initially assessed with schizophreniform disorder are at a higher risk for developing schizophrenia (Morrison, 2007). Figure 6.7 is the conceptual map that guides your assessment.

Schizoaffective Disorder

Schizoaffective disorder is characterized by the presence of both psychotic and mood disturbances. This is generally a confusing disorder and it is unclear whether it is better to diagnose the presence of schizoaffective disorder or if you should consider the presence of a bipolar (or major depressive) disorder and schizophrenia separately. Some hold that schizoaffective disorder is an entirely separate type of psychosis while others believe this is simply a collection of confusing and contradictory symptoms (Barlow & Durand, 2005).

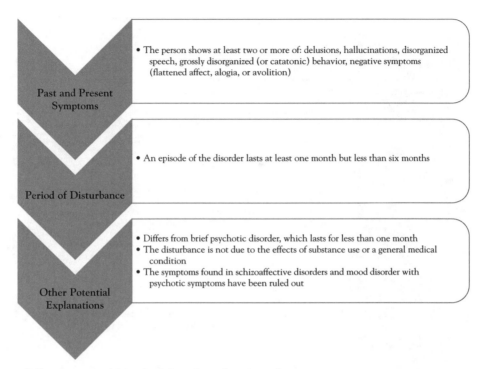

Past and Present Symptoms

- The person shows at least two or more of: delusions, hallucinations, disorganized speech, grossly disorganized (or catatonic) behavior, negative symptoms (flattened affect, alogia, or avolition)

Period of Disturbance

- An episode of the disorder lasts at least one month but less than six months

Other Potential Explanations

- Differs from brief psychotic disorder, which lasts for less than one month
- The disturbance is not due to the effects of substance use or a general medical condition
- The symptoms found in schizoaffective disorders and mood disorder with psychotic symptoms have been ruled out

Figure 6.7 Conceptual Map for Schizophreniform Disorder

When considering a schizoaffective disorder, look for both a mood episode and the psychotic features of schizophrenia that are present concurrently and for a substantial and uninterrupted period of time. During this period of time there must be at least two weeks of delusions or hallucinations in the absence of a mood episode. However, the person's mood should be seen as a significant part of the picture. The person's mood is evident as either a major depressive episode, manic episode, or mixed episode. If the depression (or mania) is brief in relation to the symptoms of schizophrenia, the presence of schizophrenia is first considered. However, if the depressive symptoms are present for longer periods of time, then a mood disorder or schizoaffective disorder should be considered. Figure 6.8 is a conceptual map that helps to plot a course through the confusing symptom picture of schizoaffective disorder.

Delusional Disorder

As the name implies, the delusional disorder is characterized by the presence of delusions that last for at least one month and often involve prominent psychotic themes; for example, grandiosity, persecutory, erotomanic, and/or somatic. The person maintains a persistent belief about something that is contrary to reality and tends to imagine events that could be happening but in fact they are not. The delusions are not considered bizarre and on the surface might look like plausible situations that can happen to

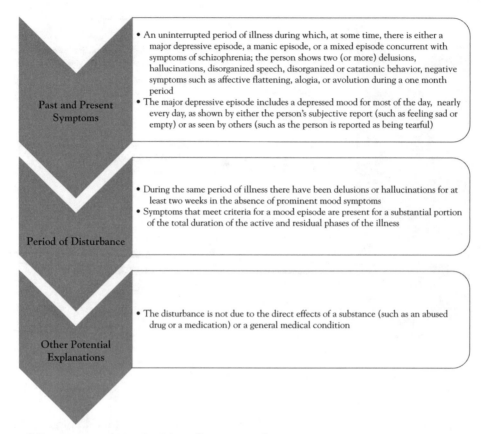

Past and Present Symptoms

- An uninterrupted period of illness during which, at some time, there is either a major depressive episode, a manic episode, or a mixed episode concurrent with symptoms of schizophrenia; the person shows two (or more) delusions, hallucinations, disorganized speech, disorganized or catationic behavior, negative symptoms such as affective flattening, alogia, or avolution during a one month period
- The major depressive episode includes a depressed mood for most of the day, nearly every day, as shown by either the person's subjective report (such as feeling sad or empty) or as seen by others (such as the person is reported as being tearful)

Period of Disturbance

- During the same period of illness there have been delusions or hallucinations for at least two weeks in the absence of prominent mood symptoms
- Symptoms that meet criteria for a mood episode are present for a substantial portion of the total duration of the active and residual phases of the illness

Other Potential Explanations

- The disturbance is not due to the direct effects of a substance (such as an abused drug or a medication) or a general medical condition

Figure 6.8   Conceptual Map for Schizoaffective Disorder

anyone as long as you do not touch on any of the person's delusional themes, such as being followed, poisoned, infected, being loved at a distance or deceived by a spouse or lover, or having some kind of disease (APA, 2000). However, the disorder differs from schizophrenia because hallucinations are not prominent unless they are related to the person's delusions.

Compared to the other psychotic disorders, the delusional disorder is considered quite rare and generally starts late in a person's life; usually between 40 to 49 years of age (B. Sadock & Sadock, 2007). Other disorders might better explain the presence of delusions and it is useful to start with a consideration of the use of substances such as drugs or alcohol. Additionally, medical conditions such as a brain tumor, vascular dementia, and cognitive-type dementia also show similar features of a delusional disorder and should be excluded. Sensory input (such as being unable to hear or to see) or social isolation (for example, being an immigrant in a foreign country) may contribute to the development of delusional disorder. The added stressors of living in poverty, experiencing an important change in jobs or relationships, or facing chronic tension and hostility at home can increase the chances of a delusional disorder for a person

Figure 6.9   Conceptual Map for Delusional Disorder

who is predisposed to the disease. Those who have effective skills for managing stress may be less susceptible to its negative effects. The person's social and occupational functioning may be less impaired because he or she is often able to perform self-care or hold a job. When recording delusional disorder, be sure to specify the type based on the person's theme of delusions; that is, erotomanic, grandiose, jealous, persecutory, somatic, mixed, or unspecified. A conceptual map to chart the symptoms of delusional disorder looks like Figure 6.9.

Brief Psychotic Disorder

Brief psychotic disorder, formerly called brief reactive psychosis in earlier *DSM* editions, is characterized by a symptom picture that lasts between 1 and 30 days. More than likely you will not often see this disorder in your practice. Typically, the person has experienced some overwhelming and stressful situation such as the death of a relative, a life-threatening accident, or even the birth of a child. Consider some kind of major life event that would cause significant emotional distress. Persons with this disorder experience delusions, hallucinations, and/or disorganized speech and behavior that last for at least one day. However, these symptoms remain within one month and the person's behavior returns to normal. Those who remain symptomatic after that period of time need to be considered for another diagnosis.

Past and Present Symptoms

- The person shows one (or more) delusions, hallucinations, disorganized speech (such as frequent derailment or incoherence), grossly disorganized or catatonic behavior

Period of Disturbance

- Duration of an episode of the disturbance is at least one day but less than one month and the person eventually completely recovers

Other Potential Explanations

- The presence of a mood disorder with psychotic features, schizoaffective disorder, or schizophrenia do not better explain the person's symptoms
- The direct physiological effects of a substance (such as a drug of abuse or a medication) or a general medical condition does not account for symptoms

Figure 6.10   Conceptual Map for Brief Psychotic Disorder

If the person's observed psychotic symptoms are seen as having been due to a preexisting mental illness (such as a mood disorder, schizophrenia, or schizoaffective disorder) or due to substance use or from a preexisting medical illness (such as a head trauma) then the assessment of brief psychotic disorder is not made. To determine the impact of a stressor, you might want to talk with family members or friends to learn about the person's past reactions to similar stressors and the chronological relationship between the current stressor and the onset of symptoms. Figure 6.10 is a conceptual map that outlines the symptoms characteristic of brief psychotic disorder.

Shared Psychotic Disorder

Shared psychotic disorder, formerly known as folie a deux (double insanity), is a dramatic and seldom diagnosed condition. One of the persons is independently psychotic and through a close and often dependent relationship the other has come to believe in the delusions and experiences of the first. These individuals are often closely related and reinforce each other for their psychopathologies. Shared psychotic disorder occurs when an otherwise healthy person develops delusions after associating with one (or more) person (or people) with independently psychotic delusional symptoms. In other words, this diagnostic category best "fits" those who have been isolated and "brainwashed" or to groups that have what is seen as delusional and dogmatic agendas.

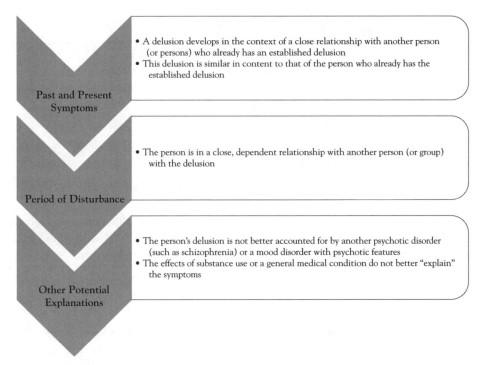

Figure 6.11   Conceptual Map for Shared Psychotic Disorder

The content of the delusion is usually believable. Aside from the shared delusion, these persons generally do not exhibit any other associated psychotic features. These delusions develop gradually and the disorder usually remits spontaneously when the parties are separated. The task becomes more complicated when the delusions involve religious themes in that religious convictions cannot be argued in rational, logical terms. Instead, they are articles of faith. The conceptual map charting your assessment looks like Figure 6.11.

FINAL THOUGHTS

This chapter provides an overview of the psychotic disorders that you can expect to see in your practice. Also addressed are the disorders you will less likely encounter in order to help refine the assessment process. They are delusional disorder, brief psychotic disorder, and shared psychotic disorder. Schizophrenia, often used interchangeably with psychosis, is characterized by a complex set of symptoms. The competency-based assessment highlights each person's highly individualized path with a mental illness and further refines the process of making distinctions in what is often a complicated symptom picture. In some instances, individuals can show symptoms of schizophrenia but they are not at the same level as those found in full-blown schizophrenia. Perhaps the greatest distinction among the disorders is the severity and duration of symptoms. Following is a summary of the disorders reviewed in this chapter.

Schizophrenia and Other Psychotic Disorders

Schizophrenia	Individuals with schizophrenia experience changes in their behavior and a number of other symptoms, most commonly delusions and hallucinations, which persist for at least six months. These persons usually experience a decline in work, school, and social functioning.
Schizophreniform disorder	People with this disorder have symptoms of schizophrenia but the symptoms last more than one month but less than six months.
Schizoaffective disorder	Individuals with this disorder have symptoms of both schizophrenia and a mood disorder such as depression or bipolar disorder.
Delusional disorder	Individuals with this diagnosis have delusions involving a real-life situation that could be true but is contrary to reality. For example, the person believes there is a conspiracy against him or her.
Brief psychotic disorder	Those individuals with this disorder have sudden, short periods of psychotic behavior, often as a response to a very stressful event. The individual quickly recovers usually in less than a month.
Shared psychotic disorder	This occurs when the individual by virtue of an intensely close relationship with another person who already has his or her own delusions come to share the same delusions.

PRACTICING THE COMPETENCY-BASED ASSESSMENT

Schizophrenia is a serious mental illness that affects a broad range of functioning and contributes to substantial impairment over time. Essentially it consists of three major groups of symptoms and they are psychotic symptoms, negative symptoms, and cognitive impairments. The following series of case vignettes provide opportunities to practice formulating your assessment.

Case Illustrations

The following case illustrations are amenable to adaption, modification, and embellishment according to your needs and interests. For instance, when you read through the vignette you might want to develop a list of questions that will help to ensure that you will make the correct competency-based assessment. In this way, the material learned in this chapter can be adapted to your own practice situation.

The Case of John Potter

John Potter is a tall and somewhat thin 45-year-old African American male who walked unannounced into the counselor's office at the Deliverance Rescue Mission. He had frequently attended the daily meal services and was recently admitted to the short-term homeless shelter. He seemed quiet, reserved, and somewhat aloof but got along with staff and fellow residents. He attended all of the required rehabilitation programs; for example, support groups and employment counseling. All of his identification recorded by the admissions department of the mission had the name of John Potter, but one day he just walked into the counselor's office and announced that his real name was Jackson. "This has been on my mind for a while now and I figured when I got the signal earlier today that I had to 'come clean' with you folks." The counselor was surprised and asked, "Is that your first name or your last name?" John responded, "We're not allowed to give out our full names. Protocol, you know. This much I can tell you."

He went on, "I sorta feel bad taking up a bed for someone who really needs it but I'm on a special mission for the Police Special Investigations Unit. The real John Potter is a narcotics dealer who often poses as a homeless person in order to go undercover for narcotics deals. Clever, don't you think? The police would never imagine a homeless man running international drug deals. I've been following Potter for some time throughout the Dade and Broward areas and recently lost track of him. I figured that if I took on his identity he would get really pissed and surface. Well, from all the signals I've been getting from my superiors in the unit, that's not working." "Signals?" asked the counselor. "Yeah, it's pretty obvious," responded Jackson. "When I was in the day room between meetings, I caught a glimpse on TV of the promo for Anderson Cooper's news program *AC360* and it hit me. That's our secret code from the captain in the investigations unit to let me know when to make a move. I guess I can tell you this much," added Jackson. "You see, all my official orders are in code. My job is to stay alert in order to read them. Sometimes they come in numbers, like 360. Other times they come in secret words." He went on, "It's something like that Lowe's home supply store advertisement. Let me try to explain my coded word system. Have you seen that advertisement on TV where the 'T' mysteriously appears next to the sign for the Lowe's store making it look like the word 'lowest'? Say for instance the one where the kid is in the backseat of a car in a parking lot and looks over his shoulder. He sees a shopping cart with a rake in full view of the Lowe's store sign making it look from his point of view like the word 'lowest.' Well, that's kind of how I get my signals. You look at something but really get the message for something else or a 'sign.'"

At first, the counselor was nonplussed by John Potter's revelation. John was initially pleasant and generally cooperative but when the details of his story were challenged, he became defensive insisting that he was telling the truth. Sensing that he was getting nowhere, the counselor ended the interview and suggested that John come back tomorrow morning. John agreed but remained adamant about his story.

The counselor reviewed John Potter's chart and noticed that a release to contact the next of kin, John's sister Mary Potter Jameson, had been signed. The counselor decided to call the sister for more information before seeing John the next day. Mary Jameson sounded relieved to hear from the counselor. She indicated that John had been living on and off with her for the past year "until he can get on his feet. As a matter of fact, my brother has been living with me and my kids for the past several years. He's got mental problems and needs a little help, as you probably already know." According to his sister, John has been able to work sporadically and apparently quit his last job as a dishwasher before disappearing. His sister went on, "John always manages to find work and his income is a big help. He's good with the kids, too. They really like his stories. I love my brother, or else I wouldn't take him in, but sometimes he can behave in such unconventional ways. I guess he's what you could call 'eccentric.' Has been for a long time, too. I remember when we were growing up, John was always somewhat isolated, even from me, his sister no less! Ever since kindergarten, he was always suspicious when one of the other kids wanted to talk to him. I thought he acted strange but Mom always insisted that John was just nervous. Back then he rarely smiled or showed much of his feelings. While he's nice enough to me and the kids, he's uncomfortable around other people. I guess that's why he changes jobs so much . . . and I've never seen him go steady or be with a woman, if you know what I mean. Sometimes he distorts things, too. It's like he doesn't think the way everybody else does. I remember when he was about 12 years old he decided that he wanted to be a minister. He would spend hours reading the Bible in his room. Geez! He even had us singing gospel songs before supper. I think we were all relieved when he finally gave up on that idea. It was something about the devil testing his dreams. I really think it was just his first erection! Oh, dear, am I talking too much? It's just that I've been so worried about my brother."

The counselor assured Ms. Jameson that she had been extremely helpful and encouraged her to continue. Mary Jameson added that her brother would often disappear without explanation for days but this time was the longest. Mary Jameson confirmed that her brother had bouts of homelessness interspersed with psychiatric admissions. She could not recall her brother's diagnosis and remarked, "But I'm sure it was pretty serious because they would give him medications and keep him for a couple of days." She had not witnessed any medical or substance-use problems. "He just does not take his medication from the psychiatrist like he's supposed to. Do you think that's his problem?" she asked.

How would you formulate your competency-based assessment for John Potter?

The Case of Hubert Estevez

"The best way I can describe my client is that he is very likeable but in sort of an odd way. He tries so hard but he just makes no sense at all," mused his counselor, Tony Vitalle. This was Hubert's 10th hospitalization. This time he was brought to the mental health center by the police who found him wandering around the shopping mall half dressed. A security guard saw Hubert Estevez coming out of one of the major department stores wearing only a do-rag, slippers, and a scruffy overcoat. He was naked underneath his coat. When his mother was notified, she started to cry over the phone. Tearfully she commented, "A do-rag? My Hubert has such beautiful curly hair. Why would he cover it up with such a ridiculous bandanna?" His mother indicated that her daughters were pressuring her not to have him come back home when he is ready to be discharged from the center. "I'm not getting any younger and what with my heart condition I'm afraid I just can't manage him by myself anymore," added Mrs. Estevez. "My Hubert is in good health. He does not drink or take drugs so I expect he will live a long time," stated Mrs. Estevez. She added that Hubert stopped taking his medications about a month ago and has since begun to hear voices and to look and act more bizarrely.

The practitioner noted in Hubert's chart, "The client's spontaneous speech is incoherent and marked by frequent rhyming and clanging associations and neologisms. Client shows flat affect and poor eye contact." When interviewed, Hubert seemed preoccupied by the influence of "the eagles" and stated, "I said the toot and read the loot and fed the eagle on the boot." This statement struck Tony Vitalle as so odd that he had to write it down immediately after he heard it. In addition, Hubert interspersed comments with "threeadle," a made up word that seemed to make sense only to Hubert. Tony thought that Hubert had a childlike quality and that he seemed eager to please the interviewer. When asked about how he came to be admitted, Hubert replied in a monotone without looking at the counselor. According to Hubert, "Well, it all started with the eagles. They are very strong so I keep them in my pocket. Is that okay? They like to eat, you know. How am I doing?" Tony Vitalle reassured Hubert by commenting on how hard he was trying to communicate. Hubert then referenced the "threeadle," giggled to himself, and shifted in his chair. He was still wearing his overcoat and it slipped open as he moved. Hubert was oblivious to revealing himself to the counselor. Tony also noticed that as Hubert spoke he constantly moved his fingers as if he was playing an invisible guitar or piano. "Early signs of tardive dyskinesia," thought Tony.

Further reviewing the social history in his client's chart, Tony Vitalle noted that Hubert was first hospitalized when he was age 16.

Hubert received tutoring at home after he was no longer able to be maintained in the classroom. Eventually home schooling was terminated when his teacher reported Hubert's lack of interest in his studies. Sometimes he would lock himself in his room when the teacher showed up. Hubert tried to work and his first (and only) job was in a fast-food restaurant. He was fired for what was described as sporadic work habits. Apparently he was unable to concentrate and would simply wander away from the counter oblivious to a long line of customers. It was hard for Mrs. Estevez to determine exactly when her son started to change. "He was never a sociable child and going to school at home didn't help, either. At one time he started to think the neighborhood kids didn't like him. Hubert was convinced that they made fun of him behind his back but I helped him to understand that was really not the case at all. At least I think I did. I guess Hubert never really enjoyed anything and he hardly ever laughed himself. You know we Cubans are a warm and expressive people but not my Hubert. He was sort of distant, almost cold. You might say he was a loner. Hubert has always lived with me and never seemed able to work. It's like he had no goals in life. He never had any friends let alone a girlfriend. I guess grandchildren are out of the picture for me," she said.

Mrs. Estevez sighed and continued, "To top it off, a couple of years ago Hubert stopped going to the store with me all together. He told me that he had better things to do. I haven't seen any of those 'better things' though. All he does is sit in his room with those earphones on his head. Sometimes I think he doesn't even turn on his DVD player. Hubert doesn't drink, never smoked a day in his life, and his health is good so I really don't understand why he acts this way." She then went on to describe Hubert's recent sleep habits. "Seems like he stays up all night. I can tell 'cause I hear my Hubert pacing around in his room. My bedroom is on the first floor just under-neath his. Sometimes I hear him banging his closet doors open and shut into all hours of the night. I'm not exactly sure but looking back I think he would throw things, too," she added.

During his prior hospitalizations Hubert was treated with neuroleptics and improved but he was noncompliant with his medication after discharge. As a result, he quickly became disorganized again. Mrs. Estevez noted that Hubert has a habit of disappear-ing, sometimes for weeks at a time. Eventually he is picked up by the police for minor infractions, such as being a public nuisance or wandering the streets. Tony wondered what could be done for Hubert during his current admission to the center.

How would you formulate your competency-based assessment for Hubert Estevez?

PRACTICAL APPLICATIONS

The psychotic disorders have the potential to profoundly affect a person's entire life and create a great deal of stress on interpersonal relationships. Poor premorbid social functioning has been found to pave the way for the onset of schizophrenia. For instance, people who are more socially isolated, never had a boyfriend or girlfriend or had few friends in childhood and adolescence are at a higher risk for developing schizo-phrenia. School problems are common, too. It has also been known that there is an association between poverty and schizophrenia. Environmental stress is another con-tributor. A series of three practical applications help you to better distinguish between expected developmental milestones and precursors to schizophrenia.

1. There are a number of biographies and novels highlighting experiences of individuals and their families with schizophrenia and the other psychotic disorders. Following is a suggested list of readings. If you know of others, review them with the intent of looking at the impact of the psychotic disorders not only on the individual's life but also on his or her family. If you have a close relative or friend who is diagnosed with schizophrenia or one of the other psychotic disorders, compare their personal experiences with those delineated in the following list of readings (or other personal biographies or novels you have read).

   Angelhead written by Greg Bottoms in 2000 and published by the University of Chicago Press tells the story of the author's brother, Michael, and the repercussions of an eventual diagnosis of schizophrenia on his family. After reading this book, consider:
   - What resources were available for this family? Can you think of what was missing that would have been helpful to them?
   - Critique the counselor's interventions chronicled in this book.
   - What was the influence of other co-occurring conditions on Michael (his substance use, for example)?
   - Describe the impact of Michael's behavior and diagnosis of schizophrenia on the family.

   A Beautiful Mind written by Sylvia Nasar in 1998 and published by Touchstone Books tells the story of John Forbes Nash, Jr. After reading this book, consider:
   - Do you think John Nash's experiences with schizophrenia are typical to those persons you see (or anticipate that you might encounter) in your practice?
   - Describe the effects his struggles with the diagnosis of schizophrenia had on his social and occupational functioning.
   - Imagine for a moment that John Nash was your client; how would you attempt to work with him?
   - Imagine for a moment that John Nash was your brother; how would having someone like him as your sibling affect you and your family?

   Daddy's Girls written by Suzanne Gold in 2000 and published by Ilibris is a novel that revolves around Cherie. She is introduced to the reader wearing strips of aluminum foil in her hair while in a state hospital in order to ward off spying black helicopters. The story revolves around one family's experiences with a member who struggles with schizophrenia. After reading the book, consider:
   - What was Cherie's impact on this family?
   - Imagine for a moment that you are working with this family, how would you respond?

- Critique the influence of this family on the development of Cherie's struggles with schizophrenia.

  Wrestling with the Angel was written by Michael King in 2000 and published by Counterpoint. The book is lengthy (500 pages) and provides an account of the author Janet Frame's life and experiences living in mental hospitals. The book provides insight into the early mental health system. Though focused on New Zealand, it provides a historical perspective on past norms of treatment, the dehumanizing attitudes of service providers, and the stigma of a mental health diagnosis. The reader also gains added insights into Frame's writings. After reading this book, consider:

- Early approaches to mental health practices and treatment.
- Whether aspects of this book are problematic for those who currently struggle with schizophrenia.
- Janet Frame eventually encounters a mental health provider (psychiatrist) who provides her with helpful care. Do you think this kind of practice is "doable" today; explain why or why not?

2. Movies are another source of information about persons struggling with mental illness and contribute significantly to public perceptions of the mentally ill, both good and bad. There are a number of films that depict schizophrenia and the other psychotic disorders; for example, *Amadeus, Bonnie and June, A Beautiful Mind, David and Lisa, Dressed to Kill, Fisher King, I Never Promised You a Rose Garden, Madness of King George, Misery, The Ruling Class, Shine, The Snake Pit, Taxi Driver,* or *One Flew Over the Cuckoo's Nest.*

   - Rent one of these movies (or others that you may have discovered). After you enjoy the plot, the action, and the movie star's portrayal, take a step back and look closely at the characters. Ask yourself:
     - What does the symptom picture look like?
     - Is the film an accurate portrayal of schizophrenia and the other psychotic disorders that you've encountered in your practice?
     - How does the character's mental illness affect relationships?
     - How much insight does the movie character have about his or her mental illness?
     - Would you consider asking one of your clients struggling with schizophrenia or one of the other psychotic disorders to view a particular film as a part of your work with them; why or why not?

3. Most states and jurisdictions have laws that make it possible to involuntarily hospitalize someone who is considered to be a danger to themselves or others for a limited period of time.

- Do you advocate that people with schizophrenia be hospitalized against their wishes?
- If not, what alternative services might be more helpful?
- How would an advocate (for example, a family member or someone affiliated with the National Alliance for the Mentally Ill) for the mentally ill respond to this question?

Appendix

Competency-Based Assessments for Chapter 6 Case Examples: Listing of Case Diagnoses

Figures 6.A1 through 6.A4 provide the diagnostic assessment for each of the cases illustrated. They are organized in the order that they appear in each chapter.

CASE REVIEW FOR JOHN POTTER

John Potter's sister, Mary Potter Jameson, describes a number of premorbid aspects of John's personality that preceded his diagnosis of schizophrenia, paranoid type. In particular, she described her brother as a loner who never had friends or even a girlfriend, and he was uncomfortable around others. Mary remembered her mother characterized her brother as "nervous" as a way to explain his odd behaviors when they were growing up. Ms. Jameson and her children seem to love John, and she characterizes her brother as "eccentric." She goes on to say that John has been able to work holding down different jobs for a short period of time. He also helps her out financially although Mary does admit that John tends to work sporadically. In addition, John's nieces and nephews seem very fond of him.

John meets the basic criteria for schizophrenia. He is preoccupied with the delusion of tracking a known international narcotics smuggler and the hallucinations of communicating with his superiors via a special code. Although you, too, might characterize him as a little odd, John is able to relate to the shelter counselor. The symptoms of

Figure 6.A1   The Conceptual Map for John Potter

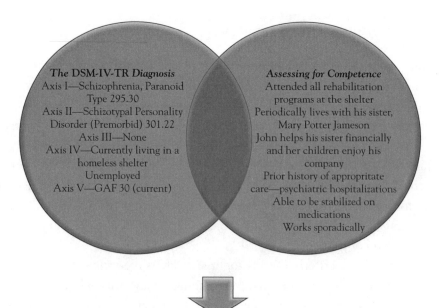

Figure 6.A2   The Competency-Based Assessment for John Potter

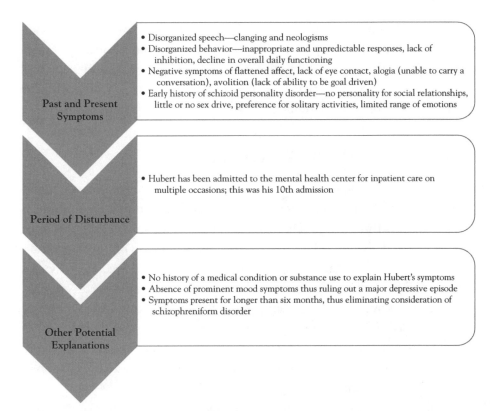

Figure 6A.3   The Conceptual Map for Hubert Estevez

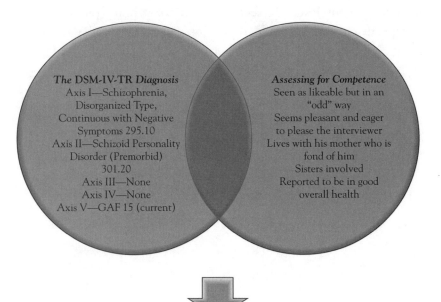

Figure 6A.4   The Competency-Based Assessment for Hubert Estevez

disorganized speech, disorganized behavior, inappropriate or flat affect and catatonic behavior are missing. The competency-based assessment points to the uniqueness of John's experience with his schizophrenia, paranoid type. Typical of this diagnosis, we could consider John as someone who is higher functioning than someone who struggles with another subtype of schizophrenia, such as disorganized type.

CASE REVIEW FOR HUBERT ESTEVEZ

Hubert meets the basic criteria for schizophrenia. He had several psychotic symptoms. Hubert does not display the motion characteristic of the catatonic type of schizophrenia, but he did show three symptoms required for the disorganized type; his affect was described as flat and inappropriate as seen by his laughter without apparent cause. Hubert also showed a disorganized speech pattern marked by frequent rhyming and clanging associations and neologisms. Finally, his behavior could be described as disorganized. Hubert's symptoms have been present for longer than a year, so the specifier continuous is added. From his mother's description, a premorbid disorder of schizoid personality disorder seems warranted. Hubert was seen as having no close friends, was not sociable, and never had a girlfriend and presumably no sexual experiences. He was further isolated by being home schooled.

Hubert's distinctive symptom picture challenges the exploration of strengths and resilience that are a part of the competency-based assessment. Yet while Hubert shows the classic patterns of talking gibberish and neglecting his appearance, there was also a childlike quality about him. He seemed eager to want to please the interviewer. Further, despite his current appearance and long-standing problems, family members are concerned about him and very much a part of Hubert's life. As far as we know, Hubert is in good general health and does not take drugs or alcohol.

The Mood Disorders

INTRODUCTION

Mood refers to a person's consistent emotion and tends to color how we view life. At one time or another, just about everyone reading this book will experience an episode of some form of sadness and despair. It could be related to a serious setback, a romantic heartbreak, the death of a loved one, loss of a job, financial troubles, or learning that you have a diagnosis of a serious illness. The related feelings of profound despondency, grief, or distress are expected responses. You could even say that something is "wrong" if you have no reaction at all. However, this normal sadness or grief seems to run its course and eventually you begin to pick up the pieces of your life and move on.

The mood disorders are different. They are more intense, pervade all aspects of somebody's life, and are more difficult to manage. For instance, some of the symptoms characteristic of a major depressive disorder such as anhedonia (or the inability to experience pleasure), weight gain or loss, problems sleeping, speeded up (or slowed) activity levels, fatigue, feelings of worthlessness or guilt, problems concentrating, or thoughts about suicide only rarely accompany the feelings of normal sadness. We do not know what contributes to the development of a mood disorder but current research suggests that it could be attributed to a range of genetic, familial, biochemical, physical, psychological, and social factors (Barlow & Durand, 2005; Hersen & Thomas, 2006; B. Sadock, Sadock, & Ruiz, 2009). The competency-based assessment is a useful tool to look at all aspects of a person's life and to help distinguish between the normal feelings of sadness and a mood disorder.

INCIDENCE AND PREVALENCE

Mental disorders are common in the United States and internationally. An estimated 9.5% of Americans ages 18 and older suffer from a diagnosable mental disorder in a given year (Kessler, Chiu, Demler, & Walters, 2005). This is in contrast to a little more than 10 years ago when about 7% of Americans were reported to suffer from a mood disorder over a one-year period (U.S. Department of Health and Human Services, 1999). Looking at lifetime prevalence, the National Comorbidity Survey (NCS) was replicated and updated between 2000 and 2003 and found that nearly one fifth of Americans reported meeting criteria for a mood disorder at some point in their lives or 20.8% of the general population (Kessler et al., 2005). This category of disorders ranks among the top 10 causes of disability.

On an international level, the World Health Organization (WHO) has recently undertaken a global survey of 26 countries in all regions of the world based on the *International Classification of Disease* (ICD) and DSM criteria and found the mood disorders to be ranked as the second most common group of mental illnesses in all but two countries with a 12-month prevalence of 0.8% to 9.6% (Kessler & Usten, 2009). Waraich, Goldner, Somers, and Hsu (2004) reviewed a series of surveys of mood disorders in different countries up to the year 2000. They found 12-month prevalence rates for the following mood disorders:

- 4.1% for major depressive disorder with an average lifetime prevalence of 6.7%.
- 2% for dysthymic disorder with an average lifetime prevalence of 3.6%.
- 0.72% for bipolar 1 disorder with an average lifetime prevalence of 0.8%.

The median age of onset for the mood disorders in the United States is 30 years (Kessler et al., 2005) and women are most frequently affected. Worldwide, the lifetime prevalence for mood disorders in women is 10% to 25% and the rates for men are 5% to 12% (Waraich et al., 2004). A summary of incidence and prevalence rates for each of the more common mood disorders is as follows.

Incidence and Prevalence Rates for the Common Mood Disorders

Major depressive disorder	Leading cause of disability in the United States for persons age 15 to 44 years (WHO, 2004).
	Affects almost 14.8 million American adults or about 6.7% of the U.S. population age 18 or older in a given year (WHO, 2004). Median age of onset is 32 years of age and more prevalent in women (Kessler et al., 2005).
Dysthymic disorder	Affects approximately 1.5% of the U.S. population age 18 or older in a given year (U.S. Census Bureau, 2009).
	Median age of onset is 31 years of age (Kessler et al., 2005).
Bipolar disorders	Affects approximately 2.6% of the U.S. population age 18 and older in a given year (Kessler, 2005).
	Median age of onset is 25 years (Kessler et al., 2005).

Suicide and Other Potential Risks

Suicide is the eighth leading cause of death among adults in the United States and a complication of the major depressive disorders. Approximately 10% to 15% of those hospitalized with depression have attempted suicide (Barlow & Durand, 2005). Looking at all deaths by suicide, approximately one fourth or 20% to 25% are attributed to those who struggle with major depression. Completed suicide is more common among those persons who experience the more severe symptoms of depression, have been diagnosed later in life, and have other coexisting disorders such as the substance use or anxiety disorders (Kessler et al., 2005). In addition, those with depression also have an increased risk of death from coronary artery disease. Hypertension and arthritis are also found to coexist with the mood disorders.

BUILDING BLOCKS FOR THE MOOD DISORDERS

We have all heard the rhetorical question "Is the glass half empty or half full?" Those who generally feel happy tend to see the proverbial glass as half full. In contrast, those who feel sad and hopeless will usually describe the glass as half empty. The mood disorders have many qualifiers and levels of severity making the diagnosis seem complicated. However, they are built on four mood episodes that are not coded in the *DSM* but serve as what are considered as the building blocks for the actual diagnosis. A mood episode can be seen as any period of time when a person feels unusually sad or happy. Most people struggling with a mood disorder will have one or more of the following episodes.

Building Blocks for the Mood Disorders

Major Depressive Episode

Quality of mood	Depressed or loss of interest or pleasure.
Duration	Feels sad most of the day, nearly every day for two weeks.
Impairment	Severe enough to impair work, school, social life.
Exclusions	Substance use, general medical condition, or bereavement within last two months.

Manic Episode

Quality of mood	Euphoric, expansive, irritable.
Duration	Minimum of one week.
Symptoms	At least three manic symptoms.
Impairment	Wreaks havoc in most areas of life.
Exclusions	Substance use or a medical condition such as hyperthyroidism.

(Continued)

Mixed Episode

Quality of mood	Fulfills criteria for both major depressive episode and manic episode.
Duration	Nearly every day for a week or more.
Symptoms	Severity may cause psychotic features.
Impairment	Impairs functioning in many areas of life.
Exclusions	Substance use and general medical conditions.

Hypomanic Episode

Quality of mood	Euphoric but not driven, irritable, different from usual mood.
Duration	Minimum of four days.
Symptoms	At least three manic symptoms.
Impairment	Minor but depends on subjective judgment.
Exclusions	Substance use or a general medical condition such as hyperthyroidism.

A major depressive episode is the most common reason that clients seek help. In order to consider a major depressive episode, a person must have a total of five of the following for at least two weeks:

Major Depressive Episode

Mood—The person feels depressed or others see them as depressed.

Interests—There is a loss of interest or pleasure in nearly all activities (anhedonia).

Eating and weight—Although the person is not dieting, there is a loss or gain of weight or their appetite decreases or increases.

Sleep—The person sleeps excessively or not enough.

Psychomotor activity—Activities are slowed down or speeded up.

Fatigue—The person reports tiredness or a loss of energy.

Self-worth—The person feels worthless or inappropriately guilty.

Concentration—The person has trouble thinking or concentrating.

Death—The person has repeated thoughts about death or about suicide (with or without a plan) or has made a suicide attempt.

Either a depressed mood or decreased interest in pleasurable activities *must* be one of the five symptoms listed above. The person shows a marked impairment in social or occupational or personal functioning. In addition, a general medical condition or the use of substances (including prescription medications) does not better explain the person's mood. The practitioner also considers that the onset of symptoms have not started within two months of the loss of a loved one (or the process of grief and bereavement).

A manic episode is another building block for considering the presence of a mood disorder. It is less common than the major depressive episode and affects men and women equally. The three most common symptoms reported are a sense of heightened self-esteem, increased motor activity, and pressured speech. These behaviors seem exaggerated and outrageous. The person feels elated (or sometimes only irritable) and may be grandiose, talkative, hyperactive, and distracted. I remember a former client once described her lack of sleep as, "I don't need to sleep because I'm young and I have a lot to do. I can catch up on my sleep when I'm old." For at least one week (or less if the individual has been hospitalized), the person's mood is exceptionally and persistently high, irritable, or expansive. They also show three or more of the following symptoms:

Manic Episode

Grandiosity—Or exaggerated self-esteem (and may become delusional).

Sleep—The person has less need for sleep.

Talkativeness—Increased chattiness.

Flight of ideas—Or racing thoughts.

Distractibility—The person is easily distracted.

Psychomotor activity—Activity levels are speeded up.

Judgment—Judgment is poor and can be seen in spending sprees, sexual adventures, or foolish investments, for example.

If the person's mood is primarily one of irritability, then they *must* show four of the above listed symptoms. The severity of the person's symptoms may result in the presentation of psychotic features or bad judgment, which leads to marked social or work impairment. Often the person needs to be hospitalized for his or her protection (or to protect others). Similar to the major depressive episode, a general medical condition or the use of substances does not better explain the person's mood.

A mixed episode is the third building block for the mood disorders, consisting of symptoms of both a major depressive and manic episode. The major difference is that the symptoms can last for as briefly as one week (but they may last longer). When symptoms are severe, psychotic features are evident. Additionally, the person may require hospitalization and their work, social, and personal functioning becomes impaired.

The hypomanic episode is the fourth building block for the mood disorders. Symptoms are like those of the manic episode but they are of a shorter duration and far less severe. The person must have had symptoms for a minimum of four days, much less time than the time required for considering a manic episode. In particular, the person does not require hospitalization. However, without treatment, the person may eventually show symptoms of a manic episode. There are a number of warning signs for the mood disorders:

Key Warning Signs for the Mood Disorders

Sadness, or expansive mood or irritability, argumentativeness

Easily distracted

Racing thoughts

Trouble concentrating

Somatic symptoms (appetite, sleep patterns)

Tired, loss of energy

Low self-worth

Repeated thoughts of suicide (or attempted suicide)

Poor judgment

Change in personal appearance

Withdrawal from and loss of interest in previously pleasurable activities

Decline in social or job performance

Absenteeism

We now turn to an overview of the specific mood disorders beginning with the depressive disorders. Figure 7.1 summarizes the depressive disorders.

THE DEPRESSIVE DISORDERS

Major depressive disorder, commonly called *depression*, is characterized by an all encompassing low mood accompanied by a person's sense of low self-esteem and loss of interest in activities that are normally pleasurable. This is the person who may be preoccupied with thoughts or feelings of worthlessness, inappropriate guilt or regret, helplessness, hopelessness, or self hatred. Unfortunately all aspects of a person's life may change. For instance, family and personal relationships, work or school life, sleeping and eating habits, or overall general health are affected.

Figure 7.1   The Depressive Disorders

Major Depressive Disorder or MDD

Sometimes referred to as clinical depression, major depressive disorder (MDD) is the most common of the mood disorders. Once thought of as the common cold of mental disorders, a major depressive disorder is a potentially chronic and disabling syndrome that is distinguished from the other more transient states of sadness by the duration, intensity, and pervasiveness of symptoms. Unlike the common cold that causes some degree of discomfort but eventually goes away, MDD is known to cause clinically significant distress or impairment in the person's social, vocational, or other important areas of functioning. I recall the experience of one client who described best herself when she said, "I just feel sad all the time. I don't even want to get up to answer the door. If I do, then I'll have to talk to the person . . . and I really don't want to." Others may report feeling dejected, low, or blue. Many people lose interest in what were once pleasurable activities. This disorder often goes undetected even though it is associated with considerable disability. When the person's depressed state is associated with an illness, a drug, or the consequence of a medication, then the diagnosis of mood disorder due to a general medical condition or substance-induced mood disorder is made.

Comorbid conditions. Comorbidity is the co-occurrence of two or more mental disorders or one or more mental disorders with one or more general medical conditions. It occurs most often in the mood disorders and a large majority of persons with MDD may also meet criteria for other syndromes particularly the anxiety disorders, substance abuse disorders, eating disorders, and personality disorders as well as general medical disorders (Grant et al., 2005; Hettema, Prescott, & Kendler, 2003). Looking at the anxiety disorders on the whole, the diagnoses of agoraphobia, generalized anxiety disorders, and posttraumatic stress disorder have the highest comorbidity with MDD (Kendler, 2001). Those who do not meet criteria for a co-occurring anxiety disorder may still have a significant amount of anxiety as they struggle with their depression (Fava et al.,

2004). It is common to find depression co-occurring with alcohol and substance abuse (Grant et al., 2005). Of interest, nicotine dependence is found to correlate with depression. For example, people diagnosed with MDD are twice as likely than the U.S. general population to smoke cigarettes (Grant, Hasin, Chou, Stinson, & Cawson, 2004).

Certain medical disorders such as hypertension, diabetes, or heart disease increase the risk for developing depression and the risks are even higher with some malignancies and endocrine disorders (Bair, Robinson, Katon, & Kroenke, 2003; Kennedy, Lam, Nutt, & Thase, 2004). A common symptom of depression is somatization, which helps to explain why those who struggle with depression are often high users of medical resources (Bair et al., 2003). These are people who often seek relief from their doctors for nonspecific aches and pains, fatigue, or gastrointestinal disturbances (Kroenke, 2003).

Specifiers for major depressive disorder. MDD shows a diverse grouping of presentations and the *DSM-IV-TR* provides a series of descriptive episode specifiers (Table 7.1). The first distinction, single versus recurrent, is an important aspect of a person's prognosis

Table 7.1 Major Depressive Disorder Specifiers

Specifiers	Essential Features
Single	Indicates only one depressive episode with symptoms present for at least two weeks.
Recurrent	Recurring episodes of depression show at least a two-month interval where criteria are not present for major depression.
Without psychotic features	Absence of hallucinations or delusions.
With psychotic features	Hallucinations or delusions are demonstrated.
With chronic pattern	The person meets full criteria for major depressive episode that lasts for two years or more.
With catatonic features	Although not commonly seen in practice, the person shows catalepsy (waxy flexibility), catatonic excitement, negativism or mutism, mannerisms or stereotypes, echolalia or echopraxia.
With melancholic features	The person has a nonreactive mood, anhedonia, weight loss, guilt, psychomotor retardation (or agitation), morning worsening of mood, awakens early in the morning.
With atypical features	The person shows evidence of mood reactivity (or mood improves in response to positive events) and there are two or more of: weight gain or appetite increase; oversleeps, leaden paralysis; or interpersonal rejection sensitivity (to the extent there is resulting social or occupational impairment).
With postpartum onset	Onset of the person's depressive episode occurs within four weeks postpartum.
With seasonal pattern	During a particular season (usually in the fall or winter) the person experiences the regular onset and remission of depressive episodes.

with the disorder. In particular, once a pattern of recurrent episodes has been established, the interval of being "well" typically diminishes over time.

Typically, MDD runs a variable course and for many people the episodes are short-lived. For almost half of those who are struggling with MDD, the depressive episodes will remit within six months (Boland & Keller, 2002). Once remission occurs, there is about a 20% risk for relapse across one year (Boland & Keller, 2002). Looking at the "chronic" specifier more closely, the chronic pattern is assigned when the person has experienced a depressive episode lasting for at least two years. Unfortunately, once a chronic pattern develops the chances of a spontaneous remission diminish.

Double depression. In practice, it is often hard to distinguish a chronic episode of MDD from recurring episodes of MDD that are superimposed on the antecedent dysthymic disorder (or a relatively low grade but chronic depression), a condition referred to as double depression (Sadock et al., 2009). More simply, this is a pattern of recurrent MDD with incomplete remission between discrete depressive episodes. Typically, the dysthymic disorder develops first and then one or more major depressive episodes follow (Klein, Schwartz, Rose, & Leader, 2000). These three forms of depression are often grouped together (McCullough et al., 2000).

Coding. The first three digits assigned to MDD are 296. The fourth digit assigned is either a 2 indicating only a single major depressive episode or a 3 signifying recurrent major depressive episodes. The fifth digit of the diagnostic code assigned provides for a rating of severity ranging from mild (assigned a number 1), moderate (number 2), severe without psychotic features (number 3), or severe with psychotic features (number 4). If full criteria for MDD are not currently met, then the person is considered to be in partial remission (and assigned number 5) or in full remission (number 6). If severity or clinical status is unspecified, the fifth digit becomes a zero.

Adding a number of additional specifiers to the diagnosis provides further diagnostic specificity. "With catatonic features" refers to the rarest form of depression. Here, the person shows markedly disturbed psychomotor features characterized by catalepsy ("waxy" flexibility) or stupor and extreme negativity. For example, the catatonic person may sit in one position for hours. However, this feature is more commonly found in schizophrenia than in depression. Other catatonic features can include periods of excessive and apparently purposeless motor activity, echolalia, and echopraxia. "With melancholic features" refers to the vegetative symptoms of severe depression; that is, sleeping difficulties, reduced appetite and weight loss, a lack of pleasure in usual activities. Depression "with atypical features" has an earlier age of onset and tends to show a more chronic and less episodic course (Parker et al., 2002). The person does not quite fit neatly into other categories and yet looks suspiciously like they are experiencing a major depressive episode. The specifier "with postpartum onset" applies only to depressed women and is used when the depressive episode begins within four weeks of childbirth. This form of depression can be seen as potentially severe, show psychotic features, and can threaten the life of the infant as well as the mother, as opposed to the more common and far less serious baby blues (Spinelli, 2004). "With seasonal pattern" refers to those who regularly suffer depressive episodes in the fall and winter season (or less commonly in the spring and summer).

An example of how to code a mood disorder with specifiers might look like:

Diagnostic Code	Diagnosis
296.34	Major Depressive Disorder, Recurrent, Severe, With Psychotic Features

The clinical picture. Depression is closely associated with a number of general medical illnesses (Kroenke, 2003). If you are working in a medical hospital or health-related setting such as a nursing home, you might want to include a checklist review of the *DSM* criteria for depression in order to distinguish the diagnosis of MDD. The core issue when assessing for MDD is evaluating whether a person's symptomatic features are the primary problem or are related to another disorder.

Figure 7.2 is a conceptual map to navigate the symptom picture for MDD.

Although symptoms must be present most of the time over a two-week period, you may come across a client who has been symptomatic for a number of months or even

Figure 7.2 Conceptual Map for Major Depressive Disorder

years before asking for help. MDD causes clinically significant distress or impairment in the person's social, vocational, or other important areas of functioning. Additionally, the symptoms are not the direct consequence of a drug or medical condition and there is no history of manic or hypomanic episodes.

Differential assessment. The first step in a differential assessment is to identify the person's current (and previous) mood states. Dysthymic disorder and MDD are differentiated based on duration, severity, chronicity, and the persistence of a person's symptoms. For example, the diagnosis of MDD is considered when the person's depressed mood is present for most of the day, nearly every day, for a period of at least two weeks in contrast to dysthymic disorder where symptoms must be present for more days than not for at least two years. Individuals with MDD generally experience one or more discrete major depressive episodes while those with dysthmic disorder experience a more chronic pattern of less severe depressive symptoms.

If the person has a history of manic, mixed, or hypomanic episodes, then the diagnosis of MDD is ruled out. If the mood symptoms alternate between periods of highs and lows, then consider the presence of bipolar disorder. When the person's symptoms are directly produced by the physiological aspects of a medical illness, a "mood disorder due to a general medical condition" is assigned. Some people drink more when they are depressed. If substances are involved then a diagnosis of "substance-induced mood disorder" would be more appropriate.

Depressive symptoms may be present during a psychotic disorder, such as schizoaffective disorder, schizophrenia, delusional disorder. To rule out a psychotic disorder, look for psychotic symptoms to occur in the absence of prominent mood symptoms. When the person with major depression also describes symptoms of the anxiety disorders, for example panic disorder or generalized anxiety disorder, then two diagnoses may be assigned on Axis I; usually the mood disorder is listed first.

A Note on Minor Depression

Minor depression is a proposed diagnostic category for the kind of depression that is not severe enough to meet criteria for a major depression and has not lasted the two years necessary for dysthymic disorder. The most common symptoms for minor depression are a sad mood, irritability, anxiety, a sadness that is clearly different from the grief process, problems concentrating and difficulty making decisions, pessimism, a lack of involvement, and a reduced capacity to experience pleasure. Less common are changes in sleep patterns, appetite, and weight. Suicidal thoughts are rarely seen. Those individuals struggling with minor depression frequently describe a history of episodes of major depression and may even report having relatives with a history of major depression.

Dysthymic Disorder

Those who struggle with dysthymic disorder (DD) are chronically depressed. Often, these are people who have constantly suffered a low mood to the point where they think this is "normal." They will show many of the same symptoms found in major depressive episodes including low mood, fatigue, feelings of hopelessness, difficulty concentrating, and problems eating and sleeping, but the key difference is the absence of thoughts of death or suicidal ideation. The vegetative features (for example, eating and sleeping) are not considered to be central features of the syndrome.

There is some evidence that persons with DD have had poorer relationships with their parents as compared to those with MDD and have experienced some degree of childhood adversity (Klein & Santiago, 2003). As adults, expect these individuals to less likely be in partnered relationships and that they will probably have limited social support networks. However, because levels of social and occupational functioning are not severely impaired overall, these individuals will probably not come to your attention until a major depressive episode occurs. Most people who struggle with DD will later develop episodes of major depression. An early onset of DD sets the stage for a chronic and often disabling course of illness.

There are three specifiers for DD (Table 7.2).

The clinical picture. It is important to consider the onset of DD; for example, dysthymia should be found before the beginning of a major depressive episode by at least two years. Figure 7.3 is a conceptual map to plot the course of symptoms for dysthymic disorder (see pg. 225). Note that the person *must* show fewer symptoms (two to four symptoms) in contrast to MDD (where the person must show five or more symptoms).

Differential assessment. Differentiating DD from MDD revolves around the intensity of the person's symptom picture. For instance, those who struggle with DD have a chronic low mood rather than clearly delineated episodes of severe depressive symptoms. The foremost and essential feature of DD is a long-standing depressed mood. Similar to MDD, the practitioner also rules out the presence of a "mood disorder due to

Table 7.2 Dysthymic Disorder Specifiers

Specifiers	Essential Features
Early onset	Symptoms appear to begin before the person is 21 years of age.
Late onset	Symptoms begin after 21 years of age.
With atypical features	Within the most recent two years, the person shows evidence of mood reactivity (or mood improves in response to positive events) and there are two or more of: weight gain or appetite increase; oversleeps, leaden paralysis; or interpersonal rejection sensitivity (to the extent there is resulting social or occupational impairment).

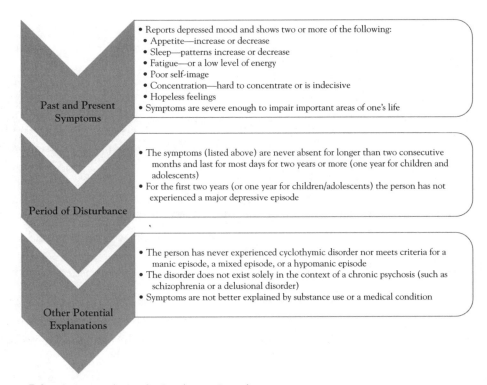

Past and Present Symptoms

- Reports depressed mood and shows two or more of the following:
  - Appetite—increase or decrease
  - Sleep—patterns increase or decrease
  - Fatigue—or a low level of energy
  - Poor self-image
  - Concentration—hard to concentrate or is indecisive
  - Hopeless feelings
- Symptoms are severe enough to impair important areas of one's life

Period of Disturbance

- The symptoms (listed above) are never absent for longer than two consecutive months and last for most days for two years or more (one year for children and adolescents)
- For the first two years (or one year for children/adolescents) the person has not experienced a major depressive episode

Other Potential Explanations

- The person has never experienced cyclothymic disorder nor meets criteria for a manic episode, a mixed episode, or a hypomanic episode
- The disorder does not exist solely in the context of a chronic psychosis (such as schizophrenia or a delusional disorder)
- Symptoms are not better explained by substance use or a medical condition

Figure 7.3   Conceptual Map for Dysthymic Disorder

a general medical condition" and "substance-induced mood disorder." A co-occurring personality disturbance can often be present. For example, if the person struggles with a poor self-image and meets the criteria for a dependent personality disorder (as well as symptoms of dysthymic disorder), the practitioner assigns a second Axis II diagnosis of dependent personality disorder.

Depressive Disorder Not Otherwise Specified (NOS)

A brief overview of depressive disorder not otherwise specified completes our discussion of the depressive disorders. When considering this diagnosis, the person obviously has depressive features but they are not quite yet recognized to be given a specific diagnosis of their own. The symptom picture must also not fulfill criteria for an adjustment disorder with depressed mood or an adjustment disorder with mixed anxiety and depressed mood. Here are a few examples:

- *Minor depressive disorder*—Minor depressive disorder is the term used for those who have had two or more weeks of depressive symptoms but fewer that the five symptoms required for a major depressive episode.

- *Postpsychotic depressive disorder of schizophrenia*—Once the acute phase of psychosis subsides, many individuals who have been diagnosed with schizophrenia will go on to develop a major depressive episode.
- *Major depressive episode superimposed on a psychosis*—The person's psychosis could be recognized as delusional disorder, psychotic disorder not otherwise specified or even the active phase of schizophrenia. The difference between this and the preceding diagnosis is timing, and in this instance, the depression occurs with the psychosis.

We now turn to a review of the bipolar disorders. They are summarized on Figure 7.4.

THE BIPOLAR DISORDERS

The bipolar disorders describe a category of mood where the person has one or more episodes of elevated mood referred to as mania (or hypomania if less severe) with or without depressed episodes. A mixed episode is seen when both mania and depression are present at the same time.

Distinguishing the Bipolar Disorders From the Depressive Disorders

Formerly known as manic depression, the bipolar disorders represent a cyclic mood disorder. This includes at least one manic or hypomanic (a milder and not psychotic) episode. These disorders were formerly recognized as manic-depressive illness and a few mental health practitioners still continue to refer to them in this way. For some people, their diagnosed mood episode may shift as a consequence of their treatment for depression. In contrast, the bipolar disorders refer to a distinct period when the predominant mood is elevated, expansive, or irritable accompanied by symptoms such as high energy, rapid or pressured speech, racing thoughts, inflated self-esteem, and a decreased need for sleep (or about 2 to 4 hours a day), distractibility, and excessive involvement in potentially dangerous self-destructive activity. The impulsivity found in mania can result in violent outbursts, spending sprees, and poor decisions, which may involve those close to the affected individual. Often people deny this manic phase because they never felt better. A former client once described her experience of mania like feeling "on top of the world." She simply could not remember any better time in her life.

Bipolar disorder usually begins with depression. Mania or the period of abnormally elevated mood in the absence of depression is less frequently seen. Unfortunately, the depression that follows a period of mania is usually severe and the person may become

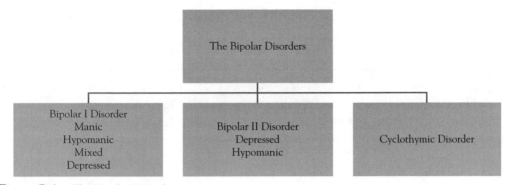

Figure 7.4   The Bipolar Disorders

suicidal. Some individuals will abuse drugs or alcohol in an attempt to medicate the mood swings.

When evaluating the person's mood in order to consider a "new" episode, it must show one of two attributes. One is that the mood represents a change of polarity; for example, the person changes from a major depressive episode to a manic episode. Another shift to look for is a separation from the previous episode by a "normal" mood that lasts for at least two months. The person may experience a spectrum of mood symptoms ranging from mild to severe over months or even within the same day.

We now turn to a differentiation among the three types of bipolar disorders.

Bipolar I Disorder

Bipolar I disorder refers to severe manic symptoms accompanied by one or more periods of major depression. The main feature that distinguishes bipolar I disorder from MDD is the presence (or history) of one or more manic or mixed episodes (a condition in which the person experiences both elation and depression or anxiety at the same time). Often individuals have also had one or more major depressive episodes (American Psychiatric Association, 2000), but that is not a requirement for the diagnosis of bipolar I. In other words, the person may or may not have had a major depressive episode but has clearly had one or more manic episodes. Rapid cycling occurs when four or more separate bipolar episodes (in any combination) are experienced within a one-year period. A seasonal affective pattern is when individuals tend to experience episodes during a particular time of the year, for example, late fall or early winter.

Specifiers for bipolar I disorder. Similar to MDD, there are a number of specifiers for bipolar I disorder. Once full criteria are met, the following may be used to further describe the current status of the episode and the features of the episode. They are summarized as follows:

Bipolar I Disorder, Single Manic Episode
- Presence of only one manic episode and no past major depressive episodes.
  Note: Recurrence is defined as either a change in polarity from depression or an interval of at least two months without manic symptoms.

- Specifiers:
  Mixed—If symptoms meet criteria for a mixed episode.

  Severity—Mild, moderate, severe without psychotic features; severe with psychotic features.

  With catatonic features.

  With postpartum onset.

  In partial (or in full) remission.

Bipolar I Disorder, Most Recent Episode Hypomanic
- Currently (or most recently) in a hypomanic episode.
- There has previously been at least one manic episode or mixed episode.
- Mood symptoms cause clinically significant distress or impairment in social, occupational, or other important areas of a person's functioning.

- Specifiers:
  Longitudinal course specifiers—With (and without) interepisode recovery.

  With seasonal pattern.

  With rapid cycling.

Bipolar I Disorder, Most Recent Episode Manic
- Currently (or most recently) in a manic episode.
- There has previously been at least one major depressive episode, manic episode, or mixed episode.

- Specifiers:
  Severity—Mild, moderate, severe without psychotic features; severe with psychotic features.

  With catatonic features.

  With postpartum onset.

  In partial (or in full) remission.

  Longitudinal course specifiers—With (and without) interepisode recovery.

  With seasonal pattern.

  With rapid cycling.

Bipolar I Disorder, Most Recent Episode Mixed
- Currently (or most recently) in a mixed episode.

- There has previously been at least one major depressive episode, manic episode, or mixed episode.

- Specifiers:
  Severity—Mild, moderate, severe without psychotic features; severe with psychotic features.
  With catatonic features.
  With postpartum onset.
  In partial (or in full) remission.
  Longitudinal course specifiers—With (and without) interepisode recovery.
  With seasonal pattern.
  With rapid cycling.

Bipolar I Disorder, Most Recent Episode Depressed
- Currently (or most recently) in a major depressive episode.
- There has previously been at least one manic or mixed episode.

- Specifiers:
  Severity—Mild, moderate, severe without psychotic features; severe with psychotic features.
  Chronic.
  With catatonic features.
  With melancholic features.
  With atypical features.
  With postpartum onset.
  In partial (or in full) remission.
  Longitudinal course specifiers—With (and without) interepisode recovery.
  With seasonal pattern.
  With rapid cycling.

Bipolar I Disorder, Most Recent Episode Unspecified
- Criteria, except for duration, are currently (or most recently) met for a manic, hypomanic, mixed or major depressive episode.
- There has previously been at least one manic episode or mixed episode.
- Mood symptoms cause clinically significant distress or impairment in social, occupational or other important areas of a person's functioning.
- The person's mood symptoms are not due to the direct effects of a substance or a general medical condition.

- Specifiers:
  Longitudinal course specifiers—With (and without) interepisode recovery.
  With seasonal pattern.
  With rapid cycling.

Episodes. The first three digits of the diagnostic code designate the bipolar I disorder and they are 296. The fourth digit notes the nature of the current episode. They are:

Diagnostic Codes for Bipolar Episodes

Zero	A single manic episode
4	Current or most recent (or currently in partial or full remission) episode is a hypomanic episode or a manic episode
5	A major depressive episode
6	A mixed episode
7	Current (or most recent) episode is unspecified

Severity. The fifth digit indicates severity except for the designation bipolar I disorder, most recent episode hypomanic and for bipolar I disorder, most recent episode unspecified. For the remaining bipolar episodes (manic, mixed, or major depressive), severity is indicated as follows:

Diagnostic Codes for Bipolar Severity

1	Indicates mild severity
2	Moderate severity
3	Severe without psychotic features
4	Severe with psychotic features
5	Indicates in partial remission
6	Indicates full remission
Zero	Severity cannot be determined or if the diagnosis is unspecified

The fifth digit is always a 0 for the diagnostic category of bipolar disorder, most recent episode hypomanic, and there is no fifth digit for bipolar disorder, most recent episode unspecified.

Here are two examples showing how to record a bipolar disorder.

Examples of Recording Bipolar Disorders

Diagnostic Code	Diagnosis
296.44	Bipolar I Disorder, Most Recent Episode Manic, Severe With Psychotic Features, With Postpartum Onset
296. 64	Bipolar I Disorder, Most Recent Episode Mixed, Severe with Psychotic Features, With Full Interepisode Recovery

Similar to MDD, the diagnosis can further add specifiers to describe the current episode; for example "with postpartum onset" or "with full interepisode recovery."

The clinical picture. For all types of bipolar episodes, be sure that the diagnostic criteria for the specific mood episodes are not better accounted for by schizoaffective disorder and are not superimposed on schizophrenia, schizophreniform disorder, delusional disorder, or psychotic disorder not otherwise specified. The variations of bipolar disorder refer to severe manic symptoms generally accompanied by one or more periods of major depression. Figure 7.5 is a conceptual map to navigate the different symptom pictures.

Differential assessment. It is helpful to remember the building blocks for the mood disorders in order to determine the specific criteria for each of the bipolar disorders. Looking at the manic episode, occasionally the person's "mania" can be characterized by psychotic ideation, which makes a differential assessment difficult for the practitioner. A bipolar disorder is more likely if the person has shown significantly more lucid thinking between episodes and the psychotic signs are relatively brief; for example, only one or two weeks per year (Judd et al., 2002). The hypomanic episodes are similar to the manic episode but of lesser intensity and duration (at least four days). The mixed episodes are particularly insidious because they involve at least a week of symptoms that meet criteria for both mania and a major depressive episode. When considering the presence of a depressed episode, it is helpful to remember that the person's

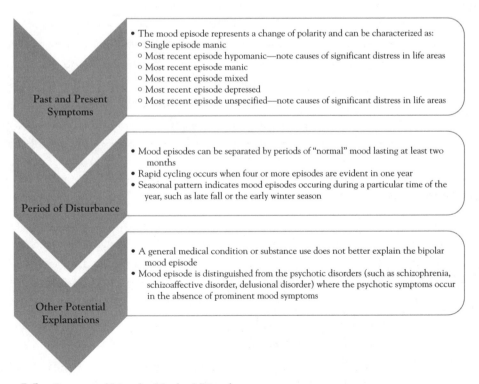

Figure 7.5   Conceptual Map for Bipolar I Disorder

symptom picture must show at least one of the two necessary features from the building block of a major depressive episode (sad mood or anhedonia) and a total of at least five symptoms total.

Assess for a general medical condition because some medical problems, for example hyperthyroidism, or multiple sclerosis could cause symptoms of a bipolar I disorder. Also consider the presence of substance-use disorders that may better explain a person's symptoms. Although it is possible for someone to have experienced depression that would meet the criteria for a major depressive episode, the current mood episode (or history of the presence of other mood episodes) would obviate a diagnosis of MDD. In order to rule out cyclothymic disorder, evaluate the severity of hypomanic symptoms; in other words, determine if they meet criteria for a manic episode and if the depressive symptoms meet criteria for a major depressive episode. However, if a person experiences a manic or mixed episode after the first two years of being diagnosed with cyclothymic disorder, then both cyclothymic disorder and bipolar I disorder would be diagnosed on Axis I.

Bipolar II Disorder

Bipolar I and bipolar II have similar symptoms but the major distinction between the two categories is that bipolar II disorder does not lead to psychotic behavior nor does it typically require hospitalization. An episode of hypomania is not associated with marked impairments in a person's judgment or performance. In fact, some people with bipolar II disorder will often describe a longing for those periods of productive energy and heightened creativity typified by the hypomanic phase of the disorder. The essential feature of bipolar II disorder consists of one or more major depressive episodes accompanied by at least one hypomanic episode. In other words, the most pronounced feature in the person's history is the presence of depression but there have also been intermittent symptoms of hypomania in the past. Figure 7.6 is a conceptual map to chart bipolar II disorder.

Cyclothymic Disorder

Cyclothymia seems to be a hybrid between dysthymia and a form of rapid cycling bipolar disorder; that is, it is characterized by manic and depressive states but neither is of sufficient intensity (or duration) to warrant a diagnosis of bipolar disorder or MDD. Symptoms must last at least two years (or one year for children and adolescents) with no symptom-free intervals extending two months or more during this time span. Essentially it is a milder form of bipolar disorder consisting of recurrent hypomanic and dysthymic episodes. Sometimes it can be hard to distinguish cyclothymia from some of the personality disorders (especially borderline personality disorder) where a chronic mood liability is a distinguishing diagnostic feature.

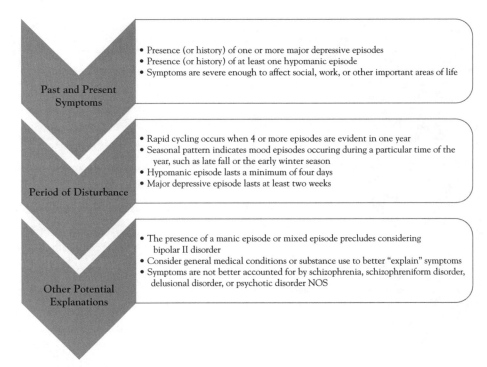

Figure 7.6   Conceptual Map for Bipolar II Disorder

Figure 7.7 is a conceptual map to help plot a course for the symptom picture for cyclothymia.

In sum, the diagnosis for cyclothymia is appropriate if there is a history of hypomania but no prior episodes of mania or major depression.

THE OTHER MOOD DISORDERS

In this chapter, we have made several references to mood disorders due to general medical conditions and the substance-induced mood disorders. In order to complete our discussion, this section provides a brief overview of each of the other mood disorders. The diagnostic challenge is to explore the person's medical history and to consider symptoms that might have significance for a mood disorder. For instance, a person may have been taking blood-pressure medication and within a few weeks or months begins to experience the onset of a depressive episode. When this happens, assess for symptoms of a major depressive episode that may be related to the person's medical history. Sometimes you might encounter someone who does not quite "fit" into a specific diagnostic category. In those situations, the diagnosis of mood disorder not otherwise specified (NOS) is considered. The competency-based assessment helps you to carefully explore the range of factors in the person's life. The diagnosis of a mood disorder NOS expands diagnostic possibilities (see Figure 7.8).

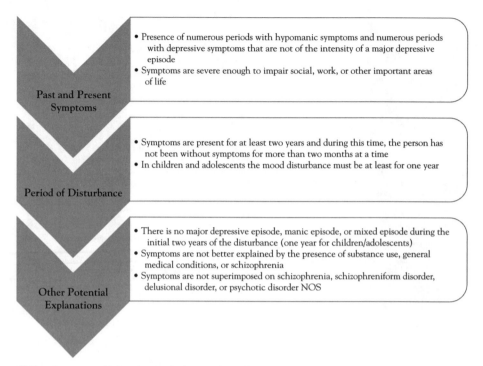

Figure 7.7   Conceptual Map for Cyclothymic Disorder

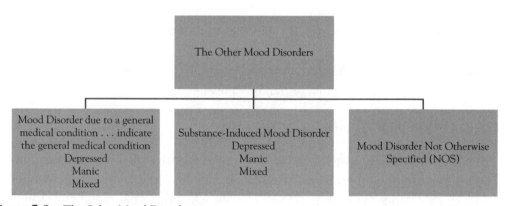

Figure 7.8   The Other Mood Disorders

Mood Disorder Due to a Medical Condition

Many medical illnesses can trigger symptoms of depression, including neurological conditions (such as Parkinson's disease), cerebrovascular disease (stroke), certain metabolic conditions (vitamin B_{12} deficiency), endocrine conditions (hypothyroidism), viral or other infections (hepatitis or HIV), and certain cancers (pancreatic cancer) (APA, 2000). In order to determine the presence of a mood disorder due to a medical condition, the mood disturbance is seen as the direct effect of a general medical condition. The symptom picture may show someone with a depressed mood, loss of interest in what were formerly pleasurable activities, or agitated and perhaps irritable. To be certain of this diagnosis, there must be evidence from the person's history, a physical exam, or laboratory findings. Be attentive to the timing between the onset (or remission) of the person's mood disturbance and his or her medical condition.

Substance-Induced Mood Disorder

A mood disorder can be diagnosed as substance-induced if the causes of the person's mood symptoms can be traced to the direct physiologic effects of a drug (prescribed or illegal) or other chemical substance or if the development of the mood disorder occurred contemporaneously with substance intoxication or withdrawal. Alternately, the person may have a mood disorder coexisting with a substance abuse disorder. Substance-induced mood disorders can have features of depressed, manic, mixed or hypomanic episodes. Most substances will affect a person's mood and can induce a variety of mood disorders. For instance, the drugs classified as stimulants such as amphetamine or methamphetamine can cause manic, hypomanic, mixed, and depressive episodes. Long-term use of benzodiazepines, commonly used to treat insomnia and anxiety, are believed to be related to increased depression (Collier, Longmore, Turmezi, & Mafi, 2009, p. 368). Depression can also be related to withdrawal from benzodiazepines but it usually subsides after a few months.

As mentioned earlier in the chapter, those who are depressed tend to drink more alcohol than they would usually consume and higher rates of MDD are found to occur in those considered to be "heavy drinkers" or who abuse alcohol. It is not clear whether those who abuse alcohol and develop depression are self-medicating a preexisting depression. However, what we do know is that in some cases, alcohol misuse can directly cause the development of depression in a significant number of heavy drinkers (Falk, & Hilton, 2008; Fergusson, Boden, & Horwood, 2009). This may be related to the distortion of the person's brain chemistry as he or she tends to improve spontaneously after a period of abstinence (Wetterling & Junghanns, 2000). Higher rates of suicide are known to occur in those individuals who have alcohol-related problems. The competency-based assessment provides the opportunity to take a thorough history helping to better differentiate between alcohol-related depression and depression that is not related to the person's alcohol use (Schuckit et al., 2007).

Mood Disorder Not Otherwise Specified (NOS)

This diagnostic category includes the presence of mood symptoms that do not seem to meet criteria for any specific mood disorder. In some situations, the practitioner may not be sure if the person struggles with a depressive disorder or bipolar disorder. This diagnosis provides a place for the practitioner's diagnostic uncertainty about a person's mood disorder.

FINAL THOUGHTS

The depressive disorders. The mood disorders are complicated by the different types of mood episodes, qualifiers, and levels of severity. As you begin to explore the person's unique history in order to differentiate the symptom picture, a good starting place is to look at current and past mood episodes; in particular the "building blocks" of major depressive, manic, mixed, or hypomanic episodes. MDD is the most common of the mood disorders affecting twice as many women than men. This disorder represents a mixed group of symptoms affecting the person's mood, affect, cognition, neurovegetative functions (or bodily symptoms such as poor appetite, insomnia, and low energy), and behavior. The substance-abuse disorders tend to co-occur with MDD. Those who are especially at risk for MDD may experience life stress, have a chronic general medical condition or a family history of depression. Additionally, those with recurrent forms of MDD are also at a higher risk for suicide. The wide range of factors that can contribute to the etiology of a major depression underscores the competency-based assessment that takes all aspects of the person's life into consideration. In addition, by identifying competencies within the person's life your focus shifts to including positive behaviors and events rather than looking solely at the so-called "defects."

Similar to MDD, dysthymic disorder also calls for a comprehensive review of the person's history of mood. Dysthymia is considered a long-term low-grade depression based on the person's chronically depressed mood for most of each day, on most days, for at least two years. Although those who struggle with DD show many of the same symptoms found in major depressive episodes, including a low mood, fatigue, hopelessness, trouble concentrating or making decisions, problems eating and sleeping, the major difference is a chronic feeling of a depressed mood. Because these symptoms have been so much of a part of the person's life, the practitioner often hears clients describe themselves like, "I've always been this way" or "That's just how I am." It is possible for episodes of major depression to be superimposed on DD and when that happens, the practitioner considers the presence of "double depression." Depressive disorder not specified was reviewed to complete the diagnostic picture.

The bipolar disorders. The chapter also explored the bipolar disorders that represent a spectrum of mood disorders. Those who struggle with these disorders experience varying degrees of a general dissatisfaction with life or feelings of unhappiness, agitation, impulsivity, euphoria, and in some cases psychotic ideation. The major distinction between MDD and the bipolar disorders is that problems associated with bipolar disorder show up in a cyclical fashion resulting in substantial interruptions in a person's life.

Cyclothymia, comprised of chronic, fluctuating mood disturbance with numerous periods of hypomanic symptoms and numerous periods of depressive symptoms lasting for at least two years in adults (one year for children and adolescents) was also reviewed. Sometimes people do not always neatly "fit" into specific diagnostic categories and the competency-based assessment provides a framework to carefully consider all aspects of a person's life. The chapter concludes with a summary discussion of mood disorders due to a medical condition, substance-induced mood disorders, and mood disorder NOS.

We now turn to the opportunity to practice making the differential assessment.

PRACTICING THE COMPETENCY-BASED ASSESSMENT

As you will see in the following case illustrations, when someone suffers from a mood disorder, his or her ability to function and lead a productive life is affected. In addition to the effects a specific mood disorder can have on people and their families, interpersonal relationships as well as career and work productivity are affected. The following cases provide an opportunity for you to differentiate between normal emotional shifts and those that seem to linger for no obvious reason.

The Case of L. C. Jones

I would like to introduce myself to you. I am Leroy Clayton Jones but most folks just call me L. C. I have "officially" had my diagnosis for at least two years now but my struggle has been for a lot longer than that. I would like to tell you my story about how this illness took over my life and how it managed to take me hostage.

My story really starts back in 1996 when I was just 10 years old. That was the year my mom died unexpectedly. Quite frankly my life has never really been the same since. You might say that I really never had a mom but she was what she was and did the best she could. See, she was diagnosed with paranoid schizophrenia. For most of the time I was growing up she was in and out of mental hospitals. My mom acted kind of crazy. I remember once she chased my dad around the kitchen with a butcher knife. What a scene that turned out to be. The police came over and Mom was right back in the hospital for a few days. She talked funny, too, and most times didn't make much sense but she was my mom and I loved her with all my heart. Sometimes I was kind of scared that I would turn out to be like her. Looking back, I guess I missed out on having a childhood because Mom was so odd and unpredictable. I couldn't have my friends over because I never knew what she might do and she would never allow me to sleep over someone else's house either. Mom worried that my friends would poison me. My dad was always busy at work. Even though he wasn't around much, like to take me to baseball games and stuff, I still knew he was concerned about me. I was never sure if he worked just to get out of the house or for the health insurance. We used it a lot what with my mom's condition. Anyway, when I was about 12 or 13 years old, I remember that he took me to see some kind of therapist who gave me all sorts of tests—I think just to make sure I was not crazy. She recommended to my dad that I take medication but I refused. My mom had died about two years before that and I was having trouble concentrating on my school work. My grades were going downhill and I was almost kicked off the baseball team.

I always loved school and was a good student. Reading all those books was a great escape. They took me away from all the commotion at home. But in my last year of high school I remember that I used to think seriously that I wanted to get away from life entirely. I just didn't know what I would do with myself but I didn't have the energy for suicide. Well here I am; 19 years old, ready to go to college, and I still feel out of place.

I've started counseling again and I am taking meds. I feel much better; like I'm finally on track with life. I even have the hope that maybe someday there will be a college degree in my future. I have to admit that I hate taking medication. Somehow I feel like I'm branded. Sort of like having an invisible tattoo right there on your forehead. After a couple of months, I experimented and took myself off my medication. A few weeks later I felt the ghost of death and destruction slowly returning. I tried to fight it without my meds but it just kept getting worse and worse. I finally decided that I could not continue like this. Funny, I didn't want to live but I didn't want to die either so I went back on my meds. I figure I will probably have to take them for the rest of my life. It was right then and there that I realized that medication does make my life a little better but I still don't like the idea. Taking that pill is a daily reminder of the ghost in my life and wishing that death would bring an end to my pain. I wonder if addicts ever feel this way. Ever since that "experiment," I've been back on my meds and have been feeling freakin' OK but I still don't like the idea of having to take a pill. I'm not feeling down or suicidal right now so they must be doing something. Is this what it feels like to be normal? For the first time I feel alive, which is a damn strange feeling for me.

Anyway, so . . . here's my story of my mental illness. For the record, I don't drink, I don't smoke or take drugs, and my health is good. My first therapist suggested it would help if I kept track of the events in my life with a journal and I would like to share some of my entries with you just so you can get an idea of the hell I lived in when it all started. You know, some of the highs, the lows, and then nothing in between.

Excerpts From L. C.'s Journal

May 2003

Even though it has been about seven years since Mom died, Mother's Day is always hard for me. My first therapist said I should write a letter to her. I did it again this year but this time it didn't seem to help as much. I also lost my job this month. I had worked for Mr. Becham at his grocery store since I was 15. It was really better working there than at the local fast-food joint. I was in charge of stocking shelves and loved the work. Mr. Becham took a fatherly interest in me and we used to have long talks about going to college. He never went to college and said that it was important for me to go in order to make something of myself. I was devastated when he told me that he was retiring and closing the store.

Then I started having trouble concentrating in school. I really think it started a couple of months earlier but it has been getting worse. I seem to be having mild mood swings, too. I can be happy one minute and rude and mean to customers the next. I was really better off than my friends. Behind my back I know they called me a "big shot" but I know that I was really doing much better than they were. When I was on top of the world, I really didn't need much sleep. It was those times that Mr. Becham would give me a lot of overtime. He said that I was the best worker he ever had. Imagine that! I had a million plans for how I would spend my overtime money. When I was in my hyper phase, I could skip from sorting cans in one aisle in the store to helping a customer in the meat department and then back to fixing the shelves. I was the best! I'm sure that's why Mr. Becham gave me all that overtime. It was hard to focus sometimes but I loved getting so much done. Well, without my job at the store I guess I don't have to worry about being distracted anymore!

June 2003

Found a new job; it's not the greatest and it's only part time on the weekends but it's a job. Have been dating a really nice girl on-and-off since Valentine's Day but I think something is still wrong with me. My concentration is getting worse. I have a hard time doing my homework and forget about trying to study for my final exams.

July–August 2003

Things are not going well on the new job. I'm so disorganized and can't seem to sleep nights. I am awake all night and then sleep until I have to go to work at 2 in the afternoon. I'm losing weight, too. Food is unappealing and I have no appetite. The mood swings are coming on more frequently. In between them I feel like I'm okay but then I go spiraling out again.

September 2003

Keeping up with school is getting harder and harder and work is a real drag. Decided to quit my job the end of this month. Things are not going well with the girlfriend, either. I get the feeling she knows there is something wrong with me because she is starting to come up with a lot of excuses when I call. We used to just go over to the mall and hang out for hours but now she's suddenly too busy. I really need a friend.

October–November 2003

Well I got the news; my girlfriend is moving away. She's only going to be an hour away and claims she still wants to date. I'm not sure I really want to keep this thing going. I need a friend right now not all the demands of a girlfriend.

Just before Thanksgiving I got in a really bad accident and practically totaled my car. It was my fault. I had trouble concentrating and smashed into the car in front of me. When they took me to the ER, I was told that I had a concussion and somehow I broke my ankle. Things are stressful at home, too. Dad complains about the bills I caused from the accident. On top of it all, he always gets stressed around the holidays. Starting to feel depressed.

December 2003

Things are really bad. I cannot sleep at all no matter when I go to bed. I am unable to concentrate on anything and doing terrible in school. Seems like I cry all day and every night. My girlfriend who moved said she would always be there for me but I know she doesn't understand what's happening to me. I try to tell her what's going on with me but she doesn't know what to say. That only makes things worse between us. Heck! I don't know what's happening to me.

The mood swings come on more often. One minute I'm crying and the next I lose self-control. That scares me. Thank goodness I have a little bit of reprieve in between the moods. I think about my mom sometimes and wonder if I'll do something crazy. You would think with all the holidays that I would have gained weight. Nope. Lost about 20 pounds so far and food is still tasteless. Now I'm afraid to drive and take the chance I might lose my concentration again and cause another accident. Got one hour of sleep on Christmas Eve. Whoop dee do!

January 2004

The mood swings keep getting worse. Those peaceful times in between are getting shorter and shorter and now I have random thoughts of death. I really think I need help. Talked to Dad and he set up an appointment for me to see a therapist. My appointment is at the end of the month. Saw the therapist and she referred me to a medical doctor.

February–March 2004

Have an appointment this month with the doctor to get some medication to help me with my moods. Things seem to be getting worse. Seems like all I think about are death and suicide.

The first medication made me sick; gave me migraine headaches. The doctor suggested that I try another one. Symptoms are only getting worse. The doctor can't seem to find a medication that works for me that has few side effects. I am consumed by the thought that life is simply not worth living. All I can think about is death and suicide.

April 2004

Finally on a medication that seems to be working; starting to feel better. Then I find out from my insurance company that I exceeded my office visits. Seems that reaching out for help didn't quite work out like I expected. Now I have no medication and no therapist. I feel so alone and this only makes my depression worse. The thoughts of suicide are all consuming. Getting desperate.

May 2004

Though she lives an hour away, I drove over to my old girlfriend's house. Showed up at midnight. Once I saw her, tears started welling up in my eyes and then I couldn't control the crying. Told her about my thoughts of suicide and begged her not to turn me away. I cried for hours and we stayed up the rest of the night talking. I was terrified to be alone and worried if another mood swing would come on. If I hit bottom again, I knew this would be the last time. She promised me that the first thing in the morning we would go back home and go together to the mental health center. I still felt hopeless and wanted to die.

My luck! We went to the mental health center the day of my final geometry exam. My grades were not the best at this point in that class and I failed the course.

How would you formulate your competency-based assessment for L. C. Jones at the time when he goes to the mental health center?

Update:

June 2004

Taking medication and it seems to be working. Starting to feel more like my old self. I still have my moments but the depression doesn't consume me like it did before. Sometimes I can even smile. Making up the geometry course in summer school and actually doing well. Still hope I can go to college in the fall. I'm sure I'll get in somewhere even if I have to start at the community college. Feel like my life is starting to be put back together.

The Case of Marilyn Greene

Marilyn Greene remembered the first day of orientation to her graduate program in mental health counseling like it was a "dream come true." She had always wanted to make a difference in someone's life and finally she was actually taking steps to become a counselor. Coming to this place in her life was not easy. Marilyn was raised in what you might call the wrong side of the tracks. She lived in a poor neighborhood. Going to school she constantly had to dodge panhandlers and drug dealers. When Marilyn was in kindergarten her mother would walk her to school every day just to make sure she got there. Marilyn never knew her father but heard that he was involved in drugs and probably died in jail. She learned the value of a good education from her mother. Marilyn's mother died of cancer when she was 12 years old and her grandmother took her in. Luckily for Marilyn, her grandmother also believed in a good education. "You gotta keep in school to make something of yourself" she remembered her grandmother saying. Now, here she was; the first in her family not only to graduate college but to be in a graduate program. Unbelievably Marilyn almost lost it all.

After Marilyn graduated from high school, she married her high school sweetheart. He worked in construction and she continued on with school working part-time in a large discount warehouse store while going to college. Marilyn was a good worker and slowly made her way up the ranks to become a department supervisor. She was also a straight A student. When she graduated college, Marilyn quit her supervisory job and started to work in the state child welfare agency just to "get my feet wet." She found she loved the job and felt challenged by the difficult cases she saw. With scholarship help, Marilyn started her graduate program in counseling. She went to school part-time and continued working days at the welfare agency. Her homework assignments and all the readings as well as spending more time away from home began to put a strain on Marilyn's marriage. Her husband wanted her home more, complained about not getting home cooked meals, and pressured Marilyn about having children and starting a family of their own. He complained about her devotion to helping other children and yet she had no interest in having children with him. He also wanted them to save money, complained when tuition bills were due, and thought it was time for them to buy their own house. It seemed that almost every day ended in an argument.

Though the couple argued almost constantly, Marilyn did not expect the divorce. It happened when Marilyn, now 30 years old, was beginning her internship in her counseling program. She continued working her job at the welfare agency and seeing clients there, doing her school internship, and taking classes. Living alone and with a reduced income to pay her rent, Marilyn began moonlighting evenings at her old job at the warehouse store.

Over several months, Marilyn began to show a profound weight loss, appeared at staff meetings at her internship agency hollow-eyed, was observed to eat only a few bites of her meals, became more withdrawn, and was visibly anxious and distracted in her classes. Exhausted, she would often go to bed as soon as she got home from her second job but would wake up at 2 or 3 in the morning worrying about how she would get through the day. The prospect of another day ahead of her seemed overwhelming. While she accomplished a lot during the day, Marilyn felt tired all the time. Going to school to become a mental health counselor was a life-long dream for as long as she could remember, but now Marilyn just did not enjoy much of anything anymore. During a meeting one evening with her supervisor at the warehouse, Marilyn became tearful and just couldn't seem to stop crying. She was told to "shake it off and be strong. At least you don't have a terminal illness." Throughout all this time Marilyn remained fully oriented, and did not abuse alcohol or drugs. Lost and confused, Marilyn made an appointment with her medical doctor who found no medical problems but suggested a referral to a mental health counseling clinic for further help. She seemed relieved at this suggestion and made an appointment the next day.

How would you formulate your competency-based assessment for Marilyn Greene?

PRACTICAL APPLICATIONS

1. After reading the case examples highlighted in this chapter, what factors do you think contributed to L. C. Jones and Marilyn Greene's reluctance to seek help?

   a. As you formulate your response, consider any feelings that these clients may evoke for you such as fear for their overall well-being or anxiety seeing a fellow counseling professional.

   b. Are there any factors that may potentially affect your ability to complete the competency-based assessment?

   c. As an alternative, share these cases with a colleague (or your supervisor) and compare your responses.

2. Interview a trusted friend (or a relative that you admire and respect) who you know has experienced a time in their life when they felt down or depressed. Explain that you want to develop your understanding of their experience of normal depression and let them know that they can end the conversation at any time if it evokes too many difficult feelings. Begin by asking what they can remember about the experience and what helped them to feel better. As you listen to the story, remember the diagnostic picture for the syndromes described in this chapter focusing on the difference between the expected ups and downs associated with life circumstances and events and those that contribute to a mood disorder.

3. Our chapter begins with the idea that all of us have experienced some form of sadness. Make a note to compare your experiences with those of the friend (or relative) you have interviewed in the above referenced practical application. Discuss these ideas with your clinical supervisor with the intent of further developing your professional insights and self-awareness into the challenges presented by the mood disorders.

———❖———

Appendix

Competency-Based Assessments for Chapter 7 Case Examples: Listing of Case Diagnoses

Figures 7A.1 through 7A.4 provide the diagnostic assessment for each of the cases illustrated. They are organized in the order that they appear in each chapter.

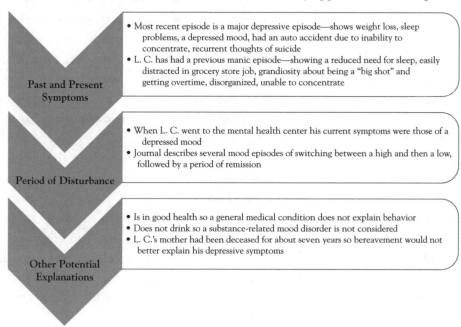

Past and Present Symptoms

- Most recent episode is a major depressive episode—shows weight loss, sleep problems, a depressed mood, had an auto accident due to inability to concentrate, recurrent thoughts of suicide
- L. C. has had a previous manic episode—showing a reduced need for sleep, easily distracted in grocery store job, grandiosity about being a "big shot" and getting overtime, disorganized, unable to concentrate

Period of Disturbance

- When L. C. went to the mental health center his current symptoms were those of a depressed mood
- Journal describes several mood episodes of switching between a high and then a low, followed by a period of remission

Other Potential Explanations

- Is in good health so a general medical condition does not explain behavior
- Does not drink so a substance-related mood disorder is not considered
- L. C.'s mother had been deceased for about seven years so bereavement would not better explain his depressive symptoms

Figure 7A.1 The Conceptual Map for Leroy Clayton (L. C.) Jones

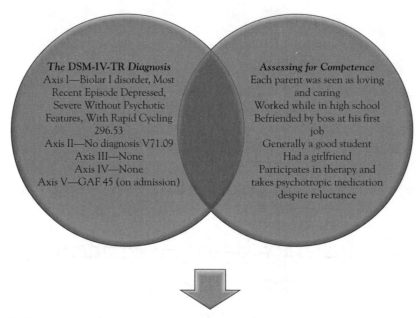

The DSM-IV-TR *Diagnosis*
Axis I—Biolar I disorder, Most
Recent Episode Depressed,
Severe Without Psychotic
Features, With Rapid Cycling
296.53
Axis II—No diagnosis V71.09
Axis III—None
Axis IV—None
Axis V—GAF 45 (on admission)

Assessing for Competence
Each parent was seen as loving
and caring
Worked while in high school
Befriended by boss at his first
job
Generally a good student
Had a girlfriend
Participates in therapy and
takes psychotropic medication
despite reluctance

Figure 7A.2   The Competency-Based Assessment for L. C. Jones

CASE REVIEW FOR L. C. JONES

A look into L. C. Jones' diary, written at the suggestion of his therapist, provides insight into his struggles with bipolar disorder. He chronicles a symptom picture of manic and depressive features beginning about seven years after the death of his mother. In particular we see his difficulties with concentration, mood swings that were initially described as mild and progressively increasing in intensity over time. Keeping up with school work becomes difficult for L. C., his girlfriend moves a short distance away, he has an auto accident due to impaired concentration, and is preoccupied with thoughts of death. Signs of manic and depressive episodes interspersed with periods of remission are described in the diary. L. C.'s mood swings increase over time, coming on more often, and, ultimately, he breaks down in uncontrollable tears in the presence of his girlfriend, leaving his last mood episode as depressed. She suggests seeking help at a local mental health clinic at L. C.'s height of depression.

Each person's experience with a mental illness is different and L. C. is no exception. The competency-based assessment reveals his early history of working and being befriended by his boss when he was an adolescent. Despite mood struggles, he remains in school and seems like a good student. In fact we learn in the update that L. C. is making up a failed course and intends to start college. Though his mother struggled with schizophrenia and multiple hospitalizations and his father seemed away from home for work, the family remained intact over the years and L. C. considers them as

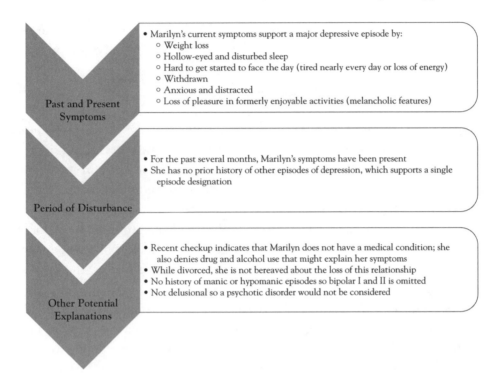

Figure 7A.3   The Conceptual Map for Marilyn Greene

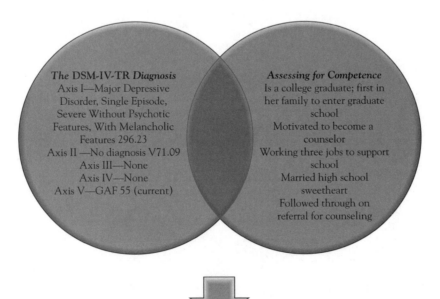

Figure 7A.4   The Competency-Based Assessment for Marilyn Greene

a part of his life. His mother's death, though a struggle for him years later, raises the question of bereavement but not to the extent to explain his depressive symptoms.

CASE REVIEW FOR MARILYN GREENE

The competency-based assessment explores the full dimension of Marilyn Greene's life history and recognizes her strengths and acknowledges her struggles with a single episode of depression. Her case story describes a life of being raised in an impoverished neighborhood where she went to live with her grandmother after her mother died. Her father was never in her life. He was reported to have been involved in drugs, and probably went to jail. Despite these adversities, Marilyn graduated from high school, married her childhood sweetheart, and continued going to school (while working) with the goal of becoming a counselor. Marilyn had no substance history and is in good health.

Marilyn's struggle with depression started after her unexpected divorce. Living alone, working several jobs, and going to school seemed to be the point in her life where symptoms of depression emerged. She was not eating well, becoming withdrawn, anxious and distracted in her classes, experienced sleeping difficulties, looked fatigued, and started each day feeling overwhelmed. Marilyn also lost pleasure in things formerly enjoyed and she became increasingly tearful. Motivated to become a counselor, she was able to reach out for help for herself.

8

Anxiety Disorders

INTRODUCTION

Although we have all worried about something at one time in our lives, there seems to be no simple explanation for why one person tends to worry more than another. The anxiety disorders seem to emerge from a complex interaction of factors and perhaps the most straightforward explanation for their etiology can be found in genetic influences. Heritable traits such as neuroticism, negative affectivity, and anxiety significantly correlate with the anxiety disorders (B. Sadock, Sadock, & Ruiz, 2009). Children of parents with an anxiety disorder are more likely to be anxious compared to children of parents without an anxiety disorder. For example, if someone has a family member with generalized anxiety disorder, the likelihood of developing the disorder seems to increase. Bowlby (1982), a seminal theorist who promoted the understanding of attachment and bonding, hypothesized that an infant's insecure attachment to the caregiver is linked with the anxiety disorders.

Those who struggle with an anxiety disorder are also more likely to describe greater unresolved feelings of anger and vulnerability toward their primary caregivers than those without the disorder. Another possible psychological contributor to the development of an anxiety disorder is how it serves to maintain worry. For instance, when a person is afraid that something bad may happen to them, it is this fear that strengthens its anxious meaning. Avoiding the potential "event" may be (negatively) reinforcing; that is, it serves to strengthen the associated fear and avoidance behavior. Borkovec, Alcaine, and Behar (2004) speculate that worrying can distract someone from their uncomfortable emotions. Overall, it appears that the interaction of genetic, biological, psychological, and social or environmental factors in a person's life, each augmenting the other, contributes to the development of an anxiety disorder. This range of potential explanations underscores the importance of the competency-based assessment that considers the multiple domains of the client's life.

INCIDENCE AND PREVALENCE

The anxiety disorders affect about 40 million American adults 18 years of age and older. This is about 18.1% of the general population in any one given year (Kessler, Chiu, Demler, & Walters, 2005; U.S. Census Bureau, 2005). The anxiety disorders commonly co-occur with other mental disorders, including alcohol or substance abuse problems, the mood disorders, and especially major depression (Kessler, Berglund, Demler, & Walters, 2005). These comorbid conditions may mask the person's anxiety symptoms or make them worse. Most people with one anxiety disorder will more than likely have another anxiety disorder.

The incidence and prevalence for each of the anxiety disorders are summarized as follows (Kessler et al., 2005; U.S. Census Bureau, 2005):

Generalized Anxiety Disorder (GAD)	Approximately 6.8 million people in the United States or about 3.1% of the population age 18 and over will struggle with generalized anxiety disorder (GAD) in a given year.
	The median age of onset is 31 years but it can begin earlier.
Panic Disorder and Agoraphobia	The incidence rates for a panic disorder are similar. It can be found in about 6 million American adults age 18 and older (or about 2.7% in a given year). Onset typically begins in early adulthood or at age 24 but can also occur later in the life cycle.
	About one in three people with panic disorder will develop agoraphobia (a condition where the person becomes intensely afraid of being in any place or situation where escape might be difficult or help will be unavailable in the event of a panic attack and leads to avoidance of these situations). Approximately 1.8 million American adults age 18 and over (or about 0.8%) will have agoraphobia without a history of panic disorder. Onset is about 20 years of age.
Social Phobia	Social phobia is diagnosed for approximately 15 million persons in the United States age 18 and over in a given year (6.8% of the population).
	Social phobia begins earlier or in childhood and adolescence; typically around 13 years of age.
	Specific phobia or a marked and persistent fear and avoidance of a specific object or situation is found in about 19.2 million American adults age 18 and over in any given year (or 8.7% of the population). Unlike social phobia, onset typically begins earlier in childhood with 7 years as the median age of onset.

Obsessive-Compulsive Disorder (OCD)	Approximately 2.2 million Americans age 18 and older will struggle with obsessive-compulsive disorder (or 1.0% of the population). Symptoms often begin during childhood or adolescence but the median age of onset is typically 19.
Posttraumatic Stress Disorder (PTSD)	Posttraumatic stress disorder can be found in about 7.7 million persons in the United States (or about 3.5%). Although it can start at almost any time, the median age of onset is 23 years.
	War experiences increased attention to this disorder and about 19% of Vietnam veterans are reported to have experienced PTSD at some point in time after the war.

OVERVIEW OF THE MAJOR CHARACTERISTICS OF THE DIAGNOSTIC CLASSIFICATIONS

There are a lot of jokes about the anxiety disorders. However, for the person who struggles with this syndrome, anxiety is no laughing matter. Most of us have experienced an anxious moment. Remember the first time you saw a client as a professional practitioner or sat down to take a qualifying exam? Anxiety is a normal reaction to stress and experiencing some degree of nervousness or apprehension is normal and even adaptive. It helps to deal with tense situations or to motivate us to study harder for the exam or keep focused. However, if you experience ongoing anxiety on more days than not and it interferes with your day-to-day activities and relationships, then you may have an anxiety disorder.

Those who struggle with an anxiety disorder generally feel extremely fearful and unsure most of the time. It is these fears and worries that become an excessive, irrational dread of what are normal everyday situations for everyone else. Those who struggle with this level of anxiety feel as if they have no control over their life and are unable to predict what may happen to them. It is this severe anxiety that impairs relationships or makes it difficult to do ordinary everyday tasks.

Anxiety rarely occurs in isolation. It is often accompanied by physical effects such as heart palpitations, nausea and chest pain, shortness of breath, stomachaches, or headaches. This is when the body prepares to deal with what it perceives as a threat. When that happens, blood pressure and heart rate increases, the person starts to sweat, blood flow to the muscle groups increases, and immune and digestive system functions are inhibited (often referred to as the fight or flight response). External physical signs of anxiety may include pale skin, sweating, or trembling. The person may experience anxiety as a sense of dread or panic. I remember one of my clients describing her anxiety as, "I just felt like I was losing it. My heart started pounding so hard that I thought it was going to jump out of my chest. I could hardly breathe and it seemed like everything was crashing down on me. I was convinced that I was going to die right there and then. It was horrible." In addition to somatic complaints, other conditions that may accompany anxiety are depression and thoughts of suicide (Sareen et al., 2005). Keep in mind that an episode of anxiety or a panic attack is not a disorder in and of itself, but provides the foundation from which the anxiety disorders described in the *DSM-IV-TR* can be assessed.

This chapter reviews those disorders characterized by anxiety and the associated behaviors. The anxiety disorders include generalized anxiety disorder, panic disorder and agoraphobia, phobias (social phobia, and specific phobia), obsessive-compulsive disorder, posttraumatic stress disorder, and acute stress disorder.

GENERALIZED ANXIETY DISORDER

Generalized anxiety disorder (GAD) is often described as the "basic" anxiety disorder due to its early onset, persistent course, and resistance to change. Regarded as the gateway to the other anxiety disorders, GAD is more commonly found in the general population than originally thought (Kessler et al., 2005). It is twice as common in women as in men with higher rates among those who do not work outside the home (Mendlowicz, & Stein, 2000). A person's race, education, income, or religion does not seem to affect the occurrence of GAD but cultural variations can be found in how anxiety is expressed. Most people turn to their family doctor for help rather than seeking treatment from a mental health practitioner because the symptoms of anxiety can mimic physical illnesses (Wittchen et al., 2002). In fact, it is not unusual for clients to describe a wide range of physical symptoms.

The Clinical Picture

The signs of GAD are so pervasive and somewhat unfocused that it is a challenge to sort through a client's symptoms. When the level of anxiety is mild, the individual can function socially and may even be able to hold a job. To further complicate the assessment, worry is a natural part of life and many of us have experienced some of the symptoms typical of GAD. However, those with GAD worry excessively about almost everything for at least six months. This is not the anxiety level of the proverbial "worry-wart." What distinguishes GAD is the pervasive and uncontrollable quality of the person's worry that leads to the chronic feelings of anxiety. The severe form of GAD is when the person's entire life is saturated with anxiety and it significantly interferes with social functioning. Even though these individuals usually realize that their anxiety is more intense than the situation warrants, they cannot seem to get rid of their concerns. For instance, these are people who have trouble falling asleep or staying asleep. Physical symptoms may include fatigue, headaches, muscle tension or muscle aches, difficulty swallowing, trembling, twitching, irritability, sweating, nausea,

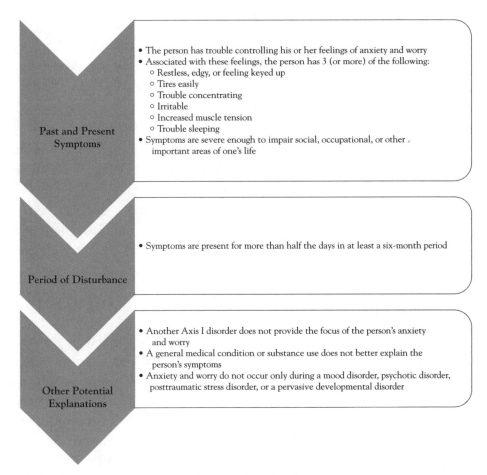

Figure 8.1   Conceptual Map for Generalized Anxiety Disorder

lightheadedness, having to frequently go to the bathroom, feeling out of breath and hot flashes.

The conceptual map (Figure 8.1) helps to guide the assessment of anxiety symptoms as distinct from a reaction to normal everyday worries in order to better determine the presence of GAD.

Differential Assessment

Those who struggle with GAD go through the day filled with multiple worries and tension even though there is really little or nothing to provoke it. They anticipate disaster and are usually overly concerned about money, family problems, or difficulties at work. One of the diagnostic challenges is that many other conditions need to be taken into account since the symptoms of anxiety can be found in nearly every other mental disorder such as the mood, eating, somatoform, and cognitive disorders. As well, a number of other disorders frequently co-occur with GAD; for example, major depressive disorder, other anxiety disorders, and the substance-related disorders.

We now turn to an exploration of panic disorder beginning with understanding the panic attack.

PANIC DISORDER

Panic disorder is one of the anxiety disorders characterized by unexpected and repeated episodes of intense fear accompanied by physical symptoms that could easily be mistaken for a physical illness. This disorder may also include a significant behavioral change typified by ongoing worry and concern or a sense of misfortune looming just around the corner. It is not unusual for the individual to worry about having another one of these attacks.

Distinguishing the Panic Attack

A panic attack is symptomatic of panic disorder and distinguished by sudden and unexpected periods of intense anxiety typically accompanied by a variety of somatic symptoms such as a pounding heart, sweatiness, and feelings of weakness, faintness, or dizziness. During these attacks, the person may flush or feel cold. Their hands may tingle or they may complain that they feel numb. The individual may also experience nausea, chest pain, or a sensation of smothering. These panic attacks can also produce cognitive symptoms such as a sense of unreality or impending doom. A panic attack

The Panic Attack

Symptoms:	Conditions:
Raging heartbeat	Occurs suddenly without any warning and the person feels unable to stop it
Difficulty breathing or a feeling of not getting enough air	Level of fear is out of proportion to the actual situation (or even unrelated)
Terror to the point that it is almost paralyzing	Passes in a few minutes
Nervous, shaking, stress	Repeated attacks can reoccur for hours
Choking, chest pains, distress	
Fearful, frightened, anxious	
Hot flashes or sudden chills	
Tingling sensation in the fingers or toes often described as "pins and needles"	
Fear of going crazy or about to die	

is not dangerous but it can be a terrifying experience largely because the person feels "crazy" and out of control. A panic attack is often described as an experience similar to a heart attack. Others may see it as if they were losing their mind. A panic attack is reputed to be one of the most intensely frightening, upsetting, and uncomfortable experience in a person's life (Bourne, 2005).

Panic Disorder Symptoms

A panic disorder is distinguished by repeated persistent panic attacks that last for several minutes (sometimes longer) or the person feels severe anxiety about having another attack, also referred to as anticipatory anxiety. The kind of panic that typifies a panic disorder is a sudden surge of overwhelming fear that comes over the person without any warning and for no apparent reason. It is far more intense than the stressed-out feeling that most of us have experienced at one time or another. The person with a panic disorder cannot predict when or where the attack may occur. Between episodes, they worry about the next attack. Some people become so worried about the possibility of the next panic attack that they begin to avoid normal activities. For example, if someone has had a panic attack in a parking garage he or she may start to avoid the garage where the panic attack first took place. When this happens, the condition is called agoraphobia (or a fear of open spaces).

Panic and Agoraphobia

Panic disorder usually occurs with agoraphobia and it is that kind of fear that ultimately restricts where a person goes or even where he or she may live. This can lead to other problems such as substance abuse, depression, or even suicide (Wittchen, Kessler, Pfister, & Lieb, 2000). Many people with a panic disorder have higher rates of chronic medical conditions compared to the general population; for example, hypertension, mitral valve prolapse, respiratory disorders, thyroid dysfunction, and migraine headaches (Goodwin, Jacobi, & Thefeld, 2003; Simon et al., 2002; Swartz, Pratt, Armenian, Lee, & Eaton, 2000).

Taken from the origins of Greek language, agoraphobia literally refers to a fear of the market place. Agoraphobia is actually not a fear of places but a fear of having a panic attack in specific places. Agoraphobia usually begins with the experience of a panic attack that seems to happen for no apparent reason (McNally, 2003). As defined by the DSM-IV-TR, agoraphobia is seen as "anxiety about being in places or situations from which escape might be difficult (or embarrassing) in which help may not be available in the event of having a panic attack" (American Psychiatric Association, 2000, p. 432). In this instance, it is the fear of recurrent attacks that causes the person to avoid leaving the safety of their home or participating in other activities. Because the person exerts so much effort to avoid a panic attack, agoraphobia can be considered as a fear of fear (Gray, 2008).

Panic disorder is associated with significant impairments in a person's quality of life, so it is helpful to look at the environment in which the person lives and works and the competency-based assessment provides a framework for looking at a range of factors in a person's life. For instance, you might explore the frequency of panic attacks, anticipatory anxiety, the presence (or absence) of agoraphobia, and overall impairment in daily activities. The more common agoraphobic venues you can expect to see in practice typically involve clusters of situations such as being outside the home alone, in a crowd or standing in a line, on a bridge or traveling in a bus, train, plane, or car where escape might be difficult or help might be unavailable if the person has a panic attack. You might also consider the influence of family and/or friends who may help out with shopping or running errands. They might even accompany the person outside his or her safety zone. In severe situations, someone struggling with panic disorder with agoraphobia may be totally unable to leave the house. This is the individual who experiences debilitating fear and dread with just the thought of walking outside. Relatively few people will have panic disorder without agoraphobia; in other words, they do not become housebound (Barlow, 2004). For some individuals, agoraphobia can develop without any preceding panic attacks (Andrews & Slade, 2002).

The Clinical Picture

The combination of panic attacks and agoraphobia support the diagnosis of panic disorder with agoraphobia. This is when the person will do just about anything to avoid a panic attack; for example, staying at home or severely restricting his or her activities. The agoraphobia usually develops within just a few weeks of a panic attack. Individuals are typically diagnosed in early adulthood and more than likely they have also experienced at least one anxiety disorder during childhood; most commonly social phobia and overanxious disorder followed by avoidant disorder, separation anxiety disorder, and agoraphobia (Barlow, 2004).

When panic disorder occurs alone, consider the diagnosis of panic disorder without agoraphobia. The symptoms are similar to the diagnostic picture of panic attack with agoraphobia except for the avoidance associated with agoraphobia. These individuals are generally not as disabled as those with agoraphobia and less likely to come to your attention.

The symptom picture is so similar, so a conceptual map of panic disorder with agoraphobia (and symptoms illustrating without agoraphobia are highlighted in parentheses) can be mapped, as in Figure 8.2.

Though it happens less frequently, agoraphobia without a history of panic disorder can be seen in Figure 8.3.

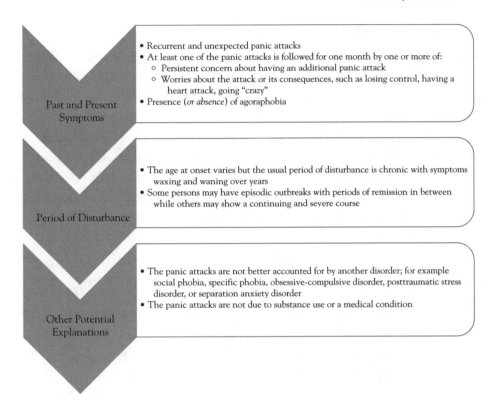

Figure 8.2   Conceptual Map of Panic Disorder with (without) Agoraphobia

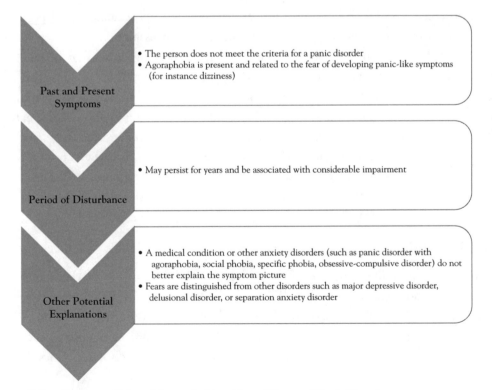

Figure 8.3   Conceptual Map of Agoraphobia without History of Panic Disorder

Differential Assessment

A panic disorder is not considered if the person's panic attacks are seen as the direct consequence of a medical condition or substance use. As a parallel, panic disorder is distinguished from other mental disorders that share the experience of a panic attack; for example, someone with a psychotic disorder. A person with another of the other anxiety disorders will experience anxiety but it is generated by different situations; for example, a social phobia is cued by social situations, specific phobia is prompted by an object or situation, generalized anxiety disorder is associated with pervasive worry, obsessive-compulsive disorder is linked to thoughts of (or exposure to) the object or situation related to an obsession, and posttraumatic stress disorder is related to stimuli triggering the stressor.

THE PHOBIAS

A phobia represents an intense, irrational fear of certain situations, activities, things, animals, or people that is so intensive that it is almost a fear of a fear. When this fear extends beyond the person's control or threatens everyday life, then one of the anxiety disorders is considered. We start with a discussion of social phobia.

Social Phobia

Social phobia, or social anxiety disorder, is distinguished by "a marked and persistent fear of social or performance situations in which embarrassment may occur" (APA, 2000, p. 450). A person often fears social gatherings, meeting unfamiliar people, situations where he or she is called on to perform and/or be assertive. Perhaps the most common presentation of social phobia is a fear of speaking in public (Stein, Torgrud, & Walker, 2000). Many individuals with social phobia avoid being in almost all social situations. Some may simply endure their discomfort but in extreme cases they may have a panic attack. Although each feared circumstance is different, it is the exposure to the feared situations that usually elicits some type of an anxious response. When individuals' fears are related to most social situations, they are considered to have generalized social phobia and the diagnosis specifies "generalized type" (APA, 2000).

The Clinical Picture

Social phobia is more commonly found among females than males (Lampe, Slade, Issakidis, & Andrews, 2003). It usually starts in adolescence, typically around age 13, and tends to follow a chronic course (Lang & Stein, 2001; Wittchen & Fehm, 2001). Those who struggle with social phobia often experience physical symptoms such as a racing heart, sweating, and trembling. Others may worry about choking on food when eating in public or being unable to urinate when others are present, also known as a bashful bladder. The fear that others may detect the nervousness or see signs of somatic distress, such as trembling hands or blushing (erythrophobia), adds to the person's distress. Although the person recognizes the excessive nature of his or her fears, he or she is still likely to either avoid or endure situations with extreme distress. It is this cycle of fear, avoidance, and distress that causes disruptions in normal routines, social activities, or relationships, work, and/or other important areas of life. When considering social phobia, take into account problems sustaining employment, a lack of career promotion, and/or severe social restrictions (Stein, Torgrud, & Walker, 2000).

Those with social phobia are distinguished by increased self-focused attention and elevated levels of public self-consciousness. These individuals tend to perceive their accomplishments more negatively than others see them and are more likely to interpret social events pessimistically (Stopa & Clark, 2000).

Figure 8.4 is a conceptual map that outlines the key features of social phobia.

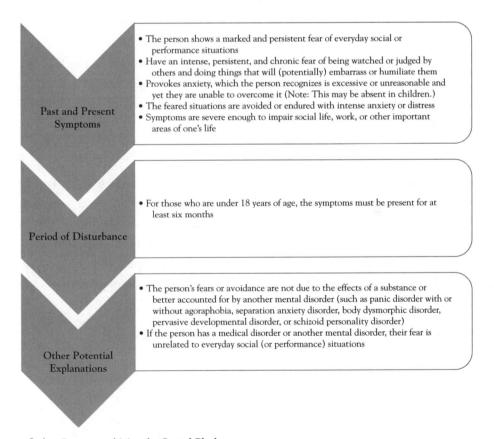

Past and Present Symptoms
- The person shows a marked and persistent fear of everyday social or performance situations
- Have an intense, persistent, and chronic fear of being watched or judged by others and doing things that will (potentially) embarrass or humiliate them
- Provokes anxiety, which the person recognizes is excessive or unreasonable and yet they are unable to overcome it (Note: This may be absent in children.)
- The feared situations are avoided or endured with intense anxiety or distress
- Symptoms are severe enough to impair social life, work, or other important areas of one's life

Period of Disturbance
- For those who are under 18 years of age, the symptoms must be present for at least six months

Other Potential Explanations
- The person's fears or avoidance are not due to the effects of a substance or better accounted for by another mental disorder (such as panic disorder with or without agoraphobia, separation anxiety disorder, body dysmorphic disorder, pervasive developmental disorder, or schizoid personality disorder)
- If the person has a medical disorder or another mental disorder, their fear is unrelated to everyday social (or performance) situations

Figure 8.4   Conceptual Map for Social Phobia

Differential Assessment

Social phobia is differentiated from the normal experience of anxiety when the person is significantly affected socially, occupationally, or in other important areas of life. Typically, social phobia can be found to co-occur with other syndromes. The more common associated comorbid conditions diagnosed on Axis I may include generalized anxiety disorder, simple phobia, major depressive disorder, and dysthymic disorder (Brown, Campbell, Lehman, Grisham, & Mancill, 2001). Social phobia is also associated with alcohol abuse and dependence. Co-occuring Axis II disorders are avoidant personality disorder or obsessive-compulsive personality disorder (Rettew, 2000).

Specific Phobia

Formerly known as simple phobia, a specific phobia is defined as an intense, irrational fear of something that poses little or no actual danger. Specific phobias interfere with a person's capacity to function well and result in the compelling desire to avoid the feared object. More than 100 specific phobias have been identified and more can be found on Internet sites (see, for example, www.phobialist.com), but the most recognized are animal, natural environment, blood-injection injury, and situational. There is an additional category characterized as "other" that receives less attention (Antony & Barlow, 2002). This is a fear that is prompted by other stimuli such as the fear of choking, vomiting, or contracting an illness; space (such as being afraid of falling down if away from some form of support like a wall); and a child's fear of loud sounds or the costumed characters one often sees in theme parks.

The Clinical Picture

The specific phobias are not extreme but they are an irrational fear of a particular thing. If the feared object can be avoided, the person usually does not seek help but if avoidance interferes with social, work, or other important areas of life it can be disabling. It is at that point that the person most commonly will come to your attention. The specific phobias usually appear in childhood or adolescence and tend to persist into adulthood. The commonly recognized specific phobia types along with examples are:

Phobia Type	Description	Examples
Animal Type	Considered the most common phobia, this is an excessive or unreasonable fear of animals and insects.	Insects, snakes, spiders, dogs, cats, birds, fish, mice
Natural-Environment Type	A fear of situations or events that occur in nature.	Heights, being near water, storms

Blood-Injection-Injury Type	The fear of seeing blood, looking at an injury, or receiving an injection (or any other invasive medical procedure).	Seeing blood, receiving an injection, having blood drawn, watching surgery
Situational Type	A fear that is cued by a specific situation.	Tunnels, bridges, elevators, flying, driving, enclosed spaces
Other Type	The fear is prompted by other stimuli.	Choking, vomiting, loud sounds, costumed characters

A conceptual map (Figure 8.5) to guide you through the symptom picture of a specific phobia follows.

Differential Assessment

The central feature of a specific phobia is an excessive and persistent fear of a specific situation (or object). While the person is aware of his or her excessive or unreasonable fear this level of insight is not necessary to consider the diagnosis in children.

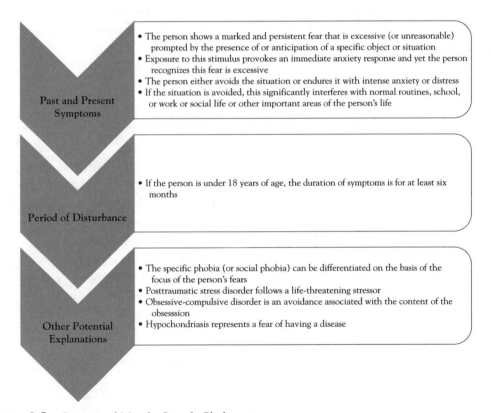

Past and Present Symptoms
- The person shows a marked and persistent fear that is excessive (or unreasonable) prompted by the presence of or anticipation of a specific object or situation
- Exposure to this stimulus provokes an immediate anxiety response and yet the person recognizes this fear is excessive
- The person either avoids the situation or endures it with intense anxiety or distress
- If the situation is avoided, this significantly interferes with normal routines, school, or work or social life or other important areas of the person's life

Period of Disturbance
- If the person is under 18 years of age, the duration of symptoms is for at least six months

Other Potential Explanations
- The specific phobia (or social phobia) can be differentiated on the basis of the focus of the person's fears
- Posttraumatic stress disorder follows a life-threatening stressor
- Obsessive-compulsive disorder is an avoidance associated with the content of the obsesssion
- Hypochondriasis represents a fear of having a disease

Figure 8.5   Conceptual Map for Specific Phobia

For most of us, fears are normal and adaptive but when they lead to significant distress or impairment in important areas of the person's life, the diagnosis of specific phobia is considered. In addition, the person's symptoms are not better explained by another mental disorder; for example, posttraumatic stress disorder, obsessive-compulsive disorder, or hypochondriasis.

OBSESSIVE-COMPULSIVE DISORDER

Those with obsessive-compulsive disorder (OCD) have persistent, upsetting thoughts referred to as obsessions and use rituals or compulsions to control the anxiety these thoughts produce. In most instances, the rituals end up controlling the person. Obsessions are defined as "persistent ideas, thoughts, impulses, or images that are experienced as intrusive and inappropriate and cause marked anxiety or distress" (APA, 2000, p 457). The most common obsession is a fear of becoming contaminated by shaking hands. Howie Mandell, the nationally recognized television personality and comedian, refers to himself as a germ-a-phobic. He popularized what has become known as the fist bump in lieu of shaking hands. Compulsions are defined as "repetitive behaviors . . . or mental acts . . . the goal of which is to prevent or reduce anxiety or distress" (p. 457). According to the *DSM-IV-TR* (APA, 2000), a person can be considered to have OCD if he or she has either obsessions or compulsions.

 The Obsessions and Compulsions

Symptoms of Obsessions:

- Recurrent and persistent thoughts, impulses, or images experienced as intrusive and inappropriate causing the person anxiety or distress.

- They are considered to be excessive in worrying about life's problems.

- Additionally, the person attempts to ignore or suppress these thoughts (impulses or images).

- And recognizes that they are an outcome of his or her own mind.

Examples:

- Fear of contamination by shaking hands.

- Repeated doubts—Wondering whether one has performed some act such as having left a door unlocked.

- A need to have things in a particular order—Intense distress when objects are disordered or asymmetrical.

- Aggressive or horrific impulses—A fear of harming loved ones, shouting an obscenity in church, thoughts of violence.

- Sexual images—Persistently thinking about performing sexual acts the person dislikes.

Symptoms of Compulsions:

- Repetitive behaviors or mental acts that the individual is driven to perform in response to an obsession or according to some form of rules that must be rigidly applied.

- These acts are aimed at preventing or reducing distress or to prevent some dreaded event or situation.

- In addition, they are not connected to what they are designed to prevent (or neutralize) and/or are excessive.

Examples:

- Behavioral—Hand washing, ordering, checking, touching things especially in a particular sequence.

- Mental—Silently repeating prayers, counting things, repeating words silently.

Many of us remember the childhood nursery rhyme, "Step on a crack; break your mother's back." Almost all of us have rituals of one kind or another. For instance, can you remember checking several times to make sure you turned off the coffee pot before rushing out of the house to be on time for an important meeting? The difference for those who struggle with OCD is that they struggle with obsessions and/or perform compulsions even when it interferes with daily life. This is the individual who is compelled to check their coffee pot over and over again to the point where they may not even be able to leave the house at all! Interestingly enough, these individuals usually find the repetition distressing and recognize that what they are doing is senseless.

The Clinical Picture

For those with OCD, both obsessions and compulsions serve to reduce distress, prevent feared harm, or to restore a sense of safety, but performing these rituals is not pleasurable. Most people who struggle with the disorder will show multiple obsessions and compulsions; for example, washing, checking, and repeating. Ritualistic washing is the most common compulsion and typically performed to decrease the discomfort associated with obsessional fears about germs or diseases. Some may wash themselves and others may clean their environment to excess. By and large the type of ritualistic washing you can expect to see in clients may involve multiple repetitions, ritualized patterns of washing, or using radical cleansers such as bleach or alcohol.

Another common compulsion is persistent checking. Typically, the person repeatedly checks to assure him- or herself that a feared catastrophe will not happen or has not happened. The more common checking behaviors are making sure that doors are locked, faucets are turned off, electrical appliances are off and/or unplugged, important items are not lost such as keys or a wallet, and that a pedestrian has not been hit while driving. Clearly the person who retraces his or her driving route to search for possible victims or constantly checks the news to make sure that no hit and run accidents have been reported shows a level of concern that is quite different from common everyday worries.

Other compulsive rituals lack a logical connection to the person's obsessional fears. These individuals perform their ritual behaviors in order to reduce stress or make sure that things feel just right rather than to prevent some type of feared disaster. For example, they may count the letters in words repeatedly in order to prevent injury or harm to a loved one. Other rituals may have no observable behavior or the overt compulsions associated with them. They are informally nicknamed Pure-O (Hyman & Pedrick, 2005). For instance, an individual may repeat songs or prayers in an attempt to negate an obsessive thought or image. I remember one client who described his need to repeat the phrase, "Blessed be our heavenly Father" over and over every time he went to church in order to try to control his fear that he might shout out an obscenity in the middle of services.

A less common form of obsessive behavior can be seen in people who accumulate excessive amounts of material. They are commonly referred to as hoarders. These individuals generally avoid discarding useless things they encounter in everyday life such as pieces of string or magazines because they are afraid they might need them at some point in the future. Some hoarded items can be of value; for example, a complete series of Barbie dolls or baseball cards. It is more difficult to assess for OCD when the hoarded items are of some financial worth. In this instance, OCD is considered when the person becomes distressed when they are unable to obtain the collectible item or their social life becomes impaired. For example, they might miss work in order to tend to a collection.

Most individuals have insight into their difficulties and often recognize the senselessness of their symptoms. However, when confronted with the feared situation, sometimes the person will lose this insight. Other factors such as mood, the presence of other people, and stress can also play a role. Some individuals, particularly children, do not recognize their obsessions or compulsions. When that happens, the specifier "with poor insight" is added to the diagnosis.

The conceptual map to OCD looks like Figure 8.6.

Differential Assessment

The course of OCD varies. In severe cases, the symptoms can keep a person from working or carrying out other responsibilities. Some may turn to alcohol or drugs to calm themselves or avoid situations that trigger the obsessions. It is far more common for OCD to co-occur with other disorders and the most common is depression (Tukel, Polat, Ozdemir, Aksut, & Turksoy, 2002). Additional comorbid diagnoses include

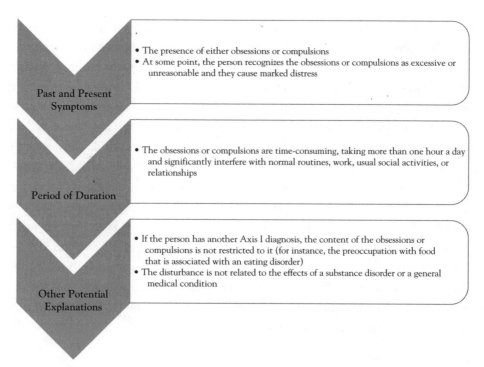

Figure 8.6   Conceptual Map for Obsessive-Compulsive Disorder

other anxiety disorders such as simple phobia or social phobia, substance use disorders, and eating disorders.

To complicate the diagnostic picture, the symptoms of OCD are similar to or overlap with other disorders (Huppert et al., 2005; Mataix-Cols, Conceicao do Rosario-Campos, & Leckman, 2005). For example, someone with posttraumatic stress disorder (PTSD) may experience intrusive, unwanted, distressing thought patterns. Similarly, the avoidance strategies used to manage the anxiety due to a simple phobia or panic disorder may be repeated in an almost ritualistic manner. The excessive worry that characterizes generalized anxiety disorder closely resembles obsessional thinking. Other diagnostic complications arise with body dysmorphic disorder (BDD) or hypochondriasis. A person with BDD is concerned about a physical defect to the extent that may seem obsessive while someone with hypochondriasis may obsess about their health and repeatedly seek medical help. In both instances, the person shows a level of constant worry often coupled with checking rituals and looking for reassurance to reduce stress.

POSTTRAUMATIC STRESS DISORDER

Posttraumatic stress disorder (PTSD) began to attract attention in relation to a growing interest in understanding how people respond to war, terrorism, and other forms of trauma. PTSD develops after a terrifying ordeal that involves physical harm or the threat of physical harm. It frequently occurs after incidents such as rape, mugging, domestic violence, car accidents, plane crashes, bombings, terrorism, or natural disasters such as earthquakes. Survivors of war are the most frequent trauma victims. In general, it is more likely that the individual will develop PTSD in response to the more horrific or enduring events. I remember how one of my clients described her rape experience that had happened almost 10 years before she came to see me. She was 23 years old when the incident took place. "If you think about it, the details would make you sick but for a long time I talked about the rape as though it was something that happened to somebody else. It went on for hours. I knew it happened to me but there was just no feeling. It took place just before Christmas. That's the time of the year when everybody is supposed to be happy but not me. You can't believe the anxiety and fear that comes over me around the anniversary date that it happened." She added, "I know I should have prevented it in the first place." The person who develops PTSD may have been the one who was harmed or the harm may have happened to a loved one. The disorder can also develop when the person may have witnessed a harmful event that happened to loved ones or even to strangers.

The Clinical Picture

Symptoms of PTSD do not usually develop immediately after the trauma. After some period of delay, the person begins to relive the event (or events) and attempts to avoid stimuli associated with the trauma or numb his or her responsiveness. The DSM specifies these conditions; in particular, the person must show three (or more) of the following (APA, 2000):

- Struggle to avoid thoughts, feelings, or conversations associated with the trauma.
- Avoidance of activities, places, or people that remind them of the original traumatic incident.
- Inability to recall an important aspect of the trauma.
- Loss of interest in things they used to enjoy.
- Difficulty feeling affectionate or detached and estranged from others.
- Sense of a foreshortened future.

Individuals with PTSD may also experience physiological symptoms; for example, to startle easily. Like my client's experience of having been raped, the person may feel a sense of guilt or personal responsibility for what happened to them. Anniversaries of when the incident happened can also be difficult. Some individuals may also be irritable, become more aggressive, or even become violent. There are a number of specifiers for the onset of the signs and symptoms of PTSD.

👉 Specifiers to Consider for PTSD

Acute	Symptoms are present for less than three months
Chronic	Symptoms present for three months or more
With delayed onset	Symptoms emerge at least six months after the stressor

Symptoms seem to be worse if the event was deliberately brought about by another person such as a mugging (National Institute of Mental Health, 2009). Most people tend to relive the trauma by thinking about it during the day and then experience nightmares when they go to sleep. When that happens, it is termed a flashback. A flashback can consist of images, sounds, smells, or feelings. They are often triggered by ordinary occurrences such as a loud noise when a door slams. During the flashback, the person may lose touch with reality and believe that the traumatic incident is happening all over again.

A conceptual map (Figure 8.7) to distinguish PTSD from the fear and anxiety normally associated with stress follows.

Differential Assessment

An anxiety disorder due to a general medical condition might be considered instead of (or in addition to) PTSD. For instance, a person may have experienced a severe head injury as a result of a violent trauma such as a car accident. In this example, note the brain damage resulting from head injury on Axis III. Situational adjustment disorder is considered when the severity of the trauma is far less than what the person experiences with PTSD. In addition, its effects are more transient and less striking.

PTSD commonly co-occurs with a number of other disorders; principally the substance-related disorders such as substance dependence or abuse, or polysubstance dependence. The other anxiety disorders may be present such as phobic disorder or generalized anxiety disorder. The mood disorders, particularly major depressive disorder and dysthymic disorder are also common. Malingering is taken into account when there may be the possibility of material gain from insurance or disability payments or the presence of legal problems.

Some Notes on Acute Stress Disorder

Acute stress disorder (ASD) is considered when the person's symptoms last for more than two days after a traumatic event but no longer than a month. This disorder is much like PTSD; that is, the person generally experiences severe stress that provokes fear, horror, or helplessness. If the symptoms persist beyond one month, then a diagnosis of PTSD is indicated. Similar to PTSD, a general medical condition,

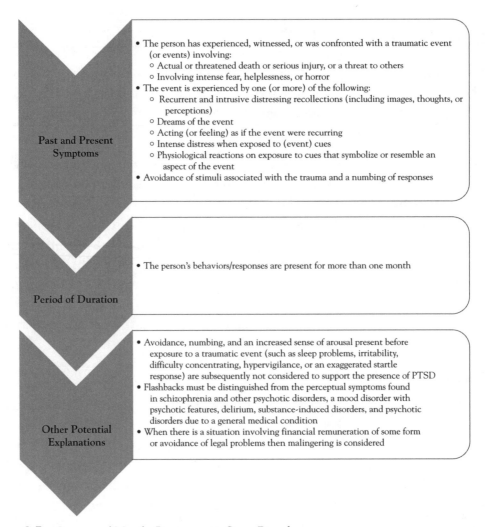

Figure 8.7   Conceptual Map for Posttraumatic Stress Disorder

substance-related disorder, or a major depressive disorder may better explain the person's symptoms. In addition, those who have been exposed to prior trauma, have had a previous diagnosis of PTSD, or have experienced other psychiatric difficulties such as depression seem to be at a greater risk for developing ASD (Bryant & Harvey, 2000).

As you begin to explore the person's experiences, the simple retelling of the story (of trauma) can be helpful. I have many friends and colleagues who have experienced hurricanes firsthand. For weeks afterward the conversation inevitably drifts back to their experiences with the storm. The telling and retelling of the event seems to help let go of some of the associated feelings. The prevalence of ASD is unknown but it is generally considered to be proportional to both the severity of the trauma and the extent of exposure to the trauma (Litz, Gray, Bryant, & Adler, 2002).

FINAL THOUGHTS

A consistent theme throughout this chapter is that anxiety is a common experience but the anxiety disorders are unique. They cause enough stress to interfere with normal everyday life. For those who struggle with an anxiety disorder, their anxiety is constant and overwhelming. These are the individuals who anticipate disaster lurking around every corner. At its most severe, just the thought of getting through the day may provoke intense worry and fear. Some people manage to perform daily tasks while others are unable to find enjoyment or pleasure in life. In general, the symptoms can include the following.

✍ Summary of the Symptoms of Anxiety

Feelings of panic, fear, and uneasiness
Uncontrollable, obsessive thoughts
Repeated thoughts or flashbacks of traumatic experiences
Nightmares
Ritualistic behaviors, such as repeated hand washing, checking, counting, or hoarding
Problems sleeping
Cold or sweaty hands and/or feet
Shortness of breath
Heart palpitations
Unable to be calm or to remain still
Dry mouth
Numbness or tingling in the hands or feet
Nausea
Muscle tension
Dizziness

The specific behaviors that a person uses to manage his or her anxiety will show up in several ways and the competency-based assessment helps to look for these individual differences. The anxiety disorders reviewed in this chapter are summarized as:

Generalized anxiety disorder—This disorder involves excessive, unrealistic worry for the person, even if there is little or nothing to provoke the anxiety. Symptoms are somewhat unfocused. Anxiety is low-key and chronic and the person does not experience panic attacks. Some individuals have insight into what generates their anxiety and others do not.

Panic disorder with and without agoraphobia—Those who struggle with a panic disorder have feelings of terror or a sense of foreboding that strikes suddenly and repeatedly with no warning. The symptoms of a panic attack may make the person feel like he or she is going crazy or having a heart attack (showing symptoms such as palpitations, rapid heartbeat) and trouble breathing (shortness of breath, chest pain). Some worry about the possibility of the next panic attack and begin to avoid normal activities. When this happens, the diagnosis is called panic disorder with agoraphobia. Others may experience agoraphobia without a history of a panic disorder.

Social phobia—Also called social anxiety disorder, social phobia involves overwhelming worry and self-consciousness about everyday social situations. Fears can range from choking when eating in public, shaking when writing, or being unable to perform when speaking in public. The anxiety associated with this disorder often centers on a fear of being judged by others or behaving in a way that might cause embarrassment or lead to ridicule.

Specific phobia—A specific phobia is an intense fear of a specific object or situation; the more common are animals, blood, heights, airplane travel, being closed in, or thunderstorms. When exposed to one of these stimuli, the person's anxiety may be experienced as a panic attack or more generalized but the worry always targets something specific. The level of fear is usually inappropriate to the situation and may cause the person to avoid common, everyday situations.

Obsessive-compulsive disorder—This disorder is characterized by constant thoughts or fears that cause the individual to perform certain rituals or routines. The disturbing thoughts are referred to as obsessions and the rituals are called compulsions. Most individuals have both obsessions and compulsions, which usually result in anxiety and dread. They generally are able to recognize them as irrational. The most common is a fear of contamination that leads to excessive hand washing.

Posttraumatic stress disorder (PTSD)—PTSD can develop following a severely traumatic and/or terrifying event. The most frequent is combat survival but it can also be found in those who have experienced a sexual or physical assault, the unexpected death of a loved one, or a natural disaster. In general, the more severe the trauma, the greater likelihood the person will develop PTSD. These individuals often have lasting and frightening thoughts and memories of the event and tend to be emotionally numb.

Acute stress disorder—Acute stress disorder is a relatively new diagnosis and follows the recognition that some people briefly develop symptoms immediately after a traumatic event. Symptoms are similar to PTSD except that they last no more than four weeks; if longer, then the diagnosis becomes one of PTSD.

PRACTICING THE COMPETENCY-BASED ASSESSMENT

We now turn to the practice cases to help you to develop your skills with the competency-based assessment of the anxiety disorders. Pay particular attention to the behaviors associated with anxiety as you formulate your competency-based assessment. As you begin to discern the person's symptom picture, consider making a summary list of these features that helped you to differentiate the anxiety disorder from common everyday anxiety.

The Case of Marybeth McKenna

Marybeth McKenna is a 32-year-old college graduate who divorced her husband about a year ago and recently started graduate school. She went back to school to improve her work skills. Although Marybeth's undergraduate degree was in elementary education she had never worked outside the home during her 10-year marriage. She presented for her appointment with the practitioner as alert, oriented, and well groomed, but seemed a little apprehensive. The practitioner's first impression was that it was just hard for Marybeth to get comfortable. Once inside the office, Marybeth settled into the chair farthest from the practitioner's desk and fidgeted with her purse. She then started to absentmindedly pull at a small string on her sleeve. Her eyes darted around the room and looked at everything but settled on nothing in particular. The practitioner began by asking Marybeth what led to her decision to seek counseling help.

Marybeth began, "I don't even know if you can help me. Quite frankly, I'm not sure why I'm here. Everybody has worries. I mean if we didn't the world would be a dull place, don't you think? Well, if you must know, I came here because of Dr. Warren Crane. He's my family physician and he said that maybe you could help. I'm not so sure. I think I just need some sleeping pills but Dr. Crane won't prescribe them for me until I see you. He believes I need to get a handle on my anxiety. I'm recently divorced and never worked outside of the house. Of course I'm a little nervous about my future. Who wouldn't be? I've had trouble sleeping, can't concentrate on my school work, and I'm a little irritable. I live alone and so I yell at my cat. What's the big deal? I didn't plan on my husband 'falling out of love' with me and into the arms of his bimbo secretary. The divorce settlement gave me a year of payments and my husband, or I should say ex-husband, sends the checks regularly but I'm anxious about what could happen to me if he misses a payment. You never know. I realize that I should move on but I'm afraid to date anyone else. Heck! If I found 'Mr. Right' he might just turn around and find someone else just like my worm of a husband did. Then I would be all alone again. Ever since my husband left, I've been feeling restless and a little uptight. Wouldn't you?"

Marybeth didn't wait for a response from the practitioner and continued, "I've been this way just about every day since he walked out eight months ago. So let's just get this over with. Fire your questions at me but if you don't mind, just ask only three at a time. You see, three is my lucky number. It used to drive my husband crazy when I started on my threes. You know, unload the grocery bags from the car three at a time or set the alarm on any number but a three. Oh! I think I'm getting off track here. What was it that you asked?"

It seemed like Marybeth was looking for a back door to escape when her eyes landed on a photo hanging on the wall of my office. She suddenly jumped up and went over to straighten the picture. "It's just a little nervous habit that I have," she added some-what sheepishly. Her eyes focused on the disarray of papers and books on my desk but she didn't move. "You see I have this thing that everything has a place and has to be exactly in its place. I know it seems crazy but I worry that people will think I'm a slob. A year ago, I would just rearrange my drawers but now I'm constantly cleaning out my drawers. If one thing is out of place then I'll take everything out and put it back again until it's all perfectly arranged. Of course, I only work on three drawers at a time. My lucky number. I don't know why. It's just a rule that I have. Sometimes it will take me hours until I get it right. I think this used to irritate the hell out of my husband! Oh, the arguments we used to have over this. Now his new squeeze of a girlfriend can take care of his sock drawer!"

I glanced at the intake form that Marybeth completed in the waiting room just before our appointment and noted that she listed a number of uncertainties in her life. Though she had been a good student in undergraduate school, Marybeth was worried about her grades since she started graduate school. She saw her professors as tough and demanding and yet was able to make straight "As." This level of performance did not reassure Marybeth. She indicated that she would worry about what would happen if she didn't get a perfect grade. Marybeth was also nervous that she would flunk out or worse yet be thrown out of school for poor performance. After spending long hours in the campus library, Marybeth would come home exhausted but had trouble getting to sleep. Once she did fall asleep, she slept fitfully and woke up exhausted. Around mid-terms Marybeth tried having a cocktail or two when she came home from school. "Yeah, it helped me relax a little but then I started to worry that I was becoming an alcoholic. I even went to a couple of AA meetings but started to feel uneasy that maybe somebody from the school would recognize me so I just stopped drinking all together," added Marybeth. There is no history of drug or alcohol abuse in her family history.

Marybeth denied having any serious physical problems, delusions, hallucinations, or extended periods of depression. "My main problem is this nagging uneasiness I have about my future. Wouldn't you feel that way, too?"

How would you formulate your competency-based assessment for Marybeth McKenna?

The Case of Tom Donohue

This is Tom Donohue's story. Tom is a 32-year-old junior account executive. Well, at least that's what he calls himself on his Facebook. In reality, he works in his uncle's real estate office selling insurance. His uncle, Howard Peterson, hired him at his wife's urging. She said to her husband, "My sister is worried about the boy. He seems to have a little trouble 'finding himself.' Just give him a chance." Although Harold had some misgivings he figured he had little to lose since Tom would receive a small salary and make most of his money through commissions. When one of the agents makes a sale and a customer needs insurance, they are usually referred to Tom. It turned out that Tom was very honest with customers. He would not sell them more insurance coverage than they needed. "Things are slow in the real estate market so this is good for business," thought Harold. He added, "We are an honest company and this just makes us look even better in the community." Despite this business relationship, nobody in the office seems to like dealing with Tom. They complain that he has a negative attitude. In fact, Tom is resentful when somebody else in the office makes a sale. He claims that their successes make him feel inadequate. Tom has a hard time making friends at the office.

Since Tom's arrival, the real estate office has changed. Instead of everybody working together and enjoying each other's company, the climate seems to have taken a turn for the worse. Nobody talks to anybody else unless they have to and mainly keep to themselves. Cracking jokes around the water cooler has become a thing of the past. Harold decided that he had it after he overheard a conversation between Tom and one of his new and promising realtors, Melissa Smithe. She made her first sale and came back to the office elated. Tom looked up from his cubicle and grumbled, "What are you trying to do, Melissa? Make us all look bad?" It was as if Tom believed that her success would make him look like he's inadequate. Harold took a deep breath and went into his office. To no one in particular he said, "That boy has got to have his head examined! The real estate market is depressed and we need all the business we can get. I just don't know what's the matter with that boy! Then I have to put up with my wife telling me that her sister overhears Tom complain about how anxious he gets when he has to come to work. Seems he's worried about how I'm going to judge him. He tells his mother that because he's my nephew he's afraid that everybody's looking at him . . . just waiting for him to make a stupid mistake. Why would I want to humiliate the kid? Good grief! He's family! If it weren't for my wife and her sister, I would have fired him long ago. However, since he's not acting right, I'm going to make sure that he does have his head examined." At that point his secretary poked her head in Harold's office. "Oh, you're alone. I heard voices and thought you might need something," she said. Harold just rolled his eyes in the direction of Tom's cubicle and added, "Sorry, but that boy is a royal pain in the butt. I think I'm going to have a 'sit down' with him. He needs to see a therapist and get his act together before people around here start quitting because of his attitude." The secretary nodded her head and added, "I think folks would appreciate that Mr. Peterson. The sooner, the better, too. Have you noticed that Tom seems lethargic, and he has trouble concentrating? One day he was on the phone with a customer and he simply stopped talking. Claimed that his mind just went blank. When I asked him if anything was wrong, he just said, 'If I think about my social responsibilities, they would scare me to death.' I've tried to talk with him about hobbies or something like that but he has little interest or pleasure in anything."

That's how Tom came to the practitioner's attention. She began the interview by asking Tom for a little information about his background. She recalled that he started by telling her his age and then added, "I know you think that's old but heck, if you're not getting older then you're dead." "He seems to have a pessimistic outlook on life," she thought. He claims that he has always felt "down" and admits to feeling depressed "for as long as I can remember. I think I've been this way since at least the first grade in school." Tom added, "The only time that I feel normal is when I'm home alone and watching TV. I can eat when I want, don't have to answer the phone if I don't want to, and just do as I please" Tom denied any history of drug or alcohol use, and has never experienced any psychotic symptoms such as hallucinations or delusions. He reported that he is in good overall health.

Tom described having no current close relationships claiming "girls are just too much trouble. All they do is want to talk. Me? I don't speak unless I have something to say." Tom wishes that he had a girlfriend but admits that his depression leaves him with little energy or interest in dating. Tom went on to reveal that he never felt comfortable with other people and generally tries to avoid social events. "They make me feel anxious but if I can't get out of it I just go and say as little as possible. I'm afraid I might say the wrong thing and then end up being embarrassed. Worse yet, people might make fun of me. I'm petrified of meeting strangers. I've always been this way."

Tom vividly remembered feeling humiliated and embarrassed when he had to give a report in fifth grade. He tried to write out everything he had to say in advance and ended up reading his presentation. He made good grades despite his struggles with class participation. Tom attended college for several semesters and once made the dean's list but ultimately dropped out when he found out that he had to take a required speech class. He subsequently got a job as a night supervisor for a small security firm. He liked the work because all he had to do was watch security monitors and had little contact with other people. Tom turned down several promotions because he was afraid of the pressure of having to supervise others. He was laid off when the company was forced to make cutbacks. He spent about a year looking for another job but never seemed to do well in the interview. "I'm self-conscious when I meet strangers. I don't think I did such a good job answering their questions," reported Tom. That's when he took the job in his uncle's real estate office.

Tom admitted that he has no friends, and avoids invitations to socialize. He describes anxious feelings that gradually build up when he anticipates social situations. He denies any sudden feelings of anxiety or having a panic attack. During the past few years Tom admitted that he had been thinking of counseling to help him to get over what he described as "shyness."

How would you formulate your competency-based assessment for Tom Donohue?

PRACTICAL APPLICATIONS

As discussed in this chapter, anxiety can exert a profound influence on how we feel, how we behave, and show some very real physical symptoms. The case illustrations have shown how anxiety can become a problem when it interferes with life in the absence of a real threat or goes on for too long after the danger has passed. Avoiding situations that provoke anxious feelings might help in the short run but when the anxiety keeps returning it can spread to other situations. In summary, anxiety can be exhausting and debilitating.

1. The cases presented in this chapter highlight the anxiety disorders and the behaviors people engage in to ward it off. When thinking about the competency-based assessment, it is important to remember that anxiety is also a symptom found in nearly all mental disorders. Reading over the case illustrations, at what point did you begin to think that Marybeth McKenna's or Tom Donohue's behavior was symptomatic of an anxiety disorder rather than something else.

    a. The anxiety disorders frequently co-occur with other diagnoses. Did you consider the presence of another co-occurring Axis I diagnosis? If so, what behaviors led you to consider another disorder? If not, how did you rule out the presence of another disorder?

    b. Rewrite the case scenario to include a symptom of a co-occurring disorder. Consider how this would play a role in Marybeth's or Tom's functioning and affect those around them.

2. As we all know, anxiety can be adaptive. For example, if a test is coming up, anxiety can help us to study harder. Uneasiness, apprehension about future uncertainties, fear resulting from a real or fantasized threat, event or situation characterizes the anxiety disorders. Sometimes people seek medical help

thinking that they might be having a heart attack or another physical illness. Imagine for a moment that an emergency room physician refers a patient to you who came to the hospital with complaints of a heart attack but no supporting medical evidence was found. What kind of questions would you ask to determine the possibility of an anxiety disorder? As a parallel, what would you ask to rule out the presence of other mental disorders that feature anxiety? Be as specific as you can.

3. Put yourself in the place of the practitioner who will be seeing the following client who was referred to you for an anxiety disorder. After introductions he begins to tell his story by stating,

"I find it hard to believe that none of my co-workers ever noticed what I was going through. If they did, thank God they didn't mention it. Heck, if anyone pointed out that I was losing it, it would have killed me, literally. Well, if you must know, you are not the first shrink I've seen. I've been to a family counselor, a hypnotherapist, and even a psychiatrist. I've tried everything from practicing deep breathing . . . I'm sure you know what that is . . . to self-hypnosis. Heck, I even discussed my relationship with my wife and mother, and even whether my father had been a strong enough influence in my life. Each time I saw a counselor, things would get a little better but nothing lasted. I once remember making it through a whole week without a major attack. It was like winning the lottery. Then in 2005, the fear came back. It was almost as strong as ever. I'm sure you can tell by my name that I'm Cuban and we have that macho image to keep up. Well, if you must know, after five years of toughing it out, I just can't take it anymore. Do you think you can help me?"

As you think about the competency-based assessment:

a. What competencies can you initially identify in this client?

b. What are your beginning thoughts about what might be this client's specific anxiety disorder?

Appendix

Competency-Based Assessments for Chapter 8 Case Examples: Listing of Case Diagnoses

Figures 8A.1 through 8A.4 provide the diagnostic assessment for each of the cases illustrated. They are organized in the order that they appear in each chapter.

CASE REVIEW FOR MARYBETH MCKENNA

Marybeth's behavior supports the presence of two commonly co-occurring disorders, generalized anxiety disorder and obsessive-compulsive disorder. Generalized anxiety disorder is difficult to assess because worry can be found in everyone's life. By exploring the range of experiences in a client's life, the competency-based assessment provides greater insight into the kind of worry that goes beyond what would be considered normal. The symptoms of generalized anxiety disorder can be seen in Marybeth's restless and keyed up feelings since her husband left her eight months ago. She has trouble sleeping and then wakes up tired. She finds herself irritable and so she yells at her pet cat. Although she is a good student, Marybeth worries about getting a poor grade. Her husband regularly sends support checks but she worries about the possibility of what would happen to her if he missed a payment.

Marybeth's obsessive-compulsive symptoms can be found in her worry that she will be seen as a slob. She recognizes that these thoughts are unreasonable when she admits

Past and Present Symptoms

- Has had multiple worries—school, dating again, support payments, concerned about being an alcoholic—and none of these adequately supported by fact
- Marybeth has been unable to control these fears aside from asking her doctor for sleeping pills (resulting in her current counseling referral)
- Has had symptoms of trouble sleeping, concentrating, fatigue, and irritability causing her distress
- Obsesses around keeping her drawers orderly and is compelled to organize them knowing it's excessive taking up several hours in her day—sees it as a "bad habit"
- Cleaning out her drawers is not related to any specific events and the behavior is clearly excessive for its purpose; does things in threes

Period of Disturbance

- Has had her "worries" and physical symptoms since her husband left eight months ago

Other Potential Explanations

- In good health and denies excessive drinking or taking drugs
- Symptoms do not support the presence of eating, somatoform, major depressive, or cognitive disorders

Figure 8A.1   The Conceptual Map for Marybeth McKenna

The DSM-IV-TR *Diagnosis*
Axis I—Generalized Anxiety Disorder 300.02
Obsessive-Compulsive Disorder 300.3
Axis II—V71.09 No diagnosis
Axis III—None
Axis IV—Recently divorced
Axis V—GAF 75 (current)

Assessing for Competence
Bright and articulate
Willing to follow through on her physician's recommendation to see the practitioner
Graduated from college
Returned to school for graduate studies
Married for ten years
Able to live on her own
In good health
Does not drink or take drugs

Figure 8A.2   The Competency-Based Assessment for Marybeth McKenna

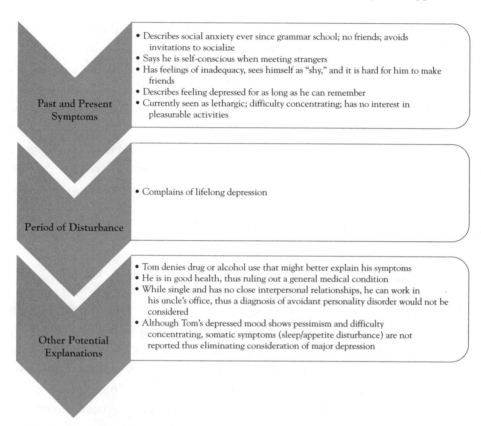

Past and Present Symptoms
- Describes social anxiety ever since grammar school; no friends; avoids invitations to socialize
- Says he is self-conscious when meeting strangers
- Has feelings of inadequacy, sees himself as "shy," and it is hard for him to make friends
- Describes feeling depressed for as long as he can remember
- Currently seen as lethargic; difficulty concentrating; has no interest in pleasurable activities

Period of Disturbance
- Complains of lifelong depression

Other Potential Explanations
- Tom denies drug or alcohol use that might better explain his symptoms
- He is in good health, thus ruling out a general medical condition
- While single and has no close interpersonal relationships, he can work in his uncle's office, thus a diagnosis of avoidant personality disorder would not be considered
- Although Tom's depressed mood shows pessimism and difficulty concentrating, somatic symptoms (sleep/appetite disturbance) are not reported thus eliminating consideration of major depression

Figure 8A.3   The Conceptual Map for Tom Donohue

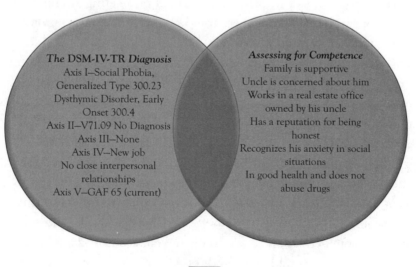

The DSM-IV-TR Diagnosis
Axis I—Social Phobia, Generalized Type 300.23
Dysthymic Disorder, Early Onset 300.4
Axis II—V71.09 No Diagnosis
Axis III—None
Axis IV—New job
No close interpersonal relationships
Axis V—GAF 65 (current)

Assessing for Competence
Family is supportive
Uncle is concerned about him
Works in a real estate office owned by his uncle
Has a reputation for being honest
Recognizes his anxiety in social situations
In good health and does not abuse drugs

Figure 8A.4   The Competency-Based Assessment for Tom Donohue

that others might see her as "crazy." She currently compulsively cleans out her drawers and must do things by three, her lucky number.

Marybeth tried drinking to relax but then worried she might be an alcoholic and so she attended a few AA meetings. However, she stopped drinking on her own when she worried someone she knew might see her in recovery meetings. Marybeth denies any medical problems and states that she is in good overall health.

The competency-based assessment draws attention to the fact that Marybeth is bright, articulate, and followed through with her physician's referral to the mental health professional. Though recently divorced, she was able to maintain her relationship with her ex-husband for 10 years. She is able to live alone and has recently returned to college where she gets good grades.

CASE REVIEW FOR TOM DONOHUE

Sometimes it is hard to shift one's lens away from pathology when looking at a client's struggles. The competency-based assessment considers a range of influences in a client's life, including a parallel exploration of the positives in someone's life. For instance, while the case illustration supports a symptom picture of social phobia, Tom Donohue somehow manages to maintain a positive reputation for being honest. Though it does cause problems for him, for example, problems making friends, anxiety about coming to work, and fears that others' successes will make him feel inadequate, Tom still manages to work in his uncle's office. He claims that he is anxious about social events and generally tries to avoid them. In fact, he's petrified of meeting strangers and has felt that way for as long as he can remember. Tom has also turned down promotions out of a fear of having to interact more with others.

Symptoms of dysthymia can be seen in Tom's long history of feeling down or depressed for as long as he could remember. The secretary at work noticed Tom's lethargy and apparent inability to concentrate. Tom has no hobbies and seems to take little interest or pleasure in anything.

Despite what could be considered potentially debilitating conditions, Tom seems to be coping. When exploring a client's struggles with the symptoms representative of a particular diagnosis, the competency-based assessment integrates strengths and resilience into the picture. As an example, Tom admits that he has been thinking about going to counseling for a number of years for his shyness and he did follow through with his uncle's recommendation to see someone. He seems to be a bright and sensitive young man who is in good health and, by history, does not drink nor take drugs. Tom's family seems to be interested in and concerned about him, to the extent where his uncle offered him a job.

Somatoform, Factitious, and Malingering Disorders

INTRODUCTION

You might know someone who is constantly going to the doctor even though there is nothing really wrong with them. For some people, this preoccupation with health or appearance becomes so great that it takes over their lives. When that happens, the person may have a somatoform disorder. Physical symptoms and concerns about health can have an emotional origin. When there is no identifiable medical condition causing the complaint, the person is at risk for any one of the somatoform disorders making them one of the most challenging and controversial disorders. Be on the lookout for the presence of a somatoform disorder if your client has any one of the following problems:

- Pain that is excessive or chronic.
- Conversion symptoms or the presence of a neurological deficit when there is no supporting evidence.
- Chronic, multiple symptoms that do not seem to have a sufficient explanation.
- Complaints that do not get better despite treatments that help most people with the same problem.
- Extreme concerns with health or body appearance and perhaps multiple cosmetic surgeries.

The somatoform disorders represent a group of disorders characterized by physical symptoms that cannot be fully explained by a medical disorder, substance use, or another mental disorder. These are individuals who go from doctor to doctor seeking relief from their medical symptoms. Diagnosing a somatoform disorder can be complicated.

For example, if someone has a genuine physical condition that previous doctors failed to diagnose, it would not be outlandish to visit as many doctors as necessary in order to get needed treatment. For us, the first step is to take our client's claims seriously and consider if the symptoms might match any known condition. By considering a range of explanations for someone's behavior, along with a review of the stresses and supports in his or her life, the competency-based assessment helps to sort through a client's symptoms in order to determine the presence of a somatoform disorder.

INCIDENCE AND PREVALENCE

The somatoform disorders are not particular to any specific age group but are more prevalent in women than in men (Fink, Hansen, & Oxho, 2004). Looking at the specific disorders, the female-to-male ratio for somatization disorder is estimated to be 10:1, from 2:1 to 5:1 for conversion disorder, 2:1 for pain disorder, and 1:1 for hypochondriasis (Yates, 2008). The somatoform disorders frequently co-occur with the anxiety and depressive disorders (de Waal, Amold, Eekhof, & van Hemert, 2004). Additionally, alcohol and drug abuse are common; that is, the person may attempt to treat his or her somatic pain with alcohol or other drugs.

The prevalence rates for the most restrictive somatoform diagnosis of somatization appear to be low or 0.1%. Prevalence rates for the other somatoform disorder rates vary according to specific populations (Yates, 2008). For example hypochondriasis approaches 4% to 6% in general medical clinic populations. Body dysmorphic disorder can be seen in as many as 2% of plastic surgery clinics. Conversion disorder is reported in 5% to 15% of general hospital patients seen for a psychiatric consultation.

It is not clear why the somatoform disorders appear but like many medical problems that often run in families, genetic influences seem to contribute to somatization. As well, children raised in homes with a high degree of parental somatization may model somatization. Factors that put people at a higher risk for the somatoform disorders seem to be family stress, parental modeling, cultural influences, and biological factors (Andreasen & Black, 2006). Looking at the role of stress, when a person encounters many stresses or cannot cope with the stress, physical symptoms worsen (Hollifield, 2005). It is hypothesized that the person unconsciously seeks relief through physical symptoms.

OVERVIEW OF THE MAJOR CHARACTERISTICS
OF THE DIAGNOSTIC CLASSIFICATIONS

The somatoform disorders are a group of conditions where the person's physical pain is related to psychological factors. People with a somatoform disorder go through numerous medical evaluations and tests to be sure that they do not have an illness, only to find that the medical test results are either normal or do not explain the physical symptoms (Ferrari, Galeazzi, Mackinnon, & Riquelli, 2008). People with this disorder are not reassured when doctors are not able to find a cause for health problems. In fact, they often become even more worried. Some become so preoccupied with their health or appearance that it dominates their lives. Symptoms are similar to the symptoms of other medical illnesses and may last for years at a time. Excessive preoccupation with the functioning or appearance of one's body is a central feature of the somatoform disorders.

Some medical tests can even be dangerous. You might have a client who has a history of multiple abdominal surgeries only to find that nothing is wrong with them. Without meaning to, people with somatoform disorders may inflict great suffering on themselves and on those close to them. Mental factors play a large role in the onset, severity, and duration of a person's symptoms. The somatoform disorders are not the result of malingering or factitious disorders where symptoms are exaggerated or contrived. Those with a somatoform disorder are not overstating or faking their symptoms. The pain they feel is real. It comes as no surprise that when the person's chief complaint is some type of physical symptom, you can expect to find this disorder revealed in a general medical setting.

SOMATIZATION DISORDER

Somatization, also known as Briquet's disorder, is relatively rare and associated with a high use of medical resources. Many times the person's symptoms do not reach the threshold for a clear diagnosis but the person may still be functionally impaired. The distinguishing feature of somatization disorder is a pattern of recurring, multiple, and clinically significant somatic complaints. As a consequence, the individuals seek medical treatment and/or they experience significant distress in social life, work, or other important areas of life. They may describe their symptoms in colorful and exaggerated terms but often without specific information. These individuals will doctor shop or go from physician to physician seeking relief. Sometimes medical tests or treatments will only serve to reinforce the person's fears that he or she has some kind of rare medical condition. The person's life revolves around these symptoms and almost becomes his or her identity. Interestingly, the person's medical complaints cannot be explained by any known medical condition. Alternatively, if the person actually does have a medical condition, the related complaints are in excess of what would normally be expected.

The Clinical Picture

Making the diagnosis for somatization disorder is difficult and the DSM (2000) has identified a series of physical symptoms that follow a specific pattern. That is, the person must have a history of pain in at least four different sites. There must be a history of gastrointestinal symptoms other than pain. There must also be a history of at least one sexual or reproductive symptom and finally, there must be a history of at least one symptom, other than pain, that suggests a neurological condition. Basically, begin thinking about somatization disorder when your client complains of multiple and chronic unexplained physical symptoms that may occur in different sites simultaneously. They are summarized as follows:

Summary of the Symptom Picture for Somatization Disorder

Symptom:	Example:		
Four pain sites	Head, abdomen, back, joints, extremities, chest, or rectum or symptoms related to bodily function such as menstruation, urination, or sexual intercourse.		
Gastrointestinal	Nausea, abdominal bloating, and less commonly reported vomiting, diarrhea, and food intolerance.		
Sexual or reproductive	For men	For women	Both
	Erectile or ejaculatory dysfunction	Irregular menses, menorrhagia (or abnormally heavy or extended menstrual flow), or vomiting throughout pregnancy	Sexual indifference
(Pseudo) neurological condition	Impaired coordination, paralysis, or localized weakness, difficulty swallowing, or a lump in the throat (globus hystericus), aphonia (or loss of voice), urinary retention, hallucinations, loss of touch or sensation, vision problems, deafness or seizures, dissociative symptoms such as amnesia or loss of consciousness other than fainting.		

In essence, the person is concerned with the symptoms themselves and not what they might mean. The individual has an extensive medical history that may be expensive, time-consuming, and sometimes even dangerous. An important distinction is that these individuals are not faking symptoms and often believe that they have something seriously wrong with them. The assessment becomes complicated if the person actually develops a serious medical condition or another mental illness. These diagnostic challenges underscore the value of the competency-based assessment that looks into the multiple experiences in a client's life and resilience or how the person manages in the face of adversity with illness, whether it is real or not. Figure 9.1 is a conceptual map to guide you through the symptom picture for somatization disorder.

All of the person's symptoms do not have to be occurring at the same time but may occur over the course of the disorder. In addition, two of the symptoms cannot

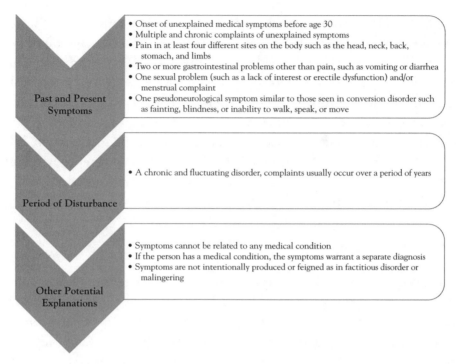

Figure 9.1   Conceptual Map for Somatization Disorder

be counted for the same diagnostic criteria. For example, if someone experiences pain during intercourse and this is seen as a sexual symptom it cannot be taken into account again as a pain symptom to support somatization disorder.

Differential Assessment

Somatization disorder usually co-occurs with other psychological disorders; in particular the mood or anxiety disorders (Yates, 2008). Substance-related disorders may also be present. Other somatoform disorders can be confused with the symptoms found in somatization disorder. For example, in pain disorder the person focuses on severe and often incapacitating somatic pain. Conversion disorder may partially explain a person's somatic symptoms. Those with hypochondriasis can have multiple physical symptoms but tend to focus on a fear of having a specific organic disease.

Cultural Considerations

Certain symptoms may vary across different cultures in that someone from another culture may experience persistent somatoform-type illnesses but do not meet the full criteria for somatization disorder. These symptoms may be better explained as a culture-bound syndrome. One example is neurasthenia, which is commonly seen in Asian countries such as China. Here, the person experiences a variety of symptoms related to the central nervous system such as weakness or fatigue, which may be accompanied by chest pain or a rapid heartbeat (palpitations or tachycardia), painful sensations, numbness in parts of the body, stomach upset, anxiety, depression, chronic hyperventilation that causes a dizzy or faint feeling, and even sighing periodically or sweating for no apparent reason. Cultural schemas influence the social construction of a person's distress. When the cultural significance of the person's symptoms of neurasthenia is taken into account, he or she may not fully meet the somatization disorder criteria as outlined in the *DSM*, despite their suffering. The competency-based assessment becomes a useful tool to consider the wide range of personal and social influences affecting people and their struggles with illness, real or imagined.

CONVERSION DISORDER

Conversion disorder, formerly known as hysteria, is where the person's senses or mobility are impaired. For example, these individuals go blind but their optical functions are perfectly normal, or they might have a seizure when there is no viable neurological explanation. Originally considered to be on the decline, recent research suggests that this fascinating disorder is more common than originally thought (Akagi & House, 2001). Like somatization disorder, conversion disorder is found primarily in women (APA, 2000). Interestingly, conversion disorder is rarely seen in mental health settings and this is more than likely related to the complexities of the diagnostic process (Snijders, Leeuw, Klumpers, Kappelle, & van Gijn, 2004). In particular, people will seek health care and not a counselor or therapist when they are not well. Since the diagnosis of conversion disorder calls for psychological factors such as stress or conflict to be associated with a person's symptoms, an additional mental health evaluation is needed to confirm the diagnosis. However, few patients in medical settings with unexplained neurological symptoms will actually be referred, thus leaving the definitive diagnosis of a conversion disorder uncertain (Crimlisk et al., 2000).

The Clinical Picture

Being able to distinguish among conversion reactions, real physical disorders, and outright faking (or malingering) is at the heart of conversion disorder. This diagnosis consists of three elements. First, the person experiences the sudden loss of neurological functions usually the result of experiencing severe stress. Voluntary and/or sensory functions are affected and the person shows symptoms such as blindness, mutism, paralysis, or loss of feeling. In some instances you might find what is commonly referred to as glove anesthesia. This is when the person claims that the entire hand, or the area a glove would ordinarily cover, is affected. Real nerve damage would not affect the entire hand. Second, these symptoms are not intentionally induced, nor are they associated with any medical illness. Lastly, there is a psychological cause. The psychological component is the most difficult aspect of conversion disorder because it calls for a determination of preceding stressors or conflicts that are linked to the development of the disorder.

Several factors can help to distinguish this psychological component. As you listen to your client, you may sense a level of indifference or a relative lack of concern about the neurological symptoms. This is commonly referred to as la belle indifference. Although this is not a foolproof sign, it is considered to be a trademark of conversion reactions. Second, the incidence of marked stress more often than not precedes a conversion symptom. Finally, someone with conversion symptoms can usually function normally although they are unaware they can do so. For instance, someone with the conversion symptom of paralysis of the legs might suddenly get up and run if confronted with an emergency. Later, they are astonished that they could do this. This symptom picture points to the competency-based assessment that provides a framework to look at the whole person and consider all aspects of psychosocial functioning as an integral part of the assessment.

Common Conversion Symptoms

Weakness or paralysis of a limb or the entire body

Impaired vision or hearing

Loss or disturbance of sensation

Impairment or loss of speech

Pseudoseizure

Fixed dystonia (ability to control the motion and function of the muscles in the body)

Tremor, myoclonus (sudden, involuntary jerking of a muscle or group of muscles) or other movement disorders

Gait problems (or the inability to stand or walk in a normal manner also called astasia-abasia)

Fainting (or syncope)

Another important feature associated with conversion disorder includes what the person gains through his or her symptoms. A primary gain is when the person's somatic symptoms serve as a symbolic resolution of unconscious psychological conflicts, reduces anxiety, and serves to keep the conflict outside of his or her awareness. This allows for the person's continued escape from or avoidance of an unpleasant situation such as having to work in an intolerable job. Secondary gain is when benefits are obtained and may help to maintain the disorder. For example, someone with a mysterious back pain

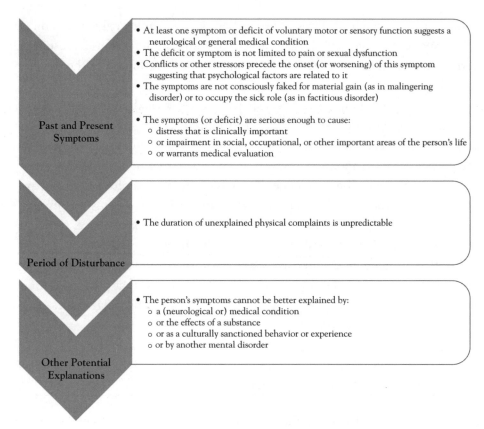

Figure 9.2   Conceptual Map for Conversion Disorder

may not only avoid a job seen as intolerable but might also receive encouragement and support from others that otherwise might not be given.

Figure 9.2 is a conceptual map of the conversion disorder symptoms.

There are four subtypes of conversion disorder assigned based on the nature of the presenting symptom (or deficit).

Conversion Disorder Subtypes

With motor symptom or deficit	Includes symptoms such as impaired coordination or balance, paralysis or localized weakness, difficulty swallowing, or a lump in the throat, aphonia, and urinary retention.
With sensory symptom or deficit	Includes symptoms such as loss of touch or pain sensation, double vision, blindness, deafness, and hallucinations.
With seizures or convulsions	Includes seizures or convulsions with voluntary motor or sensory components.
With mixed presentation	This subtype is assigned if the person's symptoms represent more than one category.

Differential Assessment

When considering a conversion disorder, the first and foremost step is to rule out a general medical condition that may explain symptoms, even if the person describes his or her health as good. You also might want to ask about the symptoms of somatizaion disorder where conversion symptoms are encountered. If the person seems afraid of having some type of serious disease, consider the presence of hypochondriasis. As well, when the person experiences pain as a symptom that is caused or increased by psychological factors, consider the diagnosis of pain disorder. Rule out factitious or malingering disorders if the person's symptoms are not consciously faked or used to occupy the sick role (Krahn, Hongzhe, & O'Connor, 2003).

It is also important to consider the influence of social and environmental factors. For instance, rates of conversion disorder have been found to be higher in rural and lower socioeconomic groups and where the highly technological investigations of illness are limited (Kuloglu, Atmaca, Tezcan, Gecici, & Bulut, 2003).

PAIN DISORDER

Pain disorder, much like conversion disorder, appears to largely have roots in psychological factors. This might include, for example, stress resulting from relationships, work, and finances. It is more common in women than men and usually begins in the thirties and forties (Andreasen & Black, 2006). With this disorder, the person complains of severe pain that cannot be attributed to or related to a specific medical disorder. The pain cannot be relieved by analgesics (medications that reduce or eliminate pain) and can arise in one or more anatomical site. Frequent complaints are pain in the lower back, head, pelvis, and temporomandibular joint (joint connecting the lower jaw called the mandible to the temporal bone at the side of the head). It is not intentionally induced by the people who have it.

The Clinical Picture

One of the diagnostic challenges to pain disorder is that pain is a subjective experience and each person will experience it differently. As such, it is hard to measure. Begin to consider pain disorder when someone experiences pain that is usually severe and often chronic. It frequently occurs after an accident or during an illness that has caused genuine pain in the first place. However, this pain subsequently takes on a life of its own. As the pain continues, it often leads to increasing incapacity and sometimes to complete invalidism. The pain can last for a few days to as long as several years. The distinguishing characteristic of pain disorder is when a person experiences chronic pain in one or more areas and it is thought to be caused by psychological stress.

Figure 9.3 is a conceptual map useful for sorting out the symptoms of pain disorder.

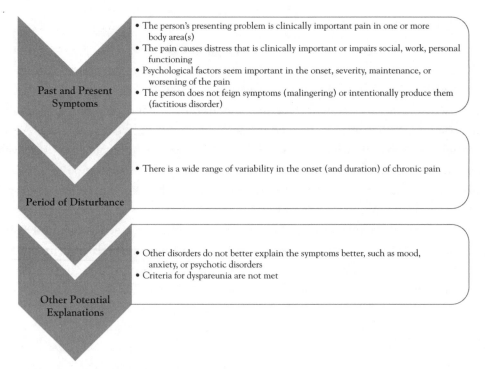

Past and Present Symptoms
- The person's presenting problem is clinically important pain in one or more body area(s)
- The pain causes distress that is clinically important or impairs social, work, personal functioning
- Psychological factors seem important in the onset, severity, maintenance, or worsening of the pain
- The person does not feign symptoms (malingering) or intentionally produce them (factitious disorder)

Period of Disturbance
- There is a wide range of variability in the onset (and duration) of chronic pain

Other Potential Explanations
- Other disorders do not better explain the symptoms better, such as mood, anxiety, or psychotic disorders
- Criteria for dyspareunia are not met

Figure 9.3   Conceptual Map for Pain Disorder

Differential Assessment

There are three factors to keep in mind when making the diagnosis of pain disorder. The first is to code the diagnosis according to the predominant cause of a person's pain, in particular:

- *Pain disorder associated with psychological factors*—This is assigned when the person has a general medical condition but psychological factors are considered to have a major role in the onset, severity, exacerbation, or maintenance of a person's pain.
- *Pain disorder associated with both psychological factors and a general medical condition*—This is considered when both psychological factors and a general medical condition seem important in the onset, maintenance, severity, or worsening of the person's pain.

Specifiers are also added. Acute is assigned when the person's pain has lasted less than six months and chronic is given when the pain has lasted at least six months or longer.

A third aspect of the diagnosis is to consider the diagnosis of pain disorder associated with a general medical condition or when the person has pain but psychological factors play a minor role, at most. When that happens, this designation is not regarded as a mental disorder per se and is recorded on Axis III with code numbers allocated according to the person's pain site. For example, someone who experiences pain in the lower back the code of 724.2 would be assigned and recorded on Axis III.

Somatoform disorder might be considered if the distribution, timing, or description of a person's pain is atypical of a general medical condition. Malingering is taken into account if the person receives some form of compensation for his or her pain. Pain could be seen as a symptom of depression and a mood disorder might better explain a person's complaints. Persons with hypochondriasis have a tendency to have other symptoms beyond pain. Conversion disorder does not include the presence of pain in someone's life. Sometimes the person is unable to describe the related emotional component of the pain. When that happens, this is referred to as alexithymia.

HYPOCHONDRIASIS

Hypochondriasis or hypochondria is generally related to an excessive preoccupation with or worry about having a serious illness. Fears of aging and death are common. It is marked by fear and efforts to reassure the person that he or she is okay do not seem to help. The person continues to be concerned even after they are presented with the results of a medical evaluation that do not support the presence of an illness. Hypochondriasis is no longer a disorder for adults but can now be found in adolescents and children. This disorder is characterized by unexplained physical symptoms that can be directly related to a fear that the person is contracting disease or a fear that he or she may acquire a particular disease. Although people with hypochondriasis place greater importance on physical health, they generally have no better health habits, like maintaining a healthy diet or regular exercise, than those without the disorder. If there is a medical illness, the person's concerns are far in excess of what one might expect for the level of disease. Many worry about a particular symptom. For these people, a headache becomes a feared brain tumor.

The Clinical Picture

Many of us at one time or another have had a cough, a minor pain, or perhaps even a small mole. If these minor ailments do not get worse, most of us simply ignore them. We generally accept our doctor's opinion that these conditions are not serious. For someone with hypochondriasis, the experience is quite different. That benign skin mole becomes a sign of having cancer. Hypochondriasis is distinguished by fears that a minor bodily symptom may indicate a serious illness. Despite reassurance that the person does not have a life-threatening medical condition, the person who struggles with hypochondriasis remains unconvinced. Many will seek constant reassurance from doctors, family, or even friends. Doctor shopping and a deterioration in the doctor-patient relationship, with frustration and anger on both sides, is common. Those who struggle with hypochondriasis often believe that they are not getting proper medical care and frequently resist a referral to a mental health professional. Given the strained relationship with health-care providers, the person may receive a cursory evaluation and the presence of a general medical condition might actually be missed thus complicating the diagnosis of hypochondriasis.

Others may completely avoid any reminder of illness. These are the individuals who claim to be afraid of going to the doctor despite the belief that they are gravely ill. Still others may refuse to talk about their fears convinced that they will not be taken seriously. Unfortunately, the torment of thinking that one has a serious illness continues to dominate the person's life. Family life may become disrupted as it becomes centered on the individual's physical well-being. Often the preoccupation with health interferes with job performance and causes the individual to miss time from work. Some people are certain that they have a life-threatening disease beyond any medical help and consider this as some form of punishment for past misdeeds (Fallon, Qureshi, Laje, & Klein, 2000). This fear can become completely paralyzing. In more severe cases, the person may become a complete invalid.

The conceptual map (Figure 9.4) to outline the symptoms of hypochondriasis follows:

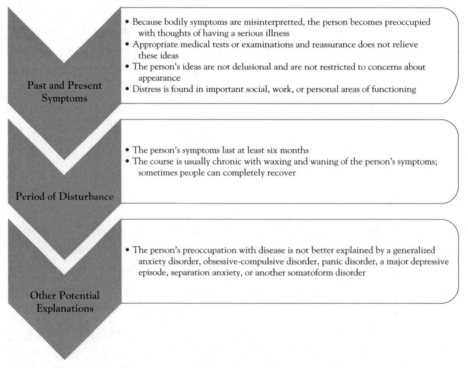

Past and Present Symptoms
- Because bodily symptoms are misinterpretted, the person becomes preoccupied with thoughts of having a serious illness
- Appropriate medical tests or examinations and reassurance does not relieve these ideas
- The person's ideas are not delusional and are not restricted to concerns about appearance
- Distress is found in important social, work, or personal areas of functioning

Period of Disturbance
- The person's symptoms last at least six months
- The course is usually chronic with waxing and waning of the person's symptoms; sometimes people can completely recover

Other Potential Explanations
- The person's preoccupation with disease is not better explained by a generalized anxiety disorder, obsessive-compulsive disorder, panic disorder, a major depressive episode, separation anxiety, or another somatoform disorder

Figure 9.4   Conceptual Map for Hypochondriasis

Variations of Hypochondriasis

There are a number of interesting variations of hypochondriasis. One is colloquially referred to as cyberchondria (White & Horvitz, 2009). The easy access to medical information with detailed explanations for any and all rare diseases and related symptoms via the Internet has spawned this relatively recent phenomenon. This technological variation of hypochondriasis is typified by the excessive use of Internet health sites to fuel a person's health anxiety. Known as a cyberchondriac, the person is often convinced that he or she has the disorder researched on the Internet. For example, this is the person who visits an Internet clinic and will self-diagnose his or her drowsiness as chronic fatigue.

Another variation of hypochondriasis is referred to as medical student syndrome (Hodges, 2004). This is a condition frequently found in medical students who are studying a number of diseases. As they learn about the symptom picture, students ultimately perceive themselves (or others) to be experiencing the symptoms or they have a fear of contracting the disease in question.

Differential Assessment

Hypochondriasis can co-occur with other disorders and the most common are depression, obsessive-compulsive disorder, phobias, somatization, and generalized anxiety disorder. However, hypochondriasis is not diagnosed if symptoms occur only in the course of another somatoform disorder or an anxiety disorder. Depression and anxiety can produce physical symptoms. Depression, for example can contribute to changes in appetite and weight fluctuation, fatigue, and a diminished interest in sex. Anxiety is associated with the physical symptoms of palpitations, sweating, a rapid heartbeat, and muscle tension to list a few. For the person struggling with hypochondriasis, these signs can be interpreted as actually having some kind of illness.

There is a great deal of overlap between hypochondriasis and somatization disorder (Noyes, Stuart, Watson, & Langbehn, 2006). When distinguishing between the two, people with hypochondriasis are fearful that their symptoms indicate a serious disease whereas those with somatization disorder typically do not progress beyond a concern with the symptoms themselves.

Many of the symptoms of hypochondriasis are closely related to obsessive-compulsive disorder (Abramowitz & Braddock, 2006). For example, many with hypochondriasis will experience a cycle of intrusive thoughts about their illness followed by compulsive checking. The difference is that those with obsessive-compulsive disorder worry about getting an illness while those with hypochondriasis are afraid of essentially having an illness. These diagnostic distinctions underscore the value of the competency-based assessment that promotes a careful exploration of the multiple dimensions of a person's life.

BODY DYSMORPHIC DISORDER

Most of us care about how we look and make an effort to improve our appearance. We may wear makeup, buy flattering clothes, carefully shave, curl, or straighten our hair. If asked, most people will describe something about their appearance they want to improve but for somebody with body dysmorphic disorder (BDD), these concerns are extreme. They worry about their looks to the point where it interferes with their lives. These are the individuals who think of themselves as so ugly that they are unable to interact with others or otherwise function without impairment. BDD is characterized by a focus on defects not seen by others or considered to be minimal and reassurance does not seem to help. Some will search endlessly for a cure for their imagined defect by going from doctor to doctor. Unfortunately, this does not relieve the person's concerns. Others may have surgery after surgery without ever being satisfied with how they look. When the imagined ugliness is not seen by others, the person might feel lonely, isolated, and misunderstood. Suicidal ideation or attempts are common (Phillips & Menard, 2006).

It is estimated that as many as 2% of the U.S. general population is affected by this diagnosis (Phillips, 2004). Unfortunately we do not know exactly what causes BDD because each person's experience is different but it seems to be the end result of a combination of biological, psychological, and environmental factors, including a history of abuse and neglect (Didie et al., 2006). The competency-based assessment provides a systematic approach to carefully examining these aspects of a client's life and evaluating his or her potential contributions to the development of BDD.

The Clinical Picture

In essence, the person who struggles with BDD is excessively concerned about and preoccupied with a perceived defect in his or her physical features. Some people may actually have a slight imperfection but their constant obsession with it is what distinguishes the diagnosis of BDD. The most commonly affected areas are on the face, hair, and the head area especially the skin and the nose. Some may see defects in more than one location or as a vaguely defined feature of their general appearance. Katherine Phillips (2005) studied more than 500 patients and identified the commonly reported complaints of imagined defects. The most common locations reported by percentages are:

Commonly Reported Locations of Imagined Defects in Body Dysmorphic Disorder

Skin (73%)
Hair (56%)
Nose (37%)

Toes (36%)
Weight (22%)
Abdomen (22%)
Breasts/chests/nipples (21%)
Eyes (20%)
Thighs (20%)
Teeth (20%)

Unfortunately, the person sees these problems as hideous and repulsive. You might hear clients talk about frequently checking their presumed ugly features to the point where they become fixated on mirrors; that is, to compulsively look at themselves or to avoid mirrors entirely. The smallest wart or mole for example is perceived to be as big as a baseball. These individuals typically think about their appearance for at least 1 hour a day. Expect to find clients in your practice with ideas of reference or thinking everything that goes on in their world is somehow related to them; in this instance to their imagined defect (Phillips, 2004). In severe cases, the person may stop all social contact and become a recluse. Because appearance is so closely linked to self-value, you can also expect to see a low sense of self-esteem along with BDD.

The conceptual map for BDD would look like Figure 9.5.

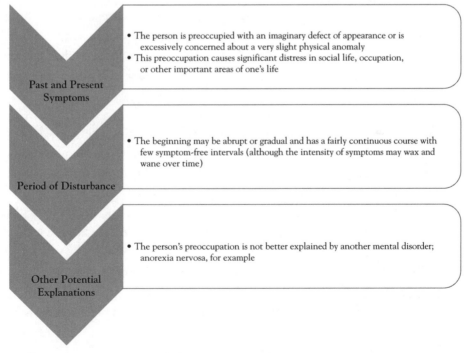

Figure 9.5   Conceptual Map for Body Dysmorphic Disorder

Differential Assessment

BDD often occurs with other disorders and it is helpful to carefully consider the symptoms for other disorders. The most common is major depression. BDD may also coexist with generalized anxiety; that is, the person worries excessively to the extent that daily life is disrupted, often causing exaggerated or unrealistic anxiety. However, the focus of worries may revolve around a perceived flaw or defect in appearance as found in BDD. The avoidant personality disorder and dependent personality disorder traits of being introverted and shy are also seen in BDD. Other comorbid disorders are social phobia or obsessive-compulsive disorder.

BDD is differentiated from hypochondriasis in that it is not appearance that preoccupies the person but the fear of having a disease. Those with anorexia have a distorted body image but it is in the context of the irrational fear of being fat. Persons with schizophrenia may complain about their appearance but the comments are often bizarre. Someone with delusional disorder, somatic type, lacks insight that his or her complaints might be unreasonable.

SOMATOFORM DISORDER NOT OTHERWISE SPECIFIED (NOS)

The somatoform disorder not otherwise specified diagnostic category is for those persons whose somatic symptoms do not meet criteria for any of the other somatoform disorders discussed up to this point. The *DSM* (APA, 2000) addresses clusters of symptoms that include:

- *Pseudocyesis*—This category refers to those who incorrectly believe that they are pregnant. You will find a client who develops the visible signs of pregnancy such as a protruding abdomen, nausea, amenorrhea (or the absence of menstruation), breast engorgement, and even labor pains.
- *Transient hypochondriacal states*—This is reserved for unexplained physical symptoms that meet criteria for hypochondriasis except that they have not lasted for the required six-month time period.
- *Environmental illness or total environmental allergy syndrome*—People claim to be allergic to most foods, clothing, perfumes, gasses, or many compounds found in chemicals with which they come into contact. This is the client who is allergic to almost everything. These unexplained physical complaints last less than six months and are not due to another mental disorder.

RELATED DISORDERS CAUSING SOMATIC COMPLAINTS: MALINGERING AND FACTITIOUS DISORDER

Malingering and factitious disorder are two conditions that are related to the somato-form disorders. They are briefly reviewed here to expand your diagnostic understanding because someone with these conditions can show symptoms having no clear-cut evidence of a physical or psychological condition. Collectively, they are considered to have their origins in the unconscious. A person who malingers is intentionally using false or grossly exaggerated physical (or psychological) symptoms motivated by an external reason; for example, to avoid going to work. As soon as the person who malingers gets what he or she wants, the physical symptoms will stop. With factitious disorder, a person intentionally produces physical (or psychological) symptoms because the person wants to gain attention; for example, they may deliberately add blood to their urine and claim hematuria (or blood in the urine), which might indicate a more serious problem such as kidney stones or even cancer.

Malingering

It is estimated that malingering is reported at a rate of 1% among mental health patients in the U.S. civilian population and about 5% in the military context (Singh, Avasthi, & Grover, 2007). Further, psychological symptoms after a personal injury can be found at a rate of 1% to 50%. Although almost any disorder can be faked, those who malinger tend to replicate psychiatric disorders since they are more difficult to expose (Mills & Lapian, 2000). Mental retardation or some form of mental deficiency, dementia, or cognitive disorders, amnesia, psychosis, which may include hallucinations or delusions (or both), and the residual symptoms of posttraumatic stress disorder are some of the more common disorders you can expect to see (Knoll & Resnick, 2006). The motives behind faking these symptoms are usually to obtain disability or social benefits, claim compensation after an accidental injury, or to settle scores with a despised employer.

The Clinical Picture

Malingering is distinguished by the intentional production of false or grossly exaggerated physical or psychological symptoms, motivated by external incentives (APA, 2000). Malingering is difficult to detect and you should begin to suspect this disorder in situations involving atypical, bizarre, or absurd presentation in the context of external motives. As the person tells his or her story, consider:

- The medical and legal context to the referral; for example, a client is referred to you by an attorney for evaluation of disability or work compensation or a criminal case related to an evaluation of competency or criminal responsibility.

- A discrepancy between a person's subjective complaints and objective findings.
- The extent of cooperation during the interview.
- The presence of a prior diagnosis of antisocial personality disorder.

Types of Malingering

Pure	The false production of nonexistent symptoms
Partial	The person exaggerates preexisting symptoms
Positive	Involves feigning symptoms of an illness
Negative	Hiding or misreporting the symptoms

It is hard for someone with malingering to maintain his or her guard for prolonged periods of time, so F. Othmer and Othmer (2000) recommend conducting a long and detailed interview as soon as possible after the event in question. The competency-based assessment is a good fit with this approach as it organizes an in-depth look at a wide range of factors in a client's life. As a part of looking into the client's history, you might also want to think about having a conversation with collateral sources that may refute or confirm what your client is telling you. They can also provide additional diagnostic information (Hall & Pritchard, 2000). When possible, review any available records documenting the person's prior level of functioning in order to verify or disprove any evidence of the person's claimed disability. In addition, take into account any history of substance abuse, other psychiatric illnesses, or antisocial acts.

Factitious Disorder

It is hard to determine the prevalence of factitious disorder because it involves willful deception and may be easily missed. In addition, people with this disorder tend to seek treatment at many different health-care facilities, which can make collecting accurate data difficult. The essential feature of factitious disorder is the intentional production of physical or psychological signs or symptoms. The primary motivation for the person's behavior is to assume the sick role in contrast to the external incentives found in malingering. A person may feign illness in several ways. The person may make up a history of having an illness such as claiming to have had a syncopal episode (or a brief fainting incident) that may be a sign of a more serious illness. Alternatively, they may actually induce a medical condition such as injecting themselves with bacteria to produce an infection. They might even manipulate assessment instruments like maneuvering a thermometer so that it will show a temperature high enough to indicate a fever.

The Clinical Picture

When assessing with someone with factitious disorder, expect the individual to present his or her history with dramatic flair. However, they will often become vague and inconsistent when questioned in greater detail (Wang, Nagida, & Jenson, 2005). Savino and Fordtran (2006) have identified a number of clues that can alert you to the presence of a factitious disorder. They are:

Clues That an Illness May Be Factitious

Employment in the health-care field

An unusual grasp of medical terminology

Numerous previous surgeries and resulting physical scars

Pathology reports lacking evidence of an authentic disease

Ability to tolerate intractable disease with equanimity and are unrealistically cooperative

Endures the discomfort of diagnostic procedures and surgery without complaint

Can be very good mimics and actors (or actresses)

Past history of feigning illness

Typically, these are individuals who have an extensive medical record with multiple admissions at numerous hospitals. When asked about their illnesses, do not be surprised to hear them provide you with an almost textbook description. When test results are negative or inconclusive, a new set of symptoms may quickly emerge.

There are three criteria for diagnosing factitious disorder:

1. The person intentionally feigns physical or psychiatric symptoms.
2. The apparent motive for this behavior is to assume the role of a sick person.
3. There are no other motives such as those found in malingering.

Factitious disorder is distinguished from the somatoform disorders in that the person is truly experiencing the symptoms. The factitious disorders are organized into four subtypes.

Subtypes of Factitious Disorders

Factitious disorder with predominantly psychological signs and symptoms	The person mimics behavior typical of a mental illness such as schizophrenia.
With predominantly physical signs and symptoms	The person claims to have symptoms related to a physical illness such as chest pain, stomach problems, or fever.

(continued)

With combined psychological signs and symptoms; neither predominates	Both symptoms of physical and mental illness are reported.
Not otherwise specified	People with this disorder produce or fabricate symptoms in another person under their care, called Munchausen syndrome by proxy or factitious disorder by proxy.

Munchausen by Proxy

Munchausen by proxy is a form of a factitious disorder and refers to the abuse of another. Specifically, it involves the involuntary use of another person, typically a child, to play the sick role. For instance, a caregiver, usually the mother, produces symptoms in her child or may provide a misleading medical history. Occasionally the caregiver may actually injure the child. Parents who commit this form of abuse often struggle with other psychiatric problems like depression, spouse abuse, sociopathy, or psychosis (Feldman, 2004). This is the parent who enjoys the attention that they might not otherwise receive from having a sick child.

FINAL THOUGHTS

In summary, the somatoform disorders involve physical complaints where no physical or organic cause can be found. Keep in mind that the clients are not faking and their symptoms are very real to them.

Somatization disorder. Somatization disorder involves multiple complaints over a long period of time. Symptoms must be present in four specific areas involving four pain symptoms, two gastrointestinal symptoms, one sexual symptom and at least one pseudo neurological symptom. Conversion disorder involves the idea that unbearable unconscious anxiety is converted into a physical illness, which is more tolerable for the person. Dramatic neurological symptoms are usually involved such as blindness, paralysis, or a loss of feeling. La belle indifference or glove anesthesia usually suggests the presence of conversion disorder. The main symptom of pain disorder is the person's complaint of pain that is significant enough to cause disruption in normal activities.

Hypochondriasis. Hypochondriasis, perhaps the most common somatoform disorder, is where the person believes that he or she has a single serious disease.

Body dysmorphic disorder. Body dysmorphic disorder is diagnosed when the person is obsessed with a real or imagined bodily flaw. The most common areas are found in the skin followed by hair and nose. The person repeatedly seeks out cosmetic surgery and often without success. Somatoform disorder not otherwise specified is used when the person does not clearly meet diagnostic criteria for the specific somatoform disorders.

Malingering and factitious disorder. Two related disorders involving somatic (or psychological) complaints are malingering and factitious disorder. Malingering is used for someone who is faking an illness for some type of gain such as getting out of work or to collect insurance. Factitious disorder applies to the person who seeks out the sick role for various psychological reasons. Unlike malingering, the individual will use drugs or other methods to induce real symptoms. In comparison people with conversion disorders who typically will be glad to discuss their symptoms at length, people with factitious disorders are guarded, defensive, and reluctant to talk about their symptoms.

PRACTICING THE COMPETENCY-BASED ASSESSMENT

At the heart of the somatoform disorders are the person's concerns with the appearance or functioning of their bodies. These are the clients who usually seek help from the professional with no identifiable or clear-cut medical basis for their physical complaints. Reflect on the following case illustrations to test your ability to sort out the specific type of somatoform disorder or to distinguish malingering and factitious disorder.

The Case of James LaDuke

This is the story of James LaDuke and his relentless search for explanations for his symptoms that have taken a toll on his life. He is 45 years old, recently unemployed, and desperate for solutions. James has been referred to you by his physician after his last round of tests showed no evidence of physical illness. James reluctantly admits, "I've thought that I've had heart attacks. I once even thought that I had bowel cancer. And I've had hundreds and hundreds of tests. It's like once I get into this pattern of thinking nothing can convince me that I'm not sick. I just want to feel better again. Can you help me? I'm willing to try anything to get better. Cognitive behavioral therapy, relaxation, meditation, hypnosis . . . you name it and I'll do it. I'll be your best client!"

He continues, "I've had this really frustrating relationship with my doctors over the years. When I see somebody new, they are really very sympathetic and send me off for tests and everything. At first, they seem really glad to have me as a patient but when the tests come back negative, they say, 'The problem is in your head.' The last one insisted that I see a shrink. No offense to you, miss." James added, "I just can't accept that all of this is psychological."

You respond that you are not offended and ask James for more details about his health history. He looks directly at you and admits, "I've done the lymphoma thing, too." You are a bit surprised at his candor and invite him to continue. James replies,

"I remember finding a bump on the front part of my neck that did not match on the other side. I immediately went to my doctor who said it was fine and that I shouldn't be concerned. I must have looked pretty pathetic at that point so he ordered some tests but they all came back normal. Well, that didn't stop me from poking and prodding around. Pretty soon my neck was sore and a bit inflamed so the doctor did another round of tests. They all came up okay."

James resumes, "I know this is irrational but I seem to be spending my entire life worrying about my health. It's gotten so that it's constantly on my mind. It all started about five years ago when I donated my kidney. Maybe you saw my story on TV?" You respond that you did not see his story on TV and ask if he would share the details.

Without hesitation, James answers, "Well, I used to drive a cab for a living. Not much money in it but it paid the bills and kept me off the streets. I live alone. The wife and kids deserted me almost 20 years ago. We were young and wild when we met. Both of us drank pretty heavily, but after a while, it seems she couldn't put up with my drinking. Well, I'm sober now and been that way for a good 20 years but they just don't want anything to do with me. I guess I must have been a pretty bad husband and father."

James looked lost in thought for a moment. "Where was I? Oh, yeah! Driving a cab. Well, I used to have a regular pick up. It was this older lady. Whoo whee! She was a mean one! Seems I could do nothing right by her. She would complain that I picked her up late. The next time she complained I was early. And that's when she was talking to me. Mostly she would just stare out the window. Well, a man's got to make a living so I figured if I could talk to her then maybe I could get to know her a little better. Turns out my cab trips were to take her to the hospital for dialysis. Seems if she did not get a new kidney soon that she would die. Well, here I am with nothing to show for my life so I offered her mine. Turns out we were a match so I donated my kidney. Even though I feel pretty good about what I did, ever since then things have not been right for me."

You ask James to explain. He says, "Well, when I was going through the tests a young doctor listened to my stomach. I remember it as if it was yesterday. He ooohed and ahhhed and then said it sounded like I had something wrong with my abdominal aorta. He solemnly announced that they were not going to go through with the operation until they found out what was wrong with me. I was terrified. After all, I was just trying to help out some lady. I spent the next few weeks convinced that I was dying. A few weeks later the head of the surgical team told me that everything was fine. The other doctor should not have said anything about my aorta and there was absolutely nothing wrong with me. Boy, was I relieved, and they went ahead and removed my kidney. That old lady I was driving around was really grateful, to say the least. Well, here I am five years later still worrying about my health. I have this back pain that comes on suddenly. I worry because I have only one kidney now and wonder if it's acting up.

Sometimes my heart beats rapidly and I swear my hands get clammy. I've had a couple of ultrasounds but they all come back normal. I don't smoke, I don't have high blood pressure, as you can see my weight is pretty good, and there's no family history of diabetes but I'm sure that having only one kidney puts me at high risk."

James looks directly at you and says," I wish you could give me some kind of guarantee that I'll live to the ripe old age of 85 and then just die peacefully in my sleep. Of course, life doesn't come with any guarantees does it?" You respond that this must be very hard for James.

He goes on to state, "My flare ups come at predictable times, usually when it's raining. Of course, if a new symptom comes up I can get pretty nutty about it. This time cancer is the only suggestion I can come up with for the back pain. It just has to be something serious. You just can't control your mind to think that it's just a sore back, can you?"

How would you formulate your competency-based assessment for James LaDuke?

The Case of June Dwyer

June Dwyer is a 28-year-old nursing student who was admitted to the hospital after she went to the emergency room for complaints of blood in her vomit (hematamesis). June was requesting surgery to resolve the problem. X-rays and blood work were ordered immediately. June was asked if she had any serious medical problems such as heart or lung disease and if she had any allergies or if she had swallowed anything unusual. When she responded negatively, an endoscopy was scheduled.

The admitting physician, Dr. Burnes, explained that this procedure will help to look for an inflammation or smaller abnormalities such as ulcers or tumors that may be the cause of her bleeding. June had a handkerchief covering her mouth, coughed, and discretely spit into it. Dr. Burnes, then went on to explain the details of the procedure stating, "June, you can expect to have your throat sprayed with a numbing solution. You will probably be given a sedating and pain-alleviating medication through the vein." June looked rather calm at this point and Dr. Burnes asked if June had any questions before proceeding. She said, "No" and he continued, "While lying on your left side, the flexible endoscope, the thickness of my finger," at this point he raised his pinkie finger, "is passed through your mouth and into your esophagus, stomach, and duodenum. This procedure will not interfere with your breathing. Most patients experience only minimal discomfort during the test." He added, "In fact, most sleep throughout the entire procedure. At the very worst you'll be left with a sore throat and some mild distention." He added reassuringly, "These are very mild side effects and soon enough you can be eating normally again." Dr. Burnes thought it was somewhat unusual that June seemed so cooperative about having this procedure done.

Up to this point, June's medical history has been unremarkable. Dr. Burnes noted that June reported a past history of prior hospital admissions where gastritis was ultimately diagnosed. A little more than one year ago, she had a miscarriage. She has been married for five years. She is a good student, works part time to help with school expenses, and shares that her husband is very proud of her decision to go back to school. June denies any history of drugs or alcohol.

You are seeing June for routine screening for discharge planning. The resident internist on the medical team, Dr. Mayhew, stopped by June's room to complete her medical history and you decide to sit in on the interview.

June:	"When I first went into the hospital they did some tests and they found nothing at all. I thought I had an ulcer. You see, I had nausea, and my stomach felt bloated."
Dr. Mayhew:	"Were you taking any medicines at the time?"
June:	"No. Nothing at all."
Dr. Mayhew:	"Were you taking laxatives at that time?"
June:	"Yes."
Dr. Mayhew:	"What happened after that . . . after you left the hospital the first time?"
June:	"Well, I was better for a while and then I got worse a few months later and went into another hospital and had the same tests done again. I don't remember exactly what they were but the only thing they found was that I had gastritis."
Dr. Mayhew:	"I'm sure that the tests that were done on you were painful and expensive and probably a lot of trouble for you. I'm curious about what you thought about that when all they found was a mild case of gastritis."
June:	"I really thought that there must be something seriously wrong for me to be feeling so bad."
Dr. Mayhew:	"Did the doctors ever ask you at that time about laxatives and if you were taking them?"
June:	"No."
Dr. Mayhew:	"If the doctors had told you at that time that you needed an operation, let's say to find out what was wrong with you, how do you think you would have responded?"
June:	"I would have gone ahead with whatever they said,"
Dr. Mayhew:	"An operation is pretty serious. Why would you just go along?"
June:	"I don't know."
Dr. Mayhew:	"Can you tell me a little more about taking the laxatives and specifically why you picked laxatives as opposed to something else?"

June:	"I found I could eat anything I wanted to and not have to worry about what I ate and still not gain any weight."
Dr. Mayhew:	"So, it was to keep your weight down."
June:	"Right."
Dr. Mayhew:	"You were taking 'Correctol,' I think. Is that correct?"
	June nodded affirmatively.
Dr. Mayhew:	"How many did you take? Let's say in a day's time on average?"
June:	"I guess it was about 40 a day."
Dr. Mayhew:	"Forty tablets a day. That's a lot."
June:	"Yes, but after they found that I had gastritis, I stopped right away. Now I have this blood in my vomit. Do you think it's something serious? Do you think I need surgery?"

The intern concluded his conversation with June by assuring her that once the tests were done that the medical team would have a better idea of what was wrong with her and recommend the appropriate treatment. Once outside of June's hospital room, he shares with you that he does not feel quite right about June's story and writes an order for staff to observe her closely over the next few days.

The next day, you review June's chart. You notice an entry by the nurse on the evening shift who observed seeing June stick her finger up her nose causing it to bleed into the back of her throat. She then swallowed the blood. June's tests ultimately failed to reveal any area of bleeding in the stomach. June was confronted with her behavior by the medical team who recommended a psychiatric evaluation. She became angry and denied having any psychiatric problems. She insisted that it was the medical system that had failed her and signed herself out of the hospital.

How would you formulate your competency-based assessment for June Dwyer?

PRACTICAL APPLICATIONS

1. Although there is no known cure for the somatoform disorders, they can be managed by helping the person who has the disorder to live as much of a normal life as possible despite some pain or other symptoms. Keep in mind that if a somatoform disorder is not properly treated the potential consequence is that the person may become even more handicapped. Given these psychological underpinnings, a good relationship with your client is essential.

   a. Reviewing the somatoform disorders and the malingering and factitious disorders discussed in this chapter, make a list of those features that might interfere with objectivity when exploring the client's history.

   b. As an alternative, ask a colleague for their ideas about 'what may chal-
      lenge their diagnostic objectivity and compare their thoughts with
      your listing.
   c. Share these ideas with your supervisor and discuss strategies to maintain
      objectivity and acceptance of your client's "illness."
   d. Review the case stories of James LaDuke and June Dwyer and think about
      how you would attempt to empathize with their struggles as a part of your
      competency-based assessment interview. What might get in your way?

2. Imagine for a moment that you have been asked to develop a brochure that
   provides information about when to contact a medical professional for a
   local walk-in clinic. What would you say? In particular, think about how you
   would describe the symptoms of the somatoform disorders in a way that could
   be easily understood by the general public. Keep in mind that some people
   mistakenly believe that psychological pain is not real and ought to be controlled without medical or mental health treatment. Others may not recognize
   that physical symptoms can be related to psychological factors. Remember the
   stigma associated with psychological disorders in the eyes of the general public
   as you develop this brochure.

3. Often considered synonymous with faking, lying, and fraud, malingering
   can evoke a number of negative feelings. It is a difficult disorder to detect.
   The client's motives behind faking symptoms can further complicate making
   an accurate diagnosis. Develop a relationship with your client as a first step
   in taking an accurate history but when you begin to find a discrepancy
   between a client's subjective complaints and objective findings, your impar-
   tiality can potentially be compromised. What steps can you take to ensure
   your professional objectivity when interviewing a client you suspect may be
   struggling with malingering?

Appendix

Competency-Based Assessments
for Chapter 9 Case Examples:
Listing of Case Diagnoses

Figures 9A.1 through 9A.4 provide the diagnostic assessment for each of the cases illustrated. They are organized in the order that they appear in each chapter.

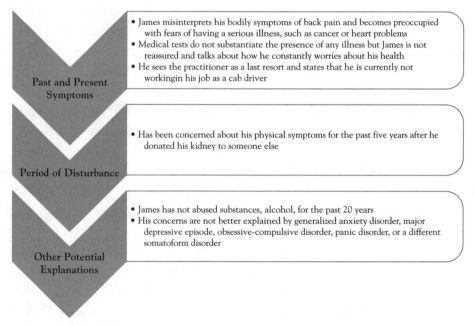

Figure 9A.1 The Conceptual Map for James LaDuke

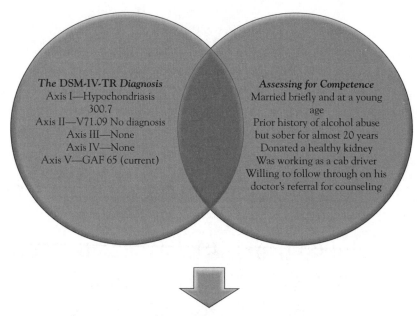

The DSM-IV-TR Diagnosis
Axis I—Hypochondriasis
300.7
Axis II—V71.09 No diagnosis
Axis III—None
Axis IV—None
Axis V—GAF 65 (current)

Assessing for Competence
Married briefly and at a young
age
Prior history of alcohol abuse
but sober for almost 20 years
Donated a healthy kidney
Was working as a cab driver
Willing to follow through on his
doctor's referral for counseling

Figure 9A.2   The Competency-Based Assessment for James LaDuke

CASE REVIEW FOR JAMES LADUKE

James begins his story by telling the practitioner about his decision to donate his kidney. Unfortunately, this seemed to be the beginning of his preoccupation with his health and fears that he has a serious illness. Despite the fact that his medical tests come back normal, he continues to worry. James talks about having been to a number of doctors. The competency-based assessment individualizes each client's experience with a mental illness, in this case James's diagnosis of hypochondriasis. For someone with this disorder, he or she may actually develop a physical illness that may be overlooked due to long-standing complaints unsubstantiated by medical tests.

The competency-based assessment reminds the practitioner to consider James's current status of living with one kidney. This approach to the assessment also includes a parallel assessment of strengths. In particular James's motivation to help someone else who would have died without a kidney replacement. In addition, James does seem aware of his physical complaints, and follows through on the referral for counseling with the hope of living a life without the uncertainties of having a serious illness. He has a prior history of alcohol abuse but has maintained his sobriety for the past 20 years.

Of interest, his predominant complaint is back pain, a symptom of an abdominal aorta aneurysm. Though James is not at high risk (that is, he does not smoke, has no history of diabetes, is not overweight, nor does he have high blood pressure) he continues to worry about his health and more so since he legitimately has only one kidney. His fears about his health have lasted for the past five years or since he donated his kidney.

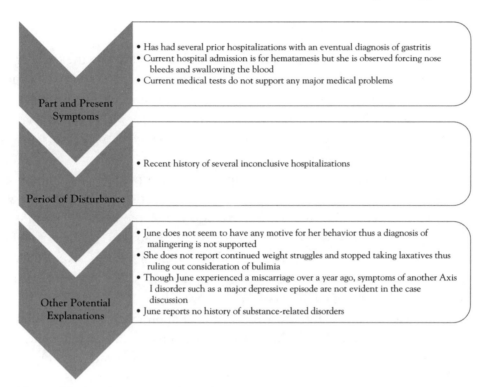

Figure 9A.3   The Conceptual Map for June Dwyer

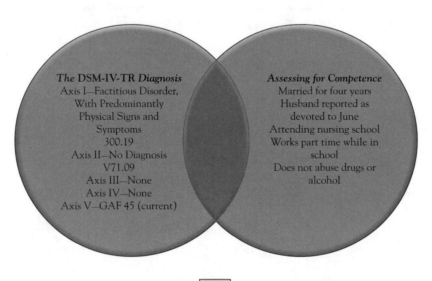

Figure 9A.4   The Competency-Based Assessment for June Dwyer

CASE REVIEW FOR JUNE DWYER

We know little of June Dwyer's social background in this case because the focus of the discussion is on her medical experiences during her most recent hospital admission. However, the competency-based assessment takes into account a parallel exploration of client strengths and June's five-year marital history emerges with a report that her husband is proud of her decision to return to school. She is seen as a good student who works part time to offset expenses.

June's symptoms of factitious disorder are supported by her previous hospitalizations, inconclusive test results, and an ultimate diagnosis of gastritis. Interestingly, she was taking up to 40 laxatives a day, but did not volunteer this information. Her motivation for taking the laxatives was to eat whatever she wanted and not have to worry about gaining weight, which would support consideration of a diagnosis for bulimia. However, she reported that she stopped taking the laxatives. The case includes no further discussion of weight or efforts to control her weight.

The case dialogue highlights June's tolerance of uncomfortable medical tests and the willingness to endure surgery, if it would have been recommended. Her evasiveness can be noted when the internist asks June if she ever volunteered that she was taking laxatives and she responded that she did not share this information. June's current hospitalization was for hematamesis and she was observed forcing nose bleeds and swallowing the blood. Test results did not support any major medical problems. There seemed to be no motives for her behavior, such as financial gain or revenge against anyone, thus ruling out a consideration of malingering. One is left to wonder about the psychological impact of her miscarriage a little over a year ago.

10

The Dissociative Disorders

INTRODUCTION

Everyone occasionally fails to remember something or loses track of time, but for the person with a dissociative disorder the experience is entirely different. People with this disorder can totally miss out on a series of normal behaviors for minutes, hours, or even days at a time. In other words, certain areas of their lives are simply not working. The specific symptoms of the dissociative disorders generally develop as a reaction to overwhelming stress or a traumatic ordeal and make it easier to keep difficult memories at bay.

The dissociative disorders found in the *DSM-IV-TR* are dissociative amnesia, dissociative fugue, dissociative identity disorder (formerly known as multiple personality disorder), and depersonalization disorder. Each of these disorders shares a set of common features. They are:

Common Features of the Dissociative Disorders

Onset	Each specific disorder typically begins and ends suddenly.
Memory	Most of the dissociative disorders show a profound disturbance of memory (with the exception of depersonalization disorder).
Precipitants	Episodes tend to be precipitated by psychological conflicts (such as an overwhelming stress generated by traumatic events or by intolerable inner conflict).
Prevalence	The dissociative disorders are considered rare and not often seen in practice.
Functioning	Impaired functioning or a subjective feeling of distress is shown (with the exception of dissociative identity disorder).

Let's now turn to an overview of the incidence and prevalence of the dissociative disorders.

INCIDENCE AND PREVALENCE

The dissociative disorders essentially involve disruptions or breakdowns of a person's memory, awareness, identity, and/or perception. The individual experiences responses ranging from detachment of self or surroundings (depersonalization), an inability to remember after experiencing an emotional trauma (amnesia), confusion about one's identity (dissociative fugue), to assuming two or more different personality states (dissociative identity disorder). These are controversial disorders and some practitioners do not even believe they exist thus making it hard to estimate the actual prevalence rates (Kihlstrom, 2001). Real or not, the symptoms interfere with a person's functioning.

Prevalence

Studies have found that the prevalence rates for a diagnosable dissociative disorder range anywhere from 2% to 3% to approximately 10% of the general population. It is estimated that 73% of persons who have been exposed to a traumatic incident will experience some type of a dissociative state either during the incident or in the following hours, days, or weeks. The dissociative experience can be either acute or chronic. For most people, these experiences will subside on their own and are not diagnosed as a dissociative disorder (Martinez-Taboas & Guillermo, 2000).

OVERVIEW OF THE MAJOR CHARACTERISTICS OF THE DISSOCIATIVE DISORDERS

Dissociation refers to the lack of connection between things usually associated with each other. Dissociated experiences are those that are not integrated into the usual sense of self—resulting in discontinuities of conscious awareness (Simeon, Guralnick, Schmeidler, & Knutelska, 2001). The *DSM-IV-TR* (American Psychiatric Association, 2000) distinguishes dissociation as a key feature of the dissociative disorders. The main symptom cluster for the dissociative disorders includes dissociative experiences characterized by a disruption in consciousness, memory, identity, or perception, causing significant distress in a person's social and/or occupational functioning. Organized around the competency-based assessment, there are a number of questions you might consider asking your clients to determine the presence of a dissociative disorder:

What to Ask When Exploring the Symptom Picture for a Dissociative Disorder

Personal:

1. At what point did you (or those close to you) first notice your problems with . . .

   - Not fully being there (consciousness).
   - Missing things or found things and you have no idea how this happened (memory).
   - Not feeling like yourself (identity).
   - Being in a strange place (perception of the environment) and unable to figure out how you got there.

2. Are there periods of time in your life (including childhood experiences) that you don't remember?

3. Do others recognize you but you do not know who they are?

4. Have you ever found yourself some distance away from home (or work) and did not know how you got there?

5. Do you ever have the feeling like you are outside of your body and looking at yourself?

6. Do you sometimes hear voices and no one else is around?

7. Do you feel as though there is more than one person or perhaps many people living inside your head? If yes, ask:

   - Do these people have names?
   - Are these people of the same age or gender?
   - Do these people have a special relationship with the others inside of your head?
   - Does any one of those individuals take charge?

8. How often do you feel anxious or depressed?

9. Do you drink alcohol or use illicit drugs? If yes, ask how often.

Interpersonal:

10. Were you physically abused or neglected as a child?

11. Was anyone in your family abused during your childhood?

12. Have you ever been touched against your will?

13. Have you ever thought about harming others (or yourself)?

Community and Environmental:

14. Are you currently being treated for any other medical conditions (including another mental illness)? Listen carefully for conditions such as a head injury, certain brain diseases, or sleep deprivation that can cause symptoms such as memory loss or a sense of unreality.

15. Do you now or have you ever served in the military? If yes, listen carefully for traumatic combat experiences.

Risk Factors Associated With the Dissociative Disorders

Individuals who have experienced chronic physical, sexual, or emotional abuse during childhood are at the greatest risk for developing a dissociative disorder. Experiences with other traumatic events such as natural disasters, kidnapping, invasive medical procedures, war, or torture can also place a person at risk. The dissociative disorders tend to be more apparent among those who are plagued with problems in relationships or at work. These are the individuals who are unable to cope well with emotional or professional stress and their dissociative reactions may range from simply tuning out to disappearing entirely. As a consequence, coworkers will see them as unreliable or loved ones may worry about them.

In addition to risk factors, there are a number of related problems you can expect to find in someone with a dissociative disorder:

Complications Associated with the Dissociative Disorders

Self-mutilation

Suicide attempts

Sexual dysfunction (including sexual addiction or avoidance)

Difficulties sleeping, insomnia, sleepwalking

Depression

Anxiety

Severe headaches

Eating problems

Dissociative Disorder Not Otherwise Specified (NOS)

When a person shows symptoms that represent a change in the normally integrative functions of consciousness memory or identity but does not meet criteria for one of the specific dissociative disorders, the diagnosis of dissociative disorder not otherwise specified (NOS) is assigned. For example, you might encounter an individual who feels as though their exterior world is unreal or odd (derealization) but they do not have a sense of being cut off or detached from one's own self (depersonalization). In contrast, the specific diagnosis of depersonalization disorder would be made when the symptoms of depersonalization *and* derealization are persistent or recurrent causing significant distress or impairment in functioning.

It is also helpful to remember that the symptom picture for the dissociative disorders may closely resemble other disorders. For example, individuals struggling with post-traumatic stress disorder may not be able to remember parts of their personal histories, especially those events that were extremely stressful. In other instances, individuals who are drinking or using drugs may experience blackouts and may not be able to remember what happened when they were intoxicated. A person with a long history of numerous physical symptoms, and diagnosed with somatization disorder, may conveniently forget important parts of his or her personal history. Another diagnosis is malingering disorder. In this instance, the person consciously fakes symptoms of memory loss, to avoid punishment or to obtain money or drugs.

Culture and the Dissociative Disorders

Cultural factors are more evident in the dissociative disorders than in the other classes of disorders found in the *DSM-IV-TR*. When considering the influence of culture on the diagnostic process, it is important to differentiate between expressions of pathology and the normally accepted experiences of dissociation found in some social contexts. The competency-based approach to the assessment helps to discern how social and culturally sanctioned norms are understood, refining how you would evaluate the extent of distress and impairment in a person's life.

The dissociative trance disorder is a diagnostic category that considers cultural expressions of dissociation and is currently listed in the *DSM-IV-TR* appendix as an area for further study (APA, 2000). Aspects of this disorder, the possession trance component (where the person enters an altered state of consciousness and feels as if he or she is taken over by a spirit, power, deity, or other person who takes control over their mind and body), may be moved from the appendix and subsumed into an existing disorder in the upcoming *DSM-5*; in particular, dissociative identity disorder. The trance component (a narrowing of one's attention so that some things, such as sight or movement, are placed outside the person's awareness) is projected to remain as a part of the dissociative disorder NOS (APA, 2000). The person generally has no recall of these experiences. If you think about it, this is not far from such nonpathological states as hypnosis and meditation. Although trance states are common experiences in many cultures, it is helpful to remember that in Western industrialized cultures such experiences are seen as not normative and may lead to inappropriate diagnoses (Behrend & Luig, 2000).

At this point, the dissociative trance is seen as an unofficial diagnostic category and informally used by mental health practitioners to accommodate dissociative syndromes. As outlined in the *DSM*, the dissociative trance disorder is applied only when it leads to distress or dysfunction and is probably more common than originally thought.

Not all possession trance states are pathological. Castillo (1997) argues that a trance is essentially adaptive and allows the person to escape from the constraints of reality. The competency-based assessment provides an avenue to fully assess the culture-based sources of stress as well as the social and environmental supports that may impact a person's level of functioning. By looking at the full range of the client's experiences, do not prematurely assume that your client has a dissociative disorder, but take into consideration the adaptive aspects of behaviors, even those that may be culturally unfamiliar to you. Some examples of culture-bound syndromes that may or may not be linked to a particular *DSM* diagnostic category are:

Ataques de nervios is a culturally accepted dissociative experience commonly seen as a response to acute stress in Latin American and Hispanic cultures (Lopez & Guarnaccia, 2000). The major features include uncontrollable crying, screaming, shouting, seizure-like behaviors, and the individual's failure to remember the episode afterward.

Amok is generally seen in Malaysia and Indonesia. This is a trance syndrome characterized by sudden outburst of unrestrained violent and aggressive behavior, usually of a homicidal nature. It generally involves a person losing his or her sense of self, grabbing a weapon such as a machete, and running through the village slashing at people. The person has no memory of what they have done and are typically excused from any damage (Lewis-Fernandez, 1994). In Puerto Rico, it is referred to as *mal de pelea* and among the First Nation's Navajo it is called *iich'aa.*

Falling out is a trance syndrome commonly found among southern Blacks in the United States and the Bahamas. It is characterized by falling to the ground, apparently comatose, but the person can still hear and understand what is going on around him or her (Weidman, 1979).

Fits are seen in India involving a seizure-like response by some women to family stress. It is considered curable by either exorcism or by the woman simply telling her husband to protect her from her in-laws.

Grisi siknis is found among teenage girls and young women of the Miskito Indians in Nicaragua. Features include a trance, amnesia, and leaving home. The young girls may also run wild with machetes, occasionally assaulting others or mutilating themselves (Dennis, 1985).

Indisposition, found in Haiti, is a possession trance understood as a response to fear. Here, the person falls to the ground in a trance but is not able to understand anything that is heard or said (Philippe & Romain, 1979).

Latah is primarily seen as a Malay-Indonesian syndrome (although it can occur elsewhere) involving a trance characterized by an extreme response to startling stimuli. It involves violent body movements, taking unusual postures, trance dancing, mimicking other people, or throwing things (Simons, 1985).

Pibloktog is found among the native Artic people, (Gussow, 1985). For anywhere from a few minutes to an hour, a polar Eskimo takes off his or her clothing and runs screaming through the snow and ice as if in response to a sudden fright.

Every client encountered in practice has a unique history. A thorough assessment, including the cultural realities in a client's life, will provide information that will help make an accurate diagnosis of the dissociative disorders. The comprehensive nature of the competency-based assessment becomes a useful tool for looking into the client's personal, social, and cultural patterns. Anchored in this approach to the assessment process, some questions to ask your clients as well as yourself in order to fully explore the interplay of cultural influences in the client's life are:

☞ What to Ask Your Clients and Yourself When Exploring Cultural Influences

Personal:
1. How does the client describe his or her cultural identity?
2. Do I need to consult with other sources of cultural expertise to fully understand the cultural meaning system of my client; for example, colleagues or community experts? (This serves to look carefully at how culture can potentially shape your client's subjective experience of illness and distress.)
3. Is there a specific cultural meaning attributed to the client's key symptoms or the distress experienced; for instance, a client's symptoms may have a specific meaning in the client's culture?

Interpersonal:
4. How does the client's family or others close to your client "explain" the symptoms of distress? Be sure to consider the nature of relationships as a part of this inquiry.
5. What are the effects of the client's symptoms on his or her family, friends, and/or coworkers?
6. What role does your own potential ethnocentric bias play in the assessment; for example, do your questions reflect any bias about certain cultures or a lack of knowledge of culturally syntonic behaviors? (This fosters a careful look at your own ideas about what you think a client's symptom picture should look like.)
7. How can I avoid the presumption of pathology and consider alternative explanations for my client's behaviors?

Community and Environmental:
8. What are the reactions to the client's symptoms in community settings; for example, at church or school?
9. Does your client encounter any forms of stigma or other negative social responses to his or her symptoms?
10. How would you characterize your client's cultural and psychosocial environment? Be sure to consider culture-based sources of stress as well as support that may play a role in your client's functioning.

In essence, culture-bound syndromes are "recurrent, locality-specific patterns of aberrant behavior and troubling experience that may or may not be linked to a particular *DSM-IV-TR* diagnostic category" (APA, 2000, p. 898). Each has a unique set of symptoms, which tend to be specific to a particular geographic, ethnic, or cultural group (Barker, 2003).

THE DISSOCIATIVE DISORDERS

Dissociative amnesia is one of several of the dissociative disorders. Take dissociative amnesia into account when someone experiences a stressful or traumatic event and subsequently blocks out certain information or has long gaps in memory that go far beyond normal forgetfulness. This is not the same as simple amnesia or when the person simply experiences a loss of information from memory.

Dissociative Amnesia Disorder

The major feature of dissociative amnesia is an inability to recall important information that cannot be explained by ordinary forgetfulness. More often, the person is responding to some sort of emotional trauma or extreme stress rather than from some kind of physical disturbance. Some people forget some but not all of the stressful events over a period of time. Others cannot recall their previous lives or forget things as they happen. Dissociative amnesia has two subtypes. Those who are unable to remember anything, including who they are, struggle with generalized amnesia. This may extend from about six months to a year. The second subtype is localized or selective amnesia. This is a failure to recall specific events, usually of a traumatic nature, that occur during a specific period of time. In most cases, you can expect to see a pattern of forgetting that is selective for traumatic events or memories rather than generalized.

The Clinical Picture

In dissociative amnesia, the most common symptom is memory loss involving information that is usually part of people's routine conscious awarenesses; for example, who they are, where they have gone, who they spoke to, or what they did. Often it is the information about the traumatic or stressful event that is forgotten. A good example is what happened to Sirhan Sirhan, the young man who made history when he assassinated potential presidential candidate Robert F. Kennedy on June 4, 1968. Sirhan fatally shot Kennedy in the kitchen of the Ambassador Hotel in Los Angeles shortly after the latter was victorious in the California presidential primary. Sirhan was unable to remember this event after his arrest. When hypnotized, Sirhan was able to recall what had happened and even reenact the episode. These memories were not accessible to him after hypnosis (Diamond, 1969; 1980).

People who have been exposed to physically or emotionally traumatic events are at a higher risk for developing dissociative amnesia and it is commonly found among those who have been involved in accidents, natural disasters, or war (Brandt & Van Gorp, 2006). Stresses such as a physical injury, guilt about having an extramarital affair, or abandonment by a spouse can also contribute to dissociative amnesia. Dissociative amnesia usually begins suddenly and the person typically has gaps in his or her memory, which may span up to a few minutes, hours, days, or even his or her entire life. A central feature of the disorder is the inability to remember significant events. The more common patterns of forgetting can be summarized as follows:

- *Localized*—This is when the person has recall for none of the events during a particular time, such as a natural disaster.
- *Selective*—This type of forgetting is less common and is where certain portions of a time have been forgotten by the individual, such as the birth of a child.

There are other patterns of forgetting but they are rarely seen in practice. A competency-based assessment is helpful in looking at all features of the person's life and carefully sorting through the symptom picture. This approach helps to sort through the different patterns of forgetfulness because these symptoms may support the diagnosis of another dissociative disorder, for example, dissociative identity disorder. The other and less common patterns you might encounter in practice are:

- *Generalized*—This is when the person forgets all of the experiences during his or her lifetime.
- *Continuous*—Considered extremely rare, this is when the person forgets events from a given time forward to the present.
- *Systematized*—This pattern of forgetting is when the person has forgotten certain classes of information, for example, relating to work or to family.

In most situations, a person is unable to remember accounts of his or her life and personal identity even though the person is able to learn new information and carry out everyday functions without any problems. Some people spontaneously recover memories. Dissociative amnesia is common across cultures but dissociative amnesia as a separate mental disorder is found mostly in modern societies.

Figure 10.1 delineates the characteristics of dissociative amnesia.

A Quick Guide to Dissociative Amnesia

Typically brought on by a traumatic event or stress

Memory gaps are related to traumatic or stressful events and are too extreme to be considered normal forgetfulness

Memory usually returns with time

Past and Present Symptoms
- The person's main problem is at least one episode of the inability to recall important information; this forgotten information usually concerns trauma or stress and is more extensive than what could be explained by common forgetfulness
- Significant distress is experienced by the person
- Work, social, or personal functioning is impaired

Period of Disturbance
- Onset can be sudden and usually follows severe stress or trauma

Other Potential Explanations
- Symptoms do not occur solely during dissociative identity disorder, dissociative fugue, posttraumatic stress disorder, acute stress disorder, or somatization
- A general medical condition or the use of substances (including medications) does not better explain symptoms

Figure 10.1   Conceptual Map for Dissociative Amnesia

Differential Assessment

There are a number of factors that can cause amnesia and it is especially helpful to look at all aspects of a person's life because there are a number of diagnoses that include an inability to recall important information such as organic mental disorders, dementia, delirium, transient global amnesia, Korsakoff disease, post concussion amnesia, any of the other dissociative disorders, and malingering of factitious disorder.

The memory loss found in organic mental disorders is typically gradual and incomplete. Unlike dissociative amnesia, memory loss due to substance abuse is seldom reversible. As such, for people with a pattern of substance use the symptoms of memory difficulties might be better understood by the diagnosis of substance-induced persisting amnestic disorder. Korsakoff disease is associated with heavy and prolonged alcohol use and the person is not able to learn new information. In addition, the individual often experiences significant deterioration in personal functioning. When someone has amnesia due to head trauma his or her symptoms might be better explained by a diagnosis of amnestic disorder due to concussion. If a person seems confused about his or her personal identity and reports having traveled from home, you might consider dissociative fugue. Forgetfulness associated with malingering is typically connected to an obvious motive to avoid punishment or acquire a gain of some type. Some individuals with amnesia are also mute and it is important to rule out the symptom picture for schizophrenia catatonic type or a catatonic disorder due to a general medical condition.

Dissociative Fugue Disorder

Fragmentation of identity and memory characterize dissociative fugue disorder. The person experiences one or more episodes of amnesia where he or she cannot recall some or all of the past. These people either lose their identities or form entirely new ones. These episodes are called fugues and are the upshot of trauma or stress. For example, a person might be in an embarrassing situation such as finding his wife in bed with another man and escape this painful reality through a fugue state. A fugue could also be a response to suicidal or homicidal impulses. Dissociative fugue appears suddenly, is unexpected, and often involves unplanned travel or wandering away from home.

The Clinical Picture

Typically a fugue may range from hours to months. Occasionally it may last longer. More often than not, the person will assume a new identity and appear to be acting normally. The person may show some mild confusion. Sometimes it can be stressful when the person becomes confused about the newly assumed identity or when he or she is made aware of the amnesia related to their original identity. In essence, when the fugue ends the person now must deal with the problems they left behind. In addition, the inability to remember what happened during the fugue may create distress or even a sense of horror for the individual. For instance, if someone married during a fugue he or she may have inadvertently become a bigamist. Imagine how they might feel when they find out what they have done. When the fugue state comes to an end, most individuals can remember their past lives and the events that led up to the onset of the fugue. A limited number of people remember nothing or almost nothing about their past.

A Quick Guide to Dissociative Fugue

Most often happens during extreme stress such as after a natural disaster or war

Involves abrupt travel away from home

The person is unable to remember important aspects of his or her life

Adopts a new identity or a partially new identity

Rarely lasts longer than a month

A fugue state is rarely recognized in progress and the diagnosis is usually made retrospectively. If you are working with a client who seems confused about his or her identity, puzzled about the past, or confrontational when their identity is challenged, consider the presence of a dissociative fugue. At the point when you begin to suspect a fugue, it is helpful to explore the individual's circumstances before travel, the travel experience itself, and the beginnings of the individual's alternate life. Sometimes a definitive diagnosis cannot be made until the person abruptly returns to his or her pre-fugue identity and is distressed to find themselves in unfamiliar circumstances. Figure 10.2 is a conceptual map of the signs of a dissociative fugue.

Differential Assessment

Before considering the diagnosis of dissociative fugue, it is important to rule out other causes of a person's inability to recall information or confusion about his or her identity. Dissociative fugue-like symptoms includes seizure disorder, somatization, malingering, dissociative identity disorder, dementia (often Alzheimer's type), the substance-use disorders, schizophrenia, mania, and head trauma. However, the fugue differs because the flight behavior is organized and purposeful. For instance, someone with

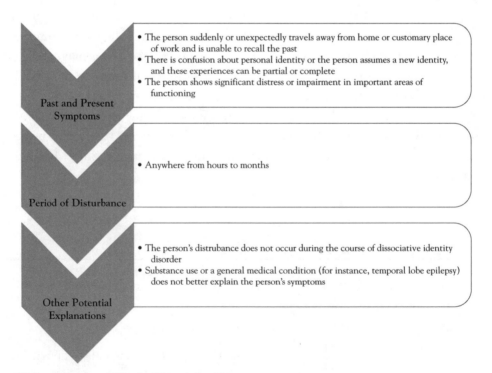

Figure 10.2   Conceptual Map for Dissociative Fugue

a seizure disorder does not assume a new identity and usually has an altered state of consciousness supported by abnormal findings on electroencephalogram testing.

Somatization disorder is suggested for those who have a history of lifelong multiple medical symptoms. The diagnosis of malingering is often mistaken for a fugue because both tend to absolve the person from accountability for his or her actions or other responsibilities or remove the person entirely from hazardous situations. However, a dissociative fugue differs because the onset is spontaneous, unplanned, and not faked by the person. If malingering is a possibility, you might consider talking with relatives or friends about your client's previous behavior.

One experience of dissociative fugue is the common pattern for about half of those with this diagnosis. If the dissociative fugue occurs more than a few times, you might want to consider an underlying dissociative identity disorder; that is, the person switches repeatedly between identities. Individuals with dementia, particularly Alzheimer's type, may wander aimlessly but they do not purposefully travel. Another option to explain episodes of an inability to recall information about one's past would be a substance-related disorder, especially alcohol. Symptoms of wandering and other bizarre behaviors are also found in those diagnosed with schizophrenia. Sometimes for people who have a rigid conscience, the only acceptable means of escape would more than likely be a dissociative fugue state (B. Sadock & Sadock, 2003).

The Dissociative Identity Disorder

Individuals with dissociative identity disorder (DID) adopt several different identities that simultaneously coexist inside the body and mind. The person must have at least two distinct personalities or personality states to make this diagnosis but the number can range as high as 200. The defining feature of DID is that certain aspects of the individual's identities are dissociated. In some instances the identities, called alters or alter egos, are complete; each has its own distinctive behavior, tone of voice, and gestures. These identities may even have their own names or may be of a gender that is different from the person's own gender. Others may be symbolic; for example, they might be known as the protector or the worker. Physical transformations can also occur. Posture, facial expressions, and even physical disabilities may emerge. For example, Chris Sizemore, whose history of DID was dramatized in the movie *The Three Faces of Eve,* had one personality who showed an eye problem called transient microstrabismus (or a divergence in the conjugant lateral eye movements) that was not seen in the other personalities. The personalities can also vary widely in age and relationship style. For instance, someone who is quiet and reserved may have another personality that is loud and vulgar. In other cases, the identity has only a few distinct characteristics. This happens when the identities are only partially independent from one another. In either case, the person's identity has fragmented.

The Clinical Picture

Persons with DID generally have one personality that attempts to hold together the various other identities, commonly referred to as the host personality. The personalities may be aware of one another to some degree though only one interacts with the environment at a time. The changeover from one personality to another is referred to as a switch. This transition is rarely seen in practice. The change usually happens suddenly and for the most part is precipitated by stress. Most of the personalities are aware of the loss of time that happens when another personality takes over.

Diagnostic controversy. There is a great deal of controversy surrounding the diagnosis of DID, ranging from the idea that symptoms are an adverse side effect of therapy to whether this is even a diagnosable condition. Perhaps the most controversial issue concerns false memories or the extent to which memories of early trauma, especially sexual abuse, are accurate. If someone has suffered some form of abuse or trauma but it is not remembered, the practitioner will ordinarily work toward helping the client to re-experience the trauma in order to relieve suffering. However, if these earlier memories are inadvertently created by careless practices and yet seem real to the client then the potential for false accusations against loved ones may happen. As a consequence, families can be torn apart or the falsely accused perpetrator is sent to prison. The practitioner also runs the risk of being sued for damages resulting from inaccurate accusations.

Looking at the symptom picture for DID, the symptoms found in other disorders are more objective, empirically verified, and readily accepted such as a mood disorder. In contrast, the key feature of DID, dissociation, is primarily a subjective experience for clients. Of interest, the diagnosis of DID seems to be more prevalent in the North American continent. For example 6% to 10% of the U.S. general population are diagnosed with DID (Foote, Smolin, Kaplan, Legatt, & Lipschiz, 2006) in contrast to China, which reports a prevalence rate of 0.4% (Xiao et al., 2006). Piper and Merskey (2004) suggest that DID is a culture-bound and often iatrogenic diagnosis (or induced by the practitioner's activity, manner, or therapy). Unfortunately, there is still much debate surrounding the diagnosis of DID (Lalonde, Hudson, Gigante, & Pope, 2001).

A Quick Guide to Dissociative Identity Disorder

Often found in those who have experienced severe psychological stress in childhood, commonly ritualistic sexual or physical abuse

Existence of more than one distinct identity or personality within the same individual

The identities will take control of the person at different times

Information about the other identities are out of the person's conscious awareness

Other symptoms to look for are:

- Unexplainable headaches and other body pains
- Distortion or loss of subjective time
- Severe memory loss
- Depression
- Flashbacks of abuse/trauma
- Unexplainable phobias
- Sudden anger without a justifiable cause
- Lack of intimacy and personal connections
- Frequent panic/anxiety attacks
- Auditory hallucinations of the personalities inside the person's mind

Another diagnostic complication is that persons with DID may experience a broad array of other symptoms that resemble epilspsy, schizophernia, anxiety disorders, mood disorders, posttraumatic stress disorder, personality disorders, and eating disorders (B. Sadock & Sadock, 2003). The following conceptual map (Figure 10.3) guides the assessment of DID.

Figure 10.3   Conceptual Map for Dissociative Identity Disorder

Differential Assessment

The differential assessment for dissociative identity disorder should also include an exploration of all facets of a person's life with attention to alternative explanations for the symptom picture. This is especially relevant considering the secretive aspects of alter identities and the associated reluctance to talk about them. This competency-based approach to taking a client's history helps to distinguish among chronic amnesia, the symptoms of posttraumatic stress disorder, a history of maltreatment, and the presence of alter identities even when other comorbid disorders are present.

The competency-based assessment makes it easier to recognize the subtle distinctions in symptoms. For example, people with schizophrenia often hear voices but the difference is in how they hear voices. Auditory hallucinations, a symptom of schizophrenia, mean that the voices are within their heads and not from the outside. A personality disorder might mistakenly be considered when the person's alternating personalities are seen as the unstable mood and behavior typical of borderline personality disorder. Dissociative amnesia involves a level of amnesia but it is not recurrent and does not involve multiple distinct personalities.

Depersonalization Disorder

Depersonalization disorder is characterized by a sense of being cut off or detached from one's self, causing distress. People with this disorder also commonly experience derealization. During an episode of derealization, the person's sense of reality of the external world is lost. Depersonalization disorder is often precipitated by stress and episodes begin and end suddenly. Common symptoms are persistent feelings of being detached from one's body or mental processes, usually feeling like being an outside observer. Many report feeling unreal or as if they are in a dream and somehow detached from what is going on around them. One of my students was working with a client who described the episode as, "It was like going through the motions of life but not experiencing it. I felt as though I was watching myself in a movie." Others may report being unable to describe their emotions (alexithymia). You might even hear a client describe him- or herself as one of the "walking dead."

The Clinical Picture

Many of us have experienced an occasional moment of mild depersonalization and these episodes are seen as normal experiences (Simeon & Abugel, 2006). However, when there are strong, severe, and persistent or recurrent feelings of depersonalization and derealization then depersonalization disorder is indicated. Although the person's subjective experience of reality is altered, it is not related to the psychotic disorders because the person is able to distinguish between reality and fantasy (Simeon, 2004).

In fact, the person's grasp on reality remains stable at all times. Anxiety and depression are common.

A Quick Guide to Depersonalization Disorder

An acute stressor is often the precursor to onset

The person has feelings of unreality and that his or her body does not belong to them

Episodes begin and end suddenly, typically ending on their own after a period of time

A conceptual map charting the features of depersonalization disorder is seen in Figure 10.4.

Differential Assessment

Much like the other dissociative disorders, the first step in determining depersonalization disorder is to rule out the presence of a general medical condition or ongoing substance abuse that may better explain symptoms. There are a variety of other diagnoses that share depersonalization as a symptom, in particular the anxiety, cognitive, mood,

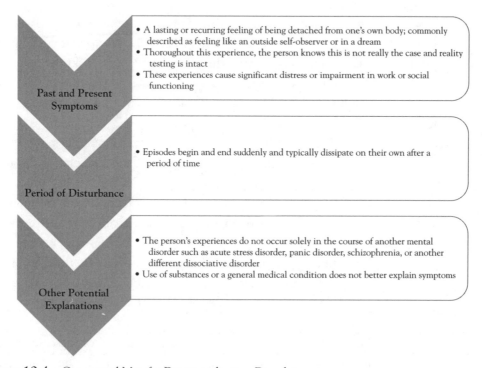

Past and Present Symptoms

- A lasting or recurring feeling of being detached from one's own body; commonly described as feeling like an outside self-observer or in a dream
- Throughout this experience, the person knows this is not really the case and reality testing is intact
- These experiences cause significant distress or impairment in work or social functioning

Period of Disturbance

- Episodes begin and end suddenly and typically dissipate on their own after a period of time

Other Potential Explanations

- The person's experiences do not occur solely in the course of another mental disorder such as acute stress disorder, panic disorder, schizophrenia, or another different dissociative disorder
- Use of substances or a general medical condition does not better explain symptoms

Figure 10.4   Conceptual Map for Depersonalization Disorder

and personality disorders as well as the psychotic disorders. Individuals with depersonalization disorder often struggle to describe their symptoms and may even be afraid that they are going crazy. However, the person knows that these odd or strange experiences are not real but simply the way they feel. It is this level of self-awareness and insight that distinguishes the depersonalization disorder from the psychotic disorders.

FINAL THOUGHTS

To summarize, the dissociative disorders are characterized by disruptions or breakdowns of memory, awareness, identity, and/or perception. The person may lose his or her identity or personal life history. There are several types of dissociative disorders and this chapter reviewed five of them:

1. *Dissociative amnesia*—Formerly known as psychogenic amnesia, the person has a noticeable impairment of recall resulting from emotional trauma. The two most common types are localized amnesia where the person has no memory of specific events (usually traumatic) that took place and selective amnesia that happens when the person can recall only small parts of events that took place in a defined period of time.

2. *Dissociative fugue*—Considered rare, this disorder is characterized by physical desertion of familiar surroundings where the person experiences impaired recall of the past. Some people with this disorder have been known to travel over thousands of miles. The person in a fugue state is unaware of his or her identity or is confused about his or her actual identity. In some cases, the person assumes a new identity.

3. *Dissociative identity disorder*—The dissociative identity disorder, formerly known as multiple personality disorder, is the most famous of the dissociative disorders. The person alternates between two (or more) distinct personality states on a recurring basis. The person shows impaired recall of important information, which varies with the different personality states, called alters or alter egos.

4. *Depersonalization disorder*—The person shows periods of detachment from one's own experience, body, or self, which may be experienced as unreal while retaining the awareness that this is only a feeling and not reality. This experience happens frequently and so severely that it interrupts the person's functioning.

5. *Dissociative disorder not otherwise specified*—The diagnosis of dissociative disorder not otherwise specified is a residual category assigned when the person does not meet the criteria for the other dissociative disorders.

When considering the dissociative disorders, the assessment needs to consider the cultural influences and a number of questions supporting the competency-based assessment were offered. There are a number of possession trance states that are considered normal experiences and several were described.

PRACTICING THE COMPETENCY-BASED ASSESSMENT

Throughout this chapter, we reviewed the dissociative disorders and discussed the various symptoms ranging from amnesia to the alternate identities that people experience. The competency-based assessment helps to keep in mind the range of life circumstances experienced by our clients in order to uncover factors such as stress or trauma that set the stage for the development of a dissociative disorder. The following cases provide an opportunity to challenge your ability to sort through a client's life story and determine the symptom picture supporting the appropriate dissociative disorder diagnosis.

The Case of Christopher Columbo

The practitioner, Angela Snow, took a long deep breath and sank back into her chair. She absently stared at the newspaper on her desk opened to the story of the man with no memory. Angela reflected, "Gosh. They don't teach you about clients like this in graduate school." She looked at the photo and thought, "There's no mistaking that beard. That's my client, John. Well, actually we found out that his name is Christopher Columbo but he preferred to be called John Doe. Claimed he felt more comfortable being a John Doe." It seemed that John believed that the negative reaction he felt to using his real name might be as a result of the guilt he had over a brief marriage that ended with his wife's death.

Reports of John's history indicated that he was married for about seven years but the marriage ended in divorce. He remarried a short time later. After less than a year the marriage abruptly ended when his second wife died after having a miscarriage. She was alone at the time. Apparently John was the one who discovered her body when he came home from work. That vivid and troubling memory was one of the first that returned to John.

Angela's thoughts drifted back to her work with John. It was seven weeks ago that Christopher Columbo was arrested in a residential neighborhood backyard in Monterey, California, with no idea of who he was or how he got there. Apparently, the family was away on an extended vacation. When they came home and found John in their yard, they called the police. John said, "I guess I must have looked pretty pathetic because they didn't want to press charges against me." The police report indicated that Christopher was unshaven, somewhat dehydrated, but neatly dressed with $100 hidden in his pants. He told the police that he had no idea how he got to California and clearly knew that he didn't live there. He was unsure of everything else. He only remembered sitting in the yard underneath the alcove by the home's pool looking out at the trees and the blue sky. The police transported Christopher to the hospital where he was kept for a few days for observation. Christopher/John was discharged in good general health. There were no medical problems noted other than mild exposure. John denied the use of drugs or alcohol. The local news ran a story about him and several of his friends and relatives recognized him as Christopher Columbo.

On discharge from the hospital, Christopher was transferred to a local shelter where he was receiving counseling from Angela Snow. The intake report noted that his estranged sister who happened to live in California was able to provide John with his driver's license, Social Security card, and other identification. Apparently, John had always been close to his sister. After the death of his second wife, he moved in with her. John lived with his sister for about a year but their relationship became strained because John was not working or helping out with the rent. Leaving his belongings behind, John simply walked out. His sister remembers that one night after dinner John announced that he was going to his room. Instead, he went out the back door never to be seen until the story about him in the newspaper.

The police investigation into the incident left little doubt that the mystery man with no memory was clearly Christopher Colombo. Unfortunately, a definitive identification could not be made until "John Doe" confirmed his identity. He did not.

What was known about Christopher Columbo's history was that he grew up just outside of Scottsdale, Arizona. He asserted that he had few memories of his childhood except that his father was an alcoholic who slapped him around when he was drinking. His mother did not drink but took a lot of pills for various aches and pains. When he was shown a picture of his family, John had no recollection of having a sister or a brother. His sister shared that their brother died in high school as a result of a freak auto accident.

The focus of Angela Snow's work was to help John find a more permanent solution for housing. They began by discussing John's strengths. According to John's sister, he was a college graduate and spent a number of years as a high school English teacher. He coached the boys' soccer team after school. Angela thought that John had a number of assets that would help him to find a job and housing. Unfortunately, their work seemed to go nowhere. Each time Angela tried to go forward with a specific action, John would talk about his frustration and overwhelming feeling of being perpetually lost. He was also afraid of losing the few connections he made in the shelter. He commented, "I'm living in a state of confusion. I've got all this information about who I was but am I going to be able to retain it? Every time I look at my photo in the paper, the bell of my name is not ringing but I know it's definitely me." For John, his life felt "superficial."

What seemed to hold up the work on getting a job was John's "fear of the unknown." Angela suggested that it might help if John contacted people who said they knew him as Christopher Columbo but John always came up with various excuses for not doing so. He claimed that he had difficulty getting numbers, didn't know "those people," or he could not figure out who he could trust from his past. "I think in most cases it's because when you show me pictures, I really don't recognize them," said John.

There was a loud knock on Angela's door that abruptly interrupted her thoughts about John and the newspaper article. A coworker stuck her head in the door and stated, "Still no sign of John. What should we do next?" John left the shelter without warning and he has been missing for the past 24 hours. Angela thought to herself that she should have seen this coming. Sometimes during their work together, John claimed that he was uncomfortable living in the shelter. He would talk about his fear of having his things stolen or being assaulted. Angela thought this discomfort would serve as motivation for John to secure more housing arrangements. "Boy was I wrong on that one," she thought.

How would you formulate your competency-based assessment for Christopher Columbo?

The Case of Illeana Rodriquez

This is Illeana Rodriquez's story. She is a 34-year-old woman who was brought to the emergency room by her husband, Hector. Illeana is the oldest girl of a large Puerto Rican family. After high school, she moved to the United States in order to find a better job. Shortly after she arrived, Illeana met and married Hector Rodriquez. She referred to him as "the light of my life."

Hector Rodriquez works as a garage mechanic and makes good money so that Illeana could fulfill her childhood dream of going to school to become a nurse. Hector is devoted to his wife and proud of her accomplishments in school. To help out with the couple's goal of moving out of their apartment in the city and into a home in the suburbs, Illeana works part time cleaning offices in the World Trade Center in New York City. Right after Hector was promoted to garage supervisor, the couple began to talk about starting a family.

According to the emergency room social worker, Illeana can be described as a pleasant woman who was extremely cooperative in the interview. She has dark hair, and is slightly heavyset. Illeana was neatly dressed wearing dark slacks, comfortable-looking shoes, and a neatly pressed shirt. Hector stood near his wife as she sat on the examining table. He held her hand and had a worried look on his face. According to Hector, his wife could not remember anything about the last eight days.

The social worker turned to Hector and asked, "I noticed on the admitting report that your wife is from Puerto Rico. Is she more comfortable speaking English or Spanish?" Hector responded that both he and his wife were bilingual. He added,

"We've been back and forth from home to the States so many times that we're pretty comfortable in both English and Spanish. Sometimes though, we tell special little secrets to each other in Spanish." The social worker asked if it would be all right to ask Illeana some questions in Spanish. Hector seemed surprised and responded with a broad smile, "You speak Spanish?" The social worker indicated that she spoke a little Spanish and thought that maybe Illeana would be more comfortable answering questions in her first language. Mr. Rodriquez seemed delighted, adding, "Well, I never thought of that, but go ahead if you think it will help Illeana to remember."

> The social worker turned to Illeana saying, "Disculpeme por hablar tan mal el espanol." Illeana smiled.
> The social worker then asked, "Sabe usted donde se encuentra?" Illeana responded, "No se."
> The social worker continued, "Pero, que dia es hoy?" At this point, Illeana looked blank.
> The social worker then asked, "Cual es la fecha?" Illeana began to look worried and turned to her husband.
> At this point, the social worker decided to stop asking further questions and said to Illeana, "Por favor, perdoname." Illeana seemed relieved and in almost a whisper stated, "Gracias."

When the physician entered the room Hector asked, "Tell me doctor, will she be all right? She tried very hard to answer all questions asked of her . . . and this nice social worker even asked her in Spanish but my Illeana does not seem to know."

The social worker briefly filled the doctor in on Illeana's status. She began, "So far she's checked out just fine. Medically at least. There are no indicators of drugs or alcohol in the lab work and her husband says there is no history of mental illness in the family." With a worried look on his face, Hector nodded affirmatively. The social worker continued, "She just can't remember anything about the last eight days. Nothing."

Hector chimed in, "It's like everything in her life just stopped. Sort of like she's frozen in time. I knew it was hard for her to see the buildings blow up . . . and then there were all the people running around. Some were screaming. Doctor, I'm sure you saw the World Trade Center explosions on TV that Tuesday. Illeana has been a changed person ever since. You see what happened was that Illeana had just finished up her shift cleaning the offices. She was walking toward the subway just like she always does when all of a sudden there was a big bang. I don't know how my Illeana ever made it home but she's not been the same since. For me . . .," Hector paused at this point and cast a worried look over to his wife. He continued saying with emphasis, "September

11, 2001, will go down in history as the worst day in my Illeana's life. It's like she can't remember anything about the last eight days. I keep asking her, 'Do you know where you are?' 'What's today's date?' but all I get is nothing. I try telling her that she's okay and that we're safe but it just doesn't seem to make a difference. Doctor, will I get my Illeana back?"

The doctor checked her chart, reviewed the lab reports and read the consult by the neurologist on call. The neurologist indicated there was no evidence of any head trauma or anything else that could explain Illeana's memory loss. On physical exam, the doctor noticed that Illeana did have a slight cough. "Probably from inhaling all the smoke from the burning buildings," he thought.

How would you formulate your competency-based assessment for Illeana Rodriquez?

PRACTICAL APPLICATIONS

The dissociative disorders come in many forms but are generally thought to stem from trauma or some type of horrible event or events that can happen to people. The dissociative aspect is thought to be a coping mechanism where the person literally dissociates him- or herself from a situation or experience too traumatic to integrate with the conscious self.

1. Working with clients who have experienced severe trauma or abuse can evoke powerful reactions. Although this can be explained away as an occupational hazard for those who work in this field, unexamined countertransference, secondary or vicarious trauma or even burnout can seriously affect one's work with clients. Individually, with another colleague or with your supervisor reflect on the following:
    a. Identify the potential problems you (or your colleagues) might encounter when working with clients who have experienced severe trauma, stress or abuse.
    b. List the ways these issues may potentially affect the competency-based assessment of the dissociative disorders, and what can be done to address them.
2. Sirhan Sirhan is mentioned in this chapter under the discussion of dissociative amnesia, a disorder where people are unable to recall recent experiences or those from the distant past. Sirhan was only able to remember his attempts to assassinate Senator Robert Kennedy when hypnotized. Apparently he had a troubled past. Sirhan was born in Jerusalem, which was part of Palestine at the time. At a young age, he witnessed bodies torn apart by bombs. At age 12, his family immigrated to the United States to escape the Israeli bombings

in Beirut. Throughout his childhood, Sirhan's father was said to be physically abusive and suddenly left the family. Aimed at refining your diagnostic thinking, put yourself in the place of a juror on Sirhan's murder trial and identify the factors you would consider to determine if he actually did struggle with dissociative amnesia at the time he assassinated Kennedy. By now you probably know that he was convicted and sentenced to a life sentence and has consistently been denied parole.

3. We often encounter clients who come from different cultural backgrounds, such as the case of Illeana Rodriquez. Imagine for a moment that you are working with Illeana and her husband.

   a. What can you do to communicate to this couple that you would like to be able to fully understand their culture?

   b. How can you ensure that your competency-based assessment considers the potential cultural influences on Illeana's memory problems?

   c. If you were working with someone from a culture that is unfamiliar to you, what can you do to better understand the client's experience with the symptoms of a dissociative disorder and respond to them in a culturally competent way?

Appendix

Competency-Based Assessments for Chapter 10 Case Examples: Listing of Case Diagnoses

Figures 10A.1 through 10A.4 provide the diagnostic assessment for each of the cases illustrated. They are organized in the order that they appear in each chapter.

CASE REVIEW FOR CHRISTOPHER COLUMBO

The competency-based assessment looks to the client's strengths and resilience. In this case, Christopher Columbo has a sister who lives nearby. Although their relationship is recently strained, they have had a longer history of being close to and supportive of each other that seems to sustain their connection. Christopher is described as bright and educated and his history notes that he is college graduate who has worked for some time as a high school English teacher and as a coach after school.

He was reported to have been married twice but both of his marriages ended; one due to a divorce and the second one from the unexpected death of his wife.

After the death of his second wife, Christopher moved in to live with his sister. The first hint of a dissociative fugue becomes apparent when, for no apparent reason, Christopher abruptly leaves his sister's home. After a period of time, Christopher was found in someone's backyard and arrested for trespassing. He claimed his identity as John Doe and had no other memories of his past. In fact, the first memory that he was able to recall was the tragic death of his wife. He is alert and his behavior does not

Figure 10A.1   The Conceptual Map for Christopher Columbo

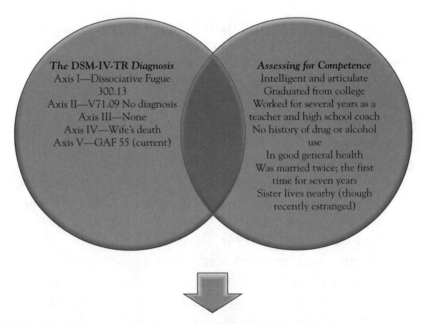

Figure 10A.2   The Competency-Based Assessment for Christopher Columbo

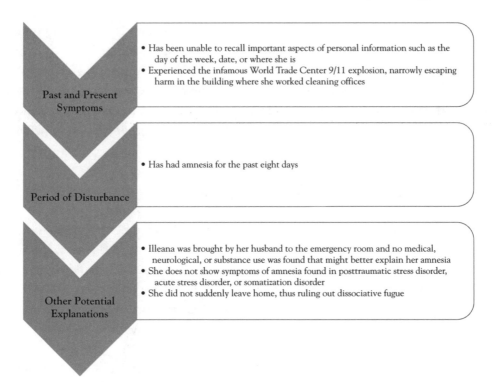

Figure 10A.3   The Conceptual Map for Illeana Rodriquez

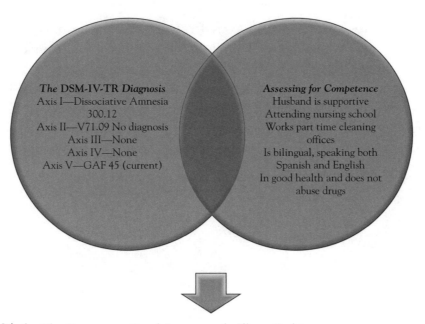

Figure 10A.4   The Competency-Based Assessment for Illeana Rodriguez

support the diagnosis of schizophrenia. He has nothing to gain from his symptoms and therefore the diagnosis of malingering would not be indicated.

After a brief hospitalization for observation, Christopher was ultimately transferred to a homeless shelter. As a positive, he has been able to make connections with others, including the practitioner during his stay in the homeless shelter. He is in good general health and has no history of substance use, thus eliminating other possible explanations for his dissociative fugue.

CASE REVIEW FOR ILLEANA RODRIQUEZ

The case discussion reveals that Illeana Rodriquez was leaving her part-time job cleaning offices at the World Trade Center when she witnessed the 9/11 destruction. She heard the explosion and saw the devastation. She had just left the building and being so close to the reality that she could have been killed by such extensive wreckage could have provided the stimulus for her dissociative amnesia. Somehow Illeana made it home but subsequently had no memory. After eight days her husband, Hector, brought her to the emergency room.

Illeana's chief complaint and source of concern for her husband was her amnesia. The doctor noted a slight cough; probably from inhaling smoke from the explosion and fire. The hospital gave Illeana a complete medical evaluation and the findings of her tests and examinations were all within normal limits. This provided no medical basis to support her state of amnesia such as a brain injury. In addition, there is no history of substance use.

The competency-based assessment considers alternative explanations for a person's behavior. The practitioner noted that Illeana was bilingual and wondered if there might have been a language barrier when she was initially interviewed. Spanish is Illeana's first language, so the practitioner asked Illeana a series of questions in Spanish to test her memory. Unfortunately, Illeana did not know the answers, so further supporting the notion that her dissociative amnesia was attributed to the traumatic experience of surviving the massive destruction of the building where she worked.

CHAPTER
11

Eating Disorders

INTRODUCTION

Do you remember the sensation of enjoying a rich, thick, gooey chocolate candy bar? Maybe potato chips and other crunchies are your favorites. But then afterward you started to feel a little guilty. The old saying, "A moment on the lips, a lifetime on the hips" begins to repeat itself over and over in your head. The loveable character Rhoda on the 1970s sitcom *The Mary Tyler Moore* show was remembered asking, "Shall I eat this candy bar or just apply it to my hips?" Okay. So you vowed to be a little more circumspect the next time you are confronted with such delicious temptations and then moved on with other activities in your life. For most of us, food is both a necessity and a pleasure. That is not the typical experience for someone struggling with an eating disorder. Serious disturbances in eating behaviors such as extreme and unhealthy reductions of food intake or severe overeating compensated by purging as well as feelings of distress about body image characterize the eating disorders. Willpower is not a part of the eating disorder symptom picture. Rather, these are illnesses where certain maladaptive patterns take on a life of their own. The third type found in the *DSM*, eating disorder not otherwise specified, is a pattern of disordered eating of severe proportions that cannot be explained by alternative diagnoses.

The eating disorders are usually divided into three main groups; anorexia nervosa, bulimia nervosa, and eating disorder not otherwise specified. The main eating disorders are anorexia nervosa, where the person is underweight but often thinks they are fat, and bulimia nervosa, characterized by binge-purge cycles (American Psychiatric Association, 2000). Individuals usually deny that they are sick, making the eating disorders one of the most difficult mental illnesses to evaluate. Another type, binge-eating disorder, has been proposed but is not yet approved as a formal *DSM* diagnosis

339

(American Psychiatric Association Work Group on Eating Disorders, 2000). It is reviewed in this chapter in order to better differentiate among the symptoms of the eating disorders recognized in the *DSM*. Binge-eating is distinguished from bulimia in that it does not involve purging. It can also be called compulsive overeating because it is marked by uncontrolled eating episodes and weight gain. It may or may not include the body image distortion experienced by those who struggle with anorexia.

Factors influencing what we eat. Eating behaviors are influenced by many factors including appetite, the availability of food, family, peer and cultural practices, and attempts at voluntary control typically referred to as dieting. Current fashion trends, sales campaigns for special foods, and some activities (such as gymnastics, cheerleading, body building, running, rowing, figure skating) and certain professions (such as actors, dancers, athletes, models, TV personalities) promote a body weight leaner than needed for one's overall health (Brubaker & Leddy, 2003; Thomas & Freyokin, 2004; Tolgyes & Nemessury, 2004). Unfortunately the self-starvation that characterizes the eating disorders has much to say about our culture that seems to place slenderness on the highest pedestal of female accomplishment (Krusky, 2002). The average U.S. woman is reported to be 5 feet 4 inches tall and weighs 140 pounds, in contrast to the average U.S. model who is 5 feet 11 inches tall and weighs far less, or an average of 117 pounds. As a matter of fact, most fashion models are thinner than 98% of U.S. women. S. Posavac, R. Posavac, and Weigel (2001) observe that it is women who are more than likely to compare their bodies with images of beauty found in the media and consequently become less satisfied with their own bodies. Although being dissatisfied with one's body image increases the risk for developing an eating disorder, shame and the related feelings of self-consciousness, inferiority, and powerless along with a wish to hide one's "deficiencies" also play an important role (Greenberg, 2002; Swan & Andrews, 2003).

Dieting. Researchers are beginning to look at how and why people eat smaller or larger amounts of food than usual and at what point move beyond voluntary control toward ultimately developing an eating disorder. There is growing evidence supporting the substantial role that genes (or stretches of DNA, a substance inherited from one's parents) can play (National Institutes of Health, 2007). For example, people who are genetically vulnerable may be more susceptible to cultural cues about the "ideal" body image. The cause of eating disorders is not clear, but those who are at risk often begin with a simple diet that eventually leads to changes in brain chemistry and in due course malnutrition. These normal dieters may progress to pathological dieting. Neumark-Sztainer (2005) found that girls who diet frequently are 12 times more likely to binge as girls who do not diet. On any given day, 45% of American women and 25% of men are on a diet (Smolak, 1996).

Dieting is big business in the United States. Americans spend more than $46 billion annually on diet products and self-help books (Hoffman & Rose, 2005). Despite the extra cost, most diet plans currently on the market are not effective. Stephen Gullo, Ph.D., author of the audio book entitled, *The Thin Commandments*, observes that diet plans are the only growth industry in the United States where most of the customers fail. If there were an effective way to lose weight, then perhaps these diet programs would be out of business. Consider that two thirds of dieters had regained all the weight they had lost in one year and 97% of dieters gained it all back in five years (Hoffman & Rose, 2005). The person with an eating disorder feels as though eating permeates every aspect of his or her lifestyle, personality, attitudes, value, quality of relationships, and overall functioning (Bachner-Melman, 2003; Ronel & Libman, 2003).

Risks associated with the eating disorders. Risk factors for eating disorders between both genders are concerns about one's appearance, substance use such as cigarette smoking and alcohol, anxiety, and depression (Croll, Neumark-Sztainer, Story, & Ireland, 2002; Granner, Abood, & Black, 2001; Krahn, Kurth, Gomberg, & Drewnowski, 2005; NIHealth, 2007). Stressful life events, a lack of self-esteem, troubled relationships, or family problems can also trigger eating disorders (Moreno, Selby, Aved, & Besse, 2000). Parents who are controlling and focus on the child's achievement, food, and weight and exercise create a family atmosphere supportive of anorexia nervosa (Bachner-Melman, 2003; Pizer, 2002). Moorhead (2001) suggests that a person who has a family member with an eating problem is at an even higher risk of developing an eating disorder.

Age is another risk factor. Although it is possible for eating disorders to happen in childhood or much later in life, onset frequently occurs during adolescence or early adulthood. About 50% of fourth-grade girls report to have dieted and the figure rises to 90% by age 17 (Dancyger & Fornari, 2009; Sohn, 2002). Croll, Neumark-Sztainer, Story, and Ireland (2002) examined the prevalence of eating disorders in a large sample of adolescents and found that 56% of ninth-grade females and 28% of males reported disordered eating behaviors. These behaviors were defined as one or more of the following: fasting or skipping meals, taking diet pills, vomiting, using laxatives, smoking cigarettes, and binge-eating. The rates were higher among 12th-grade students who showed disordered eating at a rate of approximately 57% for females and 31% for males. Some of the normal life-cycle development tasks associated with adolescence include the development of self-esteem, establishment of identity, and psychological disengagement from family. These developmental events can also be regarded as precursors to eating disorders and eating problems continue well beyond high school (Mantle, 2003).

In summary, the eating disorders are distinguished by the complex interactions among several different factors such as emotional factors and personality disorders, biological or genetic susceptibility, and a culture with an obsession for thinness (Miller & Scott-Mizes, 2000; Wright, 2003). This complexity points to the value of the competency-based assessment that provides an encompassing look at not only how people cope but the factors that influence their lives. Unfortunately, those with eating disorders are set apart by gross disturbances in eating behaviors and highly individualized extreme concerns about shape and weight.

INCIDENCE AND PREVALENCE

Unfortunately, the eating disorders have grown to epidemic proportions in our culture (Murray, 2003). Adolescents and young women, for example, account for 90% of cases and an increasing number of ethnic minorities are falling prey to this devastating mental illness (Kempa & Thomas, 2000). Overall, 4.5% of adults in the United States, or more than 9 million people, have struggled with eating disorders at some point in their lives (NIH, 2007). In general, females are at a higher risk than males to develop an eating disorder. Although rates among males are increasing, females are still 10 times more likely to develop an eating disorder. However, it seems to be increasing among men who account for 25% of Americans with anorexia or bulimia and 40% of those with binge-eating disorder (Dancyger & Fornari, 2009). The course of the eating disorders is similar for males and females; that is, both share the same concerns about body image and weight (Eliot & Baker, 2001).

Anorexia nervosa. As a whole, about 90% of those diagnosed with anorexia are female with males making up the remaining 10% (Lask & Bryant-Waugh, 2000). It is estimated that 0.6% to 3.7% of females will suffer from anorexia nervosa in their lifetimes (APA Work Group on Eating Disorders, 2000; NIH, 2007). Incidence rates are between 8 and 13 cases per 100,000 persons per year for females between 15 and 19 years of age who make up 40% of all cases (Bulik, Reba, Siega-Riz, & Reichborn-Kjennerud, 2005; Hoek, 2006). The mortality rates among those struggling with anorexia are at approximately 6%. These individuals will die due to related causes (Herzog et al., 2000). Dancyger and Fornari (2009) observe that an estimated 1,000 women die each year of complications related to anorexia nervosa. This is about 12 times higher than the annual death rate due to all causes of death among females ages 15 to 24 in the general population. The general causes of death are related to malnutrition and starvation such as cardiac arrest, electrolyte imbalance, and suicide. However, it is suicide that is the major cause of death (Pompli, Mancinelli, Girardi, Ruberto, & Tatarelli, 2004).

Bulimia nervosa. Bulimia nervosa occurs more frequently than anorexia nervosa but tends to be underassessed (APA, 2000). This may be because the symptoms are less obvious than the more visible signs of starving seen in anorexia nervosa. Someone with bulimia nervosa will more than likely have a normal or slightly overweight appearance. Approximately 1.1% to 4.2% of females are estimated to have the diagnosis of bulimia nervosa in their lifetimes (APA Work Group on Eating Disorders, 2000). The onset of symptoms occurs during late adolescence or early twenties and usually begins with an attempt to diet followed by purging behaviors (vomiting or using diuretics or laxatives to keep from gaining weight).

Binge-eating disorder. As with anorexia nervosa and bulimia nervosa, the person struggling with binge-eating disorder is usually a young woman; for example, three women for every two men with the diagnosis are affected (U.S. Department of Health and Human Services, 2001). Binge-eating disorder is currently listed in the appendix of the *DSM-IV-TR* as a potential new disorder that calls for further study (APA, 2000). Until a decision is made to include it as a formal diagnostic category, any discussion about the syndrome should be considered tentative. Though not recognized as an official psychiatric diagnosis, binge-eating disorder is by far the most common form of disordered eating affecting nearly 3% of the American population (NIH, 2007). Individuals who struggle with binge-eating often become overweight and it is more commonly found in people who are severely obese (U.S. DHHS, 2001). These are individuals who might lose and then gain weight (yo-yo dieting). They share some of the same concerns about body shape and weight as those with anorexia nervosa and bulimia nervosa (Wilfley, Schwartz, Spurrell, & Fariburn, 2000).

OVERVIEW OF MAJOR SYMPTOMS

The eating disorders frequently co-occur with other disorders such as the mood disorders, substance use, anxiety disorders, and the personality disorders (APA, 2000; Moorhead, 2001; Wright, 2003). In addition, those suffering from the eating disorders can potentially experience a range of health complications including, for example, serious heart conditions and kidney failure, which can ultimately lead to death.

Assessment challenges. An accurate diagnosis is crucial and yet you can be confronted with a number of challenges to obtaining the complete symptom picture. The competency-based assessment considers a range of factors in a client's life, including the reality that an eating disorder may be reinforced when others compliment the person's thin appearance, usually at the outset of the disorder (Bagley, Character, & Shelton, 2003). People who struggle with eating disorders may deny the severity of their illnesses compounded by cognitive impairment secondary to malnutrition, thus making them unreliable informants about their eating experiences. In addition, it is common for those with an eating disorder to have many years and cycles of care before showing improvement.

The course of recovery for anorexia nervosa may be 7 to 10 years and possibly less for bulimia nervosa (Carter, Blackmore, Sutandar-Pinnock, & Woodside, 2004; Richards et al., 2000). Between 20% and 30% of clients with an eating disorder simply drop out of treatment (Wolfe, 2003). The end result is that you will more than likely encounter a client who is an unreliable historian with a past history of treatment where the continuum of care has been broken leaving more questions than answers.

As a part of your competency-based assessment, Anstine and Grinenko (2000) suggest a series of questions to routinely include in the diagnostic interview to better screen for the possibility of the presence of an eating disorder. They are adapted as follows:

Screening for Eating Disorders

How many diets have you been on in the past year?

Has there ever been a time when people close to you (family, friends, or others) have given you a hard time about being too thin or losing too much weight?

Do you think about food a lot?

Do you feel dissatisfied with your body size (or your weight)?

Does your weight affect the way you feel about yourself?

Do you worry excessively about your weight?

Are there times when you feel badly (for example, guilty, ashamed, or depressed) after you eat?

When you start eating, are you afraid you won't be able to stop?

Do you ever eat until you feel sick?

Do you think you might have an eating problem?

It goes without saying that those who struggle with an eating disorder often deny the severity of their problem. Consider tailoring these questions to the individualized experiences of a particular client. Questioning someone about their eating patterns is a sensitive area and it is presumed that you will first develop a supportive and accepting relationship.

ANOREXIA NERVOSA

Anorexia nervosa is considered a psychophysiological disorder involving neurobiological, psychological, and sociocultural elements. Commonly found in young women who have extremely low body weight, the hallmark of this disorder is a preoccupation with food and a refusal to maintain a minimally normal body weight. These are individuals who fear becoming obese along with a distorted self-image and a persistent unwillingness to eat. They continue to believe that they look fat despite the reality that they are emaciated. Those with anorexia nervosa have a distorted body image that causes them to see themselves as overweight even when they are dangerously thin (Kohn & Golden, 2001). A client once confided to me that every time she looked into the mirror all she could see was the cellulite on her hips and thighs; all this despite weighing less than expected for someone her body size. These are people who lose large amounts of weight and yet still continue to see themselves as fat. They are obsessed with clothing size, scales, and mirrors.

Most often, those struggling with anorexia control body weight through voluntary starvation, excessive exercise, or other measures such as diet pills, self-induced vomiting (forceful expulsion of the contents of one's stomach through the mouth and sometimes the nose), diuretic drugs, laxatives, or enemas. The development of anorexia nervosa seems related to several factors with no single identifiable event that could be considered the cause of the person's struggles around eating (Austrian, 2005). The competency-based assessment provides a structure for the practitioner to examine all aspects of the person's life; for example, how one copes with life challenges, the impact of family and the supports available, and social or cultural influences.

Anorexia nervosa is the least common of the eating disorders but can be the most deadly. By the time a person with this disorder comes to your attention more than likely they will weigh less than 15% below the normal range or 85% of weight for age and height. At first glance, there is no clear boundary between the thinness of anorexia nervosa and that of an individual who is considered naturally slender. However, people with this disorder severely limit food intake. This disordered pattern of eating leads to malnourishment that often results in serious medical conditions, for example, osteoporosis and anemia, or they may even starve themselves to death. An early sign often associated with starvation is changes in brain structure and function. Anorexia is linked to a reduced blood flow in the temporal lobes, but because this does not correlate with current weight, it is more than likely a risk factor for the diagnosis rather than a consequence of starvation (Lask et al., 2005). Postmenarcheal women lose their menstrual periods or have irregular menstrual periods. There may be a decreased libido and impotence in males. The key signs of anorexia include:

Key Signs of Anorexia Nervosa

A refusal to maintain normal body weight

Intense fear of weight gain and fatness

Distorted body image

Amenorrhea

The Clinical Picture

Some of the common physical signs of anorexia nervosa are that the person's hair and nails become brittle and her or his skin becomes dry and yellow. Because the body temperature goes down, these individuals often complain of feeling cold (hypothermia). It is common to see them wearing a heavy sweater on a hot summer day. Not only does this keep the person warm but hides the thin, emaciated appearance. They may develop lanugo (the fine hair found on a newborn) on their body.

Food and weight becomes an obsession. People struggling with anorexia may develop ritualistic eating habits such as cutting food into tiny pieces and pushing it around on their plates, or refusing to eat in front of others. They are constantly thinking about the next encounter with food. They are able to control the desire to eat often ignoring hunger signals. It is common to find a preoccupation with food, recipes, or fixing elaborate meals for others, which they themselves do not eat. For some individuals the ability to control what they eat and how much they weigh helps them feel as if other aspects of their lives are under control. Research findings are now showing that some of the personality "traits" of persons with anorexia nervosa are actually risk factors for the disorder; for example, anxiety, low self-esteem, body dissatisfaction, and dieting (Berkman, Lohr, & Bulik, 2007).

Figure 11.1 is the conceptual map charting the symptoms for anorexia nervosa.

There are two subtypes of anorexia nervosa; binge-eating/purging and restricting. Specify if the person has the binge-eating/purging type of anorexia when the person restricts her or his food intake but regularly engages in binge-eating and/or purging behaviors shown by purging (self-induced vomiting, misuse of laxatives, diuretics, or enemas) or eating in binges during an anorectic episode. The less common is the restricting type where there is no bingeing and purging during an anorectic episode. The person restricts food intake and, possibly, by exercise. Sometimes the person moves back and forth between the subtypes during the course of her or his illness.

Differential Assessment

Anorexia characterizes a person's refusal to eat anything but minimal amounts of food resulting in extremely low body weight in contrast to those with bulimia who engage in uncontrolled binge-eating episodes followed by self-induced purging. A minimal body weight of 85% less than expected for normal height and age should be considered as a guide; for example, children who are still growing fall short of the 85% of expected normal weight. An individual with anorexia who experiences only a few episodes of binge-eating should not be considered for bulimia nervosa. However, if the

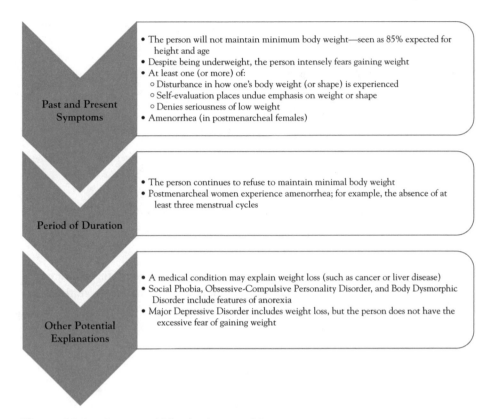

Past and Present Symptoms
- The person will not maintain minimum body weight—seen as 85% expected for height and age
- Despite being underweight, the person intensely fears gaining weight
- At least one (or more) of:
  - Disturbance in how one's body weight (or shape) is experienced
  - Self-evaluation places undue emphasis on weight or shape
  - Denies seriousness of low weight
- Amenorrhea (in postmenarcheal females)

Period of Duration
- The person continues to refuse to maintain minimal body weight
- Postmenarcheal women experience amenorrhea; for example, the absence of at least three menstrual cycles

Other Potential Explanations
- A medical condition may explain weight loss (such as cancer or liver disease)
- Social Phobia, Obsessive-Compulsive Personality Disorder, and Body Dysmorphic Disorder include features of anorexia
- Major Depressive Disorder includes weight loss, but the person does not have the excessive fear of gaining weight

Figure 11.1   Conceptual Map for Anorexia Nervosa

individual binges several (or more) times a week they would appear to have both disorders concurrently.

Other disorders may explain a loss of appetite and weight such as cancer, liver disease, or severe infections. A complete medical evaluation and tests would rule out medically based explanations. Somatization disorder is differentiated from anorexia as the person tends to have multiple somatic complaints. People with schizophrenia may have peculiar eating patterns but unless they become dangerously underweight and have distorted self-image anorexia is not considered. The diagnosis of social phobia should not be made if the person's symptoms are strictly limited to eating behaviors. The mood disorders, in particular major depressive disorder, may also complicate the assessment as part of the symptom picture includes weight loss. Obsessive-compulsive personality disorder includes rigid and perfectionistic symptoms. However, the major distinguishing factor of anorexia is the person's excessive concerns about gaining weight.

The major features of anorexia nervosa are summarized as follows:

Major Features of Anorexia Nervosa

Psychological	Preoccupation with food
	Refusal to maintain minimally normal body weight—weighs 85% less than expected for height and age
	Fear of gaining weight
	Distorted self-image
	Feelings of anxiety, low self-esteem, and/or body dissatisfaction
	Unwillingness to eat
Behavioral	May develop ritualistic eating habits
	Uses measures to control weight such as voluntary starvation, excessive exercise, or others such as diet pills, self-induced vomiting, diuretic drugs, or enemas
	Refuses to eat in front of others
	Secretive about eating
Physical	Amenorrhea in postmenarcheal women
	Decreased libido
	Impotence in men
	Malnourishment leading to serious medical conditions; for example, osteoporosis and anemia
	Complications from starvation
	Hair and nails become brittle
	Skin becomes dry and yellow
	Complaints of feeling cold (hypothermia)
	Develop lanugo

BULIMIA NERVOSA

Those with anorexia nervosa will not start eating in contrast to those with bulimia nervosa who believe they cannot stop eating. An important difference between anorexia nervosa and bulimia nervosa is that the person with bulimia does not have the extreme distortion of self-image found in those with anorexia. It is common to find a history that includes many anorexic features, but most have never had anorexia. Bulimia nervosa is especially common among young women of normal weight whose eating patterns are characterized by episodic binge-eating followed by feelings of guilt, depression, and self-condemnation. The personal characteristics found in those who struggle with bulimia can include feelings of shame, self-criticism, immediate gratification needs, a strong need for approval, and heightened interpersonal sensitivity. Despite the fact that they eat excessive quantities of food (typically junk food such as candy, doughnuts, cookies, or potato chips) people with bulimia are often able to maintain a normal weight by purging their bodies of the food and calories before it can be digested by using laxatives, enemas (less common) or diuretics, self-induced vomiting, dieting or fasting (not eating for at least 24 hours), and/or strenuous exercising (or exercising for more than an hour just to keep from gaining weight after binge-eating) (Wilson & Pike, 2001). The actual amount consumed is different for each person (Franco, Wonderlich, Little, & Herzog, 2004). The process of fasting usually backfires causing increased hunger and leading to greater overeating.

Bulimia nervosa tends to center on issues of personal identity, independence, and self-assertion leading to the development of the false self to cover a low sense of self-esteem (Mantle, 2003). These negative emotions are somehow relieved once the person's stomach is empty again. Key symptoms of bulimia nervosa include:

Key Symptoms of Bulimia Nervosa

Recurrent episodes of binge-eating

Inappropriate compensatory behaviors such as using laxatives, enemas or diuretics, self-induced vomiting or purging, dieting or fasting, and/or strenuous exercise at least twice a week

Self-evaluation influenced by body shape

The person often binge-eats in secrecy feeling disgusted and ashamed as she or he binges. Unable to control how much he or she eats, the person binges when no one else is around. I remember a client who was quite creative in replacing food so that her family would not notice how much she had eaten. She was an avid coupon collector and would go to several different supermarkets so that the checker would not know what she was up to. She became an expert at stockpiling her food stash and her favorite place was the bottom of the laundry hamper. Her husband was an early riser and usually in bed by 10 in the evening so her "best time" for gorging was late at night after everybody in the house was asleep. It is not unusual for individuals with bulimia to go to extremes to conceal their eating habits. Despite the secrecy, there are a number of warning signs and symptoms of bulimia that can alert the practitioner (Pomeroy, 2004).

Eating patterns are characterized by a destructive cycle of bingeing followed by purging or the less frequently employed "restrictive" behaviors such as dieting or exercising. In an effort to regain control and make up for the excess calories eaten, most individuals with bulimia purge to make up for bingeing. Although purging is intended to compensate for episodes of binge-eating, it actually ends up reinforcing

👉 Warning Signs of Bulimia

Lack of control over eating

Secrecy surrounding eating

Eating unusually large amounts of food

Alternating between overeating and fasting

it. A person's negative feelings about his- or herself are found to increase following binge episodes but diminish immediately before and after the compensatory activities (Lynch, Everingham, Dubitzky, & Kasser, 2007). Perhaps in the back of their minds the individuals know that they can always throw up, take a water pill, use laxatives, or go on a crash diet if they lose control of their eating again.

Telltale signs of purging. There are a number of signs of the compensatory behaviors that follow an episode of bingeing. One clue is that the person goes to the bathroom after meals. Here they throw up and maybe run the water in order to disguise the sounds of vomiting. Another indication is that the bathroom may have the telltale smell of vomit covered up by mouthwash, perfume, or air freshener. In addition to taking laxatives, diuretics, or enemas, the person may also take diet pills to curb the appetite or use a sauna to sweat out water weight. Strenuous workouts including high-intensity calorie burners such as running or aerobics may take place especially after eating. The person may decide to go on a crash diet or fast for a period of time.

👉 Compensatory Behaviors Following Binge-Eating

Going to the bathroom after meals

Smell of vomit

Using laxatives, diuretics, or enemas

Taking diet pills

Use a sauna to "sweat out" weight

Excessive exercising

Fasting or going on crash diets

Clues to bulimia. There are also a number of physical clues that can help you to recognize the presence of bulimia. One indication is known as Russell's signs where skin lesions, abrasions, small lacerations, or raised calluses are found on the top (dorsal) surface of the fingers and knuckles. This is a by-product of repeated purging behaviors caused by the constant friction of fingers scraped back and forth across incisor teeth to induce vomiting. Not everyone uses her or his fingers to induce vomiting; other techniques may include sticking coat hangers, wads of paper, or pens down one's throat. Another sign is puffy "chipmunk" cheeks caused by the salivary glands expanding from repeated vomiting. Self-induced vomiting can wear away tooth enamel. The person's teeth may be discolored as a result of repeated exposure to stomach acid when throwing up. Their teeth may look yellow, ragged, or clear. The person's weight may fluctuate by 10 pounds or more from alternating episodes of bingeing and purging (or severely restricting intake).

Physical Signs and Symptoms of Bulimia Nervosa

Calluses or scars on the knuckles or hands (Russell's signs)
Puffy "chipmunk" cheeks
Discolored teeth
Weight fluctuations (usually by 10 pounds or more)

Despite a fear of becoming fat, most persons with bulimia nervosa are usually of normal weight or can be overweight. The chronic pattern of bingeing and purging can lead to a number of health problems, especially dehydration. The gastrointestinal system may be disturbed and the person experiences heartburn, abdominal pain, cramps, and bloating. Although it may seem obvious, a sore throat and possible esophageal tears from vomiting may be evident. The constant use of laxatives, diuretics, and vomiting can cause electrolyte imbalances; most commonly low potassium levels that may lead to kidney failure. Constipation may be the upshot of taking so many laxatives. Weight gain may result from unsuccessful attempts at dieting. There are a number of complications of bulimia nervosa and they include:

Medical Complications of Bulimia Nervosa

Dehydration
Gastrointestinal system disturbances (i.e., heartburn, abdominal pain, cramps, bloating)
Acid reflux or ulcers
Chronic sore throat
Ruptured stomach or esophagus
Electrolyte imbalances (low potassium levels, kidney failure)
Swelling of the hands and feet
Broken blood vessels in the eyes
Weakness and dizziness
Constipation from laxative use
Tooth decay and mouth sores
Loss of menstrual periods
Poor hair texture
Weight gain

The Clinical Picture

The clinical picture for bulimia nervosa can be seen as a pattern of binge-eating where the person consumes enormous amounts of food (usually sweets and starches) followed by purging in order to prevent body weight and shape from ballooning. Self-induced vomiting is the most common form of purging (APA, 2000). There are two subtypes of bulimia distinguished by the methods the person uses to compensate for binge-eating. One is identified as the purging type where the person physically purges food from the body before it can be digested—by throwing up or taking laxatives, diuretics, or (less often) enemas. The person may use emetics to trigger the gag reflex to induce vomiting; for example, ipecac (a preparation made from the dried roots and rhizomes of this shrub to induce vomiting particularly in cases of poisoning and drug overdose). Diuretics such as furosemide (or Lasix for treating edema or the excessive accumulation of fluid and/or swelling) may be taken to stimulate weight control. Less common is the nonpurging type of bulimia where the person makes up for her or his lack of restraint by fasting, strenuous exercising, or going on a crash diet.

Figure 11.2 is a conceptual map of the pathway through the symptoms of bulimia nervosa.

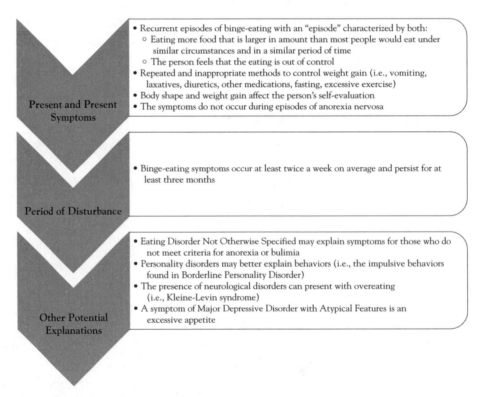

Present and Present Symptoms
- Recurrent episodes of binge-eating with an "episode" characterized by both:
  - Eating more food that is larger in amount than most people would eat under similar circumstances and in a similar period of time
  - The person feels that the eating is out of control
- Repeated and inappropriate methods to control weight gain (i.e., vomiting, laxatives, diuretics, other medications, fasting, excessive exercise)
- Body shape and weight gain affect the person's self-evaluation
- The symptoms do not occur during episodes of anorexia nervosa

Period of Disturbance
- Binge-eating symptoms occur at least twice a week on average and persist for at least three months

Other Potential Explanations
- Eating Disorder Not Otherwise Specified may explain symptoms for those who do not meet criteria for anorexia or bulimia
- Personality disorders may better explain behaviors (i.e., the impulsive behaviors found in Borderline Personality Disorder)
- The presence of neurological disorders can present with overeating (i.e., Kleine-Levin syndrome)
- A symptom of Major Depressive Disorder with Atypical Features is an excessive appetite

Figure 11.2 Conceptual Map for Bulimia Nervosa

The characteristics of bulimia nervosa can challenge your assessment skills and so it is helpful to remember that the major features tend to cluster together (Bulik, Sullivan, & Kendler, 2000; Fairburn et al., 2003; Franco, Wonderlich, Little, & Herzog, 2004; Gleaves, Lowe, Snow, Green, & Murphy-Eberenz, 2000; Keel, Mitchell, Miller, Davis, & Crow, 2000). When you determine presence of bulimia nervosa, the coding note specifies whether the disordered eating is either the purging type or the nonpurging type. As noted, the purging type is the most common. Only 6% to 8% of those with bulimia engage in nonpurging behaviors (Barlow & Durand, 2008; Striegel-Moore et al., 2004).

Differential Assessment

Rarely, neurological disorders may present symptoms of overeating; for example, Kleine-Levin syndrome (also known as Sleeping Beauty syndrome is a neurological disorder characterized by alternating periods of excessive amounts of sleep and altered behavior). Excessive appetite can also be a part of the symptom picture in major depressive disorder with atypical features. Although a person with an eating disorder may feel depressed, those with a major depressive disorder (with atypical features) do not engage in the inappropriate compensatory eating behaviors or have the concerns with body shape and weight so typical of bulimia. Binge-eating is also part of the symptom picture for borderline personality disorder. If the full criteria for both disorders are met, the practitioner may consider co-occurring diagnoses under Axes I and II respectively.

BINGE-EATING DISORDER

Although binge-eating is not fully established as a psychiatric syndrome, it is considered the most common form of disordered eating compared to the three eating disorders recognized in the *DSM* (Henderson, May, & Chew-Graham, 2003; NIH, 2007). Similar to bulimia nervosa, those with binge-eating disorder experience frequent episodes of out-of-control eating. The major difference is that these people do not purge their bodies of the excess calories. Obviously, when a person eats large amounts of calories they will gain weight. Binge-eating disorder is characterized by obesity, sustained and compulsive overeating without compensatory purging (Williams, Goodie, & Motsinger, 2008). Rather than wasting away like those struggling with anorexia nervosa, binge-eating disorder is where the person gains weight. Although obesity is characterized by a disturbance in eating, where a person's caloric intake exceeds the caloric expenditure, it is not considered a psychiatric disorder (APA, 2000).

It is possible for people with binge-eating disorder to get physically sick because they are not getting the right nutrients. They usually eat large amounts of fats and sugars that are not high in vitamin or mineral content (U.S. DHHS, 2001). People struggling with binge-eating often become overweight at a younger age than those without the disorder. Obesity is linked to an increased risk for medical problems such as diabetes, high blood pressure, high cholesterol levels, stroke, heart disease, gallbladder disease, and certain cancers (Pomeroy, 2004). The key features of binge-eating disorder are:

Key Features of Binge-Eating Disorder

Frequent episodes of uncontrolled eating

Feeling extremely distressed or upset during or after bingeing

No regular attempts to "make up" for binges (i.e., self-induced vomiting, fasting, over exercising

Obesity and related medical risks for:

- Diabetes
- High blood pressure
- High blood cholesterol levels
- Gallbladder disease
- Certain types of cancers

Most individuals have tried to control their binge-eating on their own but have not been able to control it for very long. People with binge-eating disorder are usually upset by their binge-eating and may become depressed. Many of us have had incidents where we have eaten too much and feel badly about it. After all, who has not had a whole pint of ice cream after a big fight with someone you love? Let's not even think about the overindulgences on holidays like Thanksgiving. This alone does not warrant binge-eating disorder. Some questions to help differentiate between occasional events of overeating and binge-eating are:

Distinguishing Binge-Eating

Does the person:
- Feel out of control when she or he is eating?
- Think about food all the time?
- Eat alone or in secret?
- Eat to escape from worries or for comfort?
- Feel disgusted or ashamed after eating?
- Feel powerless to stop eating?

Similar to anorexia nervosa and bulimia nervosa, people who struggle with binge-eating disorder feel ashamed and may try to conceal their problems from family and friends. They are often so good at covering up how they eat that others often do not know about the person's eating problem. These are individuals who feel guilty and disgusted by the way they eat. They worry about what they are doing to their bodies and feel badly when eating is out of control.

The following vignette of Mary Carmen Fernandez exemplifies the eating struggles that typify binge-eating disorder.

Mary Carmen Fernandez was referred to the eating disorders clinic by her family doctor for "weight loss counseling" after she had gained 50 pounds in the past six months. Mary Carmen is a pleasant and cooperative 32-year-old Cuban American who came to her appointments with the clinic practitioner appropriately dressed but noticeably overweight; she weighs about 100 pounds more than what would be considered normal for her height and age.

"I have struggled with my weight for as long as I can remember. Just look at me," began Mary Carmen. "Growing up I can always remember my mother and her mother before her being a little 'sobrepeso' so I guess that's not really unusual for me." The practitioner looked a little puzzled at this point. Mary Carmen responded, "Oh, I'm sorry but the closest English translation for what they called themselves is 'overweight.' Anyway, I remember we always grew up with the best of food and there was always a lot at the table, especially the holidays but now I'm afraid that maybe I have too much to eat. The last time my family was together I heard my sisters whispering in the kitchen. They all stopped when I came in but I know they were talking about me. I remember hearing them say that they were worried that I was . . . ," Mary Carmen pauses at this point and looks a little embarrassed. She continues, "Well that I was 'peso bruto.' Politely put, that means very overweight! Of course, they denied they were talking about me. Anyway I'm getting really scared . . . especially with the last few pounds that I've gained. I can't seem to stop. My doctor says he's concerned that if I don't drop some weight that I'll probably get diabetes. I try to diet but the pounds just keep coming on and I hate how I look."

Mary Carmen desperately wants to stop how she eats, and that's why she came to the clinic. She wants to be able to eat "sensibly" but feels that she can't. Mary Carmen was asked to describe what a typical day of eating looks like for her.

"I try to eat normally, but as the day goes on the urge to eat more and more just gets stronger," said Mary Carmen. "I'm pretty good when I'm at work but when I'm at home it's another story all together. As a matter of fact, it starts even before I get home. You see there's a great Cuban bakery that's on my way home. They have the best pastelitos (Cuban pastries). I really love the cream cheese and my second favorite is the guava. I can never make up my mind so I have a couple dozen of both! I know I shouldn't be eating all that sweet stuff so I order the beef, chicken, and ham pastelitos! I have a couple a dozen of each of those, too! Yes, to be honest I just can't stop. They're really not so big. Next I go to the grocery store that's not out of my way. I live in the Little Havana section of Miami near Calle Ocho so there are many abarroteria. Oh! There is one that makes the best croquetas (ground ham or beef or chicken in a béchamel-like paste, covered with

(continued)

breadcrumbs and fried). The ham is my favorite. And then there are the papas rellenas (fried potato balls filled with beef)! I have to have at least a few dozen of those, too. Then I buy the Cuban bread. What gives our bread such a good taste is that it's made with lard. None of that fancy oil stuff. I usually take several loaves home so I can have a couple of medianoche (known as a midnight snack, a sandwich of pork, ham, cheese, and pickles on buttered bread cooked Panini style) before I go to bed. My mother accuses me of eating like an American because I love the papas fritas (French fries) at this little hamburger place just around the corner from my condo."

Mary Carmen continued, "Forgive me but sometimes it's easier for me to talk in Spanish, especially when I feel so bad about myself. It's like I go numb when I eat like this." The practitioner offered reassurance and thanked Mary Carmen for her sincerity.

Mary Carmen explained that once she starts in on the pastelitos she does not stop eating until either all the food is gone or she is so stuffed that she feels sick. Sometimes she tries to take another route home but the thoughts of food haunt her and she ultimately gives in. "I'm such a 'puerca.' If you must know it means a dirty, untidy woman. Well, that's the polite translation!" She adds that she knows that before long she'll start eating just like this all over again. Nothing seems to help her to stop.

The Clinical Picture

Binge-eating disorder has been assigned a provisional set of diagnostic criteria in the *DSM*, so it is uncertain how many struggle with this disorder (Stunkard, 2002). Similarly, there is limited literature on the experiences of this disorder (De Zwaan, 2001). The syndrome is most like bulimia nervosa except that the person does not engage in self-induced vomiting, strenuous exercise, diuretics, or laxative misuse (Barlow & Durand, 2008). Therefore, the binge-eating disorder does not involve any of the medical complications associated with purging behaviors. It appears that those who binge-eat use food to regulate mood or difficult emotions—particularly sadness, anger, and feelings of inadequacy.

Figure 11.3 is a conceptual map to chart the path of binge-eating.

Differential Assessment

Binge-eating patterns found in binge-eating disorder do not occur in conjunction with the regular use of inappropriate alleviative behaviors, such as fasting, and does not occur solely during the course of either anorexia nervosa or bulimia nervosa. Although there is no weight range noted for those struggling with binge-eating disorder, these individuals tend to be obese. The symptom picture of major depressive disorder includes periods of overeating, but it does not involve binge-eating (APA, 2000). Eating disorder not otherwise specified is used for those who have problems related to appetite, eating, and weight but do not meet the diagnostic criteria specified in the *DSM* for anorexia nervosa or bulimia nervosa.

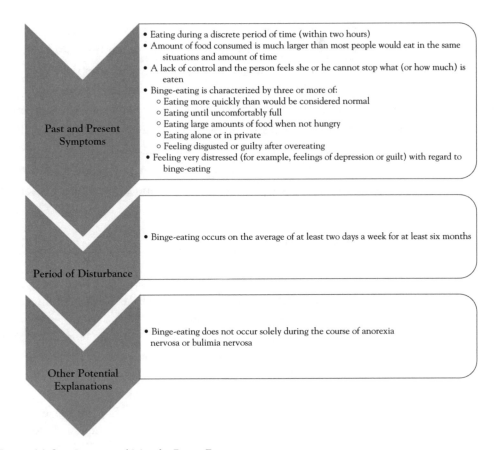

Figure 11.3   Conceptual Map for Binge-Eating

FINAL THOUGHTS

Up until recently accurate data on the extent of the eating disorders has been scarce but there has been increasing attention to this problem over the past 20 years (Gray, 2008; NIH, 2007; B. Sadock, & Sadock, 2004). What we do know is that these disorders are primarily found in females and that they start in adolescence and extend up until early adulthood. The medical complications associated with these disorders are serious and potentially fatal. Eating disorders are triggered by either a desire to lose weight and involve a fear of gaining weight or a loss of control around food. Clearly, those with disordered eating patterns have an overwhelming desire to be thin and engage in extreme behaviors to accomplish this goal. Your work is to assist the person to desist from potentially dangerous eating behaviors, a part of which requires dealing with underlying problems (Abraham & Llewellyn-Jones, 2001).

With the potential to cause serious physical harm, the eating disorders are among the most severe of the mental illnesses. Anorexia nervosa in particular has the highest mortality rate (Fairburn & Brownell, 2002). In our case examples, those with the diagnosis of an eating disorder may feel a great deal of guilt, self-loathing, and generally be ashamed of what they are doing to themselves. They may be secretive about what they actually eat or do not eat and hide their behaviors from family, friends, and others close to them. Therefore, it is helpful to look for the subtle signs and symptoms of an eating disorder. The competency-based assessment explores a range of factors in a client's life, even the reality that an eating disorder may be reinforced when others compliment the person's thin appearance, usually at the outset of the disorder (Bagley, Character, & Shelton, 2003). Comorbid diagnoses include mood, anxiety, and/or personality disorders.

Summing Up the Eating Disorders

Anorexia Nervosa	Extreme weight loss, body image disturbance, and an intense fear of becoming fat generally accompanied by an absence of three consecutive menstrual cycles in young women.
	Involves: refusing or unable to maintain at least 85% normal body weight, repeatedly checking body weight, carefully portioning foods, and eating only very small quantities of only certain foods.
Bulimia Nervosa	Secretive binge-eating episodes at least twice a week for three months followed by either self-induced vomiting, fasting, excessive exercise, or the use of laxatives, diuretics, or the manipulation of other medications.
	Involves: going to extremes to compensate for eating.
Eating Disorder Not Otherwise Specified	Eating disorder of clinical severity not explained by alternative diagnoses.
Binge-Eating Disorder	Recurrent episodes of binge-eating without the purging behavior seen in bulimia nervosa.
	Involves: feeling out of control when eating a large amount of food at least twice a week for six months, and experiencing extreme distress about overeating.

We now turn to a series of case illustrations to refine the practitioner's assessment skills.

PRACTICING THE COMPETENCY-BASED ASSESSMENT

The eating disorders involve an overwhelming desire to be thin to the point where the person engages in abnormal and dangerous eating behaviors. They are characterized by disturbances in a person's eating patterns and a distorted perception of body weight and shape. The fear of becoming overweight and the desperate attempts to control weight lead the person to engage in drastic and sometimes fatal behaviors. People with eating disorders tend to deny their problems and often feel guilty, ashamed, and secretive about what they do to themselves. This underscores the importance of the practitioner's awareness of and sensitivity to the person's struggle with food.

Case Illustrations

The following case studies are intended to extend your understanding of the eating disorders by looking beyond the person's symptom picture and considering the complex interactions of emotional, psychological, and cultural factors that also play a role in eating patterns. Each scenario offers a challenge to think about the many issues involved in the eating disorders and appreciate the connections between apparently isolated chunks of material.

The Case of Nell Jordan

Penelope Jordan (or Nell, as she was called by her family and friends), is a tall and attractive but slightly overweight 23-year-old in good health. She's not someone you would characterize as being fat; she has what would more aptly be called a soft and round figure.

The practitioner usually arrived at her office in the university's counseling center early. One morning as she was looking over her schedule of appointments for the day her eye caught the name, Nell Jordan. "I hope she keeps her appointment today. I have a sense from our earlier conversations that she's worried about something but I just can't seem to put my finger on it. Maybe I've been a counselor for a little longer than I care to admit but something just doesn't feel quite right to me," mused the counselor.

Looking back on everything, Nell remembered how glad she was when she decided to move out of her college dorm for her senior year. Walking to classes and to the library was a little longer but she thought the exercise would do her good. "Too much sitting in class and then all I do is go over to the library and sit around again," she thought. Nell also liked the added room that she now had, the privacy and close proximity to neighborhood stores, some of which were open all night. There was a fabulous 24-hour deli a block away and a bakery around the corner that made some of the best homemade bread. Nell was glad that she didn't have to contend with the student cafeteria with its bland and overly cooked buffet. Then there were the fried hamburgers. Unfortunately, these advantages ultimately turned out to be a huge nightmare for Nell and almost sabotaged her last year at school.

It started up again just after winter set in. The days were much shorter, and most of them were gloomy and gray. One morning Nell struggled more than usual to get out of bed. Lately she was finding it harder and harder to get up and face the day but this day was particularly difficult. And then those old thoughts kicked in again. "Will I be able to get through the day without thinking about food or will I blow it?" she asked herself. "I moved out here so I could exercise more but I'm still fat. I guess I'll have to start dieting again. But they never seem to work. I drop a few pounds, gain them back . . . and then some. I know I'll feel good about myself if I can just lose a few pounds and start exercising again," she thought.

After about 20 minutes or so, Nell finally gets out of bed, tiptoes across the cold wood floors, and steps into a warm shower. She starts planning her day thinking she would first do a little exercising and then have a light breakfast. She tries not to think about food because she's not really hungry. As she's getting dressed, Nell begins organizing the day ahead of her; her classes, homework, how much time she'll be in the library, and when she'll eat. Her thoughts drift to food and she plans every minute detail of her meals. She wants to fill in every minute of her time so she'll stick to her diet and not think about food.

Gradually Nell feels that dark, sinking feeling coming on. It's an old and all too familiar sensation in the pit of her stomach. All those earlier promises that she made to herself about staying on her diet came creeping back. "I just need to get my willpower back again," she sighed remembering how bad she always felt when she "slipped" and ate more than her diet allowed.

"Well, I have to eat sometime so I might as well have a little something before I leave for school. I can get my exercise walking to campus," thought Nell. She decided that a nice soft boiled egg, a little toast, no butter or jelly, and some of those canned peaches in the back of the fridge would get her day off to a good start. She gulped it down in no time. "Oh gawd, it took me longer to cook the egg than to eat it!" Nell was frantic at this point but that, too, was a familiar feeling. She started rummaging through her small kitchen for more to eat. "Nothing there," she groaned.

With an air of determination Nell puts on her coat, slips her books under her arm, and heads off to the deli. Once there she quickly grabs a handful of candy bars, a couple of those soft cakes with the crème filling inside, and two bottles of soda to wash it all down. Then she spots some of those tubs of artificial whipped topping. "Then I can dunk the cakes into the topping. These will be easy. I won't have to chew so much and I can eat them on my way to class. Now that's a plan!" She bought a huge bag of potato chips and some Doritos-like snacks "for later." Nell then proceeded around the corner to the bakery and bought a dozen chocolate doughnuts, a half-dozen éclairs, and an assortment of cupcakes. The bakery always neatly wrapped their pastries in pretty little boxes but Nell insisted that they just put them all in a bag. "Easier to carry," she told the baker who gave her an odd look. Nell had spent about $50 at this point and thought, "Great! That's most of my food budget for the next few days. Well, I'll worry about that later."

Nell immediately started eating the candy bars and then remembered her commitment to her diet. "How many calories are in all this stuff I just bought?" she asked herself. From past experience, Nell knows that she will eat until she feels bloated and uncomfortable. That will be her only reason to stop. The idea of all those calories starts to scare her. "Not to worry, I know what has to be done," she told herself. A feeling of relief starts to come over Nell. She glanced at her watch seeing that she has just enough time to head back to her apartment. "Probably easier to finish up there," she reflected.

"I might be just a little late for my first class but the 'prof' never seems to mind," she thought. Nell was a good student and worked really hard for her grades. She was fastidious and thorough and always completely researched all of her assignments. A natural "overachiever," Nell was constantly doing more than what was required for her classes. This professor recognized these traits in Nell and usually gave her a little more leeway in class than he did with the other students.

Nell turned around and headed back to her apartment. Once inside she finished eating and went straight to the bathroom. She turned down the lights and closed the blinds. Nell gulped down a couple glasses of water, bent over the toilet, and began to vomit. Somehow it was easier in the darkened room. She didn't have to see what came up. "Funny, I used to have to stick my fingers down my throat to vomit but now I can almost do it 'on demand,'" she thought. Once done, Nell stepped on the scale "just to make sure I didn't gain any weight." She still had a sour taste in her mouth but knowing she controlled her weight made it a little more palatable.

Nell initially felt really good about herself but then those bad feelings about what she had just done to herself quickly returned. "I'll never do this again. I'm going to go on a fast for the rest of today and maybe for the rest of the week. Just a little juice and coffee in the mornings to get me started and then toward the end of the week I'll add a little fruit for dinner. That always makes me feel better. I know I can change," but inside she felt so ashamed and defeated.

Nell never used drugs or alcohol but has been eating this way since high school. Back then most of the girls in her sorority did it "and it was cool." You could eat all you wanted and stay thin. We used to joke, "I can have my cake and eat it too!" At first Nell took laxatives, but found vomiting to be easier "and more efficient." When she first started vomiting, Nell instantly felt thin afterward but sticking her finger down her throat was "really gross." Then one of her sorority sisters shared her secret, "Just use a Q-tip. It's a lot more antiseptic." Initially Nell would eat this way only once or twice a month and gradually increased to once a week. By the time Nell started college, she was up to once a day but now it seemed to be happening several times a day. When she lived in the dorm, it was usually only once a day. "Too many interruptions," remembered Nell but living alone in her apartment it was a lot easier to do this a couple of times a day.

Deep down inside, Nell knows she really can't change and this probably won't be the last time. She's already thinking about eating again and wonders how many hours it will be before she gives in to the urge and begins to eat. Then she starts blaming herself for getting out of bed in the first place. With an air of resignation, Nell puts her coat back on and scoops up her books but really doesn't feel like going to school.

"I've tried so many times to stop, but I just can't seem to get out of this. Sometimes I feel like two completely different people. One is really good in school but the other . . . the one at home is a total loser. Maybe I need to be completely honest with that nice counselor I've been seeing at the health center." Nell had an instant flashback to her prior experiences with another counselor who she saw briefly just after she started high school. Even back then, Nell worried if she had problems with food. It was on her mind all the time. She finally got up enough nerve to ask the counselor if that way of thinking about food was normal. Nell remembered the counselor saying something like, "Not to worry, honey. You're not fully grown and you look fit and trim. I doubt you'll ever have problems with your weight," and then moved on to another topic. "Well, the counselor was half right on that one. I do manage to avoid getting fat," she thought. This time Nell hoped that this college counselor would be different from the other one. "I'm going to stop by her office today anyway," Nell resolved.

How would you formulate your competency-based assessment for Nell Jordan?

The Case of Carlie Walker

Carlie Walker is a 17-year-old woman who was admitted to the inpatient unit of Wren View, a hospital-based unit specializing in eating disorders. Carlie had fainted at school during a cheering practice. She was taken to the health office where the nurse immediately called her parents. Mr. and Mrs. Walker have been concerned about their daughter for some time. They noticed that Carlie started gradually losing weight after she started high school. At first she looked really attractive and received many compliments. But then Carlie's weight loss continued to the point where they started to worry that it was getting out of control. They thought that maybe Carlie was anxious about the demands of high school and keeping up with all her activities. Then the Walkers noticed that she became secretive about meals. Carlie was spending more and more time alone in her room, especially at mealtime. After Carlie fainted at school, the Walkers finally decided it was time to do something. They took her to their family doctor who suggested the eating disorders center. Carlie was admitted as an inpatient. This is Carlie's story.

"I have a problem with food. I eat. I mean I eat disgusting amounts of food and yet I'm so fat. I think about food all the time. My stomach sticks out and my rear end is way huge. I worry all the time about fitting into my skinny jeans. I mean just look at me. I'm so bloated and disgusting. Every time I pass a mirror, I have to look in the other direction. All I can see is my big fat ass," remarked Carlie. "I can't stand to see myself.

I don't date, let alone even have a boyfriend. My parents don't have to worry about me in the sex department, if you know what I mean. After all, who would even want to be seen in public with someone as fat as me," Carlie asked.

Her therapist looked at her but only saw a thin emaciated young woman who was clearly underweight for her size and body frame. Carlie's complexion was extremely pale and her eyes had a sunken appearance. They stood out like glowing black coals but were dull, giving her a haunted look. Her hair fell to her shoulders but was thin and lifeless. The practitioner remembered a note in Carlie's chart written by the center's admitting physician indicating that Carlie's weight was 15% below what could be considered "average" for her height and age. She had not had a menstrual period for five or six months. The physician noted that Carlie had no delusions or hallucinations though she admitted to a fear of gaining weight. Phobias, obsessions, or compulsions, and panic attacks were denied. She was seen as cheerful and cooperative during the intake interview.

Carlie continued, "My last therapist asked me to keep a diary of my food intake. That was awful. It only made me obsess about food even more. When I didn't complete my entries, she would pull her glasses halfway down her nose and look up at me with the most condescending look." She continued, "It was so demeaning. I didn't need to feel insulted when I'm so desperate. I feel like I'm throwing up my . . . ," she paused momentarily and then continued, "I mean throwing away my whole life. Do you think you can help me?"

The practitioner asked if Carlie could remember when her concerns about her weight began. "It all started when I tried out for cheering my freshman year in high school. After I made the team, I started comparing myself to the other girls on the squad. I was at least 20 pounds overweight compared to them. It was painful just to watch them work out in the gym. I tried to figure out who was better than me, who wasn't so good, who was fatter and who was thinner. There were three really great looking girls over on the side of the gym doing a really complicated routine. I remember that moment as if it happened just yesterday. I knew right there and then that I couldn't attempt the moves in that routine even if I tried 'cause I was so fat. I felt so inadequate. Sometimes during practice I would pretend that I left something in my locker just so I could leave. Instead I'd go into the bathroom and cry. It was awful. I don't know why they kept me on the team. Right there and then I started dieting. I would weigh myself constantly just so I could detect any minute changes and act on them immediately. Still do!"

Carlie's dieting went on for about a year. After she got tired of starving herself she started using laxatives on occasion (two or three times a week) "just to help," said Carlie. When she thought she had overeaten, Carlie would vomit. This went on for the next two years. By now she was almost 16 years old. "I learned how easy it was just to put my finger down my throat and make myself throw up," added Carlie. This continued into her senior year in high school. School reports indicated that she was a good student and involved in a number of clubs and activities.

When asked about hobbies, Carlie described how much she loved to cook and collect cookbooks. "My favorites are those with the big pictures of the food. They have
really great cookbooks for almost every season. Christmas and Thanksgiving are just
the best. Oh! But then there's Halloween. Do you know how many things you can
make with licorice and black jelly beans?" Carlie was animated at this point and added,
"I just love looking at them but sometimes I think so much about food I wish I could
die." Carlie started cooking or what she called "messing around in the kitchen" around
the time she started high school. Everybody in her family was amazed with what she
could put together. "My mom used to joke that I should write a cookbook of my own
called 'What Fell Out of the Cupboard.' I can make almost anything taste good with
whatever happens to be in the kitchen." With a note of pride, she described how much
her friends loved the snacks she would make for them. She continued, "Do you know
what you can do with chili, cream cheese, and just a touch of onion?" The practitioner gently responded, "Carlie that sounds really interesting but somehow I think we're
drifting away from why you're here. What do you think?" Carlie put her head down
and sheepishly agreed adding, "I guess it's just that food thing kicking in again but
I don't know what everybody's worried about. I do eat, you know."

Carlie did not participate in eating any of the snacks she made for her friends or
would eat as little as possible. She acknowledged that she preferred to eat alone in her
room. Her only company was her TV. Carlie would spend hours chewing her food and
then spitting it out. When she had to eat in front of her family, she would cut her food
into small portions and take the smallest bites possible. Sometimes she would break her
food into pieces that were so small they would slip through the tines of her fork. Mostly
she rearranged her food on her plate just to make it look like she was eating. She also
became pretty good at slipping it into her pockets to throw away later. There were rare
occasions when she would reward herself and eat what most would consider a full meal;
potatoes or rice, vegetables and chicken or (rarely) a steak. "Of course, when I ate that
much," added Carlie, "I would feel so bloated and stuffed that I would have to bring it
back up. After all, the only way I can be pleasing and attractive is to stay thin. I really
think I'm too fat even now."

How would you formulate your competency-based assessment for Carlie Walker?

PRACTICAL APPLICATIONS

The following series of practical applications is designed to help refine the competency-
based assessment skills useful for those who struggle with eating disorders.

1. In the case illustration about Carlie Walker, she talks about how insulting and
   demeaning it was for her when a former therapist asked her to keep a diary of
   what she ate. Do you agree or disagree with Carlie's observation?

a. Have you ever kept a diary of what you eat? If not, try it for a week or so and evaluate whether your answer to the question of keeping a journal about what you eat changes.

b. What strategies can you suggest for a client struggling with an eating disorder so that it will help better inform your competency-based assessment?

2. Interview someone you know who is currently dieting or has recently been on a diet to lose weight. Compare this person's experiences and/or expectations with the discussion of dieting reported in this chapter (for example, weight gain after dieting, the cost of diet plans, or living in a culture of thinness to list a few).

a. Have you ever been on a diet? If so, include some thoughts about your own experiences.

b. Reflect on how these experiences with attempts at losing weight can influence your competency-based assessment of clients who struggle with an eating disorder.

3. Have you ever heard of set point theory and its relationship to dieting and eating? Set point suggests that a person's body weight is regulated at a predetermined or preferred level by a feedback control mechanism. Everybody has a genetically programmed basal metabolism rate; or the rate at which the body burns calories for energy and a fixed number of fat cells that store fat for energy and can change in size. A complex interaction of metabolism, fat cells, and hormones keeps people at the weight their bodies are designed to be. Set point is the weight you stay at when you are not trying to gain or lose weight and can vary about 10% in either direction. Your body is programmed to weigh at a set point and will naturally fight to maintain that weight. The theory hypothesizes that everyone has a set point. Just like you have no control over how tall you are, the color of your eyes or hair, you also have no control over your set point weight. Your body is biologically and genetically determined to weigh within a certain weight range. Set point helps explain why dieters sometimes reach a point where they stop losing weight even when they stay on the diet. For example, when you go below your body's natural set point, your metabolism will react and start slowing down in order to try and conserve energy. Your body begins to sense it's in a state of semi-starvation and will try to use the few calories it receives more effectively, and so weight loss stops. To illustrate, let's say a woman with a set point weight of 150 pounds would probably weigh anywhere from 135 to 165. If her weight dips below 135 pounds, then her body will produce an insatiable urge to eat to bring the fat levels back into line. Conversely, if weight goes above 165 pounds then she loses her appetite.

a. What are your thoughts about set point and how it potentially relates to the eating disorders?

b. *Source:* Lissner, L., Odell, P. M., D'Agostino, R. B., Stokes, J., III, Kreger, B. E., Belanger, A. J., & Brownell, K. D. (1991). Variability of body weight and health outcomes in the Framingham population. *New England Journal of Medicine, 324,* 1839–1844.

c. *Source:* What your body is trying to tell you. (1992, June). *National Eating Disorder Information Centre Bulletin, 7*(2). (The National Eating Disorder Information Centre is a nonprofit organization founded in 1985 to provide information and resources on eating, and food and weight preoccupation.)

4. There is a popular phrase that goes something like, "A picture is worth a thousand words." Movies can provide a vivid portrayal of persons with mental illness and add to one's understanding and appreciation for their struggle. There are a number of films that depict the eating disorders; for example, *Best Little Girl in the World, Fatso, Requiem for a Dream,* or *What's Eating Gilbert Grape.*

- Rent one of these movies (or another that you have discovered). After you enjoy the plot, the outcome, and/or the movie star's portrayal, take a step back and look closely at the characters. Ask yourself the following questions:

a. What does the symptom picture of the character's eating disorder look like in comparison to the *DSM* syndromes?

b. Does the film accurately portray the eating disorders or does it present the character's struggle in an engaging or stereotypic manner?

c. Eating disorders are affected by beliefs about beauty and attractiveness, so how do the movies address these cultural influences?

Appendix

Competency-Based Assessments for Chapter 11 Case Examples: Listing of Case Diagnoses

Figures 11A.1 through 11A.4 provide the diagnostic assessment for each of the cases illustrated. They are organized in the order that they appear in each chapter.

CASE REVIEW FOR NELL JORDAN

On the face of it, Nell Jordan seems to have everything going for her. She is in college, is bright and hardworking, and in good health, though slightly overweight. However, what brings her to the college counselor's office is a symptom picture supporting bulimia nervosa, purging type. The case story describes her eating patterns and associated feelings of feeling frantic, scared, and remorseful. Although anxious (frantic) about how she eats, this underlying feeling does not support the symptom picture of an anxiety disorder. As well, there is no evidence of substance use or a neurological disorder that might better explain her symptoms. Nell talks about not feeling really good about herself but evidence supporting a major depressive disorder with atypical features is missing.

Despite this picture of pathological eating, the competency-based assessment helps to look at the client's strengths. In this case, Nell is aware of her eating patterns. Although she had a prior negative experience in counseling she remains willing to seek help and sees the college counselor. Further, she is bright, motivated, and has the reputation for being a hard worker.

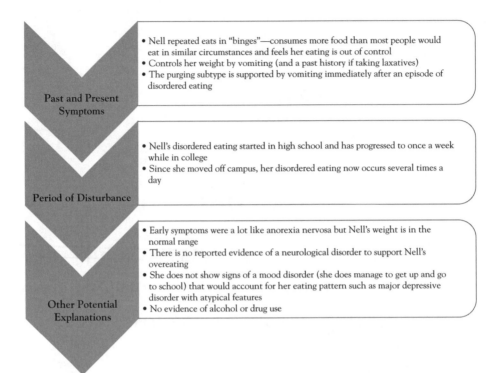

Past and Present Symptoms
- Nell repeated eats in "binges"—consumes more food than most people would eat in similar circumstances and feels her eating is out of control
- Controls her weight by vomiting (and a past history if taking laxatives)
- The purging subtype is supported by vomiting immediately after an episode of disordered eating

Period of Disturbance
- Nell's disordered eating started in high school and has progressed to once a week while in college
- Since she moved off campus, her disordered eating now occurs several times a day

Other Potential Explanations
- Early symptoms were a lot like anorexia nervosa but Nell's weight is in the normal range
- There is no reported evidence of a neurological disorder to support Nell's overeating
- She does not show signs of a mood disorder (she does manage to get up and go to school) that would account for her eating pattern such as major depressive disorder with atypical features
- No evidence of alcohol or drug use

Figure 11A.1   The Conceptual Map for Nell Jordan

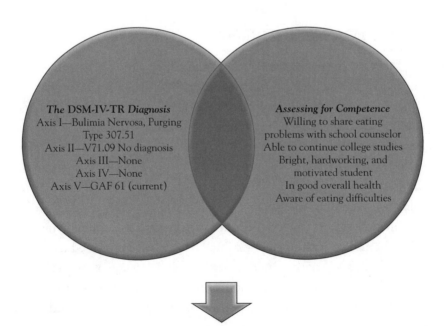

The DSM-IV-TR *Diagnosis*
Axis I—Bulimia Nervosa, Purging Type 307.51
Axis II—V71.09 No diagnosis
Axis III—None
Axis IV—None
Axis V—GAF 61 (current)

Assessing for Competence
Willing to share eating problems with school counselor
Able to continue college studies
Bright, hardworking, and motivated student
In good overall health
Aware of eating difficulties

Figure 11A.2   The Competency-Based Assessment for Nell Jordan

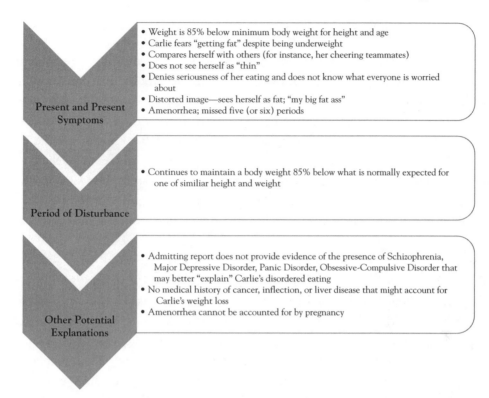

Present and Present Symptoms

- Weight is 85% below minimum body weight for height and age
- Carlie fears "getting fat" despite being underweight
- Compares herself with others (for instance, her cheering teammates)
- Does not see herself as "thin"
- Denies seriousness of her eating and does not know what everyone is worried about
- Distorted image—sees herself as fat; "my big fat ass"
- Amenorrhea; missed five (or six) periods

Period of Disturbance

- Continues to maintain a body weight 85% below what is normally expected for one of similiar height and weight

Other Potential Explanations

- Admitting report does not provide evidence of the presence of Schizophrenia, Major Depressive Disorder, Panic Disorder, Obsessive-Compulsive Disorder that may better "explain" Carlie's disordered eating
- No medical history of cancer, inflection, or liver disease that might account for Carlie's weight loss
- Amenorrhea cannot be accounted for by pregnancy

Figure 11A.3   The Conceptual Map for Carlie Walker

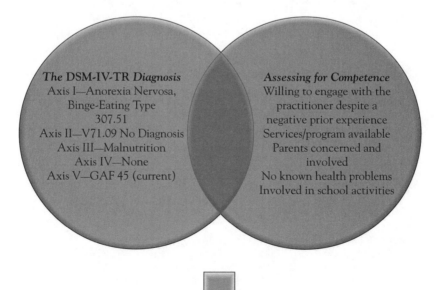

The DSM-IV-TR Diagnosis
Axis I—Anorexia Nervosa,
Binge-Eating Type
307.51
Axis II—V71.09 No Diagnosis
Axis III—Malnutrition
Axis IV—None
Axis V—GAF 45 (current)

Assessing for Competence
Willing to engage with the
practitioner despite a
negative prior experience
Services/program available
Parents concerned and
involved
No known health problems
Involved in school activities

Figure 11A.4   The Competency-Based Assessment for Carlie Walker

CASE REVIEW FOR CARLIE WALKER

As with many eating disorders, Carlie's anorexic eating patterns started gradually. When she initially joined the cheering squad in high school she began to compare herself to the other girls and concluded that her problems revolved around weight. Her parents began to notice secretive eating patterns and started to worry about her. Not until Carlie fainted in school and the school nurse notified the parents did Carlie come to the attention of professional help. By the time she was seen, Carlie showed a symptom picture typical of anorexia nervosa; her emaciated physical appearance, concerns about being fat, and missing four or five menstrual periods. Despite a limited food intake, Carlie loved to cook for others and took an interest in food recipes. Unfortunately, Carlie did not eat any of the food she prepared for others.

Despite her serious loss of weight and preoccupation with food, the competency-based assessment uncovers a number of parallel strengths in Carlie's story. Her parents are concerned about her and involved in her life. She is a good student. Counseling was not a new experience for her. Despite feeling demeaned by a prior counselor, Carlie came to see the current therapist and appeared to be engaged and willing to discuss her eating patterns. In fact, when she changed the subject Carlie responded cooperatively to the therapist's attempt to redirect her to the problem at hand. Carlie is in good general health (despite her eating patterns) and shows no symptoms to support the presence of another mental disorder such as schizophrenia, major depressive disorder, or panic disorder. Though Carlie loves to look at cookbooks and experiment with recipes, she does not particularly obsess to the point of supporting the diagnosis of obsessive-compulsive disorder.

The Personality Disorders

INTRODUCTION

The personality disorders are among the most common diagnostic categories seen in practice. Unfortunately, negative terms such as being detached, needy, hostile, antisocial, or even obsessive are usually attributed to somebody who struggles with a personality disorder. Formerly referred to as character disorders, the personality disorders were first distinguished by the DSM in 1980 as a diagnosable mental illness. Typically, these disorders highlight the pervasive, inflexible, maladaptive, and enduring expressions of a person's personality (American Psychiatric Association, 2000). In other words, those with a personality disorder struggle with inflexible and firmly entrenched behaviors across many different situations that create considerable personal and social disruption as well as general functional impairment. These difficulties are considered to be ego-syntonic (or the individual considers his or her personality traits, thoughts, behaviors, and values to be acceptable and consistent with one's true self). Behaviors that are problematic to others are perceived to be appropriate by that individual. This is the client who does not seek help but is usually referred by others. When they do seek help on their own, it is usually because of the life stresses created by the personality disorder or troubling symptoms such as anxiety, depression, or substance abuse. In general, they tend to believe their problems are caused by other people or by circumstances beyond their control. By and large, there is between 10% and 14% of adults who have not been treated for a psychiatric diagnosis but who struggle with a personality disorder (Skodol et al., 2002).

Let's now turn to an overview of the prevalence of the personality disorders.

INCIDENCE AND PREVALENCE

The prevalence rates for the personality disorders in the U.S. general population range from 6% to approximately 20% (de Girolamo & Dotto, 2000). Interestingly, one-third of those with this diagnosis were reported to be seen in primary care settings with the avoidant, dependent, or obsessive-compulsive diagnostic categories being the most common. Since persons with a personality disorder rarely seek treatment on their own, this diagnosis was infrequently the primary focus of treatment in psychiatric settings. Instead, it was the high rates of substance abuse, impulsivity, and suicidal behaviors that were the focus of attention (Ekselius, Tilfors, Furmark, & Fredrikson, 2001). Individuals with a personality disorder are more likely to have co-occurring disorders; specifically the anxiety disorders (namely panic disorder and posttraumatic stress disorder), mood disorders (depression, bipolar disorder), impulse control disorders (attention deficit hyperactivity disorder), and substance abuse or dependence (Lenzenweger, Lane, Loranger, & Kessler, 2007).

The diagnostic criteria for the personality disorders are bound to North American cultural definitions, and what is known about the personality disorders in the general population can be summarized as follows (Barlow & Durand, 2005):

Prevalence Rates for the Specific Personality Disorders

Disorder	Prevalence
Paranoid personality disorder	0.5% to 2.5%
Schizoid personality disorder	Less than 1%
Schizotypal personality disorder	3% to 5%
Antisocial personality disorder	3% in males and less than 1% in females
Borderline personality disorder	1% to 3%
Histrionic personality disorder	2%
Narcissistic personality disorder	Less than 1%
Avoidant personality disorder	Less than 1%
Dependent personality disorder	2%
Obsessive-compulsive personality disorder	4%

As you can see, a number of the personality disorders are relatively rare. For example, the schizoid, narcissistic, and avoidant personality disorders occur in less than 1% of the population.

The personality disorders are more commonly found among those who are single and in a younger age group, particularly 25 years to 44 years of age (Moran, Jenkins, Tylee,

Blizard, & Mann, 2000; Samuels, 2002). Overall, this diagnostic category is equally distributed between men and women. The one exception is the antisocial personality disorder, which is more frequently diagnosed in men. The borderline, histrionic, and dependent personality disorders tend to more frequently occur in women. When reviewing a person's history, you can expect to find a number of stressful life events such as relationship difficulties, housing problems, and long-term unemployment. It comes as no surprise that these individuals are more likely to lack social support, have conflicted marriages, trouble at work, or be unemployed, and a history of violence and criminal behaviors (Johnson et al., 2000).

Course of the Personality Disorders

Despite the paucity of empirical evidence, it is generally thought that the behavioral patterns found in the personality disorders can be traced back to late adolescence and early adulthood (Phillips, Yen, & Gunderson, 2003). In rare instances, the behaviors indicative of a personality disorder can be seen in childhood (APA, 2000). Nonetheless, it is unlikely to diagnose a personality disorder before the age of 16 or 17 years.

More recent research suggests that an individual's personality can change significantly over time and the personality disorders might not be as stable as originally thought (Lenzenweger, Johnson, & Willett, 2004; Shea et al., 2002). By and large people with the paranoid, schizoid, and schizotypal personality disorders do not improve over time in contrast to those with antisocial, histrionic, borderline, and narcissistic personality disorders who tend to improve with age (Paris, 2003). Seivewright, Tyrer, and Johnson (2002) found that the characteristic traits of the avoidant, dependent, obsessive-compulsive personality disorders can actually increase over time. In addition, those who showed increased isolation and dysphoria developed significant Axis I mood and anxiety disorder symptoms.

OVERVIEW OF THE MAJOR CHARACTERISTICS OF THE PERSONALITY DISORDERS

Each person has a set of personality traits defining his or her behaviors, thoughts, and emotions. Although some of these traits may fade with time or can be modified, many can persist throughout much of the person's life. These features become so ingrained that they usually dictate the person's worldview, lifestyle, and life choices. For instance, you might know someone who is gregarious and fun-loving and another who may be quiet and introspective. Each of us at some time in our lives may have also been gregarious and fun-loving or quiet and introspective. However, specific behaviors are considered to be an integral part of the individual's personality only if they cut across many situations and events (Barlow & Durand, 2005). Thus, having a fun-loving moment is different from being known as the proverbial "good time Charlie."

A personality disorder is considered when the person's traits become so rigid and maladaptive that they interfere with social functioning or other important areas of the person's life. In this chapter, we look at the characteristic ways of behaving as they relate specifically to the personality disorders. The *DSM-IV-TR* (APA, 2000) distinguishes 10 personality disorders and they are recorded on Axis II. Organized into three clusters, the designations are:

Cluster A	Cluster B	Cluster C
Odd and Eccentric	Emotional, Dramatic, or Erratic	Anxious, Fearful
Individuals with paranoid, schizoid, and schizotypal personality disorders.	Individuals with antisocial, histrionic, borderline, and narcissistic personality disorders.	Individuals with avoidant, dependent, obsessive-compulsive personality disorders.

Personality disorder not otherwise specified. When a person meets general diagnostic criteria for a personality disorder but has the traits of several personality disorders the diagnosis of personality disorder not otherwise specified (NOS) is assigned. The diagnoses depressive personality disorder and passive-aggressive personality disorder are listed in the *DSM-IV-TR* appendix as potential diagnoses that require further study (APA, 2000). Currently, when a person shows these features they are diagnosed in the NOS option; for example, someone with a pervasive pattern of negative attitudes and passive resistance would be considered passive-aggressive and diagnosed as having a personality disorder NOS.

As a first step in considering a personality disorder, begin by looking at the following areas and note a pattern of impairment in two (or more) of the following:

Patterns of Impairment

Cognition	Ways of perceiving and interpreting oneself, other people, and events.
Affectivity	The range, intensity, and appropriateness of emotional responses.
Interpersonal functioning	The instability of and the inability to maintain relationships, poor self-image, or self-esteem.
Impulse control	The ability to withhold inappropriate verbal or motor responses while completing a task; acting or speaking without anticipating the repercussions of one's behavior or not learning from previous negative behaviors.

Keep in mind that those who struggle with a personality disorder show personality traits that are out of proportion or so inflexible that they often cause problems for the individual as well as those around them. It is possible that these traits might have been effective in coping with conditions earlier in the client's life but they have continued for such an extended period of time that they are now causing problems (Barlow & Durand, 2005). The presence of a personality disorder is further distinguished where the individual must exhibit:

- An enduring pattern that is almost always inflexible across a broad range of personal and interpersonal or social situations.
- The enduring pattern leads to significant distress or impairment in social, occupational, or other important areas in the person's life.
- The pattern is stable and of long duration, and onset can be traced back at least to adolescence or early adulthood.
- The person's behavior is not better accounted for as the result or consequence of another mental disorder.
- The person's enduring pattern is not due to the direct physiological effects of a substance (for instance, a drug of abuse or a medication) or a general medical condition (such as a head trauma).

In the following section, the 10 descriptions of the personality disorders noted in the *DSM-IV-TR* are described. Deciding on the appropriate diagnosis based on these categories can be challenging especially when the client's behavioral pattern closely resembles what could be considered normal behavior. The competency-based assessment helps you to make this distinction more obvious by expanding the formulation of a diagnosis to a multidimensional process that includes the impact of multiple variables in the client's life. The client's life experiences are seen as far more complex than a simple listing of behavior patterns. In this way, the *DSM* is not seen as a recipe for understanding behavior but as an additional tool to be used in the assessment process.

Culture and the Personality Disorders

Another aspect to consider when assessing the personality disorders is the influence of culture and ethnicity. The *DSM-IV-TR* definition of a personality disorder is essentially a functional one in that it requires significant impairment or distress for the diagnosis to be made. However, you do need to take into account that sometimes a person's impairment or distress can be culturally specific and not a symptom of pathology. There are a number of examples where a client's cultural and ethnic experiences may influence your interpretation of the symptom picture. For instance, someone who has immigrated to the United States and is struggling to become acculturated into mainstream society may go through a sense of alienation, feelings of emptiness or abandonment, a loss of control, and anxiety. These reactions are to be expected and should not be confused with the core symptoms of a borderline personality disorder.

Another example would be the expressions of the suspiciousness found in paranoid personality disorder. Suspicion may well be an expected reaction to those situations where an individual experiences discrimination, abuse, or even humiliation based on membership in a stigmatized or oppressed population and not a symptom of the paranoid personality disorder. Another example to underscore the value of considering the influence of culture and ethnicity on the assessment process revolves around the key features that distinguish schizotypal personality disorder; in particular, the anxiety in social relationships accompanied by eccentric behavior characterized by superstitions, a preoccupation with paranormal phenomenon, magical thinking, or rituals in everyday situations (APA, 2000). Magical thinking or a belief in supernatural powers can be found in many places around the world. If someone who believed in the force of the spirits or the power of a voodoo spell immigrated to the United States, this cultural orientation could be misinterpreted as a symptom of schizotypal personality disorder. Taking the influence of culture and ethnicity is a component of the competency-based assessment and helps to place clients in their sociocultural context. In this way, you can better distinguish the potential impact of a person's culture before considering pathology.

The personality disorders are grouped into one of three clusters based on characteristics. We begin with a discussion of the Cluster A disorders characterized by odd, eccentric behavior. The paranoid, schizoid, and schizotypal personality disorders are in this category.

THE CLUSTER A DISORDERS—ODD AND ECCENTRIC

Each of the Cluster A disorders share odd and eccentric features. For example, the paranoid personality disorder typifies the individual who is distrustful and suspicious. Those who struggle with schizoid personality disorder are markedly detached from others and have little desire for close relationships. Someone diagnosed with a schizotypal personality disorder shows marked eccentricities of thought, perception, and behavior.

The Paranoid Personality

At some point in life, each of us has been a little guarded or cautious about other people. Maybe we even had some doubts about their intentions toward us. In contrast, individuals with a paranoid personality disorder are excessively mistrustful and suspicious of others and without any justification. They tend to think that other people want to harm them. As a consequence, someone with a paranoid personality disorder

(PPD) tends to be cold and distant in relationships with a need for control. When a meaningful attachment is formed, the person is apt to be jealous. For example, suspicions of infidelity can permeate the partner relationship. You could say that these are people who are generally difficult to get along with and their distrustful nature often elicits hostility from others (Kantor, 2004). Unfortunately, this negative response often only serves to confirm and reinforce the person's original pessimistic expectations of others.

There may be instances where you encounter someone who feels a sense of righteous indignation and who initiates legal action against others. Although some people with a diagnosis of PPD are bright and conscientious, the features of the paranoid personality disorder point to their need to work alone and in relative isolation with limited social interaction. Characteristics typically include:

Paranoid Personality Disorder Characteristics

Aloof and emotionally cold

Pervasive mistrust and suspicion

Fear of intimacy with a sense of vulnerability

Usually isolated and disliked

Often blames others and does not accept criticism

Rigid and may initiate conflict; for example, may be litigious

Worries that others may attempt to harm them

The Schizoid Personality

After a busy day at work have you ever come home and just wanted to sit by yourself and not talk to anybody? Magnify that need for isolation many times over and you can begin to appreciate the features of a schizoid personality disorder (SPD). Individuals with this diagnosis are characteristically detached from social relationships. They are set apart by being introverted, withdrawn, isolated, and emotionally cold and distant (Dobbert, 2007). As expected, the person's social skills are weak and they do not typically express a need for attention or approval. Often referred to as loners, these individuals fear closeness with others and are often absorbed in their own thoughts and feelings. Typically, this is someone who could be characterized as eccentric, lonely, and ill at ease in the company of others. Those with this disorder tend to lead quiet, reclusive, and unsociable lives with remarkably little need or desire for the company of others (Gabbard, 2001).

Some people with SPD are sensitive to the opinions of others but are unable or unwilling to express this emotion. For these individuals, social isolation may be extremely painful. Interestingly, beneath the surface of indifference toward social relationships, there is often a deep loneliness and a desire for close relationships. Characteristics can be summarized as:

 Schizoid Personality Disorder Characteristics

Socially detached and does not enjoy social contact

Anxious when forced into contact with others

Restricted emotional range, humorless, aloof

Often daydreams

Appears not to appreciate the care and concern of others

The Schizotypal Personality

Similar to those with a schizoid personality disorder, those with schizotypal personality disorder (STPD) are also isolated. However, they behave in ways that could be characterized as unusual and they also tend to be suspicious. These individuals are often regarded as bizarre because of how they think and behave, how they relate to other people, and even how they dress. They have what could be described as odd beliefs. I remember one client who shared concerns about her 30-year-old son's appearance and behavior. After he dyed his hair a greenish blond color, he started getting a lot of tattoos and talked about wanting to get some body piercing done . . . and in some really strange places. Her son still lived at home and aside from his mother he had no friends. He did not get along with other people, even those he had known for years, and he had difficulty keeping a job. According to his mother, he simply could not deal with public contact and she noticed that none of this seemed to bother him. Unlike someone who might be characterized as being a little eccentric, those with STPD, much like this client's son, tend to maintain behaviors to the point where they become disabling and/or distressing to others.

In addition, those with STPD may report unusual perceptual experiences or illusions such as feeling the presence of another person even when they are alone. A small proportion of these individuals go on to develop schizophrenia. Typical characteristics are:

 Schizotypal Personality Disorder Characteristics

Similar to schizoid personality disorder but also peculiar

Social and interpersonal deficits, isolated

Perceptual distortion and eccentricity; such as odd reasoning, relates strange experiences

Anxious when forced into contact with others

Odd behavior and speech that is excessively elaborate and difficult to follow

Ideas of reference, such as believing that public messages are really directed at them

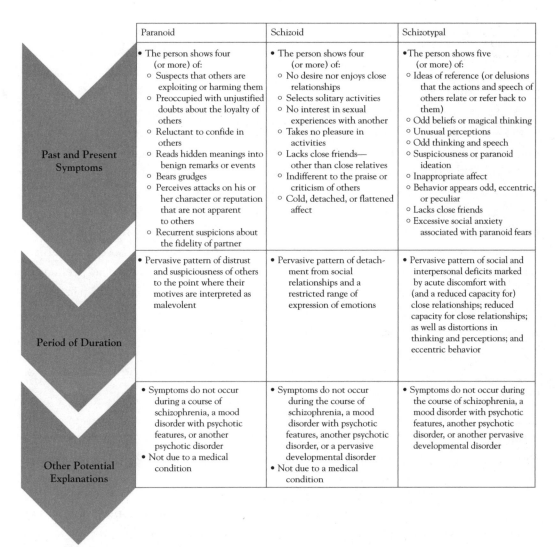

	Paranoid	Schizoid	Schizotypal
Past and Present Symptoms	• The person shows four (or more) of: ○ Suspects that others are exploiting or harming them ○ Preoccupied with unjustified doubts about the loyalty of others ○ Reluctant to confide in others ○ Reads hidden meanings into benign remarks or events ○ Bears grudges ○ Perceives attacks on his or her character or reputation that are not apparent to others ○ Recurrent suspicions about the fidelity of partner	• The person shows four (or more) of: ○ No desire nor enjoys close relationships ○ Selects solitary activities ○ No interest in sexual experiences with another ○ Takes no pleasure in activities ○ Lacks close friends— other than close relatives ○ Indifferent to the praise or criticism of others ○ Cold, detached, or flattened affect	• The person shows five (or more) of: ○ Ideas of reference (or delusions that the actions and speech of others relate or refer back to them) ○ Odd beliefs or magical thinking ○ Unusual perceptions ○ Odd thinking and speech ○ Suspiciousness or paranoid ideation ○ Inappropriate affect ○ Behavior appears odd, eccentric, or peculiar ○ Lacks close friends ○ Excessive social anxiety associated with paranoid fears
Period of Duration	• Pervasive pattern of distrust and suspiciousness of others to the point where their motives are interpreted as malevolent	• Pervasive pattern of detachment from social relationships and a restricted range of expression of emotions	• Pervasive pattern of social and interpersonal deficits marked by acute discomfort with (and a reduced capacity for) close relationships; reduced capacity for close relationships; as well as distortions in thinking and perceptions; and eccentric behavior
Other Potential Explanations	• Symptoms do not occur during a course of schizophrenia, a mood disorder with psychotic features, or another psychotic disorder • Not due to a medical condition	• Symptoms do not occur during the course of schizophrenia, a mood disorder with psychotic features, another psychotic disorder, or a pervasive developmental disorder • Not due to a medical condition	• Symptoms do not occur during the course of schizophrenia, a mood disorder with psychotic features, another psychotic disorder, or another pervasive developmental disorder

Figure 12.1   Cluster A—Odd and Eccentric: The Conceptual Map

Figure 12.1 is a conceptual map for the Cluster A disorders designed to help navigate the symptom picture for the specific diagnostic categories. Keep in mind that if the person meets criteria for the disorder prior to the onset of schizophrenia, the term "premorbid" should be added to the diagnosis as a qualifier.

Differential Assessment

Each of the personality disorders is organized into distinct clusters, but there seems to be extensive overlap of specific signs and symptoms among all the personality disorders. However, the majority of clients meet criteria for more than one personality disorder with the average number of diagnosable personality disorders for a single individual ranging from about 2 to 4. For instance, you might run across someone in your practice with any of the Cluster A disorders who may decompensate into brief psychoses, a trait in common with borderline personality disorder (Cluster B). When that happens, you will find the person diagnosed with the specific Cluster A disorder and with borderline personality disorder.

Although it could be argued that the existing *DSM* diagnostic criteria for the personality disorders seem to be imprecise, it is helpful to look for the most prototypical behavior qualities when formulating the diagnosis with considering the less descriptive behaviors at the periphery. Ideally, this approach to the diagnostic process will help you to make a precise diagnosis and lessen the overlap between the specific diagnostic criteria. For instance, persons with a schizoid personality disorder are cold and aloof and may appear distrustful but they do not have the prominent suspiciousness characteristic of those with a paranoid personality disorder. As another example, those with schizotypal personality disorder may have paranoid ideation but they also appear peculiar or odd, which would not be the case for someone struggling with a paranoid personality disorder. As a part of the differential assessment, also consider the presence of drug or alcohol use or a general medical condition that might better explain the person's symptoms for any one of the Cluster A disorders.

We now turn to the Cluster B disorders characterized by emotional, dramatic or erratic behaviors.

THE CLUSTER B DISORDERS—EMOTIONAL, DRAMATIC, OR ERRATIC

The Cluster B personality disorders typify emotional, dramatic, or erratic personality features. For example, someone with antisocial personality disorder displays a pervasive pattern of disregard for and violation of the rights of others and the rules of society. A central personality feature found in someone with borderline personality disorder is a pervasive pattern of unstable and intense relationships. The individual with a histrionic personality disorder displays excessive emotionality and attention-seeking behavior. The diagnosis of narcissistic personality disorder exemplifies qualities of grandiosity and the person usually requires almost constant admiration from others.

Antisocial Personality Disorder

Most of us have experienced the temptation to break the rules at one time or another. You know, being alone in your car and looking around a deserted highway thinking this would be a good time to accelerate until you are going 100 miles per hour just to see what your car could do. Maybe even bending the rules just a little bit did not seem like such a bad thing to do—like going only 90 miles an hour instead. In contrast, people with an antisocial personality disorder (ASPD) have a long history of failure to comply with social norms. In fact, they behave in ways that most of us would find unacceptable. For instance, they would think nothing of stealing from their own family or friends. A key feature of this disorder is the callous disregard for the rights and feelings of other people. They could be described as social predators who charm and manipulate leaving behind a trail of broken hearts and empty wallets. These are people who seem to lack a conscience and empathy for others. Some individuals may claim to have feelings of guilt but do not show genuine remorse for their behavior. Instead, they show a history of taking what they want and violating social norms without the slightest sense of guilt or remorse.

Many with ASPD have a well-developed capacity for rationalizing their behavior or blaming other people. A common justification you can expect to hear is, "They had it coming." Lying, cheating, dishonesty, and deceit permeate relationships and punishment rarely modifies their behavior. Those with ASPD are prone to impulsiveness, irritability, and aggressiveness that often lead to physical fights or assault. They often struggle with alcohol and drug use. Other comorbid diagnoses are the borderline, narcissistic, histrionic, and schizotypal personality disorders (Becker, Grilo, Edell, & McGlashan, 2000; Marinangeli et al., 2000). These individuals frequently move and have difficulty abiding by the law. They can be found in prison populations although some function quite successfully and can be found in business, entertainment, and political careers. Women with ASPD are often involved in prostitution. In order to be diagnosed with ASPD, the person must be at least 18 years old as well as have a documented history of a conduct disorder before the age of 15. Key characteristics you might look for are:

Antisocial Personality Disorder Characteristics

Disregards and violates others' rights

Aggressive, fights, difficult peer relationships

Hyperactive, irresponsible, and frequent job changes

Lying, theft, drug and alcohol abuse

No remorse for wrongdoing and lacks empathy

Anger, manipulation, lies mask fear

Sense of entitlement

Impulsive

Borderline Personality Disorder

Borderline personality disorder (BPD) is marked by an unstable self-image, mood, behavior, and relationships. These individuals, most of whom are women, tend to believe they were deprived of adequate care during childhood and often report being abused or neglected. Consequently, they feel what could be described as empty, angry, and entitled to nurturance. The person relentlessly seeks care in relationships and is sensitive in its perceived absence. When feeling the loss of a caring person, persons with BPD frequently express inappropriate and intense anger. In the movie entitled *Fatal Attraction*, Hollywood actress Glen Close portrayed the chaos and rage that followed the ending of a relationship that could best be described as a one-night stand. At first she seemed like the perfect mate for an extramarital affair with a married man named Dan, played by Michael Douglas, until he ended the relationship. In the face of rejection, the Glen Close character comes back to stalk him. She systematically terrorizes Dan's family by killing family pets and even temporarily kidnapping his daughter. Fatal attraction has become a household term for rejected love turned into a murderous obsession. Despite the drama found in this Hollywood movie, relationships for those struggling with BPD tend to be extreme and dramatic. Shifting affective states, impulsive behaviors, and inconsistency of self-concept add to the chaotic nature of their relationships.

When someone with BPD feels abandoned, they can dissociate or become desperately impulsive. Sometimes the person's concept of reality is so poor that they have brief episodes of psychotic thinking such as paranoid delusions and hallucinations. Mood shifts are typically accompanied by extreme changes in how they see the world, themselves, and other people. There is no in-between and there is an all or nothing perspective; that is, others are seen as either all good or all bad (splitting). The person with BPD frequently vacillates between overidealizing and devaluing friends, family, and romantic partners. They may engage in self-damaging behavior such as cutting themselves (self-mutilation) or attempting suicide. Approximately 10% of those with BPD ultimately commit suicide (Work Group on Borderline Personality Disorder, 2001). It is common for you to experience intense and even nurturing responses when you are trying to develop the therapeutic relationship. However, after repeated crises and failures to comply with therapeutic recommendations, the person with BPD will subsequently be seen in a more negative light or more specifically as the noncompliant client who is rejecting help. Characteristics typically associated with BPD are:

Borderline Personality Disorder Characteristics

Unstable relationships, self-image, and affect

Loneliness and sense of emptiness

Impulsive, mood lability to angry and anxious

Fears rejection and isolation

Self-destructive behavior

Alternates admiration and devaluation

Histrionic Personality Disorder

A pattern of excessive emotionality and attention-seeking that includes an excessive need for approval and inappropriate seductiveness are features of the histrionic personality disorder (HPD). Behind the person's seductive behaviors often lies a basic wish for dependency and protection. Associated characteristics may include egocentrism (an excessive preoccupation with oneself), self-indulgence, a continuous longing for appreciation, feelings that can be easily hurt, and manipulative behavior. Historically, this personality was linked to the ancient view of hysteria or a "wondering womb" (Prochaska & Norcross, 2007). Since HPD is primarily diagnosed in women, this gender bias continues (APA, 2000).

Those with HPD are also overly conscious of their appearance and are quite dramatic. Although I am not intending to diagnose the popular basketball player Dennis Rodman with HPD, one can point to his outlandish outfits, theatrical makeup, numerous body piercings, and sometimes garish hair color that often made him the center of media attention aside from his abilities on the basketball court. His personal relationships could be described as difficult. For instance, one early morning in May 2008 he was arrested in Los Angeles for domestic violence toward his girlfriend after an evening of heavy drinking in a local hotel. Rodman's reason for drinking was because of a nasty divorce and not being able to see his children for several weeks. You might say that individuals with HPD are vain and self-centered and uncomfortable when they are not in the limelight. Their expressions of emotions can seem exaggerated, childish, and superficial. Interestingly, those with HPD often easily establish relationships but they tend to be superficial and transient. The relationship may start off well but falters when depth and a sense of permanence are needed over the longer term. It is not unusual to hear a history of frequent job changes. These individuals can become easily bored and have trouble dealing with frustration. They tend to be impulsive and have difficulty delaying gratification. Somatic complaints are common. Driven by a desire for novelty and excitement they may put themselves in risky situations. Characteristics of HPD can be summarized as:

 Histrionic Personality Disorder Characteristics

Outwardly appear charming, lively, and seductive

Threatened self-esteem and sense of attractiveness

Egocentric, shallow, immature, and dramatic

Seeks excitement and attention and often exhibitionistic

Unable to focus on facts and details

Somatization

Pinkofsky (1997) offers an interesting mnemonic to help remember the features of HPD. Called "Praise me," it can be illustrated as:

✍️ **Tips for Remembering the Histrionic Personality Disorder**

P = Provocative or seductive

R = Relationships are seen as more intimate than they really are

A = Attention and the person must be the center

I = Influenced easily

S = Speech style seeks to impress others

E = Emotional liability, shallowness

M = Makeup so that the physical appearance is used to draw attention to self

E = Exaggerated emotions and tend to be theatrical

Narcissistic Personality Disorder

The narcissistic personality disorder (NPD) is seen as a pervasive pattern of grandiosity, a sense of privilege or entitlement, expectations of preferential treatment, an exaggerated sense of self-importance, and arrogant or haughty behaviors or attitudes. Often a fragile self-esteem and conscious feelings of unworthiness underlie this inflated exterior. Those with NPD can be described as being excessively preoccupied with issues of personal adequacy, power, and prestige. Self-centeredness is also a term that comes to mind. This trait makes it a formidable diagnosis for those living with NPD as well as those who have a relationship with them.

These are individuals who can be characterized as controlling, blaming, self-absorbed, intolerant of others' views, unaware of others' needs and the effects of their behavior on others, and insistent that others see them as they wish to be seen. It is common for them to make hurtful remarks and be oblivious to how these remarks affect others. The needs and feelings of others are interpreted as signs of weakness. When criticized, persons with NPD often feel rejected, humiliated, and threatened. As a way to protect themselves from these perceived dangers, they often react with contempt, rage, and/or defiance to criticism, real or imagined.

Some persons with NPD are ambitious and quite capable, but it is the inability to tolerate setbacks or criticism along with a lack of empathy that makes it difficult for them to work collaboratively with others. The person's sense of grandiosity, often coupled with a hypomanic mood, is typically not representative of his or her actual accomplishments. Central to NPD is the sense of entitlement that makes the person appear to be cold, disinterested, disdainful, snobbish, or patronizing. Major characteristics of NPD can be summarized as:

Narcissistic Personality Disorder Characteristics

Grandiosity, unrealistic self-expectation
Need for constant admiration
Impulsive and anxious
Doubts own adequacy
Alternates admiration and devaluation of others
Demanding with a sense of entitlement

A conceptual map (Figure 12.2) for the Cluster B personality disorders is presented to help sort through the client's symptom picture and determine the specific personality disorder.

Differential Assessment

Similar to the Cluster A personality disorders, there is also a degree of overlap among the Cluster B diagnostic categories. Here, too, it is common for clients to meet criteria for more than one of the personality disorders. In addition, the person with a personality disorder may have a comorbid diagnosis with the Axis I disorders (Keown, Holloway, & Kuipers, 2002). It is useful to first consider the symptom picture of the Axis I disorders before making the personality disorder as the principal (or only) diagnosis. For example, many individuals with BPD may also have a major depressive disorder or dysthymic disorder. Determine if the person's suicidal behaviors, anger, and feelings of emptiness are experienced only during episodes of depression. When considering comorbid conditions, the Cluster B personality disorders are significantly associated with the diagnostic classifications of the anxiety, eating, and psychotic disorders, as well as with alcohol abuse and dependence.

We now turn to a discussion of the Cluster C disorders.

THE CLUSTER C DISORDERS—ANXIOUS AND FEARFUL

The personality disorders organized around Cluster C organize anxious and fearful personality traits. For example, the avoidant personality disorder typifies someone who is generally very shy. Many people can show dependent qualities but someone with a

Figure 12.2 Cluster B—Emotional, Dramatic, or Erratic: The Conceptual Map

	Antisocial (Sociopath, Psychopath)	Borderline
Past and Present Symptoms	• The person shows three (or more) of: ○ Failure to conform to social norms with respect to lawful behaviors as indicated by repeatedly performing acts that are grounds for arrest ○ Deceitfulness as indicated by repeatedly lying, use of aliases, or conning others for personal profit or pleasure ○ Impulsivity or failure to plan ahead ○ Irritability and aggressiveness, as indicated by repeated physical fights or assaults ○ Reckless disregard for safety of self or others ○ Consistent irresponsibility, as indicated by repeated failure to sustain consistent work behavior or honor financial obligations ○ Lack of remorse, as indicated by being indifferent to or rationalizing having hurt, mistreated, or stolen from another	• The person shows five (or more) of: ○ Frantic efforts to avoid real or imagined abandonment (don't include self-injurious or suicidal behaviors covered below) ○ A pattern of unstable and intense relationships that alternate between idealization and devaluation ○ Identity disturbance (severely unstable self-image or sense of self) ○ Potentially damaging impulsiveness in at least two areas; such as binge-eating, reckless driving, sex, spending, substance use (don't include suicidal or self-mutilating behaviors) ○ Self-mutilation or suicide thoughts, threats, or other behavior ○ Severe reactivity of mood leading to marked instability (mood swings of intense anxiety, depression, or irritability lasting a few hours and only rarely more than a few days) ○ Chronic feelings of emptiness ○ Anger that is out of control or inappropriate and intense (demonstrated by frequent temper displays, repeated physical fights, or feeling constantly angry) ○ Brief paranoid ideas or severe dissociative symptoms related to stress
Period of Duration	• Pervasive pattern of disregard for (and violation of) the rights of others occurring since age 15 and evidence of a conduct disorder with onset before age 15 • The behavior pattern continued into adulthood and the individual is at least 18 years of age	• Pervasive pattern of instability of interpersonal relationships, self-image and affects, as well as marked impulsivity beginning by early adulthood and present in a variety of contexts
Other Potential Explanations	• Symptoms do not occur during a course of schizophrenia or a manic episode	• Often co-occurs with mood disorders, substance abuse, and other personality disorders • Distinguish from traits that emerge due to the direct effects of a general medical condition (on the central nervous system)

Histrionic	Narcissistic

• The person shows five (or more) of:
  ○ Discomfort with situations in which the person is not the center of attention
  ○ Relationships that are frequently fraught with inappropriately seductive or sexually provocative behavior
  ○ Displays emotion that is shallow and rapidly shifting
  ○ Frequent focusing of attention on self through use of physical appearance
  ○ Speech that is vague and lacks detail
  ○ Overly dramatic expression of emotion
  ○ Easy suggestibility—the person is easily influenced by opinions of other people or by circumstances
  ○ Considers relationships to be more intimate than they really are
	• The person shows five (or more) of:
	  ○ A grandiose sense of self-importance (the person exaggerates own abilities and accomplishments)
	  ○ Preoccupation with fantasies of beauty, brilliance, ideal love, power, or limitless success
	  ○ Believes that personal uniqueness renders him- or herself fit only for association with (or understanding by) people or institutions of rarefied status
	  ○ Need for excessive admiration
	  ○ Sense of entitlement (the person unreasonably expects favorable treatment or automatic granting of his or her expectations)
	  ○ Exploitation of others to achieve personal goals
	  ○ Lack of empathy (does not recognize or identify with the feelings and needs of others)
	  ○ Frequent envy of others or believes others are envious of him or her
	  ○ Arrogance or haughtiness in attitude or behavior

• Pervasive pattern of emotionality and attention seeking, beginning by early adulthood and present in a variety of contexts	• Pervasive pattern of grandiosity (in fantasy or behavior), need for admiration and lack of empathy beginning by early adulthood and present in a variety of contexts
• A substance disorder or a general medical condition does not better explain symptoms	• Distinguish from symptoms that may develop in association with chronic substance use

dependent personality disorder has an excessive need to be taken care of that results in submissive and clinging behaviors. The third personality disorder in Cluster C, obsessive-compulsive personality disorder, highlights the person's preoccupation with orderliness, perfectionism, and control.

Avoidant Personality Disorder

The avoidant personality (AVPD) or anxious personality disorder is characterized by a pervasive pattern of social inhibition and discomfort in social situations, feelings of inadequacy and low self-esteem, and extreme sensitivity to criticism or rejection. These are individuals who have difficulty joining group activities and avoid interpersonal activities although they long for close relationships. They simply assume that other people will be critical and disapproving of them and often consider themselves to be socially inept or personally unappealing.

Typically, individuals with AVPD are preoccupied with their own shortcomings and frequently feel socially incompetent, personally unappealing, or inferior to others. They are reluctant to form relationships with others and tend to be shy, inhibited, and quiet to avoid attracting attention to themselves. The person can also be hypervigilant about looking for subtle cues that might suggest even the slightest criticism or rejection. Because these individuals expect disapproval from others, they are quick to detect any indication of such disapproval and typically feel extremely hurt. The person with AVPD is able to establish friendships or intimate relationships only when he or she is assured of uncritical acceptance. Central characteristics can be summarized as:

👉 Avoidant Personality Disorder Characteristics

Socially inhibited, shy, and lonely

Sense of being inadequate with low self-esteem

Hypersensitive to criticism

Desperate for relationships but avoids social contact for fear of disapproval

Dependent Personality Disorder

The central characteristic of dependent personality disorder (DPD), formerly referred to as a passive-dependent personality in earlier editions of the DSM, is a pervasive need to be taken care of by another person that usually starts by early adulthood. This is the person who has an exaggerated fear that they are incapable of doing things or taking care of themselves on their own. As a result, they rely on other people, usually one person, to help them to get through the day. I remember one client who worked as a charter fishing captain. His wife booked all of his fishing charters. That meant that she organized his entire day and everything else that he did right down to the last detail. He relied heavily on his wife to make all of his decisions. Any disruption in his routine made him irritable and out of sorts.

Because of these individuals' dependencies on others they tend to put their own interests aside and may be found in exploitive relationships. They may even tolerate considerable abuse, including battering (Bornstein, 2006). It is not unusual for the person with DPD to have an unrealistic fear of being abandoned. Since the person is afraid to be alone or because of an exaggerated fear of helplessness, they can be seen to be going to great lengths to maintain the support of another person. For instance, they are willing to sacrifice their own opinions and are typically passive. If for some reason the relationship ends, the person with DPD will more than likely try to find someone else to replace the sense of closeness and support as soon as possible. Some of the major features of DPD can be summarized as follows:

Dependent Personality Disorder Characteristics

Need to be taken care of, passive, unsure

Submissive behavior

Fear of separation

Sensation of helplessness

May appear passive-aggressive

Exhaustive questioning

Attention to minute detail

May become upset when routines are disrupted

Distinguishing someone who tends to depend on others from a diagnosable dependent personality disorder can be somewhat subjective. Zimmerman (1994) suggests several questions that can help to make this distinction. They are adapted as follows:

✍ Assessing for Dependent Personality Disorder

The following 11 questions are aimed at assessing for the presence of dependent personality disorder:

1. Some people enjoy making decisions on their own. Other people would rather have someone they trust to guide them every step along the way. Which do you prefer?
2. Do you seek advice for everyday decisions?
3. Are there times when other people have gone ahead and made decisions about important areas in your life?
4. When you are close to someone, is it hard for you to express an opinion that is different from theirs?
5. If the person responds affirmatively, then ask, "What do you think might happen if you did share a different opinion?"
6. Do you often find yourself agreeing with others even if you do not? If the response is "Yes," then ask the person to elaborate how this happens for them.
7. Do you often need help getting started on tasks or a project?
8. Do you ever volunteer to do something that is unpleasant for you so that others will take care of you when you need it?
9. Are you uncomfortable being alone? If the response is affirmative, explore the fears or concerns the person has about not being able to take care of him- or herself.
10. Do you worry that important people in your life might leave you?
11. When a close relationship ends, have you ever been desperate to get into another relationship right away? If the response is affirmative, ask if the person would still want to get into the new relationship even if they thought it might not be with the best person for them.

Obsessive-Compulsive Personality Disorder

Obsessive-compulsive personality disorder (OCPD) describes someone who has an obsession with perfection, orderliness, and inflexibility that begins by early adulthood. These are individuals with an excessive need for control and they can feel anxious when they perceive that things are not right. They are typically preoccupied with rules, routines, lists, schedules, or other minor details, and organization. It is this rigidity, inflexibility, and stubbornness that create difficulty both in work and in personal relationships. It is hard for the person to accept new ideas or to look at alternative ways of doing things. It is not unusual for individuals with OCPD to show such a high degree of perfectionism that it interferes with getting the job done.

Some individuals will put work ahead of personal relationships and become obsessively devoted to productivity. They may hold themselves and others to unrealistic standards of morality, ethics, or values. The person with OCPD has a need to always be in the right. As you can expect, relationships with others can become difficult. Additionally, the person may spend an excessive amount of time to get a task done correctly or is reluctant to delegate to others insisting that everything must be done his or her way. The person may even take over a job that someone else is working on so that it will be done properly. Sometimes a frustration with other people not doing exactly what the person with OCPD wants spills over into anger or even violence. Unfortunately, the excessive attention to details, even the most trivial, often interferes with the person's ability to complete a task. Some individuals with OCPD, but not all, may show an obsessive need for cleanliness. Somehow uncleanliness is seen as a form of imperfection. It is these individuals who may routinely spend a considerable amount of time putting everything precisely in the right place and in precisely the right way.

Another aspect of OCPD is the individual's reluctance to throw away worthless and unsentimental objects because he or she is afraid that they might be needed at a later time. An additional feature is hoarding money or tightly controlling spending out of a fear that something could go wrong (Jefferys, 2008). To others, this behavior looks like miserliness or being stingy. Some persons with OCPD have a negative or pessimistic outlook on life (Rossi, Marinangeli, Butti, Kalyvoka, & Petruzzi, 2000), while others may have difficulty expressing emotion. Dichotomous or either-or thinking, magnification, catastrophizing, and displays of frustration and irritability can also be seen in persons with OCPD. Major aspects of this disorder are:

Obsessive-Compulsive Disorder Characteristics

Inhibited, stubborn, rigid, and perfectionistic
Preoccupied with orderliness or perfection
Mental and interpersonal control
Worry about loss of emotional control
Show a need for control

Figure 12.3 is a conceptual map that illustrates the features of each of the Cluster C disorders.

Figure 12.3   Cluster C—Anxious or Fearful: The Conceptual Map

	Avoidant	Dependent
Past and Present Symptoms	• The person shows four (or more) of : ○ Fears criticism, disapproval, or rejection to the extent of avoiding significant interpersonal contact in an occupation ○ Will only become involved with others unless certain of being liked ○ Is restrained in intimate relationships for fear of ridicule or shame ○ In social situations is preoccupied with concerns of being criticized or rejected ○ Is inhibited in new relationships, stemming from feelings of inadequacy ○ Is convinced of being socially inept, personally unappealing, or inferior to others ○ Avoids personal risk or new activities for fear of embarrassment	• The person shows five (or more) of: ○ Needs excessive advice and reassurance to make everyday decisions ○ Needs for others to assume responsibility for most major life areas ○ Fears loss of approval or support leading to difficulty with expressing disagreement (do not include realistic fears of retribution) ○ Trouble starting projects or carrying them out independently (and this must be due to low self-confidence and not from low motivation or energy) ○ Goes to excessive lengths to gain nurturance and support (even to volunteer to do something unpleasant) ○ Feels uncomfortable or helpless when alone because of exaggerated fears of incapacity for self-care ○ If one close relationship is lost, urgently seeks another to provide care and support ○ Preoccupation with unrealistic fears of being abandoned and being left to care for him- or herself
Period of Duration	• Pervasive pattern of social inhibition, feelings of inadequacy, and hypersensitivity to negative evaluation beginning by early adulthood and present in a variety of contexts	• Pervasive and excessive need to be taken care of that leads to submissive and clinging behavior and fears of separation beginning by early adulthood and present in a variety of contexts
Other Potential Explanations	• Distinguish from traits that may emerge due to a general medical condition (of the central nervous system) and chronic substance use	• Distinguish from the dependency arising as a consequence of Axis I disorders (for instance mood disorders, panic disorder, and agoraphobia) • Distinguish from a general medical condition (of the central nervous system) and chronic substance use

Obsessive-Compulsive
<ul><li>The person shows four (or more) of:<ul><li>○ Absorbed with details, lists, order, organization, rules, or schedules to such an extent that the purpose of the activity is lost—can't see the forest for the trees</li><li>○ Is perfectionistic to a degree that it interferes with completing the task</li><li>○ Is a workaholic or works to the exclusion of leisure activities</li><li>○ Is overconscientious, inflexible, or scrupulous about ethics, morals, or values to a degree that cannot be accounted for by cultural or religious identification</li><li>○ Saves worthless items of no real or sentimental value</li><li>○ Reluctant to delegate tasks unless others agree to do things exactly his or her way</li><li>○ Is stingy toward self and others, hoards money against future need</li><li>○ Is rigid and stubborn</li></ul></li></ul>
<ul><li>Pervasive pattern of a preoccupation with orderliness, perfectionism, and mental and interpersonal control, at the expense of flexibility, openness, and efficiency beginning by early adulthood and present in a variety of contexts</li></ul>
<ul><li>Often confused with obsessive-compulsive disorder</li><li>Distinguish from a general medical condition (of the central nervous system) and chronic substance use</li></ul>

Differential Assessment

As noted earlier, the diagnosis of a personality disorder on Axis II may co-occur with an Axis I disorder. In general, the personality disorders are most often associated with substance use, anxiety, and/or somatoform disorders, and least associated with the psychotic and major affective diagnoses. At the Cluster C level, these personality disorders seem to be strongly linked to the anxiety and somatoform disorders.

Another challenge to the differential assessment process is related to the etiological pathways of disorders. That is, how do you determine the direction of causality of the various co-occurring disorders (if there is a causal connection at all)? For example, someone who struggles with a DPD may develop phobias and avoidant behaviors. On the other hand, someone who struggles with phobic avoidance may develop behavior patterns that contribute to the development of a DPD. The discussion up to this point clearly indicates that those who struggle with a personality disorder rarely seek help on their own, and having a better understanding of the beginnings of the symptom picture has implications for the assessment process. The competency-based assessment provides a framework to examine the full range of the person's symptoms and offers a pathway to examine the impact on both the individual and his or her interpersonal world.

FINAL THOUGHTS

There are 10 specific personality disorders divided into three clusters, A, B, and C. Although there is considerable overlap, they are a useful way to remember each of the personality disorders. The clusters can be distinguished as follows:

Quick Guide to the Personality Disorders

Cluster A

Cluster A represents individuals who are characterized as withdrawn, cold, suspicious, or irrational. The specific disorders are:

Paranoid: These individuals are generally suspicious and quick to take offense. They often have few people that they confide in and tend to hold grudges for a long time. This person may read a hidden a meaning into remarks.

Schizoid: This is shown by the individual who cares little for social relationships, has a restricted range of emotions, and seems indifferent to criticism or praise. This person tends to be solitary and avoid close relationships.

Schizotypal: This individual appears strange or peculiar to others. Interpersonal relationships are difficult and the person lacks close friends and seems uncomfortable in social situations. Here, too, the person may show a level of suspiciousness, unusual perceptions or thinking, eccentric speech, and inappropriate affect.

Cluster B

Individuals with the Cluster B disorders tend to be dramatic, emotional, and attention-seeking. Mood is labile and often quite shallow. They often have intense interpersonal conflicts. The specific disorders are:

Antisocial: These individuals show irresponsible and often criminal behavior beginning in childhood or early adolescence (such as truancy, running away, cruelty, fighting, destructiveness, lying, and theft). In addition to the criminal behavior shown as adults, they may default on debts, act recklessly or impulsively, show no remorse for their behavior or otherwise show irresponsibility.

Borderline: These individuals are characterized as impulsive and who make recurrent suicide threats (or attempts). They are emotionally unstable, often show intense, inappropriate anger, feel empty or bored, and frantically try to avoid abandonment. They are uncertain about who they really are and lack the ability to maintain stable interpersonal relationships.

Histrionic: These individuals are overly emotional, vague, and attention-seeking. The person often needs constant reassurance about his or her attractiveness, may be self-centered, and sexually seductive.

Narcissistic: Persons with this disorder are self-important and often preoccupied with envy, fantasies about success, or ruminate about the uniqueness of their problems. The sense of entitlement and lack of empathy causes the person to take advantage of others. Criticism may be vigorously rejected. These individuals need constant attention and admiration.

Cluster C

This cluster represents people who tend to be anxious and tense. They are often overcontrolled. Specific disorders represented are:

Avoidant: This diagnostic category characterizes people who are timid and easily wounded by criticism to the point where they are hesitant to become involved with others. The person may fear the embarrassment of showing emotions or saying things that seem foolish. They may have no close friends and exaggerate the risks of taking on pursuits outside of a usual routine.

Dependent: This individual needs the approval of others to the degree that he or she has trouble making independent decisions to starting projects. Even when this person knows another to be wrong, he or she still has the need to agree. The person fears abandonment, feels helpless when alone, and when a relationship ends strives to replace it as soon as possible. These persons are easily hurt by criticism and will volunteer for unpleasant tasks to gain the approval of others.

Obsessive-Compulsive: Perfectionism and rigidity are the traits that characterize this disorder. These are people who are often called workaholics, and they tend to be indecisive, excessively scrupulous, and preoccupied with detail. This is someone who insists that things be done their way. The person has trouble expressing affection, lacks generosity, and may resist throwing away worthless objects even though they are no longer needed.

PRACTICING THE COMPETENCY-BASED ASSESSMENT

The personality disorders are considered to be an enduring pattern of inner experience and behavior that differs markedly from the person's culture. They are seen as long-standing and maladaptive patterns of perceiving and responding to other people and to stressful circumstances that lead to distress and impairment in the person's life. Review the following case illustrations and test out your skills in determining the correct competency-based assessment from the 10 personality disorders listed in the *DSM*.

The Case of Melvin Myers

At first glance, Melvin Myers seems like a pleasant, unobtrusive, and likeable guy. That is, until you spend some time with him. "He's almost too nice," thought the practitioner adding, "It seems like he's on overdrive to please others." The practitioner remembered her first impression of Melvin. He was referred by his employer's human resources department for an evaluation after he turned down a promotion for the third time. On entering her office Melvin immediately asked, "Where would you like me to sit?" The practitioner thought this question was a little odd since she only had three chairs in her office. One was behind her desk in the far corner of the room, and the other was blocked with books and files. This left an obvious choice of where to take a seat and yet Melvin seemed unsure of himself and eager to please. The practitioner had the impression that he was looking for her approval.

Melvin is a 32-year-old single man who never married. He currently lives at home with his widowed mother. The only time that he left home was to attend college. He added that he was miserable being away from friends and family and came home every chance he could. A good student, he graduated with a degree in business and accepted a job in a local bank. He went on to get his master's degree in business at a nearby college so he would not have to leave home again. He went to school part-time at night. "Mother needed me at home to help out around the house," he stated. Melvin has been with the bank for almost 10 years but still works as a teller. The practitioner thought this position was well below his level of education. Melvin saw himself as one of the best workers at the bank. When asked about his responsibilities, Melvin stated, "I keep a low profile. I really don't want to be responsible for others. Plus when you move up the corporate ladder, you have to make a lot of independent decisions and I don't want to be the one to take chances. You know with a bank you're not working with your own money. Now that the economy is so bad I think the safest thing to do is just to do what my supervisor says. One time when my supervisor was on vacation, I had to make a decision about a questionable deposit on my own. It was the worst day of my life. I had nightmares about it until my supervisor came back."

Melvin has a few close friends and one of them works at the bank with him. Both started at the bank around the same time and they have lunch together every day. Melvin added that his friend thinks the supervisor takes advantage of him. For instance, if there is an important audit coming up and the supervisor wants to leave early, it is Melvin who stays late to complete the report. Although Melvin admitted this happens more than he would like, he thinks this is just part of being a dependable worker. Melvin admitted that his relationship with his supervisor "has its ups and downs." By this he means that the supervisor gets frustrated when Melvin asks for directions, which happens most of the time, or is reluctant to start a project on his own.

The practitioner remembered thinking that Melvin did not seem to like making decisions on his own and decided to pursue this further. She asked, "Has there ever been a time in your life when somebody else made a really important decision for you?" Melvin looked thoughtful for a moment and then he responded, "Well, there was a time a couple of years ago that my mother did not like my girlfriend, Maria Helena de Castro. See, she was a Cuban girl and you know how they are . . . warm, outgoing, and they talk a lot. Mother didn't think she was a good match for me. I'm so reserved and my girlfriend was the exact opposite. Maria was so fun-loving and we did a lot of crazy things together. When I first laid eyes on her, I knew she was my soul mate. I mean we really hit it off right away." At this point, Melvin took a deep breath and slowly exhaled and appeared to look dejected. He continued, "But I'm sure that Mother was right. She always has my best interests at heart so, of course, the girlfriend had to go. Funny, I still miss Maria, but Mother was so happy when we broke up. I guess it was the right thing to do. Sometimes I get so mad at myself 'cause I just don't think I will ever find the right girl for me. I remember how Maria was so mad at me when I told her we had to end our relationship. She said I was weak and accused me of being a 'mamma's boy.' I think her reaction proves that Mother was right about her after all." The practitioner had the impression from Melvin's tone of voice that he was not so convinced that his mother was right. She thought that Melvin seemed trapped and forced to choose between two important people in his life. When Melvin decided not to go against his mother's wishes, it seemed to the practitioner that he became angry with himself for not being able to find just the right girlfriend. Now that his mother is older, Melvin expressed the fear that he worries about what he would do without her. "There's not a day that goes by when I don't ask for her opinion on things. Big things, little things . . . it doesn't matter. It just feels good knowing she's there for me."

Melvin's social history is unremarkable. He does not drink or smoke and aside from the usual childhood illnesses he is in good health. Growing up, Melvin was described as shy and introverted. He was always close to his mother who doted on him. His father participated very little in his life and died of unknown causes when he was about

10 years of age. He felt he was always close to his mother. Going off to school was diffi-cult and Melvin remembers his first day in kindergarten as the worst day of his life. He cried so hard and didn't want to go back to school the next day.

How would you formulate your competency-based assessment for Melvin Myers?

The Case of Denise McMinville

Denise begins, "My boss accuses me of being 'Miss Rules and Regulations' with 'Rigidity' being my middle name. Well, I'm not so sure I agree with that assessment. If you took one look at my staff, you could clearly see that they are lazy, a little stupid, and simply not capable of getting the job done right. Time after time I end up having to do the work myself. Then my supervisor has the nerve to blame me for not getting projects done! Me, of all people! I never take coffee breaks. In fact, I rarely go out and do things with friends or spend time just relaxing. Heck, my ex-husband . . ." Denise paused for a few seconds, seemed a little embarrassed and resumed, "Well, that was a slip. I mean my soon to be ex-husband. I married him when I was 22. I was just a kid back then and what did I know? I thought we were in this relationship for the long haul and early on I started saving for a future together. I guess it all started going down-hill when he began accusing me of being a 'penny pincher.' What's wrong with looking for a bargain? Well, after 15 years, he now decides that I'm a workaholic, too. Imagine that! Well, I don't see any good qualities in him either. Now you can understand why he's my soon-to-be ex husband. I don't drink, I don't smoke, I've never missed a day of work due to any kind of illness so what's so bad about being a workaholic?" Denise looks a little irritated and continued.

"Never mind that I go in to work early. Well, if you must know I arrive at 7 A.M. on the dot and not a minute sooner or a minute later. Yes, exactly at 7! It's my routine and it has served me well for the past five years I've been working at the hospital. It's better to get into the office before everyone else, you know? It's quiet and you can get a lot done. Most days I don't get home before 8 P.M. So what's the big deal? My husband complains that I'm not home to make him his dinner. Well, he can just make a peanut butter and jelly sandwich all on his own for dinner if he's that hungry. I have it for lunch every single day and there's nothing wrong with that. I really think he's just jeal-ous because I make more money than he does and my position is far more important than his. He's just a clerk in the admissions office. I have a lot of responsibilities but I'm healthy, I like my job, and I think I'm pretty good at it so why not put in a little extra time. What do you think?"

The practitioner wasn't sure how to respond at this point and so she paused. She then asked Denise to tell her a little about what a routine day on the job looks like. Denise immediately answered, "The first thing I do is check all of the e-mail messages that I wrote the day before. You see I write them but don't actually send them out until I can double check them. I spend about two hours just to make sure everything is spelled correctly and that it makes sense. Then I hit the send button. As a matter of fact, I check just about everything I do, including when I'm cleaning the house, working in the yard . . . even doing something as simple as rearranging my closets. I take so many breaks to admire my work. Well, that's what I call it. I'm really searching out imperfections. You might say that I like to do things my way and only my way. That's why I pay attention to the details. I just can't trust my employees to get it right. My boss says I should delegate more of the work and he claims I have a morale problem in my department but they simply just can't get it right. I have to either go in and fix their mess or just do it myself. It's easier if I do it all on my own but then there is just too much work. Sometimes I get so tied up in a project that I miss deadlines. I think that irritates the heck out of my boss, too. I'm sure you know how important it is to get things right, don't you? Gosh, I can only imagine what would happen if you gave somebody a wrong diagnosis. I wouldn't want your job. Anyway, that's why I'm concerned with details, order, and organizing my day. Lists and schedules are enormously helpful! What with all the work I do not to mention staying on top of my lazy employees, I need to keep track of my day! My boss once described me as having a one-track mind. I think that's probably very true. Keeping track of all the details I sometimes get stuck when I'm working on something. I work hard, spend long hours on the job, and now I'm going to be terminated. I've sacrificed the best years of my life for that hospital and now my position is gone. Work is my whole life. I mean I have friends and all but they are from grammar school and we don't talk as much since I've moved here."

Ms. McMinville suddenly became quiet. The practitioner decided to wait out the silence. After what seemed like a very long pause, Ms. McMinville continued, "Anyway, my boss claims the hospital is restructuring because of the economy. Last Thursday I was given two-weeks notice." Tears welled up in Denise's eyes and she looked defeated. She added, "When you asked me about my day, I answered it in the present tense when I really should have told you what I did when I had the job. It's hard to get used to being fired and I'm going to miss my work." She continued, "Am I answering your question? Do you have enough information? Is there anything else you need to know?"

The practitioner noticed on the intake report that Ms. McMinville did not come in on her own but made the appointment at her mother's suggestion. The practitioner asked how she might be of help to Ms. McMinville. "Well, my financial situation is in the cellar right now. What with the divorce, and no income except unemployment, I'm moving back home. I'm sure this will be a temporary arrangement. I have a good work history and my degree is in hospital administration. That's a really good field in today's employment market and I do work hard so I'm confident I'll find another job soon. My mother thinks the responsibilities that I had were too much for me and that's why she suggested that I come in to see you. Do you have some kind of tests that I could take to see what my problem is?" asked Denise. She went on to add, "Now that I think of it, I was always particular as a child. I have always been an orderly person and I remember that mother made me keep lists of my chores. I guess that's a habit that has just stuck with me."

How would you formulate your competency-based assessment for Denise McMinville?

PRACTICAL APPLICATIONS

1. This chapter points out that many behavioral traits that are a part of the personality disorders can also be found in normally functioning people. Reflect for a moment on the following question:

   At what point does being self-centered become a personality disorder?

2. In the 1976 book by Harvey Cleckley entitled *The Mask of Sanity*, the term *psychopath* became popularized. The 1990s revision of the *DSM* replaced the term *psychopathy* with *antisocial personality disorder (APD)*, which refers to a pervasive pattern of disregard for, and violation of, the rights of others. With that in mind, what does a charming but heartless successful business tycoon have in common with a remorseless killer? When does a certain behavior represent a personality disorder rather than expected and culturally accepted behavioral standards.

3. Imagine that you are reading the newspaper and come across a story about a brutal assault committed by a gang member during a robbery of a local convenience store. Can you assume that this individual has the diagnosis of antisocial personality disorder? Explain why or why not.

4. Sometimes it is hard for the practitioner to decide where value judgments end; for example, characterizing someone as self-absorbed, as opposed to making the distinction of a personality disorder. Cultures also differ in how they draw the line. How would you distinguish between someone with the diagnosis of narcissistic personality disorder versus being a normal member of a group or culture that encourages putting your own needs ahead of others and places a premium on youth, beauty, and attractiveness?

⫸◆⫷

Appendix

Competency-Based Assessments for Chapter 12 Case Examples: Listing of Case Diagnoses

Figures 12A.1 through 12A.4 provide the diagnostic assessment for each of the cases illustrated. They are organized in the order that they appear in each chapter.

CASE REVIEW FOR MELVIN MYERS

Melvin Myers's story is an illustration of someone who struggles with dependent personality disorder. He is employed as a bank teller and his relationship with his supervisor is reported to have its "ups and downs." He shows a lack of initiative and asks for guidance on tasks. He has refused promotions because of the increased responsibilities they would bring. He also seems to be taken advantage of by taking on extra work for the supervisor.

Melvyn's mother plays a key role in his life by making important decisions for him, including the breakup with his girlfriend. Although Melvin saw his girlfriend as his "soul mate," he subordinated his own needs and wishes to those of his mother. He currently worries about what will happen when he no longer has his mother to rely on for what sounds like making trivial everyday decisions.

Though his relationships are characterized by submission and dependence, there is more to Melvin's life story than his symptoms of a dependent personality disorder. The

401

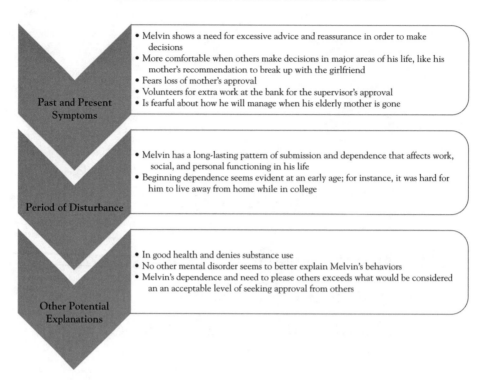

Figure 12A.1   The Conceptual Map for Melvin Myers

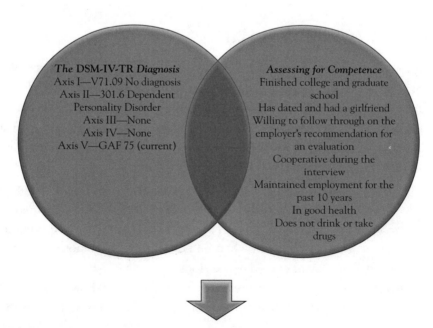

Figure 12A.2   The Competency-Based Assessment for Melvin Myers

Past and Present Symptoms

- Denise describes making lists and being preoccupied with details and organization to the point that the purpose of some of her activities is lost
- She is a perfectionist to the degree that she has difficulty completing tasks and misses deadlines
- Denise has trouble delegating tasks at work
- Is inflexible and insists work be done her way
- Her husband accuses her of being frugal (a penny pincher)

Period of Disturbance

- Beginning in her early adult life Denise shows a preoccupation with control, orderliness, and perfection
- She recalls that in childhood she liked being an orderly person and started making lists to keep track of things

Other Potential Explanations

- Denise is in good health, so a general medical condition would not better explain her behavior
- Denise claims that she does not smoke or drink, so a substance disorder is not considered
- While she recently lost her job, she seems confident of finding another, thus ruling out consideration of a major depressive disorder of dysthymia

Figure 12A.3 The Conceptual Map for Denise McMinville

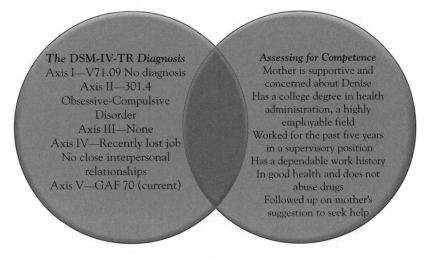

The DSM-IV-TR Diagnosis
Axis I—V71.09 No diagnosis
Axis II—301.4
Obsessive-Compulsive
Disorder
Axis III—None
Axis IV—Recently lost job
No close interpersonal
relationships
Axis V—GAF 70 (current)

Assessing for Competence
Mother is supportive and
concerned about Denise
Has a college degree in health
administration, a highly
employable field
Worked for the past five years
in a supervisory position
Has a dependable work history
In good health and does not
abuse drugs
Followed up on mother's
suggestion to seek help

Figure 12A.4 The Competency-Based Assessment for Denise McMinville

competency-based assessment helps to individualize Melvin's experiences with this disorder while looking at the full range of factors affecting his life. He shows a number of strengths. Melvin is said to be a reliable and dependable worker and has maintained steady employment since he graduated from college. He is bright and has a number of longtime friends.

CASE REVIEW FOR DENISE MCMINVILLE

Denise McMinville's husband accuses her of being a workaholic and she does put in long hours on the job. Her work habits could be described as perfectionistic and she had a great deal of difficulty delegating tasks. Despite making lists and schedules, she had difficulty meeting deadlines and these tendencies seemed to pervade her young adult life. As a youngster Denise recalls being concerned with order and started making lists for herself. Her interpersonal relationships were adversely affected; that is, her husband was seeking divorce, accusing her of being stingy and a workaholic. The employees in Denise's department had low morale; she saw them as lazy and stupid so she did all their work. Her boss accused her of being "Miss Rules and Regulations" with "Rigidity" as her middle name. These qualities support the diagnosis for obsessive-compulsive disorder.

The competency-based assessment highlights the reality that Denise's life does not take place in a vacuum. Although she did not seek out help on her own, as is typical of someone with a personality disorder, Denise did follow up on her mother's suggestion to see a practitioner. She is certainly articulate about what has been going on in her life and she appears to be intelligent. Denise has a college degree in what could be considered a highly employable field so she is optimistic about her opportunities to return to work. For the past five years, she has worked steadily in a supervisory position. Though divorcing and soon to be out of work, her family is supportive; in particular, Denise can live at home with her mother.

References

Abraham, S., & Llewellyn-Jones, D. (2001). *Eating disorders: The facts*. New York, NY: Oxford University Press.

Abramowitz, J. S., & Braddock, A. E. (2006). Hypochondriasis conceptualization: Treatment and relationship to obsessive-compulsive disorder. *Psychiatric Clinics of North America, 29*(2), 503–519.

Akagi, H., & House, A. O. (2001). The epidemiology of hysterical conversion. In P. Halligan, C. Bass, & J. Marshall (Eds.), *Hysterical conversion: Clinical and theoretical perspectives* (pp. 73–87). Oxford, England: Oxford University Press.

Allison, S., Stacey, K., Dadds, V., Roeger, L., Wood, A., & Martin, G. (2003). What the family brings: Gathering evidence for strengths-based work. *Journal of Family Therapy, 25*(3), 263–284.

American Psychiatric Association. (1980). *Diagnostic and statistical manual of mental disorders* (3rd ed.). Washington, DC: Author.

American Psychiatric Association. (1987). *Diagnostic and statistical manual of mental disorders* (3rd ed., text rev.). Washington, DC: Author.

American Psychiatric Association. (1994). *Diagnostic and statistical manual of mental disorders* (4th ed.). Washington, DC: Author.

American Psychiatric Association. (2000). *Diagnostic and statistical manual of mental disorders* (4th ed., text rev.). Washington DC: Author.

American Psychiatric Association. (2003, September 9). *American Psychiatric Association statement on diagnosis and treatment of mental disorders*. Retrieved on June 1, 2009, from http://www.psych.org/MainMenu/Newsroom/NewsReleases/2003NewsReleases/mentaldisorders0339.aspx

American Psychiatric Association. (2006, May 22). *American Psychiatric Association statement barring psychiatric participation in interrogation of detainees*. Retrieved on June 1, 2009, from http://www.psych.org/MainMenu/Newsroom/NewsReleases/2006NewsReleases/06–36positionstatementoninterrogation.aspx

American Psychiatric Association Work Group on Eating Disorders. (2000). Practice guideline for the treatment of patients with eating disorders (revision). *American Journal of Psychiatry,157*(1 Suppl), 1–39.

Andreasen, N. C., & Black, D. W. (2006). *Introductory textbook of psychiatry* (2nd ed.). Washington, DC: American Psychiatric Association.

Andrews, G., & Slade, T. (2002). Agoraphobia with a history of panic disorder may be a part of the panic disorder syndrome. *Journal of Nervous and Mental Disease, 190*(9), 624–630.

Anstine, D., & Grinenko, D. (2000). Rapid screening for disordered eating in college-aged females in the primary care setting. *Journal of Adolescent Health, 26*(5), 338–342.

Antony, M. M., & Barlow, D. H. (Eds.). (2002). *Handbook of assessment and treatment planning for psychological disorders* (2nd ed.). New York, NY: Guilford Press.

Ashford, J. B., LeCroy, C. W., & Lortie, K. L. (2005). *Human behavior in the social environment: A multidimensional perspective* (3rd. ed.). Pacific Grove, CA: Brooks/Cole.

Austrian, S. (2005). *Mental disorders, medications, and clinical social work* (3rd ed.). New York, NY: Columbia University Press.

Bachner-Melman, R. (2003). Anorexia nervosa from a family perspective: Why did nobody notice? *American Journal of Family Therapy, 31*(1), 39–50.

Bagheri, M. M., Kerbeshian, J., & Burd, L. (1999). Recognition and management of Tourette's syndrome and tic disorders. *American Family Physician, 59*(8), 2263–2272.

Bagley, C. A., Character, C. D., & Shelton, L. (2003). Eating disorders among urban and rural African American and European women. *Women and Therapy, 26*, 1–2, 57–79.

Bair, M. J., Robinson, R. L., Katon, W., & Kroenke, K. (2003). Depression and pain comorbidity: A literature review. *Archives of Internal Medicine, 163*, 2433–2445.

Baker, B. L., McIntyre, L. L., Blacher, J., Crnic, K., Edelbrock C., & Low, C. (2003). Pre-school children with and without developmental delay: Behaviour problems and parenting stress over time. *Journal of Intellectual Disability, 47*(4/5), 217–230.

Barker, R. L. (1996). *The social work dictionary* (3rd ed.). Washington, DC: NASW Press.

Barker, R. L. (2003). *The social work dictionary* (5th ed.). Washington, DC: National Association of Social Workers.

Barkley, R. A. (1998). *Attention deficit hyperactivity disorder: A handbook for diagnosis and treatment* (2nd ed.). New York: Guilford.

Barkley, R. A., & Benton, C. (1998). *Your defiant child.* New York, NY: Guilford Press.

Barlow, D. H. (2004). *Anxiety and its disorders: The nature and treatment of anxiety and panic.* New York: Guilford.

Barlow, D. H., & Durand, V. M. (2005). *Abnormal psychology: An integrative approach* (4th ed.). Belmont, CA: Thomson Wadsworth.

Barlow, D. H., & Durand, V. M. (2008). *Abnormal psychology: An integrative approach* (5th ed.). Belmont, CA: Wadsworth Cengage Learning.

Baron-Cohen, S. (2000). Is Asperger syndrome/high functioning autism necessarily a disability? *Development and Psychopathology, 12*, 489–500.

Barrett, S. P., Darredeau, C., & Phil, R. O. (2006). Patterns of simultaneous polysubstance use in drug-using university students. *Human Psychopharmacology: Clinical and Experimental, 21*(4), 255–263.

Becker, D. F., Grilo, C. M., Edell, W. S., & McGlashan, T. H. (2000). Comorbidity of borderline personality disorder with other personality disorders in hospitalized adolescents and adults. *American Journal of Psychiatry, 157*(12), 2011–2016.

Beers, C. (1980). *A mind that found itself: An autobiography.* Pittsburgh, PA: University of Pittsburgh Press.

Behrend, H., & Luig, U. (2000). *Spirit possession, modernity and power in Africa.* Madison, WI: University of Wisconsin Press.

Bell, H. (2003). Strengths and secondary trauma in family violence work. *Social Work, 48*(4), 513–522.

Bellamy, R. (1997, March). Compensation neurosis: Financial reward for illness. *Clinical Orthopaedics and Related Research,* (336), 94–106.

Bentall, R. (2006). Madness explained: Why we must reject the Krapelenian paradigm and replace it with a "complaint-oriented" approach to understanding mental disorders. *Medical Hypotheses, 66*(2), 220–233.

Bentley, K. J. (2002). *Social work practice in mental health: Contemporary roles, tasks, and techniques.* Pacific Grove, CA: Brooks/Cole.

Berkman, N. D., Lohr, K. N., & Bulik, C. M. (2007). Outcomes of eating disorders: A systematic review of the literature. *International Journal of Eating Disorders, 40*(4), 293–309.

Bernard, G. R., & Dittus, R. S. (2004). Delirium as a predictor of mortality in mechanically ventilated patients in the intensive care unit. *Journal of the American Medical Association, 291,* 1753–1762.

Bertalanffy, L. (1962). General systems theory: A critical review. *General Systems Yearbook, 7,* 1–20.

Bhugra, D. (2006). The global prevalence of schizophrenia. *Public Library of Science Medicine, 2*(5), 372–373.

Bloom, B. S. (1956). *Taxonomy of educational objectives: the classification of educational goals: Handbook I, cognitive domain.* New York, NY: Longmans.

Bockoven, J. S. (1963). *Moral treatment in American psychiatry.* New York, NY: Springer.

Boland, R. J., & Keller, M. B. (2002). Course and outcome of depression. In I. H. Gotlib & C. L. Hammen (Eds.), *Handbook of depression* (pp. 43–60). New York, NY: Guilford Press.

Borkovec, T. D., Alcaine, O., & Behar, E. S. (2004). Avoidance theory of worry and generalized anxiety disorder. In R. Heimberg, D. Mennin, & C. Turk (Eds.), *The nature and treatment of generalized anxiety disorder* (pp. 77–108). New York, NY: Guilford Press.

Bornstein, R. F. (2007). The complex relationship between dependency and domestic violence: Converging psychological factors and social forces. *American Psychologist, 61*(6), 595–606.

Bourne, E. (2005). *The anxiety and phobia workbook* (4th ed.). Oakland, CA: New Harbinger Press.

Bowlby, J. (1982). *Attachment and loss: Vol. 1. attachment* (2nd ed.). New York, NY: Basic.

Brandt, J., & Van Gorp, W. G. (2006). Functional ("psychogenic") amnesia. *Seminars in Neurology, 26*(3), 331–340.

Brookmeyer, R., Johnson, E., Ziegler-Graham, K., & Arrighi, M. H. (2007). Forecasting the global burden of Alzheimer's disease. *Alzheimer's and Dementia, 3*(3), 186–191.

Brown, T. A., Campbell, L. A., Lehman, C. L., Grisham, J. R., & Mancill, R. B. (2001). Current and lifetime comorbidity of the DSM-IV anxiety and mood disorders in a large clinical sample. *Journal of Abnormal Psychology, 110,* 585–599.

Brubaker, D. A., & Leddy, J. (2003). Behavioral contracting motivates athletes with eating disorders. *The Physician and Sportsmedicine, 31*(9), 15–18, 26.

Brun, C., & Rapp, R. C. (2001). Strengths-based case management: Individuals' perspectives on strengths and the case manager relationship. *Social Work, 46*(3), 278–288.

Bruun, R. D., & Budman, C. L. (2005). The natural history of gilles de la Tourette's syndrome. In R. Kurlan (Ed.), *Handbook of Tourette's syndrome and related tic and behavioral disorders,* (2nd ed., pp. 23–38). New York, NY: Marcel Dekker.

Bryant, R. A. (2000). Acute stress disorder. *PTSD Research Quarterly, 11,* 1–7.

Bryant, R. A., & Harvey, A. G. (2000). *Acute stress disorder: A handbook of theory, assessment and treatment.* Washington, DC: American Psychological Association.

Buckley, W. F. (1968, March). Sociology and modern systems theory. *Social Forces, 46*(3), 410–411.

Bulik, C. M., Reba, L., Siega-Riz, A. M., & Reichborn-Kjennerud, T. (2005). Anorexia nervosa: Definition, epidemiology, and cycle of risk. *International Journal of Eating Disorders, 37 Suppl,* S2–9.

Bulik, C. M., Sullivan, P. F., & Kendler, S. K. (2000). An empirical study of classification of eating disorders. *American Journal of Psychiatry, 157*(6), 886–895.

Canapary, D., Bongar, B., & Cleary, K. M. (2002). Assessing risk for completed suicide in patients with alcohol dependence: Clinicians' views of critical factors. *Professional Psychology Research and Practice, 33*(5), 464–469.

Canino, I., & Spurlock, J. (2000). *Culturally diverse children and adolescents.* New York, NY: Guilford Press.

Carey, B., & Harris, G. (2008, July 12). Psychiatric group faces scrutiny over drug industry ties. *New York Times.* Retrieved on June 1, 2009, from http://www.the-dispatch.com/article/20080712/ZNYT04/807120336

Carter, C. S., Ahnert, L., Grossmann, K. E., Hrdy, S. B., Lamb, M. E., Porges, S. W., & Sachser, N. (2005). *Attachment and bonding: A new synthesis.* Cambridge, MA: MIT Press.

Carter, J. C., Blackmore, E., Sutandar-Pinnock, D., & Woodside, D. B. (2004). Relapse in anorexia nervosa: A survival analysis. *Psychological Medicine, 34,* 671–679.

Cass, L. K., & Thomas, C. B. (1979). *Child psychopathology and later adjustment.* New York, NY: Wiley.

Castillo, R. J. (1997). *Culture and mental illness: A client-centered approach.* Pacific Grove, CA: Thomson Brooks/Cole.

Centers for Disease Control and Prevention. (2010). *How many children have autism?* Retrieved on May 3, 2010, from http://www.cdc.gov/ncbddd/features/counting-autism.html

Chapin, R., & Cox, E. O. (2001). Changing the paradigm: Strengths-based and empowerment-oriented social work with frail elders. *Journal of Gerontological Social Work, 36,* 165–179.

Christen, H. J., & Hanefeld, F. (1995). Male Rett variant. *Neuropediatrics, 26,* 81–82.

Chronicle of Higher Education. (2008, August 1). Stanford researcher, accused of conflicts, steps down as NIH principal investigator. Retrieved on June 1, 2009, from http://chronicle.com/news/article/?id=4922

Clark, A. J. (2001). Early recollections. A humanistic assessment in counseling. *Journal of Humanistic Counseling, Education and Development, 40*(1), 96–105.

Cohen, A. S., & Doherty, N. M. (2004). Affective reactivity of speech and emotional experience in patients with schizophrenia. *Schizophrenia Research, 69*(1), 7–14.

Cohen, J. A. (2003). Managed care and the evolving role of the clinical social worker in mental health. *Social Work, 48*, 34–43.

Collier, J., Longmore, M., Turmezi, T., & Mafi, A. R. (Eds.). (2009). *Oxford handbook of clinical specialties* (9th ed.). Oxford, England: Oxford University Press.

Compton, B. R., & Galaway, B. (1999). *Social work processes* (6th ed.). Pacific Grove, CA: Brooks/Cole Thomson Learning Wadsworth.

Compton, W. M., & Guze, S. G. (1995). The neo-Kraepelinian revolution in psychiatric diagnosis. *Journal of European Archives of Psychiatry and Clinical Neuroscience, 245*(4/5), 196–201.

Corcoran, J., & Walsh, J. (2006). *Clinical assessment and diagnosis in social work practice*. New York, NY: Oxford University Press.

Council on Social Work Education. (2008). *Educational policy and accreditation standards*. Alexandria, VA: Author.

Cox, E. O., & Parsons, R. J. (2000). Empowerment oriented practice: From practice value to practice model. In P. Allen-Meares & C. Garvin (Eds.), *The handbook of social work direct practice* (pp. 113–130). Thousand Oaks, CA: Sage.

Crimlisk, G, L., Bahatia, K. P., Cope, H., David, A. S., Marsden, D., & Ron, M. A. (2000). Patterns of referral in patients with medically unexplained motor symptoms. *Journal of Psychosomatic Research, 49*(3), 217–219.

Croll, J., Neumark-Sztainer, D., Story, M., & Ireland, M. (2003). Prevalence and risk and protective factors related to disordered eating behaviors among adolescents: Relationship to gender and ethnicity. *Journal of Adolescent Health, 31*(2), 166–175.

Dancyger, I. F., & Fornari, V. M. (2009). *Evidence-based treatments for eating disorders: Children, adolescents, and adults*. New York: Nova Kroshka.

de Girolamo, G., & Dotto, P. (2000). Epidemiology of personality disorders. In M. G. Gelder, J. J. Lopez-Ibor, & N. C. Andreasen (Eds.), *New Oxford textbook of psychiatry* (pp. 959–964). New York, NY: Oxford University Press.

deJong, P., & Berg, I. K. (2002). *Interviewing for solutions* (2nd ed.). Pacific Grove, CA: Thomson Brooks/Cole.

de Waal, M. W., Amold, I. A., Eekhof, J. A., & van Hemert, A. M. (2004). Somatoform disorders in general practice: Prevalence, functional impairment and comorbidity with anxiety and depressive disorders. *British Journal of Psychiatry, 184*, 465–467.

De Zwaan, M. (2001). Binge eating disorder and obesity. *International Journal of Obesity, 25*, 851–855.

Dennis, P. A. (1985). Grisi siknis in Miskito culture. In R. C. Simons & C. C. Hughes (Eds.), *The culture-bound syndromes: Folk illnesses of psychiatric and anthropological interest* (pp. 289–306). Dordrecht, Holland: D. Reidel.

Diamond, B. L. (1980). Inherent problems in the use of pretrial hypnosis on a prospective witness. *California Law Review, 68*, 313–349.

Diamond, B. L. (1969, September). Interview regarding Sirhan Sirhan. *Psychology Today*, 48–55.

Didie, E. R., Tortolani, C. C., Pope, C. G., Menard, W., Fay, C., & Phillips, K. A. (2006). Childhood abuse and neglect in body dysmorphic disorder. *Child Abuse and Neglect, 30*, 1105–1115.

Dobbert, D. L. (2007). *Understanding personality disorders: An introduction.* Santa Barbara, CA: Greenwood Press.

Dohrenwend, B. P., Turner, J. B., Turse, N. A., Adams, B. B., Koen, K. C., & Marshall, R. (2006). The psychological risk of Vietnam for U.S. veterans: A revisit with new data and methods. *Science, 313*(5789), 979–982.

Dominick, K. C., Davis, N. O., Lainhart, J., Tager-Flushberg, H., & Folstein, S. (2007). Atypical behaviors in children with autism and children with a history of language impairment. *Research in Developmental Disabilities, 28*(2), 145–162.

Doweiko, H. E. (2006). *Concepts of chemical dependency* (6th ed.). Belmont, CA: Thomson Brooks/Cole.

Dubos, R. (1968). *So human an animal.* New York, NY: Scribner.

Dziegielewski, S. F. (1998). *The changing face of health care social work: Professional practice in the era of managed care.* New York: Springer.

Dziegielewski, S. F. (2002). *DSM-IV-TR in action.* Hoboken, NJ: Wiley.

Early, T. J., & GlenMaye, L. F. (2000). Valuing families: Social work practice with families from a strengths perspective. *Social Work, 45*(2), 118–130.

Edwards, H., Harris, M. G., & Bapat, S. (2005). Developing services for first-episode psychosis and the critical period. *British Journal of Psychiatry Suppl. Aug 48,* S91–97.

Ekselius, L., Tillfors, M., Furmark, T., & Fredrikson, M. (2001). Personality disorders in the general population: DSM-IV and ICD-10 defined prevalence as related to sociodemographic profile. *Personality and Individual Differences, 30,* 311–320.

Eliot, A. O., & Baker, C. W. (2001). Eating disordered adolescent males. *Adolescence, 36*(143), 535–543.

Ely, E. W., Inouye, S. K., Bernard, G. R., Gordon, S., Francis, J., May, L., Truman, B., . . . Dittus R. (2001). Delirium in mechanically ventilated patients: Validity and reliability of the confusion assessment method for the intensive care unit (CAM-ICU). *Journal of the American Medical Association,* (286), 2703–2710.

Ely, E. W., Shintani, A., Truman, B., Speroff, T., Gordon, S. M., Harrell, F. E. Jr., Inouye, S., . . . Dittus, R. S. (2004). Delirium as a predictor of mortality in mechanically ventilated patients in the intensive care unit. *Journal of the American Medical Association, 291,* 1753–1762.

Emonson, D. L., & Vanderbeek, R. D. (1995). The use of amphetamines in the U.S. Air Force tactical operations during Desert Storm. *Aviation, Space, and Environmental Medicine, 66*(3), 260–263.

Engel, G. L. (1977). The need for a new medical model. *Science, 196,* 129–136.

Erk, R. R. (2008). Attention-deficit/hyperactivity disorder in children and adolescents. In R. R. Erk, *Counseling treatment for children and adolescents with DSM-IV-TR disorders* (pp, 114–162). Upper Saddle River, NJ: Merrill.

Evidente, V. G. (2000). Is it a tic or Tourette's? Clues for differentiating simple from more complex tic disorders. *Postgraduate Medicine, 1908* (5). Retrieved on May 1, 2010, from http://web.archive.org/web/20080731231002/http://www.postgradmed.com/issues/2000/10_00/evidente_tic.shtml

Fahn, S. (2005). Motor and vocal tics. In R. Kurlan (Ed.), *Handbook of Tourette's syndrome and related tic and behavioral disorders,* (2nd ed., pp. 1–14). New York, NY: Marcel Dekker.

Fairburn, C. G., & Brownell, K. D. (2002). *Eating disorders and obesity: A comprehensive handbook.* New York, NY: Guilford Press.

Fairburn, C. G., Stice, E., Cooper, Z., Doll, H. A., Norman, P. A., & O'Connor, M. E. (2003). Understanding persistence in bulimia nervosa: A 5-year naturalistic study. *Journal of Counseling and Clinical Psychology, 71,* 103–109.

Falk, D. D., & Hilton, M. E. (2008). Age of onset and temporal sequencing of lifetime DSM-IV alcohol use disorders relative to comorbid mood and anxiety disorders. *Drug and Alcohol Dependence, 94*(1–3), 234–245.

Fallon, B. A., Qureshi, A. I., Laje, G., & Klein, B. (2000). Hypochondriasis and its relationship to obsessive-compulsive disorder. *Psychiatric Clinics of North America, 23,* 605–616.

Fann, J. R. (2000). The epidemiology of delirium: A review of studies and methodological issues. *Seminars in Clinical Neuropsychiatry, 5,* 64–74.

Fava, M., Alpert, J. E., Carmin, C. N., Wisniewski, S. R., Trivedi, M. H., Biggs, M. M., . . . Rush, A. J. (2004). Clinical correlates and symptom patterns of anxious depression among patients with major depressive disorder in STAR*D. *Psychological Medicine, 34,* 1299–1308.

Feldman, M. D. (2004). *Playing sick? Untangling the web of Munchausen syndrome, Munchausen by proxy, malingering and factitious disorder.* New York, NY: Brunner-Routledge.

Fergusson, D. M., Boden, J. M., & Horwood, L. J. (2009). Tests of causal links between alcohol abuse or dependence and major depression. *Archives of General Psychiatry, 66*(3), 260–266.

Ferrari, S., Galeazzi, G. M., Mackinnon, A., & Riquelli, M. (2008). Frequent attenders in primary care: Impact of medical, psychiatric and psychosomatic disorders. *Psychotherapy and Psychosomatics, 77*(5), 306–314.

Fick, D., & Foreman, M. (2000). Consequences of not recognizing delirium superimposed on dementia in hospitalized elderly individuals. *Journal of Gerontological Nursing, 26*(1), 30–40.

Fink, P., Hansen, M. S., & Oxho, M. (2004). The prevalence of somatoform disorders among medical inpatients. *Journal of Psychosomatic Research, 56*(4), 413–418.

First, M. B., Frances, A., Ross, R., Widiger, F. A., Pincus, H. A., & Davis, W. W. (Eds.). (1997). *DSM-IV sourcebook,* Vol. 3. Washington, DC: American Psychiatric Association.

Fombonne, E. (2002). Prevalence of childhood disintegrative disorder. *Autism, 6*(2), 140–157.

Fombonne, E., & Tidmarsh, C. (2003). Epidemiologic data on Asperger disorder. *Children and Adolescent Psychiatric Clinics of North America, 12*(1), 15–21.

Foote, B., Smolin, Y., Kaplan, M., Legatt, M. E., & Lipschiz, D. (2006). Prevalence of dissociative disorders in psychiatric outpatients. *American Journal of Psychiatry, 163*(4), 623–629.

Forstl, H., & Kurz, A. (1999). Clinical features of Alzheimer's disease. *European Archives of Psychiatry and Clinical Neuroscience, 24* 9(6), 288–290.

Frances, A., First, M. B., & Pincus, H. A. (1995). *DSM–IV guidebook.* Washington, DC: American Psychiatric Press.

Frances, A., Mack, A. H., Ross, R., & First, M. B. (2000). The DSM-IV classification and psychopharmacology. Retrieved on June 2, 2009, from http://www.acnp.org/publications/psycho4generation.aspx

Franco, D. L., Wonderlich, S. A., Little, D., & Herzog, D. B. (2004). Diagnosis and classification of eating disorders. In J. K. Thompson (Ed.), *Handbook of eating disorders and obesity* (pp. 58–80). Hoboken, NJ: Wiley.

Fraser, M. W. (1997). *Risk and resilience in childhood*. Washington, DC: NASW Press.

Freitag, C. M. (2007). The genetics of autistic disorders and its clinical relevance: A review of the literature. *Molecular Psychiatry, 12*(1), 2–22.

Gabbard, G. O. (2001). *Treatments of psychiatric disorders* (3rd ed.). Washington, DC: American Psychiatric Press.

Gahlinger, P. M. (2004). Club drugs: MDMA, gamma-hydroxybutyrate (GHB), rohypnol, and ketamine. *American Family Physician, 69,* 2919–2927.

Gardner, F. (2001). Social work students and self-awareness: How does it happen? *Reflective Practice, 2*(1), 27–40.

Garmezy, N. (1993). Children in poverty: Resilience despite risk. *Psychiatry, 56,* 127–136.

Germain, C. B. (1973). An ecological perspective in casework. *Social Casework, 54*(6), 323–330.

Germain, C. B. (1991). *Human behavior in the social environment: An ecological view*. New York, NY: Columbia University Press.

Germain, C. B. (1994). Using an ecological perspective. In J. Rothman (Ed.). *Practice with highly vulnerable clients: Case management and community based service*, (pp. 39–55). Englewood Cliffs, NJ: Prentice Hall.

Geschwind, D. H. (2009). Advances in autism. *Annual Review of Medicine, 60,* 367–380.

Gitterman, A., & Germain, C. B. (2008). Ecological framework. In T. Mizrahi & L. E. Davis (Eds.), *Encyclopedia of Social work* (e-reference ed.). Washington, DC: NASW Press and New York: Oxford University Press. Retrieved on June 18, 2009, from http://www.oxford-naswsocialwork.com.ezproxy.barry.edu/.

Gitterman, A. (Ed.) (2001). *Handbook of social work practice with vulnerable and resilient populations* (2nd ed.). New York, NY: Columbia University Press.

Gleason, O. C. (2003). Delirium. *American Family Physician, 67,* 1027–1034.

Gleaves, D. H., Lowe, M. R., Snow, A. C., Green, B. A., & Murphy-Eberenz, K. P. (2000). Continuity and discontinuity models of bulimia nervosa: A taxometric investigation. *Journal of Abnormal Psychology, 109*(1), 56–68.

Goldner, E. M., Hsu, L., Waraich, P., & Somers, J. M. (2002). Prevalence and incidence studies of schizophrenic disorders: A systematic review of the literature. *Canadian Journal of Psychiatry, 47*(9), 833–843.

Goodwin, R. D., Jacobi, F., & Thefeld, W. (2003). Mental disorders and asthma in the community. *Archives of General Psychiatry, 60,* 1125–1130.

Gossop, M., Marsden, J., & Stewart, D. (2002). Dual dependence: Assessment of dependence upon alcohol and illicit drugs, and the relationship of alcohol dependence among drug misusers to patterns of drinking, illicit drug use, and health problems. *Addiction, 97*(2), 169–178.

Granner, M. L., Abood, D. A., & Black, D. R. (2001). Racial differences in eating disorder attitudes, cigarette and alcohol use. *American Journal of Health Behavior, 25*(2), 83–99.

Grant, B. F., Hasin, D. S., Chou, S. P., Stinson, F. S., & Cawson, D. A. (2004). Nicotine dependence and psychiatric disorders in the United States: Results from the national epidemiology survey on alcohol and related conditions. *Archives of General Psychiatry, 61*, 1107–1115.

Grant, B. F., Hasin, D. S., Stinson, F. S., Dawson, D. A., Chou, S. P., Ruan, J. W., & Huang, B. (2005). Co-occurrence of 12-month mood and anxiety disorders and personality disorders in the U. S.: Results from the national survey on alcohol and related conditions. *Journal of Psychiatric Research, 39*, 1–9.

Gray, S. W., with Zide, M. R. (2006). *Psychopathology: A competency-based treatment model for social workers.* Belmont, CA: Thomson Brooks/Cole.

Gray, S. W., with Zide, M. R. (2008). *Psychopathology: A competency-based assessment model for social workers* (2nd ed.). Belmont, CA: Thomson Brooks/Cole.

Greenberg, D. K. (2002, June). The relationship between shame, guilt, and body image dissatisfaction to disordered eating symptomatology in female undergraduates. *Dissertation Abstracts International, A: The Humanities and Social Sciences, 62*, 4332-A.

Greene, R. R. (2002). *Resiliency: An integrated approach to practice, policy and research.* Washington, DC: NASW Press.

Greene, R. R. (2007). *Social work practice: A risk and resilience perspective.* Belmont, CA: Thomson Brooks/Cole.

Greenfield, S. F., & Hennessey, C. (2004). Assessment of the patient. In M. Galanter & H. G. Kleber (Eds.), *Textbook of substance abuse treatment* (3rd ed.). Washington, DC: American Psychiatric Press.

Greisinger, W. (1882). *Mental pathology and therapeutics.* New York: William Wood.

Griffiths, R. R., Juliano, I. M., & Chausmer, A. L. (2003). Caffeine pharmacology and clinical effects. In A. W. Graham, T. K. Schultz, M. F. Mayo-Smith, R. K. Ries, & B. B. Wilford (Eds.), *Principles of addiction medicine* (3rd ed., pp. 193–224). Chevy Chase, MD: American Society of Addiction.

Grob, G. N. (1991). Origins of DSM-I: A study in appearance and reality. *American Journal of Psychiatry, 48*(4), 421–431.

Grossman, R. (2008, December 27). Psychiatric manual's update needs openness, not secrecy, critics say. *Chicago Tribune.* Retrieved on March 20, 2009, from http://archives.chicagotribune.com/2008/dec/27/health/chi-dsm-controversy-26-dec27

Gullo, S. (2004). *The thin commandments: The 10 no-fail strategies for permanent weight loss.* New York, NY: HarperCollins.

Gussow, Z. (1985). Pibloktog (hysteria) among the Polar Eskimo: An ethnopsychiatric study. In R. C. Simons & C. C. Hughes (Eds.), *The culture-bound syndromes: Folk illnesses of psychiatric and anthropological interest* (pp. 271–287). Dordrecht, Holland: D. Reidel.

Gutheil, I. A., & Congress, E. (2000). Resiliency in older people: A paradigm for practice. In R. R. Green (Ed.), *Resiliency: An integrated approach to practice, policy, and research* (pp. 40–52). Washington, DC: NASW Press.

Gutierrez, L. (2001). Working with women of color: An empowerment perspective. In J. Rothman, J. L. Erlich, & J. E. Tropman (Eds.), *Strategies of community intervention* (6th ed., pp. 209–217). Itasca, IL: Peacock.

Hall, H. R., & Pritchard, D. A. (2000). *Detecting malingering and deception: Forensic distortion analysis* (2nd ed.). Sanford, FL: DC Press.

Hardy-Bale, M. C., Sarfati, Y., & Passerieux, C. (2003). The cognitive basis of disorganization symptomatology in schizophrenia and its clinical correlate toward a pathogenic approach to disorganization. *Schizophrenia Bulletin, 29,* 459–471.

Harris, S. L. (2000). Pervasive developmental disorders. The spectrum of autism. In M. Hersen & R. T. Ammerman (Eds.), *Advanced abnormal child psychology* (2nd ed., pp. 357–370). Mahwah, NJ: Erlbaum.

Harvard Medical School. (2004). An update on attention deficit disorder. *Harvard Mental Health Letter, 20*(11), 4–7.

Harvey, A. G., & Bryant, R. A. (2002). Acute stress disorder across trauma populations. *Journal of Nervous and Mental Disease, 187,* 443–446.

Hassett, A., Ames, D., & Chiu, E. (Eds.). (2005). *Psychosis in the elderly.* London: Taylor & Francis.

Hausman, K. (2003). Controversy continues to grow over DSM's GID diagnosis. *Psychiatric News, 38*(4), 25.

He, W., Sengupta, M., Welkoff, V. A., & DeBarros. K. A. (2005). *65+ in the United States: 2005. U.S. Census Bureau Current Population Reports.* Washington, DC: U.S. Government Printing Office, 23–209.

Hearn, G. (1979). General systems theory and social work. In F. J. Turner (Ed.), *Social work treatment: Interlocking theoretical approaches* (2nd ed.). New York: Free Press.

Henderson, E., May, C., & Chew-Graham, C. A. (2003). Binge eating disorder: General practitioners' constructs of an ambiguous pathology. *Primary Health Care and Research and Development, 4,* 301–306.

Herbert, L. E., Scherr, P. A., Bienias, J. L., Bennett, D. A., & Evans, D. A. (2003). Alzheimer disease in the U.S. population: Prevalence estimates using the 2000 census. *Archives of Neurology, 60*(8), 1119–1122.

Hersen, M., & Thomas, J. C. (Eds.). (2006). *Comprehensive handbook of personality and Psychopathology.* Hoboken, NJ: Wiley.

Herzog, D. B., Greenwood, D. N., Dorer, D. J., Flores, A. T., Ekeblad, E. R., Richards, A., Blais, M. A., & Keller, M. (2000). Mortality in eating disorders: A descriptive study. *International Journal of Eating Disorders, 28*(1), 20–26.

Hettema, J. M., Prescott, C. A., & Kendler, K. S. (2003). The effects of anxiety, substance use and conduct disorders on the risk of major depressive disorder. *Psychological Medicine, 33,* 1423–1432.

Ho, B. C., Black, D. W., & Andreasen, N. C. (2003). Schizophrenia and other psychotic disorders. In R. E. Hales & S. C. Yudofsky (Eds.). *Textbook of clinical psychiatry* (4th ed., pp. 379–438). Washington, DC: American Psychiatric Press.

Hodges, B. (2004). Medical student bodies and the pedagogy of self-reflection, self-assessment, and self-regulation. *Journal of Curriculum Theorizing, 20*(2), 41–51.

Hoek, H. W. (2006). Incidence, prevalence and mortality rates of anorexia nervosa and other eating disorders. *Current Opinion in Psychiatry, 19*(14), 389–394.

Hoffman, L., & Rose, L. (2005). *Costly calories*. Retrieved on April 23, 2009, from http://www.forbes.com/health/2005/03/30/cx_dietland.html

Hollifield, M. A. (2005). Somatoform disorder. In B. J. Sadock & V. A. Sadock (Eds.), *Comprehensive textbook of psychiatry* (8th ed., pp. 1810–1828). Philadelphia, PA: Lippincott Williams and Wilkins.

Honos-Webb, L., & Lietner, L. M. (2001). How using the *DSM* causes damage: A client's report. *Journal of Humanistic Psychology, 41*(4), 36–56.

Hughes, J. R. (2004). Nicotine-related disorders. In B. J. Sadock & V. A. Sadock (Eds.), *Comprehensive textbook of psychiatry* (8th ed., pp. 1033–1037). Philadelphia, PA: Lippincott Williams and Wilkins.

Huppert, J. D., Moser, J. S., Gurshuny, B. S., Riggs, D. S., Spokas, M., Filip, J., . . . Foa, E. B. (2005). The relationship between obsessive-compulsive and posttraumatic stress symptoms in clinical and non-clinical samples. *Journal of Anxiety Disorders, 19*(1), 127–136.

Hyman, B. M., & Pedrick, C. (2005). *The OCD workbook: Your guide to breaking free from obsessive-compulsive disorder* (2nd ed.). Oakland, CA: New Harbinger.

Janssen, I., Krabbendam, L., Bak, M., Hanssen, M., Vollenbergh, W., de Graaf, R., & van Os, J. (2004). Childhood abuse as a risk factor for psychotic experiences. *Acta Psychiatrica Scandinavica, 109*(1), 38–45.

Jefferys, D. (2008). Pathological hoarding. *Australian Family Physician, 37*(4), 237–241.

Johnson, J. G., Cohen, P., Smailes, E., Kasen, S., Oldham, M. J., & Skodol, A. E. (2000). Adolescent personality disorders associated with violence and criminal behavior during adolescence and early adulthood. *American Journal of Psychiatry, 157*, 1406–1412.

Jordan, C., & Franklin, C. (2003). *Clinical assessment for social workers: Quantitative and qualitative methods* (2nd ed.). Chicago, IL: Lyceum.

Judd, L. L., Akiskal, H. S., Schettler, P. J., Endicott, J., Maser, J., Solomon, D. A., ... Keller, M. B. (2002). The long term natural history of the weekly symptomatic status of bipolar I disorder. *Archives of General Psychiatry, 59*(6), 530–537.

Juliano, I. M., & Griffiths, R. R. (2004). A critical review of caffeine withdrawal: Empirical validation of symptoms and signs, incidence, severity, and associated features. *Psychopharmacology, 176*(1), 1–29.

Kantor, M. (2004). *Understanding paranoia: A guide for professionals, families, and sufferers*. Santa Barbara, CA: Greenwood Press.

Katz, S. E. (1985). Psychiatric hospitalization. In H. L. Kaplan & B. J. Sadock (Eds.), *Comprehensive textbook of psychiatry/IV* (pp. 1576–1582). Baltimore, MD: Williams and Wilkins.

Kazdin, A. E. (2000). *Psychotherapy for children and adolescents: Directions for research and practice*. New York, NY: Oxford University Press.

Keel, P. K., Mitchell, J. E., Miller, K. B., Davis, T. L., & Crow, S. J. (2000). Predictive validity of bulimia nervosa as a diagnostic strategy. *American Journal of Psychiatry, 157*(1), 136–138.

Kempa, M. L., & Thomas, A. J. (2000). Culturally sensitive assessment and treatment of eating disorders. *Eating Disorders: The Journal of Treatment and Prevention,* 8(1), 17–30.

Kendler, K. S. (2001). Twin studies of psychiatric illness: An update. *Archives of General Psychiatry, 58,* 1005–1014.

Kennedy, S. H., Lam, R. W., Nutt, D. J., & Thase, M. E. (2004). *Treating depression effectively: Applying clinical guidelines.* London, England: Martin Dunitz.

Keown, P., Holloway, F., & Kuipers, E. (2002). The prevalence of personality disorders, psychotic disorders and affective disorders amongst patients seen by a community mental health team in London. *Social Psychiatry and Psychiatric Epidemiology, 37,* 225–229.

Kesaree, N. (2003). Tic disorders. In G. P. Mathur & S. Mathur (Eds.), *Movement disorders in children and adolescents,* (pp. 69–74). New Dehli, India: Jypee.

Kessler, R. C. (2002). Epidemiology of depression. In I. H. Gotlib & C. L. Hammen (Eds.), *Handbook of depression* (pp. 23–42). New York, NY: Guilford Press.

Kessler, R. C., Berglund, P. A., Demler, O., Jin, R., & Walters, E. E. (2005). Lifetime prevalence and age-of-onset distributions of DSM-IV disorders in the National Comorbidity Survey Replication (NCS-R). *Archives of General Psychiatry, 62*(6), 593–602.

Kessler, R. C., Berglund, P., Demler, O., Jin, R., Koretz, D., Merikangas, K. R., . . . Wang, P. S. (2003). The epidemiology of major depressive disorder: Results from the National Comorbidity Survey Replication (NCS-R). *Journal of the American Medical Association,* 89(23), 3095–105.

Kessler R. C., Chiu, W. T., Demler, O., & Walters, E. E. (2005). Prevalence, severity, and comorbidity of twelve-month DSM-IV disorders in the National Comorbidity Survey Replication (NCS-R). *Archives of General Psychiatry, 62*(6), 617–627.

Kessler, R. C., & Usten. T. B. (Eds). (2009). *The World Health Organization mental health surveys: Global perspectives on the epidemiology of mental disorders.* Cambridge: Cambridge University Press.

Kihlstrom, J. F. (2001). Dissociative disorders. In P. B. Sutker & H. E. Adams (Eds.), *Comprehensive Handbook of Psychopathology,* 3rd ed. (pp. 259–276). New York, NY: Kluwer Academic/Plenum.

Kim, J. A., Szatmari, P., Bryson, S. E., Streiner, D. L., & Wilson, F. (2000). The prevalence of anxiety and mood problems among children with autism and Asperger syndrome. *Autism, 4,* 117–132.

Klein, D. N., Schwartz, J. E., Rose, S., & Leader, J. B. (2000). Five-year course and outcome of dysthymic disorder: A prospective, naturalistic follow-up study. *American Journal of Psychiatry, 157*(6), 931–939.

Klein, D., & Santiago, N. J. (2003). Dysthymia and chronic depression: Introduction, classification, risk factors, and course. *Journal of Clinical Psychology, 59,* 807–816.

Klin, A., Volkmar, F. R., & Sparrow, S. S. (Eds.) (2000). *Asperger syndrome.* New York, NY: Guilford Press.

Knoll, J., & Resnick, P. J. (2006). The detection of malingered post-traumatic stress disorder. *Psychiatric Clinics of North America, 29*, 629–647.

Kohn, M., & Golden, N. (2001). Eating disorders in children and adolescents: Epidemiology, diagnosis and treatment. *Paediatric Drugs, 3*(2), 91–99.

Krahn, D. D., Kurth, C. L., Gomberg, E., & Drewnowski, A. (2005). Pathological dieting and alcohol use in college women—A continuum of behaviors. *Eating Behaviors, 6*(1), 43–52.

Krahn, L., Hongzhe, L., & O'Connor, K. (2003). Patients who strive to be ill: Factitious disorder with physical symptoms. *Journal of Psychiatry, 160*(6), 1163–1168.

Kreisler, J. D., & Lieberman, A. A. (1986). Dorothea Lynde Dix. In W. I. Trattner (Ed.), *Biographical dictionary of social welfare in America* (pp. 241–244). New York, NY: Greenwood Press.

Kristensen, H. (2000). Selective mutism and comorbidity with developmental disorder/delay, anxiety disorder, and elimination disorder. *Journal of the American Academy of Child and Adolescent Psychiatry, 39*(2), 249–256.

Kroenke, K. (2003). Patients presenting with somatic complaints: Epidemiology, psychiatric comorbidity and management. *International Journal of Methods and Psychiatric Research, 12*, 34–43.

Kruger, A. (2000). Empowerment in social work practice with psychiatrically disabled: Model and method. *Smith College Studies in Social Work, 70*, 427–440.

Krusky, M. S. (2002). Women and thinness: The watch on the eve of the feast. Therapy with families experiencing troubled eating. *Journal of Systemic Therapies, 21*(1), 58–76.

Kuloglu, M., Atmaca, M., Tezcan, E., Gecici, O., & Bulut, S. (2003). Sociodemographic and clinical characteristics of patients with conversion disorder in Eastern Turkey. *Social Psychiatry and Psychiatric Epidemiology, 38*(2), 88–93.

Kumra, S., Shaw, M., Merka. P., Nakayama, E., & Augustin, R. (2001). Childhood-onset schizophrenia: Research update. *Canadian Journal of Psychiatry, 46*(10), 923–930.

Kurlan, R., McDermott, M. P., Deeley, C., Como, P. G., Brower, C., Eapen, S., . . . Miller, B. (2001). Prevalence of tics in schoolchildren and association with placement in special education. *Neurology, 57*(8), 1383–1388.

Kutchins, H., & Kirk, S. A. (1997). *Making us crazy: DSM: The psychiatric bible and the creation of mental disorders*. New York, NY: Free Press.

Labruzza, A., with Mendez-Villarruba, J. M. (1997). *Using DSM-IV: A clinician's guide to psychiatric diagnosis*. Lanham, MD: Jason Aronson.

Lalonde, J. K., Hudson, H. I., Gigante, R. A., & Pope, H. G. (2001). Canadian and American psychiatrists' attitudes toward dissociative disorders diagnoses. *Canadian Journal of Psychiatry, 46*(5), 407–412.

Lampe, L., Slade, T., Issakidis, C., & Andrews, G. (2003). Social phobia in the Australian National Survey of Mental Health and Well-Being (NSMHWB). *Psychological Medicine, 33*, 637–646.

Landreth, G. L. (2002). *Play therapy: The art of relationship* (2nd ed.). New York, NY: Brunner-Routledge.

Lang, A. J., & Stein, M. B. (2001). Social phobia: Prevalence and diagnostic threshold. *Journal of Clinical Psychiatry, 62*, 5–10.

Lask, B., & Bryant-Waugh, R. (Eds.). *Anorexia nervosa and related eating disorders in childhood and adolescence*. Hove, England: Psychology Press.

Lask, B., Gordon, I., Christie, D., Frampton, I., Chowdhury, U., & Watkins, B. (2005). Functional neuroimaging in early-onset anorexia nervosa. *International Journal of Eating Disorders, 37*(Suppl.), S49–51.

Latest Findings in Children's Mental Health. (2004, Winter). Institute for Health, Health Care Policy, and Aging Research: Rutgers University. Retrieved May 10, 2010, from http://www .ihhcpar.rutgers.edu

Lawlor, P. G., Gagnon, B., Mancini, I. L., Pereira. J. L., Hanson, J., Suarez-Almazor, M. E., & Bruera, E. D. (2000). Occurrence, causes, and outcome of delirium in patients with advanced cancer: A prospective study. *Archives of Internal Medicine, 160*(6), 786–794.

Leenders, M. R. M., Mauffette-Leenders, L. A., & Earskine, J. A. (2001). *Writing cases* (4th ed.). London, ONT: Ivey Publishing, Ivey School of Business Administration, the University of Western Ontario.

Leiby, J. (1978). *A history of social welfare and social work in the United States*. New York, NY: Columbia University Press.

Lenzenweger, M., Johnson, M., & Willett, J. (2004). Individual growth curve analysis illuminates stability and change in personality disorder features: The longitudinal study of personality disorders. *Archives of General Psychiatry, 61*, 1015–1024.

Lenzenweger, M. F., Lane, M. C., Loranger, A. W., & Kessler, R. C. (2007). DSM-IV personality disorders in the National Comorbidity Survey replication. *Biological Psychiatry, 62*(6), 553–564.

Levy, S. M., Mandell, D. S., & Shultz, R. T. (2009). Autism. *Lancet, 374*(4), 1627–1638.

Lewis-Fernandez, R. (1994). Culture and dissociation: A comparison of ataque de nervios among Pureto Ricans and possession syndrome in India. In D. Spiegel (Ed.), *Dissociation, culture, mind, and body* (pp. 123–167). Washington, DC: American Psychiatric Press.

Lifton, R. J. (1999). *The protean self: Human resilience in an age of fragmentation*. Chicago, IL: University of Chicago Press.

Lincoln, C., & McGorry, P. (1999). Pathways to care in early psychosis: Clinical and consumer perspectives. In P. McGorry & H. Jackson (Eds.), *Recognition and management of early psychosis: A preventative approach*. Cambridge: Cambridge University Press.

Lindesay, J., Rockwood, K., & Macdonald, A. (2002). *Delirium in old age*. Oxford, England: Oxford University Press.

Lindsey, B. R., Piacentini, J., & McCracken, J. T. (2002). Prevalence and description of selective mutism in a school based sample. *Journal of the American Academy of Child and Adolescent Psychiatry, 41*(8), 938–946.

Litz, B. T., Gray, M. J., Bryant, R. A., & Adler, A. B. (2002). Early intervention for trauma: Current status and future directions. *Clinical Psychology—Science and Practice, 9*, 112–134.

Lopez, S. R., & Guarnaccia, P. J. J. (2000). Cultural psychopathology: Uncovering the social world of mental illness. *Annual Review of Psychology, 51*, 571–598. Report submitted to the Clinical Administration Task Force on Health Care. *Dissociation, 7*, 3–11.

Lord, C., Cook, E. H., Leventhal, B. L., & Amaral, D. G. (2000). Autism spectrum disorders. *Neuron, 28*, 355–363.

Lum, D. (Ed.). (2007). *Culturally competent practice: A framework for understanding diverse groups and justice issues* (3rd ed.). Belmont, CA: Thomson Brooks/Cole.

Lynch, P. D., & Pocinki, D. M. (Eds.). (2007, April). *Progress report on Alzheimer's disease: Journey to discovery*. Rockville, MD: U.S. Department of Health and Human Services, National Institutes of Health, National Institute on Aging. NIH Publication Number 06–6047.

Lynch, W. C., Everingham, A., Dubitzky, J., & Kasser, T. (2007). Does binge eating play a role in the regulation of moods. *Integrative Psychological and Behavioral Science, 35*(6), 298–313.

Manassis, K. (2009). Silent suffering: Understanding and treating children with selective mutism. *Expert Review of Neurotherapeutics, 9*(2), 235–243.

Mantle, F. (2003). Eating disorders: The role of hypnosis. *Paediatric Nursing, 15*(7), 42–46.

Marinangeli, M. G., Butti, G., Scinto, A., Di Cicco, L., Petruzzi, C., Daneluzzo, E., & Rossi, A. (2000). Patterns of comorbidity among DSM-III R personality disorders. *Psychopathology, 33*(2), 69–74.

Marshall, H. (1937). *Dorothea Dix: Forgotten samaritan*. Chapel Hill: University of North Carolina Press.

Marshall, R. E., Spitzer, R., & Liebowitz, M. R. (2000). New DSM-IV diagnosis of acute stress disorder. *American Journal of Psychiatry, 157*, 1890–1891.

Martinez-Taboas, A., & Guillermo, B. (2000). Dissociation, psychopathology and abusive experiences in a nonclinical Latino university student group. *Cultural Diversity and Ethnic Minority Psychology, 6*, 32–41.

Marx, O. (1972). Wilheim Greisninger and the history of psychiatry: A reassessment. *Bulletin of the History of Medicine, 46*, 519–544.

Mash, E. J., & Wolfe, D. A. (2010). *Abnormal child psychology* (4th ed.). Belmont, CA: Wadsworth Thomson Learning.

Masten, A. (1994). Resilience in individual development: Successful adaptation despite risk and adversity. In M. C. Wang & E. E. Gordon (Eds.), *Educational resilience in inner-city America: Challenges and prospects*, (pp. 3–25). Hillsdale, NJ: Erlbaum.

Mataix-Cols, D., Conceicao do Rosario-Campos, M., & Leckman, J. S. (2005). A multidimensional model of obsessive-compulsive disorder. *American Journal of Psychiatry, 162*, 228–238.

Mattila, M. L., Kielinen, M., Jussila, K., Linna, S. L., Bloigu, R., Ebeling, H., & Moilanen, I. (2007). An epidemiological and diagnostic study of Asperger syndrome according to four sets of diagnostic criteria. *Journal of the American Academy of Child and Adolescent Psychiatry, 46*(5), 636–646.

Mayer, J. D. (2006). A classification of DSM-IV-TR mental disorders according to their relationship to the personality system. In M. Hersen & J. C. Thomas (Eds.), *Comprehensive handbook of personality and psychopathology*, (pp. 443–453). Hoboken, NJ: Wiley.

Mayes, R., & Horwitz, A. V. (2005). DSM-III and the revolution in the classification of mental illness. *Journal of the History of the Behavioral Sciences, 41*(3), 249–267.

McCullough, J. P., Klein, D. N., Keller, M. B., Holzer, C. E. L., Davis, S. M., Kornstein, S. G., . . . Harrison, W. M. (2000). Comparison of DSM-III-R chronic major depression and major depression superimposed on dysthymia (double depression): Validity of the distinction. *Journal of Abnormal Psychology, 109*, 419–427.

McNally, R. J. (2003). *Remembering trauma.* Cambridge, MA: Harvard University Press.

McNicoll, L., Pisani, M. A., Zhang, Y., Ely, E. W., Siegel, M. D., & Inouye, S. K. (2003). Delirium in the intensive care unit: Occurrence and clinical course in older patients. *Journal of the American Geriatric Society, 51*, 591–598.

Meagher, D. (2001). Delirium episode as a sign of undetected dementia among community dwelling elderly subjects. *Journal of Neurology and Neurosurgery and Psychiatry, 70*(6), 821.

Mellon, M. W., Whiteside, S. P., & Friedrich, W. P. (2007). The relevance of fecal soiling as an indicator of childhood sexual abuse: A preliminary study. *Journal of Developmental and Behavioral Pediatrics, 27*(1), 25–32.

Melvin, L. (Ed.). (2002). *Child and adolescent psychiatry: A comprehensive textbook* (3rd ed.). Philadelphia, PA: Lippincott, Williams and Wilkins.

Mendlowicz, M. V., & Stein, M. B. (2000). Quality of life in individuals with anxiety disorders. *American Journal of Psychiatry, 157*, 669–682.

Meyer, C. H. (1993). *Assessment in social work practice.* New York, NY: Columbia University Press.

Miller, J. (2002). Social workers as diagnosticians. In K. J. Bentley (Ed.), *Social work practice in mental health: Contemporary roles, tasks and techniques* (pp. 43–72). Pacific Grove, CA: Brooks/Cole.

Miller, K., & Scott-Mizes, J. (2000). *Comparative treatments of eating disorders.* London: Free Association.

Mills, M. J., & Lapian, M. S. (2000). Malingering. In B. J. Sadock & V. A. Sadock (Eds.), *Comprehensive textbook of psychiatry* (8th ed., pp. 2247–2258). Philadelphia: Lippincott, Williams and Wilkins.

Mokdad, A. H., Giles, W. H., Bowman, B. A., Mensah, G. A., Ford, E. S., Smith, S. M., & Marks, J. S. (2004, May/June). Changes in health behaviors among older Americans. *Public Health Reports, 119*, 356–361.

Montes, G., & Halterman, J. S. (2007). Psychological functioning and coping among mothers of children with autism: A population-based study. *Pediatrics, 119*(5), 1040–1046.

Moore, D. P., & Jefferson, J. W. (2004). *Handbook of medical psychiatry* (2nd ed.). New York, NY: Mosby.

Moorhead, D. J. (2001, July). Early risk factors and current functioning of young adult women with full or partial eating disorders. *Dissertation Abstracts International, A: The Humanities and Social Sciences, 62*, 332-A.

Moran, P., Jenkins, R.,Tylee, A., Blizard, R., & Mann, A. (2000). The prevalence of personality disorder among UK primary care attenders. *Acta Psychiatrica Scandanavica, 102*, 52–57.

Moreno, J. K., Selby, M. J., Aved, K., & Besse, C. (2000). Differences in family dynamics among anorexic, bulimic, obese and normal women. *Journal of Psychotherapy in Independent Practice, 1*(1), 75–87.

Morrison, J. (2007). *Diagnosis made easier: Principles and techniques for mental health clinicians.* New York, NY: Guilford Press.

Mueser, K. T., & McGurk, S. R. (2004). Schizophrenia. *The Lancet, 363,* 2063–2072.

Mulvany, F., O'Callaghan, E., Takei, N., Byrne, M., & Fearon, P. (2001). Effects of social class at birth on risk and presentation of schizophrenia: Case-control study. *British Medical Journal, 323*(7326), 1398–1401.

Munson, C. E. (2001). *The mental health diagnostic desk reference: Visual guides and more for learning to use the Diagnostic and Statistical Manual (DSM-IV-TR)* (2nd ed.). New York, NY: Haworth Press.

Murphy, B. A. (2000). Delirium. *Emergency Medicine Clinics of North America, 18*(2), 243–252.

Murray, R. M., & Jones, P. B. (2003). *The epidemiology of schizophrenia.* New York, NY: Cambridge University Press.

Murray, T. (2003). Wait not, want not: Factors contributing to the development of anorexia nervosa and bulimia nervosa. *The Family Journal: Counseling and Therapy for Couples and Families, 11*(3), 276–280.

Myers, S. M., Johnson, C. P., & Council on Children with Disabilities. (2007). Management of children with autism spectrum disorders. *Pediatrics, 120*(5), 1162–1182.

Nair, J., Ehimare, U., Beitman, B. D., Nair, S. S., & Lavin, A. (2006). Clinical review: Evidence-based diagnosis and treatment of ADHD in children. *Mo Med, 103*(6), 617–621.

National Association of Social Workers. (2009, April). Association urges inclusion in DSM-V group. *NASW News, 54*(4), 5. Washington, DC: Author.

National Institute of Mental Health (NIMH). (2009). *Anxiety disorders.* Retrieved on October 15, 2009, from http://www.nimh.nih.gov/health/publications/anxiety-disorders/complete-index .shtml

National Institute on Aging (2005). *Alzheimer's disease fact sheet.* Washington, DC: National Institutes of Health.

National Institute on Drug Abuse. (2005). *Cigarettes and other nicotine products.* NIDA Info Facts. NIF—010 National Institutes of Health—U.S. Department of Health and Human Services.

National Institutes of Health (NIH). (May 2007). *News in health.* Bethesda, MD: Department of Health and Human Services. Retrieved April 16, 2009, from http://newsinhealth.nih .gov/2007/May/index.htm

Nelson, T. S., Chenail, R. J., Alexander, J. F., Crane, D. R., Johnson, S. M., & Schwallie, L. (2007). The development of core competencies for the practice of marriage and family therapy. *Journal of Marital and Family Therapy, 33*(4), 417–438.

Neumark-Sztainer, D. (2005). *I'm, like, so fat!* New York, NY: Guilford Press.

Newhill, C. E., & Korr, W. S. (2004). Practice with people with severe mental illness: Rewards, challenges, burdens. *Health and Social Work, 29*(4), 297–305.

Noble, D. N., Maluccio, A. N., Whittaker, J. K., & Jones, B. L. (2008). Children. In T. Mizrahi & L. E. Davis, *Encyclopedia of social work* (e-reference ed.). Washington, DC: NASW Press and New York: Oxford University Press. Retrieved on May 9, 2010, from http://www .oxford-naswsocialwork.com/entry?entry=t203.e50-s1

Noyes, R., Stuart, S., Watson, D. B., & Langbehn, D. R. (2006). Distinguishing between hypo-chondriasis and somatization disorder: A review of the existing literature. *Psychotherapy and Psychosomatics, 75*(5), 270–281.

O'Connor, K. P. (2001). Clinical and psychological features distinguishing obsessive-compulsive and chronic tic disorders. *Clinical Psychology Review, 21,* 631–660.

O'Gorman, F. (2004). The anatomy of resilience. What makes some clients bounce back better than others? *Counselor Magazine—The Magazine for Addiction Professionals, 5*(1), 14–17.

O'Neill, S. E., & Sher, K. J. (2000). Physiological alcohol dependence symptoms in early adult-hood: A longitudinal perspective. *Experimental and Clinical Sychopharmacology, 8*(4), 493–508.

Orsmond, G. I., & Seltzer, M. M. (2007). Siblings of individuals with autism spectrum disor-ders across the life course. *Mental Retardation and Developmental Disabilities Research Review, 13*(4), 13–20.

Ostrander, R. (2004). Oppositional defiant disorder and conduct disorder. In L. B. Silver & F. M. Kline (Eds.), *The educator's guide to mental health issues in the classroom* (pp. 267–286). Baltimore, MD: Paul H. Brookes.

Othmer, F., & Othmer, S. C. (2000). *Falsifying and lying: In American Psychiatric press, the clinical interview using DSM-IV, the difficult patient* (pp. 349–384). Washington, DC: Author.

Pace, P. R. (2008, January). Evidence-based practice moves ahead. *NASW News, 53*(1), 4.

Palmer, B. A., Pankratz, V. S., & Bostwick, J. M. (2005, March). The lifetime risk of suicide in schizophrenia: A reexamination. *Archives of General Psychiatry, 62*(3), 247–253.

Paniagua, F. A. (2005). *Assessing and treating culturally diverse clients: A practical guide.* Thousand Oaks, CA: Sage.

Paris, J. (2003). Personality disorders: A biopsychosocial model. *Journal of Personality Disorders, 7*(3), 255–264.

Parker, G., Roy, K., Mitchell, P., Wilhelm, K., Malhi, G., & Hadzi-Pavlovic, D. (2002). Atypical depression: A reappraisal. *American Journal of Psychiatry, 159,* 1470–1479.

Parrillo, V. (2008). *Encyclopedia of social problems.* Thousand Oaks, CA: Sage.

Parsons, R. J. (2002). Guidelines for empowerment-based social work practice. In A. R. Roberts & G. J. Greene (Eds.), *Social workers' desk reference.* New York, NY: Oxford University Press.

Parsons, R. J. (2008). Empowerment practice. In T. Mizrahi & L. E. Davis (Eds.), *Encyclopedia of social work* (e-reference ed.). Washington, DC: NASW Press and New York: Oxford University Press. Retrieved on September 11, 2009, from http://www.oxford-naswsocialwork .com/entry?entry=1203e104

Pederson, P. B. (2008). Ethics, competence, and professional issues in cross-cultural counseling. In P. B. Pederson, J. G. Draguns, W. J. Loner, & J. E. Trimble (Eds.), *Counseling across cul-tures* (6th ed., pp. 5–20). Los Angeles: Sage.

Perkins, K., & Tice, C. (1999). Family treatment of older adults who misuse alcohol: A strengths perspective. *Journal of Gerontological Social Work, 31*(3/4), 169–185.

Philippe, J., & Romain, J. B. (1979). Indisposition in Haiti. *Social Science and Medicine, 138,* 129–133.

Phillips, K. A., & Menard, W. (2006). Suicidality in body dysmorphic disorder: A prospective study. *American Journal of Psychiatry, 163*(7), 1280–1282.

Phillips, K. A. (2004). Body dysmorphic disorder: Recognizing and treating imagined ugliness. *World Psychiatry, 3*(1), 2–17.

Phillips, K. A. (2005). *The broken mirror: Understanding and treating body dysmorphic disorder* (Rev. and expanded ed.). Oxford, England: Oxford University Press.

Phillips, K. A., Yen, S., & Gunderson, J. G. (2003). Personality disorders. In R. E. Hales & S. C. Yudofsky (Eds.), *Textbook of clinical psychiatry* (4th ed., pp. 804–832). Washington, DC: American Psychiatric Press.

Pinkofsky, H. B. (1997). Mnemonics for DSM-IV personality disorders. *Psychiatric Services, 48*(9), 1197–1198.

Piper, A., & Merskey, H. (2004). The insistence of folly: A critical examination of dissociative identity disorder. Part I. The excesses of an improbable concept. *Canadian Journal of Psychiatry, 49*(9), 592–600.

Pizer, A. G. (2002, August). The relationship between general parental controllingness and eating disorder symptomatology in mothers. *Dissertation Abstracts International, A: The Humanities and Social Sciences, 63*(2), 758-A.

Pliszka, S. R. (2003). Psychiatric comorbidities in children with attention deficit hyperactivity disorder. *Pediatric Drugs, 5*, 741–750.

Pomeroy, C. (2004). Assessment of medical status and physical factors. In J. K. Thompson (Ed.), *Handbook of eating disorders and obesity* (pp. 81–111). Hoboken, NJ: Wiley.

Pompli, M., Mancinelli, I., Girardi. P., Ruberto, A., & Tatarelli, R. (2004). Suicide in anorexia nervosa: A meta-analysis. *International Journal of Eating Disorders, 36*(1), 99–103.

Posavac, H. D., Posavac, S. S., & Weigel, R. G. (2001). Reducing the impact of media images on women at risk for body image disturbance: Three targeted interventions. *Journal of Social and Clinical Psychology, 20*(3), 324–340.

Prochaska, J., & Norcross, J. (2007). *Systems of psychotherapy: A transtheoretical analysis.* Belmont, CA: Thomson Brooks/Cole.

Reamer, R. G. (2006). *Social work values and ethics* (3rd ed.). New York, NY: Columbia University Press.

Reisberg, B. (1984). Functional assessment staging (FAST). *Psychopharmacology Bulletin, 24*, 653–659.

Rettew, D. C. (2000). Avoidant personality disorder, generalized social phobia, and shyness: Putting the personality back into personality disorders. *Harvard Review of Psychiatry, 8*, 283–297.

Richards, P. S., Baldwin, B. M., Frost, H. A., Clark-Sly, J. B., Berrett, M. E., & Hardman, R. K. (2000). What works for treating eating disorders? Conclusions of 28 outcome reviews. *Eating Disorders: The Journal of Treatment and Prevention, 8*, 189–206.

Rockwood, K., & MacKnight, C. (2001). *Understanding dementia: A primer of diagnosis and management.* Halifax: Pottersfield.

Ronel, N., & Libman, G. (2003). Eating disorders and recovery: Lessons from overeaters anonymous. *Clinical Social Work Journal, 31*(2), 155–171.

Rose, S. (1990). Advocacy/empowerment: An approach to clinical practice. *Journal of Sociology and Social Welfare, 17*, 41–51.

Rossi, A., Marinangeli, M. G., Butti, G., Kalyvoka, A., & Petruzzi, C. (2000). Pattern of comorbidity among anxious and odd personality disorders: The case of obsessive-compulsive personality disorder. *CNS Spectrums, 5*(9), 23–26.

Rutter, M. (1987). Psychological resilience and protective mechanisms. *American Journal of Orthopsychiatry, 57,* 316–331.

Rutter, M. (2000). Genetic studies of autism: From the 1970s into the millennium. *Journal of Abnormal Child Psychology, 28,* 3–14.

Sadock, B. J., & Sadock, V. A. (2003). *Kaplan and Sadock's synopsis of psychiatry: Behavioral sciences, clinical psychiatry* (9th ed.). Baltimore, MD: Williams and Wilkins.

Sadock, B. J., & Sadock, V. A. (2004). *Concise textbook of psychiatry* (10th ed.). Philadelphia, PA: Lippincott, Williams and Wilkins.

Sadock, B. J., & Sadock, V. A. (2007). *Synopsis of psychiatry* (10th ed.). Philadelphia, PA: Lippincott, Williams and Wilkins.

Sadock, B. J., Sadock, V. A., & Ruiz, P. (Eds.). (2009). *Kaplan and Sadock's comprehensive textbook of psychiatry* (9th ed.). Philadelphia, PA: Lippincott Williams and Wilkins.

Saleebey, D. (1996). The strengths perspective in social work practice: Extensions and cautions. *Social Work, 41*(3), 296–305.

Saleebey, D. (2008). *The strengths perspective in social work practice* (5th ed.). Boston, MA: Allyn & Bacon.

Saleebey, D., & Scanlon, E. (2005). Is a critical pedagogy for the profession of social work possible? *Journal of Teaching in Social Work, 25*(3/4), 1–18.

Samuels, J. (2002). Prevalence and correlates of personality disorders in a sample community. *British Journal of Psychiatry, 180,* 536–542.

Sareen, J., Cox, B., Afifi, T., de Graaf, R., Asmundson, G., ten Have, M., & Stein, M. (2005). *Anxiety disorders and risk for suicidal ideation and suicide attempts.* Retrieved September 30, 2010, from Archives of General Psychiatry: http://archpsyc.ama-assn.org/cgi/content/full/62/11/1249

Savino, A. C., & Fordtran, S. S. (2006). Factitious disease: Clinical lessons from case studies at Baylor University Medical Center. *Proceedings (Baylor University Medical Center), 19*(3), 195–208.

Schenkel, L. S., Spaulding, W. D., Dilillo, D., & Silverstein, S. M. (2005). Histories of child maltreatment in schizophrenia: Relationships with premorbid functioning symptomatology, and cognitive deficits. *Schizophrenia Research, 76*(2–3), 273–286.

Schonwald, A., & Lechner, E. (2006). Attention deficit/hyperactivity disorder: Complexities and controversies. *Current Opinion in Pediatrics, 18*(2), 189–195.

Schuckit, M. A., Smith, T. L., Danko, G. P., Pierson, J., Trim, R., Nurnberger, J. I., . . . Hesselbrock, V. (2007). A comparison of factors associated with substance-induced versus independent depressions. *Journal of Studies on Alcohol and Drugs, 68*(6), 805–812.

Sciutto, M. J., Nolfi, C. J., & Bluhm, C. (2004). Effects of child gender and symptom type on referrals for ADHD by elementary school teachers. *Journal of Emotional and Behavioral Disorders, 12*(4), 247–253.

Seivewright, H., Tyrer, P., & Johnson, T. (2002). Change in personality status in neurotic disorders. *Lancet, 359,* 2253–2254.

Selten, J. P., Cantor-Graae, E., & Kahn, R. S. (2007). Migration and schizophrenia. *Current Opinion in Psychiatry, 20*(2), 111–115.

Shea, M. T., Stout, R. L., Gunderson, J. G., Morey, L. C., Grilo, C. M., McGlashan, T., . . . Keller, M. B. (2002). Short-term diagnostic stability of schizotypal, borderline, avoidant, and obsessive-compulsive personality disorders. *American Journal of Psychiatry, 159,* 2036–2041.

Sheafor, B. W., & Horjesi, C. R. (2003). *Techniques and guidelines for social work practice* (6th ed.). Boston, MA: Allyn & Bacon.

Shear, K., Jin, R., Ruscio, A. M., Walters, E. E., & Kessler, R. C. (2006). Prevalence and correlates of estimated DSM-IV child and adult separation anxiety disorder in the National Comorbidity Survey Replication. *American Journal of Psychiatry, 163,* 1074–1083.

Shreeram, S., Jian-Pinghe, J., Kalaydjian, A., Brothers, S., & Merikangas, K. R. (2009). Prevalence of enuresis and its association with attention-deficit/hyperactivity disorder among U.S. children: Results from a nationally representative study. *Journal of the American Academy of Child and Adolescent Psychiatry, 48*(1), 35–41.

Siegel, H. A., Rapp, R. C., Kelliher, C. W., Fisher, J. H., Wagner, J. H., & Cole, P. A. (1995). The strengths perspective of case management: A promising inpatient substance abuse treatment enhancement. *Journal of Psychoactive Drugs, 27*(1), 67–72.

Sim, K., Chua, T. H., Chan, Y. H., Mahendran, R., & Chong, S. A. (2006). Psychiatric comorbidity in first episode schizophrenia: A 2 year longitudinal outcome study. *Journal of Psychiatric Research, 40*(7), 656–663.

Simeon, D, (2004). Depersonalization disorder: A contemporary overview. *CNS Drugs, 18*(6), 343–354.

Simeon, D., & Abugel, J. (2006). *Feeling unreal: Depersonalization disorder and the loss of self.* New York, NY: Oxford University Press.

Simeon, D., Guralnick, O., Schmeidler, J., & Knutelska, M. (2001). The role of childhood interpersonal trauma in depersonalization disorder. *American Journal of Psychiatry, 158*(7), 1027–1033.

Simon, N. M., Blacker, D., Korbly, N. B., Sharma, S. G., Worthington, J. J., Otto, M. W., & Pollack, M. H. (2002). Hypothyroidism and hyperthyroidism in anxiety disorders revisited. New data and literature review. *Journal of Affective Disorders, 69*(1–3), 209–217.

Simons, R. C. (1985). The resolution of the latah paradox. In R. C. Simons & C. C. Hughes (Eds.), *The culture-bound syndromes: Folk illnesses of psychiatric and anthropological interest* (pp. 43–62). Dordrecht, Holland: D. Reidel.

Singh, J., Avasthi, A., & Grover, S. (2007). Malingering of psychiatric disorders: A review. *Psychiatry, 10,* 126–132.

Skodol, A. E., Gunderson, J. G., Pfohl, B., Widiger, T. A., Livesley, W. J., & Siever, L. J. (2002). The borderline diagnosis I: Psychopathology, comorbidity, and personality structure. *Biological Psychiatry, 51,* 936–950.

Small, B. J., Gagnon, E., & Robinson, B. (2007). Early identification of cognitive deficits: Preclinical Alzheimer's disease and mild cognitive impairment. *Geriatrics, 62*(4), 91–23.

Smith, O. (2000). *Aging in America.* New York, NY: Wilson.

Smolak, L. (1996). *National Eating Disorders Association/Next door neighbors puppet guide book.*

Snijders, T. J., Leeuw, F. E., Klumpers, U. M., Kappelle, L. JJ., & van Gijn, J. (2004). Prevalence and predictors of unexplained neurological symptoms in an academic neurology outpatient clinic—an observational study. *Journal of Neurology, 251*(1), 66–71.

Sohn, E. (2002). The hunger artists: Are genes and brain chemistry at the root of eating disorders. *U.S. News and World Report, 132*(20), 44–48.

Solomon, B. (1976). *Black empowerment: Social work in oppressed communities.* New York, NY: Columbia University Press.

Spinelli, M. G. (2004). Maternal infanticide associated with mental illness: Prevention and the promise of saved lives. *American Journal of Psychiatry, 161,* 1548–1557.

Staines, G. L., Magura, S., Foote, J., Deluca, A., & Kosanke, N. (2001). Polysubstance use among alcoholics. *Journal of Addictive Diseases, 20*(4), 57–73.

Stefanatos, G. A. (2008). Regression in autistic spectrum disorders. *Neuropsychological Review, 18*(4), 305–319.

Stein, M. B., Torgrud, L. J., & Walker, J. R. (2000). Social phobia symptoms, subtypes, and severity: Findings from a community survey. *Archives of General Psychiatry, 57,* 1046–1052.

Stern, H. P., & Stern, T. P. (2002). When children with attention-deficit/hyperactivity disorder become adults. *Southern Medical Journal, 95*(9), 985–991.

Sternberg, R. J., Forsythe, G. B., Hedlund, J., Horvath, J. A., Wagner, R. K., Williams, W. M., . . . Grigorenko, E. L. (2000). *Practical intelligence in everyday life.* New York, NY: Cambridge University Press.

Stopa, L., & Clark, D. M. (2000). Social phobia and interpretation of social events. *Behaviour Research and Therapy, 38,* 255–267.

Striegel-Moore, R. H., Cachelin, F. M., Dohm, F. A., Pike, M., Wilfley, D. E., & Fairburn, C. G. (2004). Comparison of binge eating disorder and bulimia nervosa in a community sample. *International Journal of Eating Disorders, 29,* 157–165.

Stromwall, L. K., & Hurdle, D. (2003). Psychiatric rehabilitation: An empowerment-based approach to mental health services. *Health and Social Work, 28*(3), 206–214.

Stunkard, A. J. (2002). Binge-eating disorder and the night-eating syndrome. In T. A. Wadden & A. J. Stunkard (Eds.), *Handbook of obesity treatment.* New York, NY: Guilford Press.

Substance Abuse and Mental Health Services Administration (SAMHSA). (2003). Results from the 2002 National Survey on Drug Use and Health: National findings (Office of Applied Studies, NHSDA Series H-22, HHS Publication No. SMA 03–3836). Rockville, MD: Author.

Substance Abuse and Mental Health Services Administration (SAMHSA). (2009). Results from the 2008 National Survey on Drug Use and Health: National Findings (Office of Applied Studies, NSDUH Series H-36, HHS Publication No. SMA 09–4434). Rockville, MD: Author.

Swan, S., & Andrews, B. (2004). The relationship between shame, eating disorders and disclosure in treatment. *British Journal of Clinical Psychology, 42,* 367–378.

Swartz, K. L., Pratt, L. A., Armenian, H. K., Lee, L. C., & Eaton, W. W. (2000). Mental disorders and the incidence of migraine headaches in a community sample: Results from the

Baltimore Epidemiologic Catchment area follow-up study. *Archives of General Psychiatry, 57,* 945–950.

Tavris, C. (1992). *The mismeasure of woman.* New York, NY: Simon and Schuster.

Thomas, C. L. (Ed.). (1997). *Taber's cyclopedic medical dictionary.* Philadelphia, PA: F. A. Davis.

Thomas, K., & Freyokin, D. (2004, July 2). Crushing weight of the tabloids: Media pressures stars to be thin. *USA Today Life Section,* 3-E.

Thyer, B. A., & Wodarski, J. S. (Eds.). (2007). *Social work in mental health: An evidence-based approach.* Hoboken, NJ: Wiley.

Tolgyes, T., & Nemessury, J. (2004). Epidemiological studies on adverse dieting behaviors and eating disorders among young people in Hungary. *Social Psychiatry and Psychiatric Epidemiology, 39*(8), 647–654.

Tukel, R., Polat, A., Ozdemir, O., Aksut, D., & Turksoy, N. (2002). Comorbid conditions in obsessive-compulsive disorder. *Comprehensive Psychiatry, 43,* 204–209.

United Nations. (2007). *World population prospects: The 2006 revision highlights.* Working Paper No. ESA/P/WP.202, Population Division, Department of Economic and Social Affairs, United Nations. Retrieved on February 14, 2008, from http://un.org/esa/population/publications/wpp2006/WPP2006_Highlights_rev.pdf

U.S. Census Bureau. (2009). U.S. Census Bureau population estimates by demographic characteristics, table 2: Annual estimates of the population by selected age groups and sex for the United States: April 1, 2000, to July 1, 2004 (NC-EST 2004–02). Retrieved on July 1, 2009, from http://www.census.gov/popest/national/asrh/.

U.S. Census Bureau Population Estimates by Demographic Characteristics. Table 2: Annual estimates of the population by selected age groups and sex for the United States: April 1, 2000, to July 1, 2004 (NC-EST2004–02) Source: Population Division, U.S. Census Bureau Release. Retrieved on June 9, 2005, from http://www.census.gov/popest/national/asrh/

U.S. Department of Health and Human Services. (1999). *Mental Health: A report of the surgeon general.* Retrieved on July 1, 2009, from: http://www.surgeongeneral.gov/library/mentalhealth/home.html

U. S. Department of Health and Human Services. (February 2001). *Binge eating disorders.* NIH Publication No. 99–3589. U. S. Department of Health and Human Services National Institutes of Health. Retrieved on April 23, 2009, from http://win.niddk.nih.gov/publications/binge.htm

van Os, J. (2004). Does the urban environment cause psychosis? *British Journal of Psychiatry, 184*(4), 287–288.

van Os, J., Krabbendam, L., Myin-Germeys, I., & Delespaul, P. (2005). The schizophrenia environment. *Current Opinion in Psychiatry, 18*(2), 141–145.

Volkmar, R. M., & Klin, A. (2000). Asperger's disorder and higher functioning autism: Same or different? *International Review of Research in Mental Retardation, 23,* 83–111.

Volkmar, R. M., & Rutter, M. (1995). Childhood disintegrative disorder: Results of the DSM-IV field trial. *Journal of the American Academy of Child and Adolescent Psychiatry, 34,* 1092–1095.

Voss, R. W., Douville, V., Little Soldier, A., & Twiss, G. (1999). Tribal and shamanic-based social work practice: A Lakota perspective. *Social Work, 44*(3), 228–241.

Vuchinich, R. E. (2002). President's column. *Addictions Newsletter, 10*(1), 1, 5.

Wakefield, J. C. (1992). Disorder as harmful dysfunction: A conceptual critique of DSM-III-R's definition of mental disorders. *Psychological Review, 90*, 238.

Waldemar, G., Dubois, B., Emre, E., Georges, J., McKeith, I. G., Rossor, M., . . . EFNS. (2007). Recommendations for the diagnosis and management of Alzheimer's disease and other disorders associated with dementia: EFNS guideline. *European Journal of Neurology, 14*(1), 1–26.

Wang, D., Nagida, D. N., & Jenson, J. J. (2005). Factitious disorders. In B. J. Sadock & V. A. Sadock (Eds.), *Comprehensive textbook of psychiatry* (vol. I, 8th ed., pp. 1829–1843). Philadelphia, PA: Lippincott Williams and Wilkins.

Waraich, P., Goldner, E. M., Somers, J. M., & Hsu, L. (2004). Prevalence and incidence studies of mood disorders: A systematic review of the literature. *Canadian Journal of Psychiatry, 49*(2), 124–138.

Webb, N. B. (2003). *Social work practice with children*. New York, NY: Guilford Press.

Weidman, H. H. (1979). Falling-out: A diagnostic and treatment problem viewed from a transcultural perspective. *Social Science and Medicine, 13*, 95–112.

Werner, E., Dawson, G., Osterling, J., & Dinno, N. (2000). Brief report: Recognition of autism spectrum disorders before one year of age: A retrospective study based on home video tapes. *Journal of Autism and Developmental Disorders, 30*, 157–162.

Werrbach, G. B. (1986). Family strengths-based intensive child case management. *Families in Society, 77*(4), 216–226.

Wetterling, T., & Junghanns, K. (2000). Psychopathology of alcoholics during withdrawal and early abstinence. *European Psychiatry, 15*(8), 483–488.

White, R. W., & Horvitz, E. (2009). Studies of the escalation of medical concerns in Web search. *ACM Transactions on Information Systems, 27*(4). Retrieved on April 3, 2010, from http://portal.acm.org/citation.cfm?doid=1629096.1629101

Widiger, F. A., Francis, A., & Pincus, H. A. (Eds.). (1994). *DSM-IV sourcebook*, Vol. 1. Washington, DC: American Psychiatric Association.

Widiger, F. A., Francis, A., Pincus, H. A., Ross, R., First, M. B., & Davis, W. W. (Eds.). (1996). *DSM-IV sourcebook*, Vol. 2. Washington, DC: American Psychiatric Association.

Widiger, F. A., Francis, A., Pincus, H. A., Ross, R., First, M. B., Davis, W. W., & Kline, M. (Eds.). (1998). *DSM-IV sourcebook*, Vol. 4. Washington DC: American Psychiatric Association.

Widiger, T. A., & Sankis, L. M. (February 2000). Adult psychopathology: Issues and controversies. *Annual Review of Psychology, 51*, 377–404.

Wilens, T. E. (2004). Attention deficit/hyperactivity disorder and the substance use disorders. The nature of the relationship, who is at risk, and treatment issues. *Primary Psychiatry, 11*(7), 63–70.

Wilfley, D. E., Schwartz, J. N. B., Spurrell, B., & Fairburn, C. G. (2000). Using the eating disorders examination to identify the specific psychopathology of binge eating disorder. *International Journal of Eating Disorders, 27*, 259–269.

Williams, J. B. W. (2008). Diagnostic and statistical manual of mental disorders. In T. Mizrahi & L. E. Davis (Eds.), *Encyclopedia of social work* (e-reference ed.). Washington, DC: NASW

Press and New York: Oxford University Press. Retrieved on May 18, 2009, from http://www.oxford-naswsocialwork.com/entry?entry=1203e104

Williams, P. M., Goodie, J., & Motsinger, C. D. (2008). Treating eating disorders in primary care. *American Family Physician, 77*(2), 187–95.

Wilson, G. T., & Pike, K. M. (2001). Eating disorders. In D. H. Barlow (Ed.), *Clinical handbook of psychological disorders* (3rd ed.). New York, NY: Guilford.

Winters, E. E. (1950). *The collected papers of Adolph Meyer, Vol IV, Mental Hygiene.* Baltimore, MD: Johns Hopkins Press.

Wittchen, H. U., Kessler, R. C., Pfister, H., & Lieb, M. (2000). Why do people with anxiety disorders become depressed? A prospective-longitudinal community study. *Acta Psychiatrica Scandinavia, 406,* 14–23.

Wittchen, H. U., & Fehm, L. (2001). Epidemiology patterns of comorbidity, and associated disabilities of social phobia. *Psychiatric Clinics of North America, 24,* 617–641.

Wittchen, H. U., Kessler, R. C., Beesdo, K., Krause, P., Hofler, M., & Hoyer, J. (2002). Generalized anxiety and depression in primary care: Prevalence, recognition, and management. *Journal of Clinical Psychiatry, 63*(Suppl. 8), 24–34.

Wolfe, K. B. (2003). Treatment transitions: Improving patient recovery through effective collaboration. *Eating Disorders Review, 14*(5), 3–11.

Wolin, S. J., & Wolin, S. (1993). *The resilient self: How survivors of troubled families rise above adversity.* New York: Villard.

World Health Organization. (2004). *The World Health Report 2004: Changing History Annex Table 3: Burden of disease in DALYs by cause, sex, and mortality stratum in WHO regions, estimates for 2002.* Geneva: WHO.

Work Group on Borderline Personality Disorder. (2001). Practice guideline for the treatment of patients with borderline personality disorder. *American Journal of Psychiatry, 158,* 1–52.

Wright, N. (2003). Are acute inpatient mental health wards an appropriate treatment setting for people with anorexia nervosa? *Mental Health Practice, 7*(2), 18–21.

Xiao, Z., Yan, H., Wang, A., Zou, Z., Xu, Y., Chen, J., . . . Keyes, B. B. (2006). Trauma and dissociation in China. *American Journal of Psychiatry, 163*(8), 1388–1391.

Yates, W. R. (2008). Somatoform disorder. *British Journal of Psychiatry, 193*(1), 5–19.

Yeargin-Allsopp, M., Rice, C., Karapurkar, T., Doernberg, N., Boyle, C., & Murphy, C. (2003). Prevalence of autism in a US metropolitan area. *Journal of the American Medical Association, 289*(1), 49–55.

Yip, K.-S. (2005). A strengths perspective in working with Alzheimer's disease. *International Journal of Social Research and Practice, 4*(3), 434–441.

Yip, K.-S. (2006). A strengths perspective in working with an adolescent with self cutting behaviors. *Child and Adolescent Social Work Journal, 23*(2), 134–146.

Zelenko, M., & Shaw, R. (2000) Case study: Selective mutism in an immigrant child. *Clinical Child Psychology and Psychiatry, 5*(4), 555–562.

Zimmerman, M. (1994). *Interview guide for evaluating DSM-IV psychiatric disorders and the mental status exam.* Philadelphia, PA: Psych Products Press.

Author Index

Subject Index